MONOLITHIC UNDERTOW

PRAISE FOR MONOLITHIC UNDERTOW

"This is a masterpiece, heavy, fun, mad, wild, inspiring, mind-blowing, massively deep though never precious, so many tangents somehow brought together with clarity and vision. I love the idea of a left-hand path history, and the connections between the begin nings of the universe, ritual music and modern electronic rock is jaw-dropping. I love it, this is the music book of the year and the ultimate book on the sound of the eternal now. This is going to drop like a true fucking monolith from the skies."
–**David Keenan**

"Every now and then a book comes out that redefines a form, creates the narrative and is a startling jolt to the culture fabric . . . [*Monolithic Undertow*] is thrilling, inspiring, informative and makes you jump all over the internet looking for the soundtrack. The book is a game changer and you will never listen to music in the same way again."
–**John Robb, *Louder Than War***

"Sword is a deeply knowledgeable and perceptive advocate for a vast range of often esoteric, sometimes challenging, always extraordinary music."
– ***The Quietus***

"*Monolithic Undertow* searches for our relationship to drone music: an epic playlist that begins in the womb, then criss-crosses an ex-haustive thread across the lo-fi Verdantic cassettes of Alice Coltrane, the 'true British blues' of Black Sabbath, infrasonic weaponry and the gritty doom-clouds of The Velvet Underground."
– ***Art Review***

"Addictive . . . Sword's is an impressively global ear."
– ***Irish Times***

"Verbose and effusive when assessing recordings, *Monolithic Undertow*'s scope is large enough that any reader will likely discover something."
– ***Buzz***

Harry Sword is a Cambridge-based writer.
He is a contributor to *The Quietus*, *Vice*, *Record Collector*, *Munchies* and *The Guardian*.
Monolithic Undertow is his first book.

Monolithic Undertow

IN SEARCH OF SONIC OBLIVION

Harry Sword

THIRD MAN BOOKS

For more information:
Third Man Books, LLC, 623 7th Ave S, Nashville, Tennessee 37203
A CIP record is on file with the Library of Congress

FIRST USA EDITION
ISBN 9781737382935
Art direction by Jordan Williams
Layout by Amin Qutteineh
Cover design by Sarah Goldstein

Cover photo (Stephen O'Malley of SUNN O))) in concert at
The Caverns outside of Nashville, Tennessee 2019) by Carissa Stolting

for Tamara, Freddie, Jack and Lana Sword

Contents

New Foreword
for the North America Edition

Third Man

Harry Sword

I started writing this book in 2017 in a very different world. By the time I was completing the last couple of chapters in 2020 — recovering from a grim bout of Covid-19 and listening obsessively to Eliane Radigue's *Tryptych* as I wrote, half hypnotised, into the late, late nights — it was clear we weren't in Kansas anymore…

The drone, however, remains immovable. At early Q and A's readers frequently asked why I was drawn to write about the drone? Well, I'd say, it's the *absoluteness* of it, the *everything* of it. After all: music is so often about wrestling with emotions so big and real and here and now that they can't be left unsaid, or unsung. Think of the love song, the protest song. Universal constants. Love and anger. Beyond reason — often beyond cold, sober analysis. So what do we do? We sing them out, we shout them out, we play them out. We do it because we *have* to do it. But what about the immensity of the infinite? The mystery of the unknown? These are also universal constants of a very different kind. And, as humans, we're unique in that we're aware — painfully aware — that our time is finite. How, then, do we wrestle with the inevitability of time, the awareness of time, the vastness of space? As we'll see, the drone — sound without beginning or end; traditional markers of time removed — is a big part of the story here.

When I was asked to write a new forward for this new American edition, I cast my mind back to my earliest experiences with hypnotic music. The memories — the riffs — came flooding back. Bands like Fu Manchu, Karma to Burn, Kyuss and Sleep opened a portal to me in the mid 1990's. For an English kid out in the sticks, this was a very different America to the stadium bands I'd grown up listening to. Here was a hallucinatory world of dune buggies and Mexican weed; muscle cars and skull bongs; late night Kung Fu triple bills and bad acid; heat haze shimmering off Arizona parking lots and monstrous, fuzzed out, brutal, cave man riffs; of beat prose and strange glowing orbs in the sky; of grease and high weirdness and humidity and condensation dripping down beer bottles in dark bars while the fan rotated above; of Melvins and Tad and the Jesus Lizard and the Butthole Surfers and all manner else. But — more than that — for the first time, here was music that took me out of myself and into outerstellar orbit. Music that removed me from the nuts and bolts, the here and now, and into a different headspace. It was, in a word, transcendent.

It's always strange looking back at teenage years. For me, it's something of an irony that this sonic awakening happened at the exact same time as britpop — a sound I disliked, with it's faux confidence and dull, myopic, meat and potatoes plod. Give me head music. Give me melting, hallucinatory, fuzzy maximalism; hypnosis and gnosis and drone and feedback. And give it to me still! As I write this, it's a freezing November morning and Endless Boogie *Admonitions* is blasting in the headphones and here we are again…the drone eternal; the riff colossal…

Peace and Love to all

Harry Sword
Cambridge
November 2021

Prologue

We'd spent three days mainlining Duvel, Oude Geneva and ludicrously strong hydroponic weed.

The only solids to pass my lips were a couple of *kapsalon* kebabs — Rotterdam's infamous grease bomb, a mound of unidentifiable meat slurry topped with gouda shavings, chips and gloopy Dutch *saus*. A fellow writer and I were covering Roadburn Festival in Tilburg for the *Quietus*, and had spent the last few hours in communion with three thousand people standing stock still, head banging slowly in perfect union.

'It's like the wailing wall in there.'

In his dazed, half-hypnotised state, my friend perfectly captured the ritualistic power of doom metal done properly. Bongripper had just finished performing their aptly named *Miserable* LP in its entirety — a slow-building endurance test of brute physical bass weight. By the time we stumbled into the clouds of weed smoke outside Tilburg's 013 arts complex (dubbed 'Freak Canyon' by locals due to the bedraggled — and often extravagantly bearded — hordes of psychedelic warriors who descend en masse to the quiet university town each April) we were in a state of advanced sonic inebriation.

Bongripper play at heinous volume — the kind that makes teeth rattle like stray dominoes and lungs disgorge forgotten matter. That the band look like trainees in a *Sunday Times* top 30 legal firm rather than grizzled doom veterans only adds to the sense of disorientation.

Roadburn is the world's foremost pilgrimage for doom, drone and the outer church of noisy psychedelia: it champions the slow, the heavy and the weird. The festival is a serious proposition. Consider: Eyehategod — New Orleans sludge forefathers, whose slow-motion beastings evoke some hellish opiate withdrawal in 100 per cent humidity — playing in a consecrated church for two successive days.

Where a chilled Sunday afternoon lull in the programming is a screening of Dario Argento's opulent *giallo* bloodfest *Suspiria*, with its creepy score performed live by Italian proggers Goblin, sending those poor souls who had indulged too freely in fungal-based hallucinogens scuttling for the back doors. Over Roadburn's four days, peals of feedback and sustain beat away at the year's residual cortisone like some cathartic audio elixir resetting wayward strands of DNA. At times, it felt like I was experiencing the sonic embodiment of a palpable universal hum — those onstage channelling a mighty audio portent as opposed to merely playing.

Music from the doom/drone continuum subverts traditional rockist tropes — the preening machismo; the virtuosity; the cult of the performer; the adolescent turbulence — leaving a bare-bones structure of primal catharsis. Chords that last a full half-hour, a maelstrom of feedback, a Jah Shaka-esque bass blanket that shakes the bodily foundation. And — though ostensibly dark and physically oppressive — the music of Sunn O))), Electric Wizard, Saint Vitus, Melvins, Neurosis, Sleep or Earth is about more than that. For me, these are agents of primordial sonic ablution, enablers of psychic transferral to a different mental plane: a punch-drunk station of gleeful oneness, a place to embrace your inner medieval psychedelic pieman or switch off the mind altogether. Records like Sleep's *Dopesmoker* or Neurosis' *Through Sliver in Blood* carry a sense of ritualistic power: you don't listen; you partake in sonic ceremony.

Sitting in the Cul De Sac, Roadburn's smallest venue and one of Holland's finest dive bars — where sweat drips from the low ceiling and the air is scented with creaking leather — the seeds of this book were formed. I was, initially, going to map the story of doom metal and its many satellites. A deeply underground affair until the mid 1990s, this scene was now a worldwide cult with the attendant infrastructure — dedicated record labels, magazines, promoters and festivals — that entails. Roadburn feels like a family of fervent believers. It struck me as odd that nobody had told the story of the music.

As I began to think more deeply, the idea of a straight-up 'history of doom' felt reductive. Doom metal is, after all, defined primarily by the use of extreme *sustain*. The drone, in other words. And the drone is found everywhere from Buddhist chant to Indian raga; free jazz to ambient techno; minimalism to industrial, not to mention the myriad drones of nature. It can underpin music as (seemingly) disparate as the crackling dub techno of Basic Channel, the ecstatic jazz of Alice Coltrane or the oppressive glory of Godflesh.

Its amorphous nature, capacity for assimilation into unlikely spaces and presence in musical traditions around the world presented an intriguing ley line. As I researched the idea of the drone, its recurrence throughout musical history and place in theology and philosophy alike, I started to consider *why* we seek immersion in slow-moving sounds. What had begun as a hazed pondering in a nicotine-stained Dutch bar had become a quest to understand the essence of the drone — both how it came to underpin such diverse forms of music and why people have been drawn to it for millennia.

Speed in music reflects change. Societal, personal or political. Disruption to an established order. In the 1950s, teenagers ripped cinema seats with flick knives as society looked on aghast at the onset of rock 'n' roll delirium. 'Young blood', pumped on the adrenalised key hammering of Little Richard, Jerry Lee Lewis et al. Fast-forward twenty years and we find punk marshalling amphetamine drive in evocation of nihilistic oblivion, political unrest and frequently both. Electronic dance music has frequently presented a similarly confrontational stance, be it drum and bass pushing a frenetic 170 beats per minute in the name of urban futurism or Detroit techno evoking the ravaged topography of the (former) motor city — a husk of staggering decrepitude reverberating to Underground Resistance.

But while velocity in music is readily associated with unrest, the left-hand path — slow-moving hypnotic sound — is a road far less travelled, at least critically. *Monolithic Undertow* explores the viscous slipstream — drone, doom and beyond — and claims the sounds uncovered, which hinge on hypnotic power and close physical presence, as no less radical. It is not, however, a history of drone as genre. Once genre lines become codified, the least interesting music happens. As Birmingham techno producer Surgeon once put it to me: 'That thing of when people say: "Right then, today, I'm going to make a *dark techno* track." That attitude is the absolute recipe for shit music. It's looking at music on the pure surface level.'[1]

So it is with all music.

Instead of gravitating to genre, this book follows an outer stellar orbit of sounds underpinned by the drone. The bulk of the narrative is concerned with the twentieth-century underground, and how so much of it came to be shaped by the drone. I was also keen to include substantive background on the vital influence of non-Western musical traditions. Too often the importance of Indian classical music, say, is relegated to a footnote or brief paragraph in discussions of the wider sixties rock lineage. But — as we'll see — were it not for the enduring influence of figures like Ravi Shankar or Pandit Pran Nath the underground landscape of today would be completely unrecognisable.

Certain topics covered in early chapters — archaeoacoustics, the ecology of background noise, the spiritual trance traditions of India and Morocco, the role of sound in Dionysian ritual — could, of course, fill many books, many times over. My hope here was not to comprehensively catalogue such venerable traditions and areas of deep scholarship, but to open potential wormholes in the minds of curious readers, and link areas that may otherwise have remained disconnected.

Monolithic Undertow thus plots a crooked path across musical, religious and subcultural frontiers. It traces the line from ancient traditions to the modern underground, navigating archaeoacoustics, ringing feedback, chest-plate sub-bass, avant-garde eccentricity, sound weaponry and fervent spiritualism. From Neolithic beginnings to bawdy medieval troubadours, Sufi mystics to Indian raga masters, cone-shattering dubwise bass, Hawkwind's Ladbroke Grove to the outer reaches of Faust and Ash Ra Tempel; the hash-fuelled fug of the Theatre of Eternal Music to the caveman doom of Saint Vitus and cough-syrup reverse hardcore of Swans to the seedy VHS hinterland of Electric Wizard, ritual amp worship of Earth and Sunn O))) and the many touchpoints between, *Monolithic Undertow* explores the power of the drone — an audio carrier vessel capable of evoking womb-like warmth or cavernous dread alike.

I was also keen to map the drone in other non-musical spaces — from the womb, to infrasonic sound weaponry to 'singing' black holes. Indeed, while I was writing — among the ever-churning maelstrom of Trump, Brexit et al. — I found myself thinking increasingly about how the drone manifests *outside* of music. The invasiveness of the 24/7 news cycle, outpouring of online anger, pressure for the instant 'hot take'; the outrage, showboating, dopamine-seeking crack monkey of social media 'engagement' — all of this increasingly seemed to me to manifest as a drone.

Perhaps it was psychosomatic? Look for patterns and they tend to appear: maybe I'd spent too long in a sleep-deprived state listening to Sunn O))) at brain-mashing volume? But the thought remained. Is the thrum of infinite information — the ceaseless fire hose of 'content' — another manifestation of the drone?

One freezing January morning, I stumbled across the following paragraph, quoted in a Velvet Underground biography, from Marshall McLuhan's seminal 1967 text *The Medium is the Massage*. In the book, McLuhan explores how new technologies play with, alter and shape human perception. Here he was, describing the time-bending effect of the Velvet Underground amid the blizzard of what was then modern life:

'Time' has ceased, 'space' has vanished. We now live in a global village . . . a simultaneous happening. We are back in acoustic space. We have begun again to structure the primordial feeling, the tribal emotions from which a few centuries of literacy divorced us. Electric circuitry profoundly involves men with one another. Information pours upon us, instantaneously and continuously. As soon as information is acquired, it is very rapidly replaced by still newer information. Our electricity configured world has forced us to move from the bait of data classification to the mode of pattern recognition. We can no longer build serially, block by block, step by step, because instant communication ensures that all factors of the environment and of experience coexist in a state of active interplay. We have now become aware of the possibility of arranging the entire human environment as a work of art.[2]

I was struck by the 'primordial feeling' that the Velvet Underground awoke in McLuhan as he wrote his book. It spoke of what I'd been connecting with and what, I think, all of us who 'get it' seek in the drone.

That primordial feeling . . .

The Universal Drone

What do we mean by drone? The word is myriad. It can carry connotations both sinister and banal. A drone can drop a cluster bomb or deliver a pizza.

In music, drone is an audio space where age-old markers, such as verse, chorus, verse or complex progressions are rendered redundant. Sounds don't (or, crucially, *appear* not to) change at all.

Static, hiss, white noise, feedback — these are all drones. In essence, drone equals sustain — sustained sustain, if you will. Environmental and mechanical drones form the auditory backbone of urban and wild spaces alike. The acoustic by-products of the natural and man-made world are inescapable. Traffic; background conversation; wind; turbines — to be alive is to live with multiple background drones, whether we're conscious of them or not.

Think of a power cut and how it brings into focus the eerie quiet that befalls a house when the various mechanical drones that our brains are so adept at tuning out — the low hum of central heating, the buzz of the refrigerator, the churn of the dryer — actually stop. The removal without forewarning of the small domestic symphony we seldom otherwise notice has a disquieting effect.

But enough of the dishwasher.

What of the cosmic infinity? What of the godhead?

I'm sitting in my kitchen with a cup of tea, listening to the sound the universe made as it expanded 600,000 years after the Big Bang. It sounds like Hawkwind. More specifically, it sounds like the band's electronics division circa 1973, Del Dettmar and Dik Mik — bearded purveyors of rare cosmic misanthropy — setting up their rickety table of rudimentary ring modulators and letting rip in some musty Ladbroke Grove squat.

I imagine the scent of Peshawar hash and patchouli oil heavy in the air, boxes of the *International Times* dotted around, Moroccan rugs lining sparse wooden floors, chipped mugs of brick-coloured tea offering some respite to the rising damp that surely permeated my imagined dilapidated seventies west London terrace.

I listen again, lost in the magic of the cosmic infinitude. It sounds viscous, alive, intelligent. I hear transmogrifying sub-bass, phasing, a creepy Doppler effect that builds with ominous portent.

That I'm sitting here — now — at my kitchen table listening through time to this universal sound feels miraculous.

In the early universe there were no atoms, only charged particles. Charged particles don't allow light to travel. The early universe was therefore black. Any light was absorbed, immediately. Eventually protons and electrons began to form hydrogen atoms — the building blocks of what we think of as life. The universe was no longer black.

At this point — as Professor John Cramer explains to me over a crackly phone line from Washington DC — 'a burst of radiation — what we call the cosmic background radiation (CBR) — was released. It has been travelling through time ever since. This is what satellites are picking up: radiation that was produced around 600,000 years after the Big Bang. As the universe expanded, it essentially became a bass instrument. The sound waves shot downwards at the same rate of expansion, which creates a Doppler effect.'

You might be wondering by this point how we can hear such an event, billions of years after the fact. Cramer took the data from a satellite system called Planck sent to measure fluctuations in temperature in the CBR. He converted it to pressure variations (all sound is created by vibration — fluctuations in pressure) and entered the data into a computer program called Mathematica which, in turn, translated it to the sound file I'm now listening to at my kitchen table.

When Cramer played it through a powerful subwoofer his dogs sat up, entranced.

'I'd never seen them behave that way,' he laughs. 'People ask, "How could there be sound waves in the early universe when space is a vacuum?" But the early universe was hardly a vacuum. It was filled with matter and had a higher density than the Earth's atmosphere. There was no problem with sound waves travelling through it. Think of it like a drum head,' he continues, 'a vibrating sphere. By analysing the frequency, you get information about what was happening. The frequencies are too low to hear — these were very large wavelengths, very low frequencies.'

Make no mistake: we're talking *very* low-frequency sound — a tumbling leviathan of universal sub-pressure, getting ever lower the further the wavelengths are stretched. Cramer had to boost the resulting frequency 100 *septillion* times (100 followed by 24 more zeroes) just to get the recordings into an audible range. Could we, I tentatively ask, say that the sound of the universe expanding was really more drone than bang?

'It wasn't really a bang at all,' he agrees. 'It sounded more like an aeroplane flying low over your house. In that respect, yes — it was more of a drone than a bang.'

Cramer's sound file feels like cosmic magic, a beautiful synergy of scientific endeavour, sonic mystery and the humbling vastness of the expanding universe. It isn't the only link between the cosmos and the drone, however. Researchers at the University of Cambridge's Institute of Astronomy recently discovered what they describe as a 'singing' black hole among a distant galaxy cluster that emits the lowest sound waves ever detected.

Situated amid a group of thousands of galaxies known as the Perseus Cluster — around 250 million light years from Earth — Dr Andrew Fabian and team found the sound it makes is a 'single note . . . really a drone'.[3] Using a middle C as reference point, Fabian determined that note was a B flat. However, this B flat is 57 octaves below middle C — approximately one million, billion times lower than the lowest sound audible to the human ear.

While Cramer measured the temperature fluctuations, Fabian and team measured the distance between enormous pressure ripples on the outside of the black hole. These ripples — caused by the rhythmic squeezing, heating and movement of cosmic gas amid the intense gravitational pressure of clustered galaxies — equate to sound waves. By measuring the location of the ripples and the speed at which sound may travel between them, the team determined the musical note of the drone.

Ambient producer William Basinski's recent album *On Time Out of*

Time works with a similar sound, sourced from MIT's Gravitational Wave Observatory in California — a piece of equipment tasked with observing cosmic gravitational waves. His album takes the sound created by these waves — what he describes as 'ripples in space-time' — and transposes them to the ambient sphere. The Berlin debut of the record reportedly opened with Basinski stating: 'This is about what happens when two black holes fuck.'[4]

It's humbling to be listening to audio fundamentals of such immense celestial force. But there is also a strange comfort in the idea of the cosmic drone. Rumbling outside the scope of human perception, a bass weight of godlike depth, out in the planetary ether.

A *living* sound that cleaves to the ultimate universal mystery.

Indeed, the idea of the drone as a singular force — *the* singular force — runs through philosophy, mathematics and theology like a gilded sonic thread. Take string theory. The theory of (almost) everything. In short: all universal matter is made up of infinitesimally minuscule vibrating strings. The Large Hadron Collider, Paul McCartney, a wooden chair — drill down far enough . . . it's all vibration.

Vibration produces sound. All matter exerts force on the airwaves surrounding it. Every object has a natural frequency at which it vibrates when struck. Can 'natural frequency' therefore be applied to the universe itself? From a spiritual perspective, this idea takes on interesting significance.

In Buddhism and Hinduism alike, the drone manifests as the sacred Om (which we'll explore more in later chapters) — the vibration of universal matter. In Hindu philosophy, sound carries uniquely sacred significance. The concept of Nadha Brahma translates as 'Sound is God' — a fundamental tenet of Vedic scripture. The divine is codified not as matter, but as *sound* vibration that runs through everything — coexisting in everything and everyone simultaneously. The unified nature of reality itself is — in theological terms — intimately tied to the drone.

The idea of celestial sound vibration was also considered by Pythagoras in the concept of *musica universalis*, the music of the spheres — the idea that celestial objects, stars and planets in orbit, emit sound. Legend has the Ionian Greek philosopher and mathematician walking past a blacksmith and noticing that the pitch of each hammer changed, depending on its size. 'Harmony' could, he deduced, be mapped: distance in sound charted in much the same way as the *physical* distance between, say, the village blacksmith and the village baker. He transposed his harmonic hypothesis to a cosmic scale — *musica universalis* — which theorised that the separation between planets should harmonically 'map' to their respective distances: 'There is geometry in the humming of the strings, there is music in the spacing of the spheres.'

Many artists have taken inspiration from the music of the spheres and the infinitude of the cosmic drone. We'll delve deep into Hawkwind's space-conquering acid maelstrom, the mystic thrum of Ash Ra Tempel and others later.

For now, though, let's take it back to our own beginnings. Humanity's relationship to the drone begins in inner, rather than outer, space.

The Sonic Womb

The womb is a dynamic audio environment. The maternal drone is our first auditory experience. Of the five senses, hearing is the first to develop. Bodily sounds — the rushing of the blood, the beating of the heart, the gurgles of the digestive tract — are not merely perceptible to a foetus *in utero* but heard, loud and clear. A 1990 study recorded levels of womb sound at around 88 decibels at full term, much higher than previously anticipated and equivalent to a food processor or a car wash at twenty feet.

Drone sounds evoke the womb. They remain demonstrably soothing for the early years of a child's life. At time of writing my infant son won't go to sleep without a drone generator. The ubiquity of these sleep aids — whereby static, wave sounds, rain or gentle traffic noise are played in a continuous loop — is testament to their effectiveness. A Pavlovian audio marker that says 'sleep time', such devices frame the drone as aural security blanket: a comforting sonic shield that leads back to the interior.

Sleep is a precious commodity for us all now. The endless drone of content and commerce has driven us to seek refuge in other, more benign, drones. Recent years have seen specific Spotify 'sleep playlists' gain popularity while drone generators and meditation apps have moved into the mainstream.

Ambient music is functional. Like an ambient temperature, it is by definition *ignorable*. This is why it facilitates creativity or relaxation. Inevitably, ambient producers have riffed on sleep, hypnosis, waking-dream states. Producer Max Richter's 2015 *Sleep* is an eight-hour piece mirroring a typical sleep cycle. Using electronic drones, field recordings, piano and strings, Richter attempts, in his words, 'an eight-hour personal lullaby for a frenetic world and a manifesto for a slower pace of existence.'

Richard D. James aka Aphex Twin sought to harness the peculiarly fertile psychic ground between wakefulness and sleep on his record *Selected Ambient Works Two*. He composed much of the album immediately on waking. Fitful sleep in the studio, then straight on the buttons in an attempt to capture the fleeting hypnagogic state that fades like mist.

At the all-night late-sixties San Francisco concerts of minimalist pioneer Terry Riley, the audience were encouraged to bring hammocks and sleeping bags and be lulled to sleep by cyclical tape loops and, no doubt, pungent herbaceous smoke. Riley's somnambulant sounds were a letting go of the pinpoint focus of the avant-garde, anticipating ambient with its use of the drone as sleep aid.

For some the idea of 'sleep as muse' — not to mention the ambient predilection for surrender, passivity and beatific calm — is anathema, an insult to artistic motion, a mollifying tonic that disavows the very pulse of life and creativity. When confronted with the twee commodification of YouTube's audio 'wellness' division it's hard to disagree. Here, the drone is deployed in gratingly winsome terms. A cursory search for 'meditation music' or similar will bring up thousands of hours of polished pre-set mulch accompanied by questionable descriptive claims: 'remove *all* negative thoughts'; 'find *instant* bliss' et cetera. However, this does the real thing a disservice — and we'll investigate the fundamental difference between ambient as quick-fix wellness product and considered artistry later.

It makes sense that in times of stress we seek solace in sounds that evoke a return to the cocoon — to stasis and the fugue state of womb-like immersion; indeed that descriptor comes up time and again. Some composers have gone direct to the source, with viscerally arresting results. *Biostasis* (1974) — by minimalist composer Éliane Radigue — combines slowly unfurling synthesiser tones with the heartbeats of her son and unborn grandchild. In her words, a 'hymn to the perpetuation of life', it's simultaneously comforting and mysterious. The merest hint of a synth drone is offset against a gentle pulse, evoking an amorphous, aquatic state.

Radigue is a master of using the drone to traverse both the beauty and sadness of life. *Trilogie de la Mort* (1988) was inspired by the death of her son and follows the journey stages of the *Tibetan Book of the Dead*: *Kyene* (birth), *Milam* (dream), *Samtem* (meditation), *Chikai* (death), *Chonye* (clear light) and *Sippai* (crossing and return), playing like an attempt to articulate what she described as the 'mysterious power of the infinitesimal',[5] forging a sonic path through to the beyond.

Is the drone fundamentally transformative? Is it mentally cleansing, having a similarly positive effect on the mind as exercise does to the body? If so, then what of catharsis? Are the harsher metallic landscapes of Sunn O))), Neurosis, Sleep and the like — where expurgation, as well as transcendent meditation, is a primary goal — so far removed from the works of Radigue, Eno and others?

This meditative aspect is, however, but one side of our complex relationship with the drone. Amorphous, uncontrolled and mysterious tones can also be a source of anxiety, frustration and pain — not to mention the odd outlandish conspiracy theory. Noise pollution is the drone in its most dismal incarnation. Think of the average open-plan office. The audio soup is ceaseless: murmured telephone conversations; printer on overdrive; opposing ringtones; the hum of overhead strip lighting; the low rumble of some distant boiler.

The Boiler Room

Beyond mere irritation, background noise is a proven health hazard. Sound stripped of easily digestible 'meaning', in the conversational sense, has been shown to increase negative 'cognitive load'. Lack of acoustic control — spaces, like the now ubiquitous open plan, that offer no audio respite or means of shutting oneself off from others — can lead to feelings of powerlessness.

Here there are parallels with Oscar Newman's defensible space theory. His book *Defensible Space* (1972) observed higher rates of crime and anti-social behaviour in New York's high-rise as opposed to ground-level projects, although both were occupied by people of broadly similar backgrounds.

He theorised that an area is healthy when residents feel an individual sense of agency, and therefore have the onus to 'defend' — both metaphorically and literally — their homes. Communities — through insensitive planning, lack of amenities, disenfranchisement of residents and lack of investment — become dangerously alienating if people begin to feel powerless over their surroundings and therefore lose the incentive to care. Social problems and crime are — so goes the theory — logical outcomes of bad housing.

His book was seized on as a damning indictment of the folly and insensitivity of post-war social housing around the world.

It would be churlish to suggest lack of defensible audio space in the average open-plan office results in anything like the same level of stress that beset post-war estates that have suffered decades of criminal neglect, but there are parallels. Aside from the visual stress of being 'on display' at all times, the open plan offers scant audible respite.

A creeping sense remains that perhaps the true purpose is — rather than fostering chummy collaboration in some Nathan Barley-esque 'ideasphere' — actually more akin to panopticon prison philosophy. Designed in such a way that inmates can — potentially — be observed at all times. Prisoners, housed around the perimeter, are unable to see into the inspection area while always remaining observable. In England, north London's Pentonville is an infamous example of panopticon design. French philosopher Michel Foucault framed the social theory of 'panopticism' in *Discipline and Punish: The Birth of the Prison* (1975). His central idea was that any panoptic design results from a desire for mechanistic control over any populace in 'need' of observation:

If the inmates are convicts, there is no danger of a plot, an attempt at collective escape, the planning of new crimes for the future, bad reciprocal influences; if they are patients, there is no danger of contagion; if they are madmen there is no risk of their committing violence upon one another; if they are schoolchildren, there is no copying, no noise, no chatter, no waste of time; if they are workers, there are no disorders, no theft, no coalitions, none of those distractions that slow down the rate of work, make it less perfect or cause accidents.[6]

The sonic environment in prison — where existing feelings of fear and stress are compounded by the shock of exposure to an alien audio sphere — was recently captured in the brilliant Prison Radio Association radio documentary *Sounds Inside*. It offers a cacophonous sound collage of what prison actually sounds like: reverb-laden shouts, metallic clangs, frenetic ping-pong games, echoing footsteps, screams, laughter, calls to prayer — and how it affects those who live there. In the show, producer, writer and former inmate Carl Cattermole recalls the shock that rare moments of sonic respite (in this case a quiet classroom) brought in HMP Pentonville:

The classrooms were daunting with that padded quietness . . . It was like a different world from the landings where the sound is punishingly bright — a total echo chamber.[7]

Elsewhere in the documentary an HMP Brixton inmate called Jacob describes the calming drone of the vacuum cleaner, and how it offered a distinct solace:

When I'm down here by myself and I'm hoovering I can figure out things in my head . . . I love the sound . . .[8]

Powerlessness in the face of sound — be it the acoustic footprint of city life, an institution, industrial noise or simply inane office 'banter' — has a demonstrably negative psychological effect. Attempts to negate it by tuning into hypnotic audio zones of our own — even the respite provided by a vacuum cleaner — are testament to the power of the drone as a mechanism of personal liberation.

But when does sound become noise? And who makes the distinction?

The Agony and the Ecstasy

The drone as noise, sonic backdrop to a life of servitude, is a potent symbol of capitalist overload. Canadian writer Murray Schafer spent decades researching noise as audio pollutant. He defined it as a necessary — though often unwelcome — appendage of urbanisation and rapid industrial development. In Schafer's view there are three principal noise types: unwanted noise, unmusical sound and any loud sound or disturbance in any signalling system. From an artistic perspective, however, these categories are bothersome. If 'unmusical' sound is to be declared 'noise' it poses the question: who decides? Murray Schafer? No. The ear of the beholder reigns supreme.

If the drone of a vacuum cleaner in HMP Brixton can be used as an aural escape mechanism, then surely it not only transcends the negative association of Schafer's definition but also itself: it becomes a liberatory audio talisman. If any 'unmusical sound' is to be taken as noise — relegated to a negative critical zone of Schafer's design — then you can discount any number of discordant sounds where the intention is greater than that of mere irritation.

Napalm Death blasting through a punishingly abrasive grindcore set? Merzbow at tinnitus-rendering levels? The Iration Steppas rig pumping out dub at chest-rattling volume? These sounds may have proved contrary to Schafer's personal tastes. But the idea that the wild frontier of sound should be codified in such a way — with the 'unmusical' (in the traditional harmonic sense) demoted into a sonic dead zone equated with irritation and distress — denigrates the many artists disrupting the harmonic flow and working with abrasive sound.

The drone — when deployed, as it so frequently is, in the service of the obtuse and atonal, as opposed to underpinning harmonic interplay — fits

Schafer's 'unmusical noise' definition to a tee. Indeed, generations of artists have explored the wild frontiers of 'unmusical sound'. In the early twentieth century, the Italian futurists were obsessed with the very idea of noise as an art form bonded to the factory experience and the cornucopia of peculiar — and new — sounds that emanated from these gargantuan spaces: clanging, banging, metal on metal, the brute mechanised swing of a brave new world.

Luigi Russolo's *The Art of Noises* futurist manifesto published in 1913 argued for a new order of sound — seldom, it must be noted, actually realised — that reflected a changing of the sonic guard. This was to be a celebration of mastery of resource; the thrusting, forward motion of mechanisation, a clarion call to the factory floor, a triumphant jeer in the face of what were seen as the primitive feudal orders of the (recent) past.

As it grows ever more complicated today, musical art seeks out combinations more dissonant, stranger, and harsher for the ear. Thus, it comes ever closer to the noise-sound . . . Beethoven and Wagner for many years wrung our hearts. But now we are sated with them and derive much greater pleasure from ideally combining the noise of streetcars, internal-combustion engines, automobiles, and busy crowds than from re-hearing, for example, the 'Eroica' or the 'Pastorale' . . . away! let us be gone, since we shall not much longer succeed in restraining a desire to create a new musical realism by a generous distribution of sonorous blows and slaps, leaping nimbly over violins, pianofortes, contrabasses, and groaning organs, Away![9]

The futurists took what many now take as audio pollution — industrial drones and clangs, the noise of the machine — and eulogised it to the point of fetish. There was, of course, a well-documented proto-fascistic element at play here. The futurists celebrated noise not simply because they found it sonically interesting but *because* of what it represented: the primacy of modernity over a life of agricultural drudge. Wooden-stringed instruments and the established classical oeuvre plucked and strummed upon them were — in Russolo's mind — as musically valid as a plate of stodgy pasta. (The futurists *hated* pasta. In *The Futurist Cookbook* Marinetti railed against the way that it induced 'lassitude, pessimism, nostalgic inactivity and neutralism . . . anti-virile . . . no food for fighters.')[10]

There are, of course, sonic parallels to be made with the late-twenti-eth-century noise/industrial axis here: forms in which the drone is frequently front and centre. However, while the futurists delighted in the dance of the machine, they came at it from the perspective of a modern-day middle manager measuring toilet breaks and recording 'productivity metrics'. The machine was cherished because it represented efficiency of process, the primacy of automation.

By contrast, industrial music of the late twentieth century — far from revelling in the mechanised efficacy of factory toil — looked to the dehuman-ising aspect of life and death among the smokestacks, and drew sonic pictures in the residual soot. Artists like Throbbing Gristle worked in the negative zone, clocked in at the (death) disco, but broadly eschewed gratuitousness. [gratuity = a tip etc.] At its best there was a cathartic element at play, emo-tional honesty as opposed to lecherous excess. Listen to a track like 'Medicine' (1982): a full minute of ear-piercing feedback dissolves into cavernous metallic echo and disembodied voices — 'it's really good'; 'yes, it's coming through . . . coming out'; '39 b . . . quite good'. A nightmarish evocation of nameless *procedures* — more ghost in the faculty than fly on the wall — TG use the drone to set a scene of chilly corridors, churning basement boilers, barren tumbleweed courtyards and clicked heels hurrying to observation rooms: theirs is a fundamentally visual music.

As writer David Keenan so memorably put it in *England's Hidden Reverse*, industrial music was 'an attempt to say yes to no'.[11] Throbbing Gristle hold up a mirror to humanity, in all its fallibility and grotesque *in*humanity. When Chris Carter unfurls a queasy distorted synth drone on 'Hamburger Lady' — which relates the unbearable pain of a terminal burns victim — it evokes dread and claustrophobia. But above that it relates hopelessness — the hopelessness of a situation outside the scope of imagination to anyone but the sufferer. True horror, rendered without any semblance of Hollywood excess — a drab prosaic horror. William S. Burroughs's own description of *Naked Lunch* applies here: 'The title means exactly what the words say: naked lunch — a frozen moment when everyone sees what is on the end of every fork.'

Static; subterfuge; stasis; sex. In noise and industrial music alike the drone is cast as a means of shaking up complacency. It challenges the listener to question preconceived ideas about the validity of sound and the places they are willing to go with it. Classical notions of melodic progression, virtuosity and — by proxy — exclusivity, whereby musical ability is the preserve of the practised few, are called into sharp focus. The joy of noise, the shock of the new — or as Sir Ben Kingsley's Don Logan in *Sexy Beast* would have it, '. . .

the sheer fuck-offness' involved in the visceral joy of creation — is prized. Sound is a malleable texturiser, erotic and amorphous. As prolific Japanese noise producer Merzbow put it:

> Just as the Dadaists made art from objects from the street, I made sound from the scum that surrounds my life. I'm inspired by the surrealist idea 'everything is erotic, everywhere erotic'. For me, noise is the most erotic form of sound. The word 'noise' has been used in Western Music since *The Art of Noises*. However, industrial music used 'noise' as a kind of technique. Western noise is often too conceptual or academic. Japanese noise relishes the ecstasy of sound itself.[12]

The *ecstasy* of sound.

Herein lies the rub. At its best, noise and industrial music reclaim the audio backdrop of life's darker frontiers without gloating (at its worst it does precisely that and worse) but it frequently revels in the *textural* glory of the process and, as we'll see time and again, the drone is a prime texturiser — and catharsis is never fully shorn of glee.

Field Manoeuvres

If the mechanised drone is a source of stress and anxiety, what of the drones of the natural world? These sounds can be foreboding — the howl of wind over Bodmin Moor, say, a place that seemingly crackles with dark malevolence — or offer beatific calm. Does any sound evoke languid humidity, a heat-haze crawl pace, more readily than the granular drone of cicadas?

The natural drone frequently offers solace. The return to nature is frequently tied to tropes of abandonment. Of course, it doesn't always work like that (we'll soon explore the dread and terror that can accompany natural sounds of unknown provenance) but the act of leaving behind the literal and metaphorical 'trappings' of city life — be they work, technology or stress — can indeed be intoxicating. A freeing from doleful routine drudgery, the reigniting of a palpably animal spark: at its best — and, crucially, with the right headspace and in the right surroundings and company — the sounds of nature can work as something approaching primal cathartic magic.

Recently, walking across gorse fields in Cornwall looking for the remote Neolithic burial chamber of Chun Quiot, I found myself on top of a rugged hill with both north-west and south-west Atlantic coastlines in clear view, the rush of wind all around. It was sheer exhilaration — an audio feast of near erotic intensity — the push of the wind coming from both directions, saline tang in the air, the glimpse of Chun Quiot's foreboding capstone just visible against slate-grey skies.

Sound artists working with field recordings seek to capture such sonic flashes of personal wonderment, attempting psychic access to the heart of the moment in the process. As such moments are often fleeting, they necessitate active deep listening. In a recent interview with *The Quietus*, sound artist — and former Cabaret Voltaire agitator — Chris Watson railed against the intrusiveness of noise pollution and its effect in shutting off our ability to listen closely.

> We're all damaged by noise pollution — psychologically as much as anything, and we're just not aware of it. You ring your bank and they play music at you down the phone, it's so invasive. Because of that we waste so much energy in shutting things out, we don't get the chance to listen . . . The advent of cheap fabricated build-ings means that most of those you go in have appalling acoustics. You can't have a conversation or you can hear everybody else's conversations because you're surrounded by flat parallel walls.

Watson has navigated both the beauty and strangeness of natural soundscapes in his field work and the stress buzz of scattershot mechanical audio in his earlier work with Cabaret Voltaire. His soundscapes capture the essence of the places he is recording, honing in on visceral atmospherics peculiar to a location. *Stepping into the Dark* (1996) is a case in point, and saw Watson work with powerful wind drones at Glenn Cannich, capturing the eerie multilayered tones as they whip across the glen and also the doom-laden scratch and craw of the 'parliament of rooks' at Embleton rookery. He evoked the memory of ley line pioneer T.C. Lethbridge in his liner notes.

> Lethbridge might have said that the birds come here, largely due to this always pagan site having obvious associations with the

17

strong atmosphere of its ley line and ritual past . . . The acoustic of the place spins the parliament of the rooks through the cold air, its stillness, and into the timeless chaos . . .[13]

Watson's field recordings communicate the transient nature of a natural world in flux: there is no background manipulation or editing, he simply mikes up the environment at the right time and records what is happening in front of him. I'm minded to make a comparison to the raw recording style of Steve Albini (Nirvana, Pixies, Big Black et cetera) who famously eschews post-production trickery to capture the spirit of what is happening in the *room*, as opposed to perfect performances by individual players spliced together after the fact.

Key to Watson's acoustic philosophy is the idea that each location holds a particular spirit: on the haunting *El Tren Fantasma* (2011) he evoked a ghost train journey — the now defunct railway that traversed the Mexican Pacific coast — by travelling the former line and recording the sounds, people and wildlife that once surrounded it. Natural drones place the listener in the centre of a long-gone journey, the acoustic footprint of which still resonates today, be it the thrum of buzzing flies on 'Crucero La Joya' or the menacing animal howls amid heat-haze cicadas on 'El Tajin'.

Watson's pioneering production work in early Cabaret Voltaire records also made use of field recordings (albeit layered and processed) to evoke a feeling of Dadaist multimedia overload, humanity adrift in a chaotic maelstrom of political messages, militaristic yelling, pop culture references and dystopic futurism. Repetition, tape loops and crackling white noise brought a feeling of unease, humanity adrift amid ceaseless *input*.

Other sound artists like Matthew Herbert have used field recordings as a launch point for navigating similarly dark territories. His heartbreaking *One Pig* (2011), for example, follows the journey of an animal bred for meat. Each track is named after a month in the animal's short — and entirely fore-written — life. First plaintive oinks are offset against maternal synth drones; wrenching death squeals become a grotesque sub-bass blanket; slamming doors and the click of boots are pregnant with malevolence due to the certain knowledge of the outcome — this is the end, my friend.

Herbert personalises and amplifies the process of industrialised death. He forces the listener to confront what is taking place and evaluate their own complicity.

Elsewhere, he's worked with more minimal sample material to equally devastating effect. *The End of Silence* (2013) took a five-second sample — heard untreated at the album's start — of a fighter jet dropping a bomb in Libya. The roar of the engine and the muffled boom of the explosion followed by the grotesque 'calm' of the immediate aftermath are then, over fifty minutes, sliced, rearranged, processed and scrambled into a collage by turns eerie and horrifying. Just as *One Pig* renders brutally personal that which is typically hidden, so *The End of Silence* speaks to the desensitised 24/7 news 'consumer' blunted by a barrage of familiar war imagery. The foundational sound — shorn of familial 'war report' visual signifiers and attendant grave commentary — is deeply shocking.

Again, the drone is used to wrap the listener in a false security blanket. Calm passages give way to the same moment of unadorned horror. Time and again, you're jarred awake, reminded that *every* sound, no matter what Herbert has done to it, no matter how ostensibly soothing, derives from that one moment of terror. Is *The End of Silence* industrial music in its truest, most devastating, form? It's certainly more emotionally resonant and truly shocking than any of the faux 'transgressive' posturing that came hot on the (leather) coat tails of Throbbing Gristle et al. throughout the eighties.

By manipulating a *single* sound, Herbert speaks of the sheer sonic terror of modern warfare. Indeed, the sounds of war carry a uniquely potent dread. Though the visual signifiers of wartime propaganda — gleaming fighter jets, well-drilled infantry, naval squadrons — have been used to foster feelings of patriotic pride since time immemorial, sound is a completely different matter.

Rarely do the sounds of bombs or machine guns induce anything other than fear or revulsion. During the First World War the misery and squalor of the trenches may have been hidden from public view; however, the fact that the bombs of the Somme were audible in London offered a (literal) echo of a world of horror and destruction just over the Channel.

The devastating psychological and physical effect of sound was well documented during the First World War. The world's first industrial war was unimaginably loud. Gunners operating 18-pound field guns were not issued with ear defenders — eardrums could be easily perforated on first use by sheer sonic shock; first-hand testimony often offers soldiers recalling dazed gunners stumbling around, blood pouring from burst eardrums. Such was the volume that sound was spoken of in physical terms: 'I felt that if I lifted a finger I should touch a solid ceiling of sound,' wrote one soldier of the bombardment at Vimy Ridge.[14]

Thousands suffered irreparable hearing damage amid the barrage. Others reported a fine-tuning. There could be a horribly personal aspect to the soundscape of the trenches. Soldiers undertaking hand-to-hand combat missions would become sensitised to the smallest sounds. The maximal audio carnage of the front was suddenly shrunk to an animalistic level of minute perception. In *Storm of Steel* — the first published account of trench warfare, written by German infantry soldier Ernst Jünger in 1920 — the phenomenon was recounted.

Ears are tensed to the maximum, the rustling approach of strange feet in the tall grass is an unutterably menacing thing. Your breath comes in shallow bursts; you have to force yourself to stifle any panting or wheezing. There is a little mechanical click as the safety-catch of your pistol is taken off; the sound cuts straight through your nerves. Your teeth are grinding on the fuse-pin of the hand-grenade. The encounter will be short and murder-ous. You tremble with two contradictory impulses: the heightened awareness of the huntsmen, and the terror of the quarry. You are a world to yourself, saturated with the appalling aura of the savage landscape.

Each war brings its own peculiar hellish soundscape. In the Second World War the whinnying drone of the air raid siren provided ominous forewarning of fast-approaching bombers. The German Stuka Ju 87, meanwhile, was fitted with a 70cm siren nicknamed the 'trumpet of Jericho'. This emitted a terrifying high-pitched drone as the dive-bomber hurtled towards its target — a weapon of sheer psychological warfare aimed at maximising dread from those nearby as well as those directly in the line of fire.

Far removed from shiny recruitment-centre images of camaraderie and derring-do, the field of 'sound weaponry' evokes sinister tropes: covert manip-ulation, black ops, secret bases, torture et cetera. Weaponised sound sees the drone at its most malevolent, handed to the men in black: a world of clammy dread, seedy embassies, battered suitcases and shifty emissaries.

Ghost Tape Number 10 is an unsettling case in point. During the Vietnam War an American psy-ops unit developed a tape as part of a psychological offensive called Operation Wandering Soul.

It played on the widely held Vietnamese folk belief that the dead must receive a proper burial in their homeland — or else, be destined to become an eternally 'wandering soul'. The tape encompassed eerie drones, white noise and disembodied voices calling out to 'relatives' in the Viet Cong to lay down arms. Played at high volume during night-time ground missions and via loudspeakers mounted on helicopters, the Americans hoped to stoke fear and manipulate deep-seated folk beliefs as 'ancestral' voices (Southern Vietnamese actors) called out, 'My friends! I have come back to let you know that I am dead! I am dead! . . . Don't end up like me! Go home, friends, before it is too late!'

Anecdotal evidence suggests it had some success. Though many Viet Cong soldiers realised that the tape was a work of fiction, it planted enough of a seed of doubt — playing as it did on such deep-seated belief — to cause some to turn back.

The power of sound to induce feelings of terror, awe or unease is manifest. Nowhere is this clearer than in the depersonalised horror of modern drone warfare, whereby unmanned drones wreak havoc via remote control. In a 2012 *New Yorker* feature, the Palestinian journalist Wasseem El Sarraj described the soundscape of Gaza under attack and the long-term effects such sonics had on his family.

> Drones: in Gaza, they are called *zananas*, meaning a bee's buzz. They are the incessant, irritating creatures. They are not always the harbingers of destruction; instead they remain omnipresent, like patrolling prison guards . . . it creates a terrifying sound-scape, and at night we lie in our beds hoping that the bombs do not drop on our houses, that glass does not shatter onto our children's beds. Sometimes, we move from room to room in an attempt to feel some sense of safety. The reality is that there is no escape, neither inside the house nor from the confines of Gaza.[15]

A recent study by Stanford Law Center, 'Living under Drones' — which focuses on US Army drone activity among al-Qaida strongholds in rural Pakistan — makes for equally harrowing reading. The main psychological factor cited by multiple interviewees was that of unpredictability. The buzzing drone could signal observation, or imminent attack. A villager recounted the experience: 'I can't sleep at night because when the drones are there . . . I hear them making that sound, that noise. The drones are all over my brain, I can't sleep. When I hear the drones making that drone sound, I just turn on the light and sit there looking at the light. Whenever the drones are hovering over us, it just makes me so scared.'

The (avian) drone carries dark associations in the collective subconscious, be it the terror of depersonalised warfare or creepy anonymous surveillance. However, in 2014 John Cale — ex-Velvet Underground composer — sought to recalibrate perceptions of the devices by framing them as 'airborne architecture' alongside a dronal musical backing in a Barbican installation called *LOOP>>60Hz: Transmissions from the Drone Orchestra*. On the night, Cale provided a cascade of metallic synth drones alongside vocals which were sonically 'carried' around the Barbican by a squadron of flying drones with loudspeakers — some 'dressed' in costumes — which also provided their own inescapable buzz. Playing with perceptions both of the machines, and what Cale described as the 'drone of civilisation' (60Hz being the hum of electricity), the 'idea was to make things that had no right to fly — utterly unreal, uncanny — surreal as objects.'

The acoustic by-product of the flying drone can often lead to distress, but it is not a specific part of its design make-up. Sustained infrasound tones — frequencies lower than 20Hz, i.e. the regular limit of human hearing — used in long-range acoustic devices to disperse rioters, are a different matter: here sustained tones are weaponised by design.

Able to induce a feeling of extreme unease, one 'feels' rather than 'hears' infrasound. Indeed, this is where rumours of the 'brown note' — a frequency of such depth it supposedly induces defecation — come from. The veracity of such claims remains unfounded, though — as we'll see later when discussing Sunn O))) — rumours abound. A mobile sonic device called the Mosquito, meanwhile, emits ultrasound frequencies outside shopping centres in the attempt of deterring loitering teenagers who are naturally susceptible to ultrasound frequencies, as the capacity to hear ultra-high frequencies deteriorates with age.

Infrasound will be a familiar feeling to anybody who has seen Sunn O))) play or experienced a serious dub reggae rig at full pelt. Sternum-crushing bass creates a sensation of physical movement around the lungs, sound pressure pushing against your body. This is what Bristolian dubstep producer Pinch calls 'chest-plate' bass (his early Subloaded club posters bore the legend 'if your chest ain't rattling, it ain't happening'): a physical rush of sound that exerts a palpable 'presence' inside your cavities.

One can well imagine how such a visceral sensation — shorn of any musical 'meaning' — would induce panic in a crowd.

Weaponised sound — which, by accident or design, almost always comes in the form of the drone — works as a tool of subliminal coercion for a number of reasons. In the case of flying drones, the sonic buzz forewarns of potential attack and signals instant panic. Infrasound deliberately pushes buttons known to result in psychological distress. Stukka bombers, with their screech, amplified terror itself. The fact people *know* where the sound is coming from — and know what it means — creates a feeling of powerlessness.

The Hum

Mysterious sounds of unknown provenance can have similar, albeit less viscerally distressing, effects. A strange acoustic phenomenon known as 'the hum' — a low bass drone intermittently reported in various locations around the world for decades — is a case in point.

Most closely associated with Bristol, in the 1960s people began to contact the city council complaining of a bass rumble particularly audible at night. Various theories as to the cause of 'the Bristol hum' (as it has since become known) have been put forward: factory noise, pylons, subsonic frequencies emitted from submarines, even electromagnetic radiation. Some residents reported nosebleeds and headaches. Perhaps inevitably, various conspiracy theories — UFOs, military testing or even oblique government mind-control experiments — have been propagated, too. Reports of the hum stopped in the early 1980s but started again in 2016.

Descriptions typically frame it as sounding like a truck engine or a wall fan. Film-maker and Bristol resident Jamie Brightmore described it on his blog as sounding as if 'the vibration is coming from the ground, through the foundations, heard through the structure of the building'. A YouTube video posted in 2017, meanwhile, sees a visibly distressed man peering out of his loft window as an eerie metallic drone emerges from the grey Clifton skyline: 'I don't know what it is but it's starting to freak me out a bit. I don't like it. It's been happening every ten minutes. There it is again! I'm going to stop recording now.'

'The Hum' might sound like a 1950s B movie — some Roger Corman-produced drive-in schlock — but it's a significant global phenomenon. Aside from Bristol, the most well-known 'hum' is located in the small town of Taos, New Mexico and was first reported in the early 1980s. It proved so bothersome to residents that questions were asked in Congress in 1993 and attempts were made to locate the cause.

One possibility is ELF (extra-low frequency) electromagnetic radiation waves — sometimes generated by lightning or disturbances in the Earth's electromagnetic field. Another is that the hum is caused by 'permanent free oscillations' on the seabed, whose microseismic waves can be picked up by those with particularly sensitive hearing. As is often the case, the lack of a common consensus has led to a wild array of theories and sense of unease among those living with it. Naval conspiracy theories aside (the Taos hum even features in an *X-Files* episode — *Drive* — in which Mulder investigates low-frequency emissions), the strain of living with the mysterious drone is described by some as akin to low-level tinnitus.

After hearing the hum himself during a stay in British Columbia, Dr Glen MacPherson started tracking the worldwide phenomenon on a website that allows users to report their own experiences.[18] There are currently around 10,000 reports, everywhere from Sweden to Canada. In an article for the *Conversation* MacPherson described the hum as 'like a truck engine idling. For some, it's a distant rumbling or droning noise. It can start and stop suddenly or wax and wane over time. For others, the Hum is loud, relentless and life-altering.'

In the article MacPherson quotes from a paper by a geoscientist called David Deming (who also hears the hum). Deming has conducted extensive research into the phenomenon and believes the most probable cause to be rooted in very-low frequency (VLF) radio transmissions or accumulative industrial derived infrasound.

It's appropriate that Bristol — associated as it is with the ever-morphing permutations of bass music culture — should have the most famous hum in the world. The more mischievous minded could suggest that it could be the residual audio ghost of sound systems past, a phantom loop enveloping the city.

Does the drone lend itself to mystery? To the eerie and inexplicable? The sense of deep-seated unease caused by 'the hum' is testament to the capacity of sustained tones to evoke disquiet, a sense of lifting the curtain of the everyday. Given this, perhaps it is inevitable that we also see the drone harnessed time and again in spiritual ritual — an audio emblem that transcends borders and stretches back millennia.

Chapter 1

ENTER THE CHAMBER

It's 38 degrees on the outskirts of Valetta, the capital of the island of Malta. Scrawny cats idle underneath battered cars, waiting out the fierce afternoon sun. Washing hangs from crumbling wrought iron balconies six floors up and old men in crumpled black suits play dominoes on the shady side of the street. Aside from a few tiny hole-in-the-wall bars — buzzing ceiling fans, plastic tables, corner-mounted TVs — not much is open.

Malta is the smallest country in the EU, a fifth the size of greater London. Situated 90 kilometres south-east of Sicily, it's closer to Libya than mainland Europe. The Phoenicians, Romans, Arabs, Normans and British all left their mark. Towns and villages often have Arabic names (M'dina, Rabat), Roman ruins abound, locals sometimes begin sentences in Maltese and finish them in English.

The chaotic dreamscape of ancient ramparts, imposing sea defences, watchtowers, crumbling alleys, baroque cathedrals and Neolithic remains has served as backdrop for both *Game of Thrones* and *Gladiator*. The island visually cleaves to the epic (the Knights Templar, the ancient mystic Catholic warrior order, were responsible for much of Valetta's sixteenth-century baroque architecture) but the realities of twenty-first-century life are tough.

Farming is an often thankless task. Most of the countryside is unirrigated, with cracked dry soil during the baking summers, scarce arable land and abandoned farmhouses surrounded by cracked limestone walls. That the most widely eaten meat is wild rabbit — more often than not unctuously slow braised with red wine and marrowfat peas in the form of *stuffat tal-fenek* — tells you a lot about the place.

As I travel the main island, the past is brought into vivid focus. Neolithic and Roman ruins are ubiquitous — and often mercifully free of the dainty visitor-centre vibe that plagues similar sites in England. Aside from the main sites, I stumble across unmarked remains down dirt-track roads and look for stone circles amid scrubland on the outskirts of dilapidated villages.

The ruins of Neolithic Malta offer beguiling clues of what was clearly a highly advanced civilisation but which predated the written word. There is no hieroglyphic code to decipher here. Much remains a mystery. What we do know is that around 4000 BC the people of Malta and its smaller sister island Gozo began to build temples marking the passage between life and death. Many share similar features — curved stone facades, forecourts and decorative stones covered in spiral motifs. Amulets, beads, figurines and knives were often found. A dominant figure — the so-called 'fat woman' or Venus of Malta — is thought to have been a fertility symbol. Some historians have even speculated that the temples themselves represented the head, arms and legs of the deity and that the idea of a 'mother goddess' was central to spiritual life.

Ancient temple remains like those found at Tarxien, Hagar Qim and Mnajdra — which were built over six thousand years ago — represent incredible feats of engineering: some of the stones at Hagar Qim weighed twenty tonnes apiece. These count among the world's first known free-standing stone buildings. To contextualise just how old we're talking: by the time the Great Pyramid of Giza was finished around 2580 BC, these temples would have been in use for well over a millennium. Or, to apply Julian Cope's helpful Stonehenge analogy from his British Neolithic survey *The Modern Antiquarian*: 'If Jesus were to have stood in front of the monument during his lifetime it would have been older to him, then, than he is to us, now.'

So it is with the Maltese temples.

Ritual activity is strongly evidenced. At the temple of Mnajdra — a site long rumoured in folklore to cure illness and promote fertility — numerous flint knives and animal bones were found, while excavations at the Xaghra stone circle on Gozo brought up some 200,000 human bones. Archaeologists believe the circle acted as an above-ground 'memory monument' where an elaborate funeral rite took place — bodies appear to have been brought there, ritually dismembered and the body parts arranged ceremoniously around the site.[1]

Today, however, I don't linger above ground. I am going underground.

The Hypogeum of Hal Saflieni is the most mysterious of ancient sites in an island packed with them. A labyrinthine Neolithic burial chamber complex that was painstakingly tunnelled by hand three storeys down into soft limestone. Built over a period of centuries around six thousand years ago, it has no architectural parallels anywhere in the world. But from the outside it's as unassuming a UNESCO world heritage site as you're ever likely to stumble across.

Down a side street, off the main drag in Paola — a dusty Valetta suburb — it sits amid corner shops, bars and pizza places. Aside from a disability ramp and a black sign bearing the solitary word 'Hypogeum' — beneath which the shadows of each letter bend in a sinister, seemingly acid-tainted fashion — it looks like any other weather-beaten apartment block. Beneath the unassuming surface, however, lies an ancient netherworld that lay undisturbed for millennia. In 1902, builders installing plumbing in a new apartment block accidentally cut into the roof of the near perfectly preserved subterranean temple.

What they found was like something out of *Indiana Jones*: oblique chambers, side rooms, pits containing headless statues, geometric wall paintings and around 7,000 skeletal remains. In the decades since its discovery, a wormhole of garish folklore has built up around the place. Serpent priests, ritual sacrifice, UFOs, genetic mutation, lost children and disappearing tour groups all feature in local tales of the site, inspired not only by the singular topography of the site, but also its most peculiar acoustics.

The so-called 'Oracle Chamber' is a rectangular side room with red ochre spirals painted on the ceiling. It has a particularly disquieting aural effect. Archaeologists and historians have long speculated about both the stone shelf mounted across the back wall, which looks very much like a modern resonator panel, and the small niche into which many have speculated that an oracle or ancient priest may have spoken, their voice reverberating around the entire chamber with eerie sonority.

As *National Geographic* reported in 1920, some eighteen years after the Hypogeum's discovery: 'A word spoken in this room is magnified a hundred-fold and is audible throughout the entire structure. The effect upon the credulous can be imagined when the oracle spoke and the words came thundering forth through the dark and mysterious place with terrifying impressiveness.'[2]

The Hypogeum was likely a place of community remembrance. The dead were far from 'out of sight, out of mind'. They were laid out in their hundreds, made accessible to visitors via a complex of walkways and chambers. Primary burials would have been moved to make way for new arrivals; builders tunnelling out new niches would have fleetingly shared the fetid chambers with corpses old and new; the smell of red ochre paint and blazing torches would have mingled with the overpowering odour of rotting flesh in various stages of decomposition. In its own peculiar way, the Hypogeum would have been a *living, breathing* space.

Today I'm one of only ten people — the maximum allowed inside at one time — descending underground. A visit involves booking months in advance. The whole operation, by dint of environmental necessity, is a highly controlled business. Cameras, phones and liquids are put in lockers by stern-faced security guards. It feels more like hard-core airport security than tourist site. Atmosphere and temperature are constantly monitored for optimum humidity with hi-tech gear.[3]

As I stoop down narrow cut passageways into the main chambers, the juxtaposition between the baking urban streets a few feet away and this ancient subterranean space is eerie, sinister, claustrophobic in the extreme. Condensation drips from the ceiling and a hammy voice-over guide — complete with chinking 'tunnelling' sounds, atmospheric drones and the hushed whispers of the 'ancient builders' — plays through tinny tour headphones — but it doesn't dampen the ghostly, reverent atmosphere.

I walk the passageway in the ancient upper tier. It leads to five low-roofed burial chambers, chiselled from pre-existing caves. The middle level is spectacularly detailed. The set piece here has been dubbed the 'holy of holies' — a room carved to emulate in perfect miniature detail one of Malta's above-ground temples. Two pits at the entrance were thought to have been used to collect offerings: smashed figurines were found in both.

As we crowd into the Oracle Chamber every cough, whisper and word comes alive, imbued with resounding power and presence. The sound bounces around the dank walls for a freakishly long time. It is extraordinary. I have never heard reverberation like it. This space — indeed the entire Hypogeum — crackles with peculiar magic. Descending into its bowels feels like entering a netherworld, some *Gormenghast* fantasy, a feeling enhanced by each successive chamber being only partially visible from the next, separated by limestone walls and panelling.

It hums with *intent*, with fervency of belief. Regardless of one's own spirituality or lack thereof, when entering a space imbued with such metaphysical significance, you can't help but pick it up. Some echo from the past perhaps? A psychic residue in the crumbling limestone walls? It feels that way.

Dr Rupert Till from the University of Huddersfield has conducted extensive acoustic experiments at the site. 'We had somebody who had a very deep bass voice and when he was speaking the whole area was literally *ringing* around him,' Till tells me. 'This was clearly a space where ritual activity would have taken place. If you look at cultures around the world you find the dead still very much living. We remember the dead: but at the Hypogeum it seems likely to have been a much more *active* process, a place where you would have perhaps descended to keep the memory of the dead alive, or to ask questions of them. The expectation of going down there would perhaps have made one hypersensitive. And when you heard the voice echoing — and in the Hypogeum the bass sounds can reverberate for around fourteen seconds — it would have been a place where you could remember spirits. In that respect, perhaps their *voice* may have been kept alive.'

Immersed in the ancient acoustics, I wonder what role the drone might have played down here, under the ground, six thousand years ago.

Ritual Vibrations

The words 'sound ritual' conjure a cornucopia of camp Hammer Horror-esque imagery. Charles Grey — resplendent in velvet hood — loudly enunciating into an ancient tomb; tribal drummers in a trance; some innocent inductee lost to ritual ecstasy as the coven chants; the summoning of ancient deities through wilful incantation; torches ablaze in bucolic winter night. Hoary imagery maybe, but the fact remains: sound defines personal ritual and organised religion alike and has done for millennia. What, though, do we really mean by 'ritual'?

The dictionary definition is 'a set of fixed actions and sometimes words performed regularly, especially as part of a ceremony'. Taken on those terms, we can say with certainty that the Hypogeum was a place of ritual burial. If we take the Hypogeum as a gateway space — in which the journey of the soul from this world to another was likely to have been represented — I think it reasonable to assume the strong resonance of the chambers, the striking drone, may have been harnessed. But if so, might the Hypogeum have been 'acoustically engineered' — as is sometimes claimed — to enhance this effect? It's a question that has been debated by archaeologists, acoustic researchers and historians alike.

Dr Till believes the former proposition — that an accidental resonance was harnessed — is likely, while remaining sceptical that the Hypogeum's builders set out with acoustic intent:

There is no evidence for specific acoustic engineering. When you move close to a wall the bass resonance increases. If you go to a club and stand next to the wall, you'll notice the bass is incredibly powerful. The resonant frequencies at the Hypogeum are similarly powerful but there is no evidence that the space has been *created* to cause an acoustic effect. I have heard such stories but find no evidence to support it. What we can say is that the space has incredibly powerful acoustics that you absolutely cannot miss: you can't fail to appreciate that. But at the Hypogeum we actually found other spaces that have even *more* powerful resonances than the Oracle Chamber.

Could an ancient people have had enough understanding of acoustics to deliberately set about hollowing out limestone in order to maximise the reverberant potential of the space for a desired effect? This hypothesis is usually centred around the idea that the niche found in the wall acted as a focal point for ceremonial vocal chant or prayer, its hollow boosting the reverb. Others have hypothesised that the cut stone shelf along the back wall of the chamber acted as an acoustic panel, much like those found in classical concert halls today, which may also have increased the reverberation of the space.

There is no definitive answer. Blueprints are, after all, not forthcoming. As so often with archaeoacoustics, we're in the realm of informed speculation. After visiting the Hypogeum, I spoke to historian Katya Stroud who works for Heritage Malta. She suggested that the Hypogeum may indeed have been engineered — but only *after* the fact, once the strange acoustics had already been noted.

'The "shelf" is very suggestive,' she explained. 'The carving of what looks like a very shallow shelf along the top where the niche is found in the Oracle Chamber does suggest that this was created to enhance the acoustic effects of the chamber. The general consensus, however, is that the acoustic effect of the chamber was not created deliberately, but was most probably accidental. However, the niche and this "shelf" may indicate that measures were then taken to enhance the natural acoustic effects.'

The roof of the Oracle Chamber is covered by a distinctive red ochre spiral motif. Writer and archaeoacoustic researcher Paul Devereaux has hypothesised that this imagery perhaps served to represent what was occurring, a visual reckoning of the sound within the chamber, the motif representing a primitive waveform.

The spirals could represent foliage, yes. But in the often multifunction nature of symbols, spirals are indeed suitable visual analogues for sound. The increasing sizes of the spirals and especially of the discs could signal amplitude i.e. the special acoustic properties of the niche. The discs, after all, lead us right inside the niche. Was that from where the voices of the gods — or ancestors — emanated? We are so blasé about sound in our noisy modern world that we tend to forget that it could hold mysterious properties for early peoples who did not possess a scientific, wave model understanding — we can acknowledge this especially regarding the eerie quality of resonance and echoes. What we know from Greek oracle sites suggests that even rushing water or the soughing of wind in foliage could be read as divine communication, if often through the mediation of priests and priestesses. It is in any case a questionable assumption that the builders of the Hypogeum made a noteworthy acoustic discovery by accident . . . the creation of the Hypogeum was an intentional act. It couldn't have been otherwise.[4]

One can see why the question of deliberate acoustical engineering has inspired debate. Engineering reveals intention. And it is via *intention* — of visual imagery, written text or architectural features — that sacred buildings decree their spiritual meaning. We gaze at the foreboding gargoyles on the side of Notre Dame and understand that more than drainage systems, they show a visceral representation of the Catholic concept of evil: a physical portrayal of the unconverted soul in eternal damnation — a warning from God. Likewise, when looking at the mosaicked dome of the Great Mosque of Süleymaniye in Istanbul we understand it represents the vault of heaven. Ancient sites such as the Hypogeum — being the work of a people who left no written trace — may be bereft of the cast-iron *evidence* of intention that comes from meticulously maintained archives, architectural records, church ledgers, diaries et cetera — but that doesn't mean that these places are shorn of deeper, intentional significance.

The emergent discipline of archaeoacoustics attempts a reading of sites from an acoustic — as well as visual — perspective. It maps the literal and metaphorical resonance of spaces. In his book *Sonic Wonderland*, Professor Trevor Cox talks of developing a sense of 'aural wonderment' and learning how to 'read' your surroundings aurally. Historians sometimes talk of the sense of wonderment that surely accompanied visiting a medieval cathedral for the first time. I live near Ely cathedral. As I drive over the bleak, flood-prone fenland ('Slow Down! Don't drown on Fenland Roads!') I wonder what it must have been like some thousand years ago for a cold, hungry, illiterate peasant to have seen that immense Romanesque structure, rising out of the black loamy soil, from afar. Maybe like catching a glimpse of divinity. At the least, a temporary cerebral escape from the brutalising Fenland wind and mud.

But a preoccupation with visual impact poses a question: why do we so often associate the visual, rather than the aural, with a sense of wonder? Speaking to Paul Devereaux after my Hypogeum visit, he puts it to me that: 'archaeoacoustics is simply the recognition that ancient people had ears. We are a very visual culture. It has taken a long time for researchers to start to think about sound in relation to these sites. Sound is ephemeral and these places are very ancient and made of rock. It was anti-intuitive for a long while, but really in the last twenty years people have started thinking about sound in these places.'

Is it reasonable to assume that interesting acoustic phenomena — like those experienced in a resonant burial chamber — would likely have had an *amplified* psychological effect? Today, you're likely to experience echo every time you walk into a multistorey car park or duck into a stairwell to take a call in the office without necessarily *registering* it. But if the only time in your life you heard sound bouncing around the walls was in the Hypogeum, it's likely you'd remember it as something significant, ethereal even. Would these effects — singular and deeply pronounced as they are — have been exploited in spiritual ceremony?

Look at the central role the drone, in the form of reverberation, has since played in other sacred spaces. Reverberation is central to devotional music around the world. In Christianity for example, the church organ provides a bombastic ceremonial experience that serves to emphasise the humbling magnitude of the cathedral space, its ethereal power and fundamental separation from the daily grind. In a stone cathedral, sound will be reflected against the walls and ceiling, but it will also be reflected against other surfaces — wooden pews, wax candles, statues — creating a dramatic effect. The music becomes greater than the sum of its parts. It 'lives' in the space during the reverb, interacting with everything and everybody within that space, the air *ringing* with the vibration of belief.

Indeed, reverberation has not only influenced how we hear devotional music but also how it is composed. In sacred medieval music, the drone carries particular significance. In Byzantine chant, it's vocalised as the *ison* — a continuous bass note sung rather than played, with the church acoustics enhancing the reverb effect, as described by Greek musicologist G.K. Michalakis: 'In large churches, we have reverb . . . reverberation itself acts as *ison*, where the most important notes of a passage are to be heard more than the rest: we're into psycho-acoustics.'[7]

Reverb carries weight because it amplifies the message throughout a sacred space, like a call and response. Byzantine chant was composed for medieval cathedrals with reverberation times specifically in mind. Many of Bach's organ pieces are designed to explore the reverb as well as the notes. As organist and composer E. Power Biggs said of Bach's Toccata in D minor, 'consider the pause that follows the ornamented proclamation that opens . . . obviously this is for the enjoyment of the notes as they *remain suspended in the air.*'

A research team at UCLA recently focused on a change in Greek church architecture during the fourteenth century. There was a shift from the long basilica design — able to accommodate larger crowds — to smaller domed churches. Previously thought to be the result of shrinking congregations, the research — led by Byzantine historian Sharon Gerstel — makes a compelling case that the enhanced reverberation afforded by the dome was a significant factor behind the architectural shift.

In these churches, the singers (as well as the lyrics of the chants) were often depicted in mosaics and paintings at each far wall. At around the same time, the traditional vocal music shifted into a more complex form called 'kalaphonic' or 'beautiful voice'. Could this be, the researchers wondered, all connected? As many of the singers were depicted on opposite walls pointing at each other, seemingly communicating, perhaps the new domed design was intended to maximise the space's reverberant potential.

The team put their theory to the test in the Church of St Nicholas Orphanos. They positioned a single chanter at the east-facing opening, while Gerstel stood underneath the image of the chanters opposite. The results were surprising, as she recounted in an interview: 'The sound rolled out through the portal as if through a microphone, as if the monks in the painting were singing.'[8] Repeated experiments resulted in a similarly visceral, perceptual shift. 'You feel as if you're penetrated by the sound and at the same time, you're looking at the wall seeing these figures that appear to be moving,' Gerstel said. 'You're not standing there listening, you're enveloped.'

The powerful resonance of sacred spaces — the emotional colouring they lend sound — has also been a source of inspiration for many artists. A record like Tim Hecker's *Rave Death 1972* (2011) is a case in point. Recorded in Frikirkjan church in Reykjavik, Iceland, Hecker created an imposing dronescape using the church's fourteenth-century organ, its foggy subtones ricocheting off the rafters, ancient and decayed and immense. A former Catholic, Hecker plays with extremes of volume and sub-pressure to create what he once described as 'some kind of secular God effect through sonic power'. Hecker subverts the idea of holy reverberation being tied to an organised religion. On recording the Icelandic Choir Ensemble singing a fifteenth-century polyphonic vocal score, he reportedly told them to 'imagine you're Chewbacca and you have a saxophone and you just drank 8,000 litres of codeine — now sing 10 times slower than that.'[9] In Hecker's hands, reverberation is democratised, a tool of malleable audio potency that's there for the taking by anyone with the right intent.

It's easy in our cacophonous modern world to overlook the significance of sound to ancient people. In *Sonic Wonderland*, Cox makes the point that increased vulnerability to predators could have sharpened hearing response. Likewise, a heightened sensitivity to weather may have affected what we were hard-wired to listen for: storms that could irreversibly damage a precariously built hut; rains that could wipe out crops; the potential of wind to carry scent and alert the quarry. It's entirely possible then that unusual sounds may once have carried more psychological weight than they do today.

Just as Egyptian pyramid tombs represented a metaphorical passage to the underworld, the Hypogeum may have symbolised a similar journey — the passage from the living world to another realm. Sound is the most ephemeral of the senses. In ancient times, it existed only in the moment. All we're left with now is the resonance of ancient spaces, with how sound would have *felt*.

Down here in the Hypogeum, my imagination conjures intoxicating glimpses into what could have been experienced in the chamber, six thousand years ago. The red ochre paintings above my head would only have been visible by torchlight; as the torchlight flickered, the spirals on the ceiling would start to 'move'; the naked eye would, perhaps, be drawn from one to the next. Entranced by the flickering light and the movement of the paintings, one would become intoxicated by a sense of being outside daily reality. Perceptions of day or night would, here in the bowls of the Hypogeum, be rendered redundant. The smell of decomposing corpses would have been overpowering; the reverberant voices — which become a deep bass drone in conversation, let alone in chant — would have added to the sensory overload. Drum beats may have induced torpor or heightened trance. Anyone outside the central Oracle Chamber would have been able to hear but not see. Sacred spaces are often delineated spaces. It's tantalising to consider who might have had access to this central area and who might not. Many of the Hypogeum's attendants might only have experienced the reverberating voices as they tunnelled around the rest of the site, disconnected from any physical body. The acoustic ceremony within the Oracle Chamber might only have been created and witnessed directly by the Hypogeum's chosen few.

If we are willing to take 'a leap of faith' and accept this was a place built intentionally to mark the passing of life and facilitate inner journeying, then we're talking about the very *definition* of the psychedelic experience: 'a mental state characterised by a *profound sense of intensified sensory perception, sometimes accompanied by severe perceptual distortion*'.[10] 'The basic human need for transcendence through coloured lights and music goes back thousands of years,' Andrew Weatherall told me, the year before he sadly passed away. 'And whether that's delivered with flaming torches or state-of-the-art lighting equipment, it's the same thing.'

Though unique in its resonant qualities, the Hypogeum isn't the only Neolithic structure noted for its intense sustain.[11] Myriad other sites have been examined by archaeoacoustic researchers in recent decades. Newgrange in the Boyne Valley, Ireland, is a 5,200-year-old passage tomb, noted for its singular acoustic effects. A burial mound built by a Stone Age farming community, Newgrange is a 19-metre passage leading into a chamber with three alcoves, surrounded by ninety-seven huge stones with spiral carvings. The central chamber has an astronomical alignment with the winter solstice, when a brilliant shaft of sunlight lights up the inner passage. Like the Hypogeum, Newgrange is one of the oldest standing 'buildings' in the world, predating the Pyramids by some 500 years.

Unearthed in 1699, Newgrange was a minor local tourist attraction but remained little known beyond Ireland until the twentieth century. By the 1960s, it had become mostly overgrown. Weeds and long grass covered the majestic mound and there was no longer any public access to the passage tomb. The late archaeologist Professor Michael O'Kelly led a decade-long excavation of the site from the early 1960s. As his team undertook the Herculean task of clearing the mound, they stumbled upon a slit above the entrance, half closed by a block of crystallised quartz. Scratches on the quartz indicated that it had been used as a shutter allowing light into the main tomb — itself sealed with a five-tonne stone slab.

O'Kelly speculated that the shutter may have acted as some kind of light source when the tomb was closed. Local legend had it that the sun shone straight into the tomb at midsummer solstice but this was impossible, the alignment of the burial mound and the midsummer sun being incompatible. O'Kelly speculated that perhaps the winter, rather than midsummer, solstice produced the strange ocular effect cited by local folklore. In December 1967, he decided to put his theory to the test and drove to Newgrange in the early morning of the midwinter solstice. He recounted the experience in 1978:

I was astounded. The light began as a thin pencil and widened to a band of about 6 in. There was so much light reflected from the floor that I could walk around inside without a lamp and avoid bumping off the stones. It was so bright I could see the roof 20 ft above me. I expected to hear a voice, or perhaps feel a cold hand resting on my shoulder, but there was a silence. And then, after a few minutes, the shaft of light narrowed as the sun appeared to pass westward across the slit.[12]

Repeating the experiment with the same results throughout the 1970s, O'Kelly became convinced Newgrange was astrologically aligned to mark the winter solstice. Later, Newgrange was examined acoustically, with unexpected results. Archaeologist Dr David Keating of the University of Reading conducted tests in 2001 and noticed a strange effect: a loudspeaker set up to emit a low-frequency tone seemed to be getting quieter as he walked *towards* it, while moving towards the side chambers seemed to result in an increase in volume. Dr Keating believes this effect may have been exploited in ceremonies — the central area acting as a dramatic and unpredictable 'echo chamber' — as he explained on BBC Radio 4's documentary *Stone Age Sound* in 2001: 'It is inevitable that priests or druids would have found this effect and exploited it, or it is possible they believed that when they made this noise they were bringing the dead to life.'[13]

Keating also found that sounds in the 110Hz range triggered the strongest resonance, the 19-metre entrance passage behaving like 'a wind instrument, sound waves generated within the chamber filling it.'

Hypnagogic Intent

Search the term '110Hz' and the results will likely drive the sceptically minded into a puce-faced Dawkins splutter. Alternative therapy abounds around this frequency with claims to 'Regenerate your Cells!' and 'Cure Cancer' et cetera. The idea of a specific frequency being claimed as a 'healing mechanism' seems to hum with the scent of snake oil. An advertisement for a £275 '110Hz aluminium tuning fork' to 'Purify, Neutralise and Eliminate Negative Energies' is unlikely to dissipate any such cynicism. But while the idea of a particular oscillation 'curing cancer' may sensibly ring alarm bells, it shouldn't detract from serious scientific research that has been undertaken into what actually happens to the brain when exposed to this frequency.

Within archaeoacoustic research 110Hz is, indeed, often tested. Dr Paolo Derbertolis of the University of Trieste recently conducted research into the resonant properties of the Hypogeum's Oracle Chamber.[14] He carried out experiments on voice, traditional Maltese drums and conch shells. A strong double resonance was found to be activated between 110 and 114Hz: a low male baritone in other words. In off-site experiments, Dr Derbertolis also explored the physiological effect of the frequency range on the human brain, finding that — when exposed to such frequencies — the subject's brain activity 'is significantly reduced in language centres; this kind of brain activity is associated with the half-awake/half-asleep hypnagogic state, with vivid mental imagery and auditory hallucinations.'[15] It was concluded that the Oracle Chamber would therefore have afforded participants a profound sensory experience, visceral and perhaps even psychedelic. Archaeoacoustic researcher Paul Devereaux also conducted extensive tests at Newgrange and again, the space reverberated at the frequency range of 110Hz. As he explained to me, 'We kept picking up this frequency. The chambers were resonating at 110Hz, which is the lower baritone range. It's very dramatic at Newgrange.'

On returning to England, Devereaux and co-researcher Robert Jahn decided to investigate further. They asked another member of their team — Ian Cook, a clinical neuroscientist from UCLA — whether there was any neurological significance to their findings. 'Ian said — "I don't think so, but when I get a chance I'll do some experiments,"' recalled Devereaux. Cook later conducted experiments on regional brain activity on a group of thirty volunteers. Each was monitored via ECG while listening to varying frequencies. He found that at 110Hz patterns of brain activity changed dramatically over the prefrontal cortex, which is the part of the brain responsible for co-ordination, impulse control, attention and planning.

When exposed to sustained tones at 110Hz, activity at the left temporal region was found to be 'significantly lower' than at other tested frequencies, while activity associated with the left-hand side of the brain — namely language and emotional processing — essentially 'shifted' to the right, resulting in a temporal deactivation. Cook concluded his peer-reviewed paper with the observation that listening to tones at 110Hz is

associated with patterns of brain activity that differed from those observed when listening to tones at neighbouring frequencies . . . The left-hand brain has been associated with the cognitive processing of spoken language; lower cordance values during the 110Hz stimuli would be consistent with reduced activity under that condition.[16]

The psychoactive implications are interesting. If both language processing and cognitive function are reduced at 110Hz; if infrasonic frequencies induce mental discombobulation and physical hallucinations, then are we — to some degree — entering into the realm of hypnosis through sound? Whether or not one chooses to believe that Neolithic peoples had a sophisticated enough understanding of acoustic science to manipulate surroundings for a desired mental effect, there is sufficient evidence to suggest that these particular frequencies — even if activated by chance, rather than design — *had* such an effect. Archaeoacoustic researcher Dr Aaron Watson believes these acoustic phenomena, once recognised, would have added to the spiritual importance of sites. He wrote:

These monuments from the distant past were not the remote and silent places we visit today; they may best be understood as gateways through which people of the Neolithic period passed to gain access to dimensions far beyond the reality of their everyday lives.[17]

The Eternal Dance

In the popular imagination, hypnosis is often associated with the dark — a state of heightened suggestion in which the subject loses an essential sense of 'self' and is open to the power of suggestion and atypical behaviour. The 1980s, for example, witnessed public hysteria over explicit hip-hop lyrics and supposed hidden messages in heavy metal records. Judas Priest were involved in a lawsuit over the 1985 double suicide of two men who shot themselves after listening to the band's *Stained Class* album on repeat. The prosecution case — eventually dismissed by the judge — centred around the idea that their music contained 'backward masking': subliminal messages contained within the music. It was alleged the band had dubbed 'Do it! Do it!' onto the song 'Better by You, Better than Me'. The case personified the enduring Middle American fear of popular music.

The concern over subliminal messaging, though demonstrably false (as the band's manager noted, 'if there was going to be a message, it would say: "buy seven"[18]), played into deep-seated fears of the debasing effects of music — musicians framed as shadowy pied pipers leading the youth in a sinister dance towards sex, drugs, the devil and death. Over the years, everyone from Led Zeppelin to the Beatles has been accused of hiding subliminal messaging within music, but the hypnotic *power* of sound — its ability to confound the senses and shift consciousness — is a folkloric trope that crosses borders and spans millennia. It's not always associated with negativity, per se. Religious ecstasy, for example (which we'll discuss further in the next chapter) is often connected to repetitive sound and the evocation of blissful trance states via chant, say. However, the hypnotic element of music has also frequently been framed as a dangerous conduit, one capable of channelling the 'animal' spirit and enabling states where control, inhibition and ego are lost in a giddy dance of abandon.

The Strasbourg 'dancing plague' of 1518 was a peculiar case in point. The story goes like this: a woman started to dance outside her house and was joined by townsfolk until around five hundred people — dizzy and dehydrated — were stamping themselves to a state of sweaty delirium in the street. The authorities were worried. Stumped as to what to do, they decided to hire a ragtag band of pipers and 'herd' the frenetic horde to dance away from the streets, containing them in a central square. There, so legend has it, many dropped dead from exhaustion. The cause of the 'dancing plague' has been the subject of much speculation. Some believe a contaminated batch of rye wheat was to blame (ergot fungi, which can grow on rye, contains ergotamine — a chemical structurally related to LSD and with its own powerful psychotropic effects). Others have pointed to the legend of Saint Vitus, the patron saint of dancers, as a potential source of Strasbourg's capering scourge. Religious lore paints Saint Vitus punishing sinners by compelling them to dance, and according to this theory, this belief perhaps seeped into the townsfolk's collective subconscious, priming them for a mass breakdown of inhibition.

In seventeenth-century Italy, a phenomenon called 'tarantism' took root. People bitten by spiders in the vineyards of southern Italy (a region long associated with ritual folk magic) would take to frantic dancing in order to rid themselves of both the poison and spirit of the spider, thought to possess them after the bite. Local folklore dictated a ritual whereby the *tarantura* — as the afflicted were known — would be compelled to dance to special violin music called the *pizzica pizzica* which symbolically mimicked the *pizzoco* (bite) of the spider. After the dance, the bitten were said to be healed, though some claimed to suffer vivid (generally arachnid-based) hallucinations for the rest of their lives. The phenomenon continued until the 1960s and was recognised to the extent that, each year on 29 June, the Feast of Saint Paul, *taranturas* from around the region would congregate in the town of Salento, seeking mercy from the saint.

Eighteenth-century physician Nicola Caputo wrote the following description of the ritual:

It often happens that those who go dancing through the towns and hamlets accompanied by the usual music are brought to an orchard, where, in the shade of a tree, near a pond or brook offered by nature or prepared through craft, they abandon themselves to the dance with the greatest delight, while groups of youths in search of pleasure and pranks gather near. Among the latter mingle more than a few who are approaching old age and who, contemplating with serious curiosity the melodic frolicking, seem to exhort the youths with unspoken admonishment.[19]

In more recent decades, illegal raves evoked similar 'admonishment' among 'those approaching old age' though unlike the *taranturas,* admonishment of the participants was not left 'unspoken'. The political frenzy that greeted free parties in fields and warehouses around the M25 throughout the late eighties and early nineties was fuelled by fear — of freedom, breaking of societal norms and the idea ravers were under a spell of drug- and music-induced sensory delirium. Systems like Spiral Tribe pushed warp-speed free-party techno in sessions that went on for days — sometimes weeks — at a time. Reading back first-hand accounts of the infamous Castlemorton party where, in May 1992, 40,000 ravers congregated in the Malvern hills for a week — it's striking how many residents were disturbed, not simply by a Dionysian spectacle alien to those who had grown up in post-war middle England, but by the *hypnotic* effect of the sound.

After five days, some local residents began to crack: 'There's something hypnotic about the continuous pounding beat of the music . . . it's driving people living on the frontline into a frenzy.'[20]

The response of Castlemorton villagers speaks volumes of the power of sound to disturb the mind and upset the status quo. The drone — at a distance in the form of an incessant background throb, a wave of penetrating sub-pressure — posed the question: *when will it end?* Drugs and all-nighters were, of course, nothing new. Mods, punks and Northern soul heads were all fuelled by the jittery grind of cheap amphetamines. But there was a world of difference between sweaty lads from Bolton gurning and spin-kicking through the night out of sight, out of mind in Wigan Casino or Blackpool Winter Gardens, and the likes of Spiral Tribe or Bedlam bringing the party to your doorstep with seventy rigs and staying there for days on end. Illegal raves frequently co-opted spaces that were known — and used — by the 'straight' world: public land, industrial estates, disused airfields, car parks. They subverted the everyday environment to the wildly bacchanalian.

Techno — particularly the high-velocity free-party style favoured by early nineties systems — is sheer *primal* sonics. The 4/4 taps into the heartbeat, melody is eschewed in favour of propulsive drive. It's functional music. A force for movement. Dance for days and — drugs or no drugs — you'll find yourself in a very peculiar place. Sleep deprivation, repetitive sound and constant motion will all see to that. But while the ravers were locked in the hypnotic groove, the residents of Castlemorton found themselves, by dint of proximity, unwilling *partners* in a ritual not of their making. Two separate bodies of people were under the spell — a yin and yang of mass hypnosis dramatically unfolding. But the effect on the villagers broke the central tenet of hypnosis — that the subject should be a willing participant.

So: how does hypnotism work?

In the popular imagination, we're into the realm of mind control. Boggling eyes, clipped tones, swinging pendulums and black turtleneck sweaters. Let's step it up a notch. We are being injected with truth serum in a bland state facility somewhere in the former Eastern bloc while a grim-faced matron — now bending, now *melting* — asks the same question, over and over again. Now we're mechanically clipping a silencer onto a rifle and glacially staring through the binoculars of a seedy top-floor hotel window at a Slavic man opening a black attaché case focusing purely on the *job at hand*.

In reality, self-help hypnosis and neurolinguistic programming is mundane. It's the simple power of suggestion. Hypnosis generally works if we *want* it to work. By listening to a hypnosis audio or booking in at a clinic you are already — by dint of intention — a *willing* participant in the ritual. We've seen how specific frequency ranges can cause a demonstrable shift in consciousness from the left to the right side of the brain. Hypnosis works in much the same way, helping induce a trance-like state — not deep sleep, nor one which causes significant disconnect from surroundings as in the case of an intense hallucinatory experience — but a palpably heightened state of aware-ness. A voice will calmly use suggestive phrases in order to effect a demonstra-ble change on a part of life — addiction, lack of confidence, phobia — that a patient actively wants to address.

Dr Hilary Jones described the process thus in his book *Doctor, What's the Alternative?* 'The analytical left-hand side of the brain is turned off, while the non-analytical right-hand side is made more alert,' he wrote. 'The conscious control of the mind is inhibited, and the subconscious mind awoken. Since the subconscious mind is a deeper-seated, more instinctive force than the conscious mind, this is the part which has to change for the patient's behaviour and physical state to alter . . . progress can only be made by reprogramming the subconscious so that deep-seated instincts and beliefs are abolished or altered.'[21]

The parallels between modern hypnosis techniques and the trance-inducing potential of Neolithic ritual are manifest — both are predicated on the idea of intent. Ian Cook's UCLA study found significant deactivation to happen in left-side brain function when exposed to 110Hz drones, a frequency picked up at numerous ancient sites. But while it's interesting this is so often noted, sound is only a part of the story. Mathematician Matthew Wright was sceptical of the claim that there was any great significance in the frequency ranges recorded at Neolithic burial sites, or of any claim that spaces were specifically acoustically engineered. He authored a paper titled 'Is a Neolithic Burial Chamber Different from My Bathroom, Acoustically Speaking?'[22] and concluded that no, there was no discernible difference between a Neolithic burial chamber and his bathroom.

This is interesting from a scientific perspective. However, it ignores the crucial issue of intent. An example: if I sit on the toilet, open a newspaper and hum the *Match of the Day* theme in my sonorous baritone I may find that the 110Hz resonance has been triggered. It is unlikely, however, that any cerebral change of note will occur. Now, if I was to enter the same space with serious ritual *intent* — perhaps thinking deeply about loved ones lost, lighting candles and incense and reciting a repetitive prayer chant, I might expect to feel a different response to the resonance.

Russian director Konstantin Stanislavski — pioneer of the method acting technique — wrote along similar lines in his seminal text *An Actor Prepares* (1936):

We must have, first of all, an unbroken series of supposed cir-cumstances in the midst of which our exercise is played. Secondly we must have a solid line of inner visions bound up with those circumstances, so that they will be illustrated for us. During every moment we are on the stage, during every moment of the development of the action of the play, we must be aware either of the external circumstances which surround us (the whole material setting of the production), or of an inner chain of circumstances which we ourselves have imagined in order to illustrate our parts. Out of these moments will be formed an unbroken series of images, something like a moving picture. As long as we are acting creatively, this film will unroll and be thrown on the screen of our inner vision, making vivid the circumstances among which we are moving. Moreover, these inner images create a corresponding mood, and arouse emotions, while holding us within the limits of the play.[23]

Ritual is intrinsically bonded to the theatrical arts. The underlying motivation — the will to invoke a change in consciousness on the part of an audience — is remarkably similar. In any spiritual ceremony, as in any theatrical performance, each participant — be they worshipper or preacher — assumes a predefined role. Any religious or spiritual ceremony contains performative aspects that enable those present to 'get into character'. The Roman Catholic mass, for example — with swinging incense, robes, epic architecture and powerful, reverberant acoustics — is a fundamentally *theatrical* experience. All visual and aural stimuli are finely honed to enable a transcendent experience.

The drone — in the form of ringing reverberation of psalms, the deep bass of the organ — maximises the intention of belief. The sound becomes bigger than the sum of its parts. But the idea of ritual is by no means tied to organised religion. Non-denominational ritual tropes run like a velvet thread throughout underground twentieth-century music: the black hoods of Sunn O))), the incense, candles and extreme volume of the Theatre of Eternal Music; the crossing of the pain/pleasure barrier by dancing for twenty-four hours straight in some dank Berlin basement. The mesmerising effects of sound; the manipulation of our surroundings; the desire to make sense of, or simply to marvel at the mystery of life; the need to announce our presence; to engage in activity that goes beyond the daily grind for survival and reaches, albeit fleetingly, to the infinite? That goes back to the start — as does the drone.

Sounds of Descent

I'm speaking to Barnaby Brown: ancient-instrument evangelist, musician, scholar, Highland piper and font of esoteric Greco-Roman musical lore. A conversation with Brown is an eclectic treat: he delights in connecting points between ancient and modern traditions with an infectious enthusiasm. For the past decade he has been on a mission to rekindle understanding and appreciation of noble, often long ignored, musical traditions. Much of his work focuses on music with a strong drone element — Sardinian double and triple pipes, ancient Greek aulos and recreated Palaeolithic bone pipes included.

At the mention of the ancient drone, he becomes animated. Before written music, before it was codified in the modern sense — before, even, it was understood to be a separate entity from mere sound — would sustained tone, I ask, have held any particular power?

'We need to take this right back,' Brown explains. 'Not just to the earliest archaeological finds of instruments over 40,000 years ago, but to tens of thousands if not *millions* of years ago. The idea of the drone is imprinted into us as *Homo sapiens*. We have a connection to something that triggers a deep sense of security, perhaps awe: I think that magic and religion and other worldly sensations are key to thinking about drone sounds. Think of the use of drone instruments in sacred ceremony, kings and rulers and priests; the mystery and the magic and the feel-good factor that the drone brings. It provides comfort and a slight scariness — something awe inspiring and mighty that feels beyond the human.'

In Brown's view, the drone is likely to have been one of the fundamental tenets of early music making: perhaps *the* earliest of all.

'It comes down to the first basic instruments,' he continues. 'Putting your lips to an animal horn and producing a sound. Now the sound that comes out is a drone. It's the oldest and easiest way of making a glorious sound, a simple animal horn. We've found instruments from between twenty-eight to forty thousand years ago, made from bone. These are beautiful, sophisticated instruments. If you put a hole in the side of a mammoth tusk, it produces the most *amazingly* intense drone. It also gives us a natural organic ancestor for the Scandinavian *lure* and the trumpets that we find from the Bronze Age and Iron Age.'

Neolithic burial chambers such as the Hypogeum and Newgrange offer a visceral glimpse into a mysterious musical past — reverberant chambers still ringing — but what happens when we trace (much) further back?

The Stone Age offers, from both the visual and audio perspective, remarkably sophisticated traces of an early artistic drive. The need to create, to represent the lived experience with limited means. Bison, rendered in charcoal and ochre, charging in a spectral dance in the cave of Altamira in northern Spain; red handprints reaching down through millennia in Cueva de la Manos (the cave of hands), Argentina; images of beasts in Libya, swimmers in Egypt, numerous vivid Native American images in Santa Barbara, California. These beautifully rendered illustrations refute the outdated notion — widely held in the nineteenth century, when the majority of such images were (re)discovered — that our distant ancestors lacked either the means or motivation to leave an imprint, let alone produce images of such stunningly evocative beauty. Many archaeologists of the time held that cave paintings were forgeries — simply too sophisticated and sensitively rendered to have come from early man.

A classic Gary Larson *Far Side* cartoon from the 1980s features a T-Rex pensively considering a calendar, pencil gripped in claw. Every day's entry is exactly the same: 'Kill something and eat it'. For many years, it was assumed that the images represented in caves were similarly objective (i.e. 'I am going to paint this animal because I want to kill and eat this animal'). In more recent years, this literal interpretation has been largely revised by many archaeologists who offer a more complex reading.

Caves are — even with the benefit of modern safety harnesses, head lamps and navigational gear — extremely hazardous spaces. What, then, was the purpose of descending through the pitch black in order to paint pictures? What was the principal driver in undertaking such dangerous and — from the hunter-gatherer perspective — energy-sapping journeys? In his 2002 book *The Mind in the Cave*, archaeologist David Lewis Williams proffered the idea that altered states of consciousness offered a key motivation to the creation of cave art, and that viewing the cave paintings from a modern Western materialist viewpoint was fundamentally wrongheaded.

Williams's central hypothesis is that all human beings are neurologically hard-wired to experience — whether in the form of dreams, trance states or via the ingestion of psychoactive substances — altered states, and that visions recalled from these states led to the creation of art. However, the images that result from such states will change depending on an individual's surroundings and day-to-day experiences. Hypnagogic states (the state immediately before falling asleep), he writes, are 'part and parcel of what it is to be fully human. They are "wired" into the brain. At the same time, we must note that the mental imagery we experience in altered states is overwhelmingly derived from memory and is hence culturally specific . . . the spectrum of consciousness is "wired", but its content is mostly cultural.'[24]

But what, then, of the aural? The acoustic world inhabited by ancient man was marked — not only by extraordinary reverberant cave acoustics and the myriad sounds of the natural world — but also by musical instruments. In 2008, at Hohle Fels — a cave in southern Germany — a 40,000-year-old vulture-bone flute was discovered. Common consensus holds this to be the world's earliest recognisable instrument. Comprising a naturally hollow piece of griffin vulture bone with five finger holes and a V-shaped mouthpiece, it was discovered in near complete condition. At 8 millimetres wide and 13 inches long, it would have been a considerable labour of love for whoever made it. The craftsmanship was fastidious: using primitive stone tools, two halves were hollowed out, carved, shaped and then reattached with an airtight seal.

'I believe that we've been making music for even longer — on the evolutionary scale — than even these instruments suggest,' says ancient instrument scholar Barnaby Brown. 'Birds sing, but how far back does "music" go? You can't put a start point to it. Sound tools, when our ancestors first made tools for music making — that's a technological breakthrough, aside from just singing — so certainly it was established as far back as 50,000 years ago.'

Over the past few years, Brown has been playing a hand-built reproduction of the vulture bone flute. A precarious exercise as he had only one bone to work with, he eventually plucked up the courage to start to bore his own holes and insert a reed:

'I initially tried to play it without a reed and thought "my goodness — anyone can make a note; anyone can make a tune", but then I put the reed in. And whatever the reed would have been back then — a bit of birch bark squeezed together, a piece of elder, a bit of cane, any common reed — the results were startling. I have a repertoire of around one hundred pibrochs that I play on the pipes — and they all transposed to this ancient flute!'

Other instruments such as the bullroarer also date to the Palaeolithic. A dramatic device, a bullroarer is a flat piece of wood, bone or antler attached to a leather cord. When swung around the head at a great speed, it results in a haunting low-frequency drone. The pitch modulation can be changed depending on the speed at which it is swung and the length of cord used. Bullroarers have been found all over the world but are most closely associated with Aboriginal culture, where they are thought to ward off evil spirits and were used in burial rituals. They were also widely used by the Southern African San people to imitate the drone of bees swarming.

The didgeridoo is perhaps the world's most instantly identifiable ancient drone instrument, a vitally important part of Aboriginal spiritual life. The didgeridoo is comprised of the inner trunk of a eucalyptus tree that has been hollowed out by termites. A low drone is produced by blowing into the top of the pipe, differences in modulation occurring depending on force of breath. Circular breathing — a tricky technique whereby a player simultaneously stores air in the cheeks while exhaling down the pipe — is vital to the achievement of a continuous drone. Myriad folk traditions surround the didgeridoo, most notably the communal *corroboree* where the tribe gathers at night and a group of adult men perform stories and legends, lead chants and songs and mimic the movements of animals in ceremonies that could last several days or even weeks.

Within Aboriginal culture, the drone of the didgeridoo links the telling of stories, the passing of knowledge — a collective societal *journey*. Palaeolithic caves were places of *inner* journeying — offering both a literal and metaphorical 'trip' into the depths of the human psyche. Dr Rupert Till from the University of Huddersfield researched the psychoacoustic potential of Neolithic burial chambers. He has also researched the acoustic properties of cave networks across Europe, culminating in the multidisciplinary EMAP (European Music Archaeology Project) 'Sounds of the Caves' project, which acoustically mapped the cave networks of northern Spain.

Again, Till emphasises the journeying aspect: physical descent, and the idea that those painting and making sound in caves were seeking something beyond the everyday experience of needful survival:

"People would have been going down for significant reasons. If you spend twenty minutes in a sensory deprivation tank, you begin to hear things that aren't there; you begin to imagine things. Some begin to hear random sounds or voices — or imagine other sounds, like flowing water. Similarly, after a while deprived of light you may start to see things. These are fundamentally psychedelic effects — we understand this today. It would have been a very intense experience; a confusing experience. Half seeing things, half hearing things. You can't help but link that experience to altered states of perception. Going into caves is a journey. It's travel; the unknown, into the earth, into the underworld — a world where normal life simply doesn't exist".

The desire to reach a place where 'normal life simply doesn't exist' is a universal constant. It's why we write, paint, dance, take drugs, make love. The drone places us in a zone of mental discombobulation, a state of sonic awe. So it makes sense that it has also been harnessed for aural intoxication, not least in the spectre of the piper — frolicking, mischievous, hypnotic — leading us on a merry dance down the centuries.

In mythology the piper is framed as harbinger of Dionysian glee or malicious doom. The Pied Piper of Hamelin, for example — shunned by the townsfolk of Lower Saxony who foolishly refuse to pay him for his rat-catching services — took his retribution by leading their children away, hypnotised by his pipes. Or consider Pan — half man/half goat, Greek god of the wild — invariably depicted naked with his pipes, horns and a sinister grin.

Piper at the Gates of Dawn

In the ancient world, piping traditions were defined by the interplay between melody and the drone, a tonal dance that mirrored the thorny relationship pipers often had with the Establishment: at times venerated, more often distrusted. The Sardinian launeddas pipes are a traditional instrument that dates back to antiquity. A double pipe with an added drone, a launeddas tradition survives in Sardinia to this day although, as Barnaby Brown explains, the pipers were often viewed with wariness by the authorities due to the intoxicating effect of their music.

'The drone is the source of it all,' Brown tells me. 'The launeddas makers put an enormous amount of time into the drone. The melody pipes are tuned by picking out harmonics in the sound spectrum of the bass drone. And that is absolutely critical. Because when the notes are locked into those bass harmonics, it puts you in a trance. When you don't hit the harmonics, you get interference — and that can be very expressive to play with. Then with the ancient Greek aulos pipes, for example, you have this venerable musical tradition where they *deliberately* exploited interference tones. It makes almost a chugging sound, a bit like in heavy metal — a distortion — and that creates tension.'

'The joy comes in relishing that tension,' Brown continues. 'Conflict and resolution; dissonance and consonance. Playing with that is basically harmony. People misunderstand harmony. They think it's all about consonance. It's not! Harmony is really about the *playfulness* between dissonance and consonance. It's a game. There is a dynamism there — like a marriage, like life. Moments of tension, moments of release.'

In Sardinian legend, the launeddas player was associated with sexual energy and magical ritual. A bronze statue of a launeddas piper from around the first century BC showed a crouching naked figure blowing the pipes with a prominent erection. According to Brown, this resonates with the Scottish Highland tradition, where the exposure of the genitals during combat is recorded in various tales. This act was also known in ancient Greece as *anasyrma*. The exposed phallus was believed to bestow magical powers, avert the 'evil eye' and bring good luck. The launeddas piping tradition predated

Christianity in Sardinia, but although the pipes eventually assimilated into Christian worship, a measure of trepidation remained.

'We forget that dancing was central to early Christian worship,' says Brown. 'And the dancing was led by the piper. In Sardinia, all the pipers were kicked out of church in the 1600s. Dancing would still happen on a Sunday, but only after mass. The worshippers were kicked out into the piazza because they wanted to dance. They weren't going to change their ways just because a priest told them not to. So with the launeddas, you have this wonderful mixture of monotheistic, polytheistic and animistic elements at play.'

The animistic element in the drone of the pipes is important. In ancient Greece, Dionysus — the god of ritual madness, wine and merriment — was inextricably linked to the pipes. Musicians would come together at the Olympic Games and musical competitions across the Palaeolithic world and compete. The aulos pipes were fundamental to Dionysian rites and had a reputation for being, as Brown says, 'colourful, exciting. On the aulos you can bend, you can modulate, you can use all sorts of blues notes and play around with the pitches. Playing the aulos is like controlling a wild beast. These pipes are strongly associated with divine bliss and religious ecstasy — a state that you work yourself into, like dervish whirling.'

The drone of the aulos pipes was associated with derangement of the senses through sonic decadence. Followers of Dionysus would indulge in lavish rituals of sex and booze known as the Mysteries of Dionysus. Vast representations of phalluses would be erected, wine-drinking competitions held and bulls sacrificed in ceremonies of uninhibited excess and full-scale sensory obliteration. The heroic drinking was invariably accompanied by drums and pipes. Initiates into the Dionysian cult were known as *maenads*, usually depicted on vases led by a team of aulos players. They counted among their number women, slaves, outlaws and 'non citizens' and this subversion of normative societal hierarchy — along with the drunkenness, fornication and dancing — combined to position the maenads as a real and present danger to the Establishment. Festivities could be bloody affairs — historian Daniel Boorstin described grotesque rituals laid on in service to divine intoxication:

These drunken devotees of Dionysus, filled with their god, felt no pain or fatigue . . . they enjoyed one another to the rhythm of drum and pipe. At the climax of their mad dances the maenads, with their bare hands would tear apart some little animal that they had nourished at their breast.[25]

51

The music mirrored the frenzy of the gathering and the comedown alike: frenetic disordered rhythms tempered with the ceaseless drone of the aulos. There was a distinction between Apollonian and Dionysian music. The former was the god of reason and light — his music was therefore measured, rhythmically steady, harmonically ordered. In contrast, Dionysian music was wild and droning, the aulos pipes 'not giving the brain one minute to return to acoustic normality.'[26]

The drone has always been inextricably bound to the human needs of identity, spirituality and escapism. Like a feedback loop, the drone recurs time and again — from the reverberating potential of Neolithic burial chambers, the evocation of mental delirium in ancient pipes to the transcendent resonance of sacred spaces. In European traditions, the drone has often been a hidden hand evoking a spiritual response. In Eastern traditions — Buddhism and Hinduism, in particular — the drone is a central tenet of theology.

It represents life, the universe and the godhead itself.

Chapter 2

CHANT ECSTATIC

Chant conjures potent imagery. Medieval monks in some dank abbey, shrouded in mist, pallid faces distorted by flickering candlelight, hoods up, voices rising as haunting Gregorian madrigals fill the hall; Tibetan Buddhists standing in a circle amid fluttering prayer flags, the drone of the Om ringing in the mountain pass; the cross-legged guru, beatific smile on face, chanting between mighty blasts on a charas pipe; the hypnotic call and response of the Master Musicians of Joujouka as they call forth the mischievous Bou Jeloud — sewn into fresh goatskins — to frolic amid the wood smoke and thwack assembled dancers with inflated bladders and branched olive sticks.

Repeat a familiar word for long enough and it becomes alien. Focus shifts from literal meaning to the physicality of the sound itself. The chanter becomes unaware of the physical process involved — intake of breath, vocalisation, muscles contracting. It becomes automatic, like taking a familiar route and arriving at the destination without a conscious memory of the drive itself.

Chant, then, is the sound of belief beyond sober theology, where fervency reaches to epiphany. Chant is the channelling of primal transcendence through repetition: an attempt to fling aside the flimsy curtain of day-to-day reality in order to access a higher truth.

To Buddhists and Hindus alike, the Om is the sound of the universe: the literal vibration of universal matter. It personifies the oneness of everything, an ultimate reckoning with reality. When Om is chanted it contains all knowledge, all life, all *everything*. The Chandogya Upanishad — the oldest sacred Hindu text — begins with the instruction, 'let a man meditate on Om, the essence of all'. Om is the essence of life itself.[1]

Before matter, before the formation of the universe, there was *sound*. Celestial vibration.

'You need to understand the concept of creation in order to understand the drone and its significance,' explains master sitarist Dharimbir Singh, his voice blending into a background of students tuning sitars. 'Indian thinking is rooted in the idea of the "one" — the one manifested in the many; the totality of white light refracting into colours, colours refracting back into white light.

'That is the significance — non-duality. The whole of creation is the same thing,' continues Singh. 'Om is the representation of the one. The *whole* bedrock of creation is in sound — the concept of Nadha Brahma. Om is the significance. Whatever we do — music, medicine, anything — we never forget the basic fact: everything is interconnected. What is the spiritual effect? You never forget that you are coming from the one.'

In devotional music, the drone is — time and time again — cast as the foundation stone on which melody is layered, and on which musical structure begins to takes shape. Certain instruments — the organ, sitar and tanpura for example — produce a drone for this purpose. The drone carries a spiritual significance that goes beyond melodic aesthetics or musical structure, however. Fostering feelings of warmth and calm, the drone is a tonal swaddle that facilitates meditative contemplation and sonic awe. It helps remove the thrust of time itself.

No longer anticipating development, we focus on the present. Slow-moving sound stimulates the perceptual mechanism. As sound artist Laurie Spiegel once said: 'The mind doesn't perceive constancy after a while. It habituates what is unchanging and listens for something that it hasn't yet sensed.'[2]

Chanting removes one incrementally further away from the boundaries of the sound itself, the physicality invested in 'making' it, until it becomes something else — an amorphous entity with a strange life of its own, shedding literal linguistic meaning like a snake sheds its skin.

Chant can go *beyond* sonic reverence, of course: in the mind of the believer, it can be used as a mechanism for the incarnation of God. Devotees of Hare Krishna take the words of their famous 'Hare Krishna, Hare Rama' chant to manifest the presence of the godhead. There are parallels here with the Roman Catholic communion, worshippers taking bread and wine not as 'representation' but the *literal* body and blood of Christ. So it is with chant — not the representation or evocation of the godhead but a mechanism for its actual manifestation.

The Overtone Drone

It's midnight and I'm listening to a recording of the Gyuto Monks Tantric Choir, headphones on, rain lashing at the windows. The monks push the bottom end of their vocal range to cavernous depths, reverb adding a thrilling tactile resonance. Overtones — two or more bass notes sung at once — come in great undulating waves. Voices connect via a hive mind, rising, falling, rising again as one in a viscous wave of tactile sound. The sound of the chanting feels ancient, laden with portent. It emits a sense of transience but also immovability — not of the fleeting nature of life — but of *sound itself*. The drone of the Om cast as undulating universal locked groove, a viscous sonic wall I can almost touch.

Sacred music can exert power, even on the non-believer. Much like visiting hallowed ground, the fervency of belief is palpable but *malleable*, transferable to the unconscious gut level. It's too easy to section off religious music as 'other', a source of hushed reverence that cannot possibly be understood by anybody but the believer, to feel it isn't available on a spiritual level unless you, too, 'believe'. But just as it is possible to separate a novelist or painter from their personal or political affiliations, sacred music can be freed from formal liturgy. For me — tonight — the chant of Tibet's Gyoto monks connects me back to the amorphous sense of hypnotic ritual that opened this book — Bongripper at Roadburn festival in the Netherlands and the 'wailing wall'.

Sound waves either connect with us or they don't. These connections can span across cultures, beliefs, the ages. I was recently sent a collaborative record by Blackmoon1348, a drone metal band who recorded with the Tibetan monks of the Tashi Lhunpo monastery. It's a powerful, heavy listen. The slow-burning riffs unfurl at glacial pace, underpinned by the monks' overtone chanting, which alternates between monolithic bass weight and ethereal dynamism. The chanting acts as a sub-blanket, underpinning the mix with oscillation that's as thick as molasses. It sounds like serendipity. Here is the perfect connection of the duality of the drone — the sacred and the lay — woven together in harmony, vocal overtones and the churning maelstrom of feedback connecting across traditions, time and space on the sonic highway.

Closely related is overtone singing — an intoxicating wormhole to tumble down late at night, and practised in myriad musical traditions from Tibet to Sardinia. A complex technique — a type of throat singing that takes years of vocal conditioning — it sees a singer open and close their vocal chords at rapid speed, enabling them to produce two — sometimes up to *four* — tones simultaneously; a steady drone atop which harmonics frolic and dance.

In Mongolia for example, overtone singing is the representation of the *sound* of nature. The overtone is of equal spiritual import as the visual appreciation of nature's physical form. Birdsong, the foreboding howl of wind across the barren steppe, the rush of the mighty Orkhon river. These sounds are held in the deepest spiritual regard by herdsmen on the Mongolian plain, imbued with a life force all of their own that Mongolian throat singing singers seek to mirror.

The sound is extraordinary. A grounding rumble topped with ethereal whistles and pure melodic interplay, like slowly turning the dial on a celestial radio. Swirling harmonics weave around *elemental* bass notes, not only the sound of mountain meeting sky but also the sound of what lies underground.

Developed out on the steppe — where sound travels a great distance — and traditionally used by nomadic herds-people, throat singing was originally associated with shamanic practice and dates back millennia. A force of nature — both literally and metaphorically — from the throat of a skilled practitioner it sounds *beyond* human, a physical impossibility where one voice channels many. As traditional Mongolian throat singer N. Sengedorj says, he is able to 'speak to the mountains, lake and grass . . . nature is a great compos-er and transmits its own creation to human beings and gifted performers.'3

The intensity of overtone singing has lent itself to some thrilling juxta-positions between the modern and ancient. The HU are a Mongolian metal band who describe their sound as 'hunnu rock' — human rock. They combine Mongolian throat singing with an epic metal bearing that evokes nomadic life and shamanic legend. 'Wolf Totem' contrasts the sturdy neigh of the Mongol horses with the revs of a motorbike, traditional flute and jaw harp with chug-ging electric guitars. It's a heady blend sonically, and their videos are visually arresting too. The band ride across the steppe on Harleys in full leathers before dismounting, lining up and chanting of the certain obliteration of tiger, bear, elephant and — finally — human who they will 'Fight! And obliterate!'

Outside of the overtone tradition, others have used similar vocal tech-nique. Avant-garde agitator Diamanda Galás has one of the world's great voices: her multi-octave range and acrobatic dexterity draw on an oeuvre of larynx-shredding screams, depth-charge chants, haunting whispers and belting operatic crests. Spending time immersed in her back catalogue is a bracing experience, to say the least. Her overtone vocalisations evoke the rich depths of human despair, bodily degradation, caustic rage at the evils of religious hypoc-risy and personal apathy. When studying at USCD, Galas would lock herself in the university's anechoic chamber — an acoustically dead space — where she'd 'take LSD and try everything with my voice, get into a lot of thinking that dealt with sensory deprivation . . . If I couldn't hear the reverberation inside, then nobody could hear me outside.'

Her live album *Plague Mass* (1991) features material from her *Masque of the Red Death* trilogy, inspired by the AIDS crisis that claimed the life of her brother in 1986. Recorded in New York's cathedral of St John the Divine, it's the definitive document of her lung-shattering power, primal catharsis in action.

Spoken-word sections give way to overtone shrieks, laden with vibrato, echoing around the cathedral. Galás subverts the aural accruements of sacred rite and ritual — chants, stone cathedral reverb, gospel liturgy, speaking in tongues, prayer — in a personal howl of caustic rage. Disembodied voices swipe and claw their way into your inner ear canal, approaching from all sides: the priest, the dead, different roles ducking in and out. Assuming the role of priest she asks — for five painful minutes — 'Do you confess?' before the cry, 'Yes I confess! Give me sodomy or give me death!' Galas is a spirit vessel. Chant, scream and overtone layered in a powerhouse of vocal exorcism — not of any demonic possession, but of the pain of loss and societal indifference in the face of a brutal disease: the dial reset, sonic allegory of Church and State spat back with venomous intent.

Seven Spirits

The idea of channelling an essence or calling forth a spirit — through repetition, chant and drone — is a staple of myriad musical traditions, both religious and secular, around the world. The Gnawa are a musical brotherhood descended from West African slaves who settled in Morocco. They practise a complex sonic healing ritual to contact, placate or renegotiate personal relationships with seven individual spirit entities known collectively as the *melk*, and also to ward off evil spirits known as the *djinn*. Their principal ritual — the *lila* — combines folk magic, music and numeric mysticism in a hypnotic session that lasts the whole night.

The music of the Gnawa is a swirling rhythmic thrum that pivots on chant, down-tuned *sinter* (a three-stringed lute) and drums. It's a broodingly immersive sound. On the *sinter*, the bass string is struck repeatedly by the thumb, making a pulsating bass drone while the fingers pick out a repetitious circular motif atop. Alongside this dense rhythmic undertow, powerfully hypnotic chants unfold, rendered in gruff tones. Each speaks to one of the spirits in turn. The number seven is highly significant: the Gnawa call to seven spirits and seven saints, hold seven powers to awaken, burn seven types of incense and wear clothes of seven colours throughout the night. Dancers turn in circles, spinning tasselled hats and moving in time to the music, the rhythmic drone of the lute adorned by the clatter of the *krakebs*, a castanet-like instrument. The ritual moves to a predetermined order: sound, sight, smell and movement harnessed as the individual spirits are summoned.

While expurgation may be the primary goal for some, the interplay between an individual and the spirits may also be central to the ritual. Some might seek to recalibrate their relationship, bargain with or strengthen the bond with an individual spirit.

As an oral tradition, Gnawa is passed from master to apprentice. It takes decades of devoted study to reach master level. Gnawa sects were, traditionally, itinerant outliers in Moroccan society, the music largely confined to sub-Saharan regions. While strongly influenced by the Moroccan Sufi tradition they do not always identify as Sufi per se: the connection is, rather, most strongly felt in concepts of trance, music and ecstasy that run through Gnawa and Sufi ritual alike. The Gnawa idea of *hal*, for example, relates to ecstasy through movement, a state of transcendence reached consciously or unconsciously through dance. Deep listening — *sama* — is also important, divinity reached through heightened sensual perception.

Gnawa music has become an increasingly visible musical force in Morocco in recent decades, reaching far outside its tribal origins. A huge festival attracting up to 400,000 people takes place in Essaouira every year, while musicians from far and wide have sought out Gnawa musicians to collaborate with. Bill Laswell, who coined the term 'collision music' for his myriad experimental projects, has long been a champion of the Gnawa's musical tradition. In 1994, Laswell brought Pharaoh Sanders to Morocco to record with late Gnawa master Maleem Mahmoud Guinia for the *Trance of Seven Colors* album, and also instigated the *Holy Black Gnawa Trance* album in 2016 with Guinia's brother Maleem Mokhtar Guinia.

Techno producer James Holden recently became enamoured with the trance-inducing potential of Gnawa, producing a record with Guinia in 2014 alongside Floating Points and, after his death in 2015, the *Marhaba* EP with Guinia's son. The combination of Gnawa energy alongside Holden's dronal modular excursions was a joy, hypnotic chant and lute giving rhythmic lifeblood while Holden's swathes of synth underpin the mix.

While the Gnawa have been the source of much cross-cultural inspiration in recent years, however, it's another form of mystic Moroccan music — rawer, harsher and louder than the Gnawa — which has consistently had the greatest resonance in countercultural channels for the past sixty years: the Master Musicians of Joujouka.

The Howl of the Rif

Bloody goatskins; raucous chants; hash pipes; extreme volume; tales of madness and mountains; fertility rites; sleep deprivation; ancient ritual. It's easy to understand why the Master Musicians of Joujouka were talismanic to Burroughs, Bowles, Gysin — the Beat writers who took their inspiration from the dark heat of the alleys, cafés, brothels and literary salons of the post-war Tangier Interzone.

A mystic Sufi sect based in the foothills of the Rif mountains in northern Morocco, the Masters — members of the tribe Ahl Serif — produce a narcotic cacophony that hinges on frenetic tribal drums, gruff call and response chants and the screeching drone of multiple rhaita pipes. Playing a music unique to the village and passed from father to son, the Joujouka sound is unlike any other. They've been at it for centuries. William S. Burroughs famously called them the 'world's only 4000-year-old rock band'.[4] Playing for up to twelve hours straight, musicians and audience alike entering a waking dreamscape, theirs is a brutal trip.

Joujouka music is principally about healing, delirium and fertility. Legend has it that in the fifteenth century AD, Sufi saint Sidi Hamid Sheikh arrived in the village and bestowed the ability to heal disturbed minds on a group of local musicians. As such, Joujouka musicians are said to be blessed by *baraka* — the spirit of the saint. Revered by the Moroccan court throughout the Middle Ages, the music still retains its reputation for healing. To this day, people seek respite or cure from mental illness in the village. Musicians are taught from early childhood and only gain master status after many years' practice. A flute-type instrument called the lira, double-reed rhaita pipes and powerful goatskin drums are the traditional instruments while vocals usually take the form of raucous call and response chants, rendered with an intensely throaty, guttural delivery.

Frank Rynne — beatnik authority, historian, Dubliner — has worked with a group of Joujouka musicians (there are two groups, and no small amount of animosity exists between them) for the past twenty-five years, spending extended periods living in the village, as well as recording the group. The first Westerner ever to be granted full membership of the Association of the Master Musicians of Joujouka — a fraternal guild — he was elected by the Masters to organise Joujouka business outside the country.

'The music drives some people absolutely mad,' he laughs. 'For people who grew up with the music — from the Ahl Serif tribe in the village — when it gets to a crescendo they go batshit crazy. Kids go into frenzy. The music has an extraordinary effect. They reach a pitch where you think "that is as far as they can go; they couldn't possibly keep it at that pitch" but then the lead rhaita player goes up a little bit and the drone shifts up and the drummer gets up a level. And it goes on and on and on.'

Each June, the village celebrates the festival of Bou Jeloud where a Pan-like satyr figure — half-man/half-goat, played by a villager — bestows fertility and harvest bounty on the village by striking all who come near with the branch of an olive tree. Three days and nights of frenetic music, dancing and feasting follow. Described by Rynne as 'completely primordial', the Bou Jeloud festivities are a theatrical and bloodily narcotic affair where the skins of four freshly skinned goats are sewn into the costume worn by whoever is playing Bou Jeloud that year.

The legend that birthed the festivities is a vital part of Joujouka mythology. A weary young shepherd called Attar lay down exhausted in the forbidden cave of Magara near Joujouka village, leaving his flock grazing in the fields below. After a few hours' sleep, the shepherd Attar was roused by Bou Jeloud, a half-man/half-goat figure who was playing a flute. Attar entered into a bargain with him. In exchange for Bou Jeloud gifting Attar the secrets of the pipes — a secret the young shepherd was sworn never to share — Bou Jeloud would be gifted a bride from the village. Attar didn't heed Bou Jeloud and broke the pact by sharing the music with his friends. The villagers, however, kept their side of the bargain and Bou Jeloud was duly presented with his bride — Aisha Kandisha.

She was, however, completely mad and proceeded to exhaust the goat man with her wild dancing and ceaseless frolicking. Bou Jeloud left the village — leaving his bride behind — and the villagers enjoyed great harvest and fertility. Bou Jeloud returned to the village for a number of years before disappearing, after which a villager donned the goatskins and mimicked his movements, in order that the village could continue to enjoy the fertility Bou Jeloud bestows.

'The blood of the animal is still on him,' says Rynne. 'You have a man sewn into freshly killed goatskins who is dancing to this ritual music in front of you. He's whipping you and hitting you with olive branches and sticks.'

The Bou Jeloud music played during the festival is *incessant*, pregnant with building mania. The rhaita pipes in combination with the rhythmic drumming and chanting create an audio zone of sheer psychoactive potency. Bou Jeloud is not a predefined role: he appears at different times throughout the night, depending on what the music is doing. The drone is central to this, a playful mechanism that can 'call' him back and forth, over the course of the night.

'He might not be "let go",' says Rynne. 'He might "hold on" to the role. And how does that happen, in a ritual sense? Through the drone! They play this *intense* drone. I don't know why they don't just do it for ever. For me, it's the most ecstatic music in the world. It holds a place where your brain can't function. You're captured by this insane rhythm and the basis of it is a continuous, circular-breathing enabled drone that screeches at a pitch that makes it impossible not to dance. You're sweating. In that moment there is sexual energy, ancient energy.'

Ancient and anarchic, sexual and mischievous, the music of the Joujouka plugs straight into the ley line of Dionysus. Bou Jeloud is, after all, a Pan-like character. Just as the aulos pipes of the Mysteries of Dionysus were — millennia ago — used for sensual derangement, a trance state whereby intoxication was revered and enhanced by the pipes — so it is with the Masters.

Theirs is an *extreme* music, imbued with a palpable glee. The peaks — when multiple rhaita pipes are droning at different pitches and the drums amp up to a pounding rhythmic frenzy — are unrelentingly intense.[5] The Masters are rural, tribal — essentially a musicians' guild in the service of the local community. A wedding in Joujouka isn't a wedding without the Masters. The swirl of the music underpins the community; it's woven into the fabric of village life.

It wasn't until the 1950s, however, that the Joujouka sound began to permeate beyond the Rif mountains, bewitching the emergent Beat culture as a viscerally intense audio counterpoint to the surreal dreamscape of the Tangier Interzone. That it has since been disseminated globally through counterculture figures like Brian Jones and Ornette Coleman — both of whom recorded in Joujouka — makes perfect sense. After all, the best rock 'n' roll and free jazz are about abandon, liberation, the breaking of restrictions, an embrace of the animalistic.

The Interzone Drone

Post-war Tangier has long occupied a febrile space in the underground literary subconscious, an international zone inhabited by a seamy coterie of spies, spivs, smugglers, bohemians, dealers and chancers of every conceivable persuasion and appetite.

From 1924 until Moroccan independence in 1956, the city was jointly governed by the Spanish, British and French. Contraband, information and drugs were the predominant trades and — in a beguiling fleshpot of Berber African,

Mediterranean European and Arab influence — Tangier lent itself to a peculiarly dreamlike iconography. Blind alleys, luxurious gardens unobserved behind grimy walls, portside cubbyholes, hidden courtyards, the maze-like streets of the medina little changed since the Middle Ages, offset against the elegant wrought-iron balconies, continental cafés and bookshops of the *ville nouvelle*.

This was a city of sexual, intellectual and artistic freedom immortalised in the seductive fictive universes of William S. Burroughs, Brion Gysin and Paul Bowles — a playground of narcotic literary legend. Indelibly associated with the Beats, a steady stream of bohemian tourists followed in the footsteps of Burroughs et al., seeking a mystical land of hashish and smack, cut-throats and pretty boys. Discreet pursuits could be enjoyed in Tangier that were strictly *verboten* at home. Homosexuality — though technically illegal — was broadly tolerated. The same was true of the potent Moroccan kif which — alongside endless glasses of wincingly sweet mint tea — provided psychoactive fuel for the city. As historian Barnaby Rogerson once noted, Tangier was a place where tolerance was 'practised but not preached'. The city's bohemian flotsam enjoyed intellectual and practical liberty under azure skies, a world away from the rigidly square confines of post-war America and Britain.

The literary crowd in Tangier circled Paul and Jane Bowles and Mohammed Mrabet. Bowles wrote his masterpiece *The Sheltering Sky* — a novel imbued with the hallucinatory splendour of North Africa — in the city in 1949, and went on to chronicle the mythology, surreal street life and magical underbelly of Morocco until his death in 1999. His fiction was imbued with the minutiae of daily life, rendered with the supposedly dispassionate eye of the weary Western traveller. Despite spending decades in the city, Bowles always considered himself a 'tourist', and presented Tangier as a mystery that would for ever remain unsolved.

In the 1993 documentary *An American in Tangier*, Bowles described a magical pull: 'I had based my sense of being in the world partly on an unreasoned conviction that certain areas of the Earth's surface contained more magic than others . . . A hidden but direct passage that bypassed the mind.'

His life in Tangier followed a set pattern. Mrabet — painter, writer, storyteller — would arrive at the Bowles' flats in the afternoon. (Paul lived upstairs, Jane downstairs. Neither had a phone. Rather, they communicated using toy telephones connected via a wire that dangled out of the window.) Here Mrabet would smoke a few pipes of kif, cook dinner and recount folk stories to whoever was around, many of which Bowles translated. The Beat connection — indelible to this day — was solidified in the early 1950s by the arrival of Brion Gysin and William S. Burroughs.

Tangier proved a darkly seductive muse for both. Drugs and sex were in plentiful supply, the living was cheap and the city — in all its shambling, eccentric glory — became something of an (albeit productive) isle of the lotus-eaters for both. Burroughs's Tangier days have been well documented. Myriad accounts depict him holed up in the Hotel El Muniria writing *Naked Lunch* while eating balls of mahjoun hashish fudge, leaving to score smack or cruise the beach sweltering in a full suit under the midday sun, or taking tea at the Café du Paris among the retired double agents. He remixed Tangier into his most (in)famous literary location — the Interzone — a nightmarish dreamscape controlled by the Nova Police and populated by a rogues' gallery of grotesques.

Gysin, meanwhile, wrote *the* fundamental Moroccan-influenced counter-cultural novel — *The Process* — in 1969. A thinly veiled semi-autobiographical journey across the Sahara, it was steeped in an atmosphere of Sufi mysticism and strange happenstance, rendered in vivid, hallucinatory prose. The Masters are present in a number of passages.

Here Gysin describes the essence of the Bou Jeloud ritual in fevered terms:

Bou Jeloud is fear and fucking: running wild, chasing, beating, catching, biting, tearing and fucking: again and again and again. Bou Jeloud leaps high in the air with the music to fall out of the sky on top of the women, beating them with switches so they can go on having the kids. The women all scatter, like marabout birds in a pasture . . . Bou Jeloud is after you, chasing you! You're run down, overrun, screaming with laughter and tears. You're trampling children while wild dogs snap at your heels. Everything, suddenly, is swirling around in a great ring-a-rosy, around and around and around. Go! For ever! Stop! Never! More! and: *No more!* and: *No . . . No More!* Pipes crack in your head and you can't hear a thing. You're deaf! Or, you're dead! Dead in cold moonlight surrounded by madmen and ghosts. Bou Jeloud is on you . . . frisking you, fucking you . . . beating you, butting you . . . taking you, leaving you. Gone![6]

Gysin was introduced to Joujouka music with Paul Bowles in 1951 by the painter Mohamed Hamri,[7] with the three attending a Sufi festival in Sidi Kasim together. Gysin fell in love with the sound instantly, famously proclaiming it as the music 'I wanted to hear for the rest of my life'. He struck up a friendship with Hamri who took him up to the village for the first time a few years later.

Hamri was *the* pivotal figure in the dissemination of Joujouka music outside Morocco. Born in 1932, he was brought up in Ksar el Kbir, the nearest town to Joujouka village. His uncle — Sherkin Attar — was bandleader at the time and the young Hamri knew the music and village musicians well. Aside from painting (he painted Morocco in a modernist style, and exhibited all over the world), Hamri was also an enthusiastic chronicler of Joujouka folklore, writing *Tales of Joujouka* in 1975, which collated the stories and mythology of the village.

In the early fifties, he and Gysin opened the infamous Tangier restaurant The 1001 Nights and the pair employed the Joujouka as 'house band'. Amid bottles of rough Algerian red wine, rich lamb tagine, saffron-scented fish stew and billowing clouds of hash smoke, Gysin instigated a cross-cultural scene. The Masters played, Hamri cooked, Gysin and friends read poetry. *A Night at the 1001* — released by Sub Rosa in 2001 and compiled from tapes made by Gysin in the restaurant — captures a heady atmosphere of wild music and literature, complete with coughs, chinking glasses and table scrapes.

But while Tangier provided a sanctuary to writers and artists, Joujouka was a different proposition altogether. Tangier was urbane, sophisticated. Joujouka was a rural mountain village that didn't have electricity until 1994, an agrarian economy broadly unchanged since the Middle Ages and untethered to any Western tradition — or comforts — whatsoever. Bowles and Gysin both harboured an aesthetic fondness towards the old Morocco, albeit from a position of Western privilege. Bowles, in particular, frequently railed against the 'modernisation' of Morocco in print and conversation, feeling a sentimental attachment to a way of life that he seldom engaged with on a day-to-day level, living in a *ville nouvelle* apartment complete with servants. He found the Masters' music, in the words of Frank Rynne who met Bowles on a number of occasions, 'too crude', the hardships associated with village life unseemly. Gysin, meanwhile, resented the increasing recognition that the Masters enjoyed from the 1960s onwards, a result of Hamri booking them for gigs outside of the restaurant.

'Gysin was almost bitter when Hamri brought the Joujouka to do shows in Tangier in the 1960s, as if the music should be kept secret,' says Rynne. 'I find the same thing around Paul Bowles in his writing. When I met Paul, it was very evident that he was this colonial figure who saw old Morocco — underdeveloped Morocco — as a tableau. He hated any modernisation. But that, to me, underlines a disrespect and disregard for the people. Bowles isn't kind to Moroccans in that he was writing about a *medieval-esque* Morocco. He hated to see that change. That somebody in Joujouka has a fridge is a good thing — otherwise meat goes bad and your children get sick; or you can't keep your insulin if you're diabetic. Your lifespan is going to be reduced if you don't have access to a road or a water system. I don't think that culture should be preserved at the expense of healthcare.'

Bowles on the Road

While unmoved by the frenetic drone of the Joujouka, Bowles was fascinated by other Moroccan tribal music. In 1959, he petitioned the US Library of Congress to fund him to venture across rural Morocco and record musicians on location, Alan Lomax style. He sought out a wide spectrum of traditional sounds, from Berber musicians in the highlands to the Gnawa and Jewish music, recording over 250 pieces, sweltering in the heat, buoyed up on 'hot Pepsi-Cola' and pipes of kif as he carried an Ampex 601 tape recorder that weighed as much as a bag of bricks.

Things didn't always go according to plan. In Tangier, for example, there was only one remaining muezzin who recited the call to prayer unamplified, relying on unadorned vocal force to carry the message, like an old-school town crier. He was to make one final call before getting an amplifier like everybody else. Bowles — determined to get the moment on tape — set out with Allen Ginsberg in tow. Sitting in a nearby café, they set up the tape recorder. Ginsberg became animated and started a rambling commentary about the immensity of the occasion, the power of what he was hearing, the magic of it all. Listening back to the tapes, the muezzin was inaudible — Ginsberg's monologue loud and clear.

Bowles's recordings caught a country at the crossroads of decolonisation. The French had left in 1956 and the Moroccan authorities were grappling with modernisation, King Mohammed V attempting to introduce a functioning governmental system while quelling tribal dissent and dealing with widespread poverty. Bowles however, intent on documenting ancient tribal traditions, attracted the chagrin of the Ministry of the Interior, who forbade him from recording without their express permission — a directive he studiously ignored.

Among the middle classes of Fez and Casablanca, attitudes to tribal music were frequently antagonistic, Gnawa and Berber music mistrusted as an arcane abomination; a primitive noise steeped in mischief and witchcraft, unbecoming of a thrusting nation hell-bent on modernity. By cleaving to these ancient traditions — archiving, preserving and disseminating them, while on the payroll of the American government, no less — Bowles was causing offence, flying in the face of a newly outward-facing nation, meddling in areas that didn't concern him. In his essay 'The Rif, to Music', Bowles illustrates the officious animosity he was up against:

Few of them are as frank about their convictions as the official in Fez who told me: 'I detest all folk music, and particularly ours here in Morocco. It sounds like the noises made by savages. Why should I help you to export a thing which we are trying to destroy? You are looking for tribal music. There are no more tribes. We have dissolved them. So the word means nothing. And there never was any tribal music anyway — only noise.'[8]

In reality, this was far from the truth. Tribes hadn't remotely been 'dissolved'. Moroccan society was a diverse tapestry encompassing Riffians, Berbers, Arabs, Jews, Gnawa, Haratin and many smaller tribes. Music was central to all. The sounds recorded by Bowles shared one vital trope: hypnosis. The dronal chants, screeching rhaita pipes and circular rhythms were in the service of hypnosis. Like the Joujouka, the music documented by Bowles in 1959 was, in essence, *trance* music. He was adamant that it needed to be taken in its entirety, not broken down into smaller, user-friendly, chunks:

It is essential to distinguish between static repetition and organic or deceptive repetition, in which the apparently reiterated rhythmical, melodic or textural motif is a device for capturing the attention . . . it is in this respect that good Berber music excels . . . since its aim is to cause hypnosis, to be appreciated the music must be given the opportunity to hypnotise.

Dreammachines

Like Bowles, Gysin and Burroughs were equally fascinated by hypnotic states. The viral nature of societal control mechanisms (namely the written and spoken word) — both their authoritarian effect and artistic subversion — was a lifelong preoccupation of Burroughs, in particular. In his view, every aspect of political, social and religious control was inexorably bound to particular groupings of words or images. By recognising this, repurposing the building blocks, one might curb the shackles of subliminal authoritarian control. Though generally attributed to Burroughs, it was in fact Gysin who pioneered the cut-up — whereby text from a variety of sources is physically cut into pieces and rearranged in a different order, disassociating it from its previous 'life'. The technique was then brought to wider underground consciousness by Burroughs with *Naked Lunch* and the *Nova Express* trilogy.

The pair would later publish a working manifesto — *The Third Mind* — which introduced the procedure as the hidden hand of chance working as creative catalyst. Writing created with the cut-up will 'consist of a process of decoding, of contamination and sense perversion. All this because all language is essentially mystification and everything is fiction.'[9]

The cut-up extended to sound, too. Burroughs was an early pioneer of primitive sampling. Fascinated by the subversive potential of recorded speech, spliced and edited — remixed, essentially — he conducted numerous peculiar experiments with tape recorders.[10] In his absurdist essay 'Electronic Revolution', he set out — in frequently hilarious fashion — various practical approaches for scrambling mass media and political messaging, casting a chaos boomerang into the broadcasting ether. In his hands, the firmament of the news cycle was rendered amorphous drone, targeted against itself, repurposed for nefarious means, churned to surreal slurry.

In eerily prescient fashion, Burroughs offered practical advice on the dissemination of fake news:

> You need a scrambling device, TV, radio, two video cameras, a ham radio station and a simple photo studio with a few props and actors. For a start you scramble the news all together and spit it out every which way on ham radio and street recorders. You construct fake news broadcasts on video camera. For the pictures you can use mostly old footage. Mexico City will do for a riot in Saigon and vice versa. For a riot in Santiago Chile you can use

the Londonderry pictures. Nobody knows the difference . . . you scramble your fabricated news in with actual news broadcasts . . . you have an advantage which your opposing player doesn't have. He must conceal his manipulations. You are under no such necessity. In fact you can advertise the fact that you are writing news in advance and trying to make it happen by techniques which anybody can use. And that makes you NEWS . . . cut-ups could swamp the mass media with total illusion.[11]

Brion Gysin sought to harness the subliminal power of dream imagery via self-induced trance. He invented a stroboscopic flicker contraption with the artist Ian Sommerville called the Dreammachine that was capable of inducing powerful light hallucinations.

A card cylinder with patterned slits cut in the side is placed on a turntable spinning at either forty-five or seventy-eight revolutions per minute. Inside the cylinder, a light bulb is suspended. The 'subject' sits in front of the Dreammachine, eyes closed, and is blasted with light between eight and thirteen pulses per second. This mimics, so the theory goes, alpha waves — electrical impulses in the brain present at moments of deep relaxation. The Dreammachine is dronal in its effect, inducing a hypnotic state. In an interview with the writer Jon Savage in 1986, Gysin explained the process as a form of subconscious bio-hacking, dream imagery harnessed as cranial escape mechanism.

Very often people compare it to films . . . I have seen in it practically everything that I have ever seen . . . all imagery. All the images of established religions, for example, appear — crosses appear . . . eyes of Isis float by, and many of the other symbols that appear as if they were the Jungian symbols that he considered were common to all mankind . . .[12]

It was inevitable that once on Moroccan soil, Gysin and Burroughs would be inexorably drawn to the music of the Masters of Joujouka, given their interest in serendipity, the hand of chance, the distortion of 'reality'. The literature of dreams found the music of dreams, an alchemical wedding of peculiar happenstance solidified. Soon the arrival of Rolling Stone Brian Jones was to further the legend of the music of this small Moroccan village, and result in one of the most mind-twistingly hypnotic recordings ever put to tape.

I Am the Goat!

The Masters remained a cult concern in Tangier throughout the 1960s, largely unknown outside Morocco. This changed with the arrival of the Rolling Stones and their introduction — again, via Hamri the painter — to the music of the village. The Stones had, much like the Beats before them, sought a refuge of sorts in Morocco. Pressures of fame, dodgy accounting and drug hassles had plagued the band for years but the infamous Redlands bust of 1967 had ramped the band's collective cortisone to intolerable levels. They were attracting the censure of the Establishment and tabloids to a hateful intensity: no longer framed as the totemic jesters of swinging London, but increasingly seen as a genuinely destructive force.

Convening in the aftermath while awaiting trial, the band decided on a trip to Morocco as a stress-relieving tonic. The trip was plagued with drama from the outset, however. Brian Jones was unwell, and missed the first few days. By the time he arrived, his girlfriend Anita Pallenberg and Keith Richards had embarked on an affair. The atmosphere in the band's camp was soured beyond repair. After a few sullen days taking acid, shopping in the souk and smoking the strong local hash, the rest of the Stones went home. Jones stayed on.

Invited on a trip to Joujouka by Brion Gysin and Hamri, Jones decided to record the Masters during the Bou Jeloud festivities. On arrival, an unusually blond goat was paraded around the village before being ritually slaughtered for the feast. Staring into the goat's eyes, Jones became animated, pointing and saying 'The goat is me! I'm the goat!' Later — after feasting on the animal — he reportedly said that it 'felt like communion'.

The goat incident summed up the atmosphere of bad luck and gallows humour that surrounded the Stones' camp, and Jones in particular, at the time. The music he got down on tape that night was wild and discordant, a howl of ancient spirits swirling. The leader of the group then was Mallim Ali Abeslam El Attar, one of the most legendary Joujouka leaders. Attar had led a hard life. He was conscripted — like so many Sufi musicians of the same generation — to fight for Franco in the Spanish Civil War during the 1930s. He stayed in Spain until 1948 when he returned to the village, without either pay or pension from the fascist Spanish government. He knew Hamri well and, aside from playing in the village and at the 1001 Nights restaurant, would also sometimes play on the train line that ran from the nearby town of Ksar el Kabir to Tangier.

Hamri and Brian Jones got on well. Frank Rynne frequently spoke to Hamri about him. He told me how Hamri recalled Jones reclining on a small bed in the village to listen to stories of Joujouka folklore, eyes closed. Hamri would think Jones was asleep and stop reading, upon which a hand would rise from the bed and a soft London accent call out 'and then?'

Joujouka life may have offered a brief respite from the maelstrom that surrounded the Stones back home, but the music of Joujouka was itself a mania-inducing maelstrom of another kind. The fever-pitch screech of the rhaita pipes was offset against the wet cave thwack of handheld drums and hypnotic chanting. Jones took the tapes back to London and treated them with tape echo and stereo phasing, a primitive dubbing that added a psychoactive touch to what was already deeply psychedelic music. In Jones's hands, the vocals swoosh in and out of the mix, ducking and weaving around the drums like the midnight shadow play cast by the village bonfire; occasional crowd noise — screaming and clapping, phlegmy hash-lung coughs — is audible, adding a raw dynamism. What Jones captured that night was guts music, blood music — forty minutes immersed in the febrile maelstrom. The listener is pulled around as if riding a cosmic waltzer, a rickety carriage spun relentlessly by a toothless, timeless jester: a constant audio *pressuring*.

Jones died two years later in 1969. The album he recorded in Joujouka — *Brian Jones Presents the Pipes of Pan at Joujouka* — was released two years later in 1971. It remains a psychedelic masterpiece imbued with the hallucinatory energy of the Rif. The Joujouka even honoured him with a piece played to this day in their live repertoire: 'Brian Jones Very Stoned'. After the *Pan* album, other visitors came and went — most notably Timothy Leary, who wrote of his experiences in *Jail Notes*, and Ornette Coleman, who recorded the frenetic, maddening 'Midnight Sunrise' with the Masters for *Dancing in Your Head* (1977).

The Jones album built a steady cult following, although it prefigured a confusing and acrimonious split among the Joujouka that lasts to this day. Two separate groups formed, each spelling the name of the village differently: the Master Musicians of Joujouka — whose leader is Ahmed El Attar, and who perform the same ceremonial function in the village as ever — and the Master Musicians of Jajouka, as led by Bachir Attar. The split stemmed from a disagreement in the 1970s when the musicians, who operate much like a guild, replaced Bachir's father, Hadj Abdeslam El Attar with Mallim Fudal. Attar claimed this was unjust. In his view, the role of group leader was hereditary, not open to vote. However, this has been disputed: many in the village believe the role of leader can be decided by common consensus.

Bachir Attar's Jajouka band are a different — more outward facing — proposition to the Joujouka who remain in the village. Bachir's group opened for the Rolling Stones on the *Steel Wheels* tour in 1989, they record in studios and have toured extensively worldwide, collaborating with everybody from Ginger Baker to Lee Ranaldo and Debbie Harry.

The spectre of the Jones record still hangs heavy over the village. A controversial 1995 re-release on Philip Glass's Point Music imprint had a different cover featuring a profile photograph of Bachir Attar, despite the album not featuring his playing (he was a toddler when Jones came to the village). The original sleeve notes by Gysin, meanwhile, were edited to remove any mention of it being Hamri — a long-time champion of the 'other' Joujouka group — who had, in fact, introduced Jones to the music. No royalties were shared with any of the Joujouka musicians who actually played on the record, nor were they consulted on the release.

Indeed, the album served to underline the fundamental differences in approach from the two groups. One — as led by Bachir Attar — as a more commercial touring entity, the other — the Joujouka — fulfilling the same tradition and ceremonial function as ever. Both, of course, claim to be the 'real' group, decades of vitriol and conjecture making it unlikely anyone from outside the village will ever get the full story.

Regardless of internal tensions in the village, the Masters have been weaving their hypnotic cacophony for centuries. Burroughs once said of Tangier that it was like a 'dream concocted in stone, sky supersonic, orgone blue, warm wind . . . but more than that, it's like the dream is breaking through.' The exact same could be said of Joujouka music — sensorial power reaching towards an epiphany glimpsed through the sonic ether.

The Masters will always be associated with Beat lore, Brian Jones, the peculiarly fertile psychic dreamscape of 1960s counterculture revolution. Their music is elemental, it gets under the skin, entering the subconscious. For connoisseurs, it is an addictive sound, the melodies snaking around the head for days after a listening session. Sometimes *nothing* else will do: Joujouka or bust.

However, the music proved (and remains) too fundamentally extreme — too dizzying — for mass consumption. Joujouka speaks of oblivion, ceaseless tension, building to glorious cathartic release. But if you don't get it — and many don't — that release never comes, just a building, brain-gnawing mania. Brion Gysin once said, 'you know your music when you find it. You fall into line and dance until you pay the piper.' For those who have fallen under the Joujouka spell this rings true: the pipes of Bou Jeloud will always be playing — somewhere deep within in the recesses of the mind, powering up the synapses and feeding the soul.

Chapter 3

MIDNIGHT RAGA

Indian music gained serious countercultural influence during the 1960s. By the latter half of the decade, sitar and tanpura drones were ubiquitous — as much a part of the rock lexicon as fuzz-laden guitars. Frequently enhanced by the time-stretching properties of LSD, and enthusiastically adopted by rock aristocracy including the Beatles, the Pretty Things, the Kinks, the Rolling Stones, Procol Harum and Donovan, countless others fell under the influence as the decade progressed.

To some, Indian music represented a catch-all, a hash-scented portal that led directly to perceived Eastern mysticism: a musical 'otherment' underlining sensory delirium or the ubiquitous peace and love signalling of the times. San Francisco's hapless Strawberry Alarm Clock captured the pervading spirit with their ludicrous 'Sit with the Guru' (sample lyric: 'Hip mankind on, turn your mind on / Sit with the Guru / Meditation . . . ooo-ooo'). Indeed, so enthusiastic was the adoption of the sitar that in the decades since, it has become something of a sartorial audio hallmark — as potent a signifier of perceived 'hippy guff' as Lennon specs and peace signs, used everywhere from *The Simpsons* to *Austin Powers* to *This is Spinal Tap* as a celluloid memorial device.

While the Beats often sought mystical intensity, sexual frisson and artistic freedom in Morocco, for the travel-minded hippy all roads led to India. In the UK, attitudes to travel had changed beyond all recognition since the end of the Second World War. Empire may have ended twenty years previously but by 1967 a new generation was assimilating Indian spiritualism, drugs and music in a way that would have seemed inexplicable and decadent to the gin-soaked civil servants of times gone by. The hippy trail — generally undertaken on cramped overland buses — followed a route that had been loosely established by ex-RAF engineer Paddy Barrow Fisher in 1957.

77

Staying on in India after the Second World War, and through the Indian struggle for independence, Fisher founded the Indiaman bus company in the 1950s, a ramshackle service that followed an established cross-country route[1] from London to Amsterdam, through to Greece and up through the Balkans to Turkey. Alighting in Istanbul, many would make for the infamous 'Pudding Shop' — a battered café specialising in kebabs, baklava, rose-scented rice pudding and back-door hash deals. The Pudding was the established meet for the weary international diaspora and catered to hippies, Beats and esoteric scholars of every conceivable persuasion. In the absence of an established infrastructure, the shop — specifically its walls, daubed in messages, phone numbers and no small amount of questionable poetry — acted as a bricks-and-mortar Lonely Planet guide. From Istanbul eastwards, the journey got serious. A drive over the Iranian border, on through Afghanistan and Pakistan before reaching the final destination — India or, for the hard core, Nepal.

Most, having devoured Jack Kerouac, Allen Ginsberg et al., wanted to escape the greyscale post-war social conservatism that stifled the provinces. Beat literature ensured that travel for its *own* sake, the journey being as important as the destination, was held in high spiritual regard, and hardship, frugality and sickness were worn as badges of honour. A minority held a keen interest in Indian spiritualism. Many simply relished the opportunity to beat a path to the world's finest artisan hashish, strains previously only talked about in hushed tones in musty Ladbroke Grove bedsits — temple ball, charas, malani cream — tracked down to source and consumed in the sun for a pittance.

For the hapless suburban hippy, exterior signifiers pointed to a culture steeped in laissez-faire mysticism. The semi-naked sadhus — wondering holy men who answer the call to eschew marriages, old names, jobs and worldly possessions to live a life of ascetic meditation — proved a particular fascination. With their dreadlocks, chillum pipes, ash-covered torsos and loincloths the sadhus were, ostensibly, living the endgame of the hippy ideal: a life of freedom and peace, unburdened by material concerns. The reality was, of course, infinitely more complex: there was a world of difference between the austere solitude, spiritual rigour, physical endurance and deep mental stamina required of the genuine sadhu life, and the romantic ideal. Enlightenment — as many found out — wasn't attained by a lungful of charas and a bus ticket.

No country has a closer relationship to the drone than India, and the sounds that resulted from its influence, though often magical, were inevitably fraught. Myriad claims of cultural appropriation — or simple dunderheaded misunderstanding — were levelled at those attempting to assimilate Indian music into rock 'n' roll. The story of how the drone of India came to permeate rock, the avant-garde and free jazz alike is nuanced, however. It goes beyond hippy stereotypes. Because while some took the classical traditions of India flippantly — a kitsch dalliance quickly assimilated, even more quickly discarded, others dedicated years, in some cases their entire lives — to painstaking practice, austere study and deep meditation. People like George Harrison, La Monte Young and Alice Coltrane, for example, were *serious* heads who drew abiding personal and artistic uplift from Indian music and found — in foundational artists like Ravi Shankar and Pandit Pran Nath — lifelong inspiration.

So how did the cultural accruements of the Indian subcontinent — the Om signs, chants, joss sticks, sitar drones and vivid imagery — come to be so indelibly linked to the counterculture? Why did the drone of India become *the* emblematic musical hallmark of the 1960s? From the rock perspective — and we'll come to the divergent slipstreams of Indian-influenced free jazz and minimalism later — the lineage can be traced to a fortuitous afternoon in April, 1965.

Ravi and George

In their relentless mid-sixties ascendency, the Beatles weren't accustomed to downtime. The pace was frenetic. They maintained a gruelling schedule that would make many modern bands baulk. The film world, however, is a business for which the phrase 'hurry up and wait' might well have been invented. In 1965 the Beatles were filming *Help!* — one of their dismal, rictus-grin 'capers' when, one afternoon, waiting for a scene in an Indian restaurant to be readied, a group of Indian musicians hired to provide background music began to play. George Harrison sat entranced by the drone emanating from the otherside of the room.

On tour in America the following year, he was introduced to the music of Ravi Shankar by Roger McGuinn of the Byrds. The Byrds were already big Shankar fans, with 'Eight Miles High' (1966) carrying a clear influence, McGuinn replicating the sound of the sitar on his guitar, the intro riffing on John Coltrane's 'India'. On tour, McGuinn played Coltrane and Shankar ceaselessly. 'It was the only music we had,' he remembered in 2010. 'By the end of the tour, Coltrane and Shankar were ingrained.'[2] Harrison was soon equally enamoured.

Returning to London for the *Rubber Soul* sessions, he got hold of a cheap sitar and recorded a clumsy backing to 'Norwegian Wood' — the instrument's first use in a rock context.[3] One of the strings broke during the recording. Stumped as to how to replace it, Harrison was put in touch with the Asian Music Circle — an Indian music appreciation society, run by married couple Ayana Deva Angadi and Patricia Fell-Clarke. Moving in bohemian Hampstead circles, the Angadis set up the AMC in 1946 and played host to sessions, socials and lectures from visiting Indian musicians and enthusiasts. Hungry for discovery, Harrison became a regular at their sessions. Finally introduced to Shankar in person at one of the AMC parties, he described his music as 'hitting a certain spot that I can't explain, but it seemed very familiar to me. The only way I could describe it was: my intellect didn't know what was going on and yet this other part of me identified with it. It called on me.'[4]

Shankar was *the* pivotal figure in the dissemination of Indian music in the West. He came from an international family. His father had studied law at Oxford and practised as a barrister in London. Ravi, meanwhile, had been performing since the age of ten in his brother Uday Shankar's dance troupe. They toured France and America throughout the 1930s. In Hollywood, the young Ravi — at the time considering an acting career — was introduced to stars like Jean Harlow and Clark Gable. On returning to India, however, he undertook rigorous sitar tuition with master musician Baba Allaudin Khan, who persuaded Ravi to dedicate himself to music. Shankar studied under Khan in the austere *gurukula* fashion — student as disciple to guru, setting about designated household chores with the same rigour as study, and learnt his craft the old-fashioned way.

By 1944, Ravi Shankar had completed his training and, a few years later, was appointed musical director of All India Radio. But despite this rigorous traditional apprenticeship, he was no purist. He'd think nothing of cutting traditional ragas short to fit on his records, incorporating different arrangements or shortening performances on tour to fit Western expectations. Neither was he wedded to one style: he was happy to mix and match traditions from around the Indian subcontinent; his cosmopolitan bearing was manifest, both in India and abroad. Shankar's debut album — *Three Ragas* — was released in 1956, and he again toured Europe and America in support. However, it was 1962's album *Improvisations* that set his lifelong reputation for cross-pollination in motion.

Featuring a collaboration with jazz flautist Bud Shank and bassist Gary Peacock ('Fire Night'), the album also marked the start of his professional relationship with Byrds manager Jim Dickson, who released *Improvisations* on his World Pacific imprint. Starting gently with three short ragas, Shankar warms up to a more hard-core traditional (i.e. side-long) piece on the flip side ('Raga Rageshri') that follows the classical format: slow *alap* introductory section to explore the notes and establish melodic themes, middle *jor* section which beds down the melody and rhythms, and a fast-paced *gat* — or climax — at the end. The album did the rounds in LA, in the jazz and rock 'n' roll circles alike. The enthusiastic patronage of Dickson and the Byrds ensured it reached myriad heads who hadn't been exposed to Indian music before. A word of mouth cult built up around Shankar and his mesmeric sound and, soon, his music was seen as the perfect complement to psychedelic experiences.

Among the California set, Ravi Shankar's records were often the inevitable accompaniment to early LSD voyages. As we'll soon see, Shankar himself was often scornful of those who attempted to draw the line between Indian music and the psychedelic experience. But the uncomfortable fact remains: Indian music gained a rock audience during the 1960s principally *because* of its ready assimilation with acid. When LSD hit the collective subconscious in 1966, rock 'n' roll responded by assimilating the drone; it had to — the walls were now melting . . .

Acid Raga

For many, the sitar drone and acid was sheer audio chemical alchemy. The sitar conjures hypnotic density. It sonically mirrors the acid experience to an uncanny degree. Does any sound more readily evoke the melty synaesthesia that occurs at the moment of breakthrough? The bending; the breathing; the warping of walls and curtains; the realisation that everyth*ing* has taken on palpable personality and significance that extends beyond its previous — and here, now, demonstrably *false* — inanimate status?

If there is a single common crucible of the psychedelic experience — a hive mind realisation — then it is this: everything is made of the same fundamental building block matter, and the idea of 'separation' is, therefore, illusory. It is an extraordinary sensation, once experienced never forgotten. LSD and psilocybin break down the barrier of inherent *difference*: you see the same bond between objects, people, plants, buildings. Each becomes part of a greater living whole. Inanimate objects are imbued not only with life but *personality*, soul. That said, it's when personality disappears that things get even more interesting. The idea of 'ego death' — whereby one's lived experience, memories, essential selfness disappear altogether (depending on your viewpoint either the crucible or the terrifying nadir of the psychedelic experience) melds succinctly to the drone: a free-flowing sound without beginning, middle or end, markers of time removed.[5]

Indeed, LSD has a visceral effect on the perception of sound. When 'acid' is evoked as a descriptor in music, distinct tropes are called into play: extended jams, drone elements, disembodied voices, unusual time signatures — a discombobulation of elements servicing an aural tapestry where the *texture* of the sound is of equal importance to melodic progression or hooks.

When you're tripping, music can evoke mortal terror or weeping hilarity. You may temporarily be unable to tell if you are merely 'thinking' or physically 'speaking' internal thoughts; likewise you may 'hear' inanimate objects, or 'see' sounds. This is because of what LSD does to the brain's serotonergic system, disrupting what we see and hear. Acid disrupts the frontal cortex that affects our perception of sound: time becomes blurred, sounds echoing and bleeding into one another. Acid thus creates its *own* drone. It is no accident, then, that much of what we consider acid-influenced music draws so heavily on swooshing, sweeping, droning, reverb-laden sounds: just think of how Hawkwind, say, transition from one track to the next with great swathes of electronic noise — or the way Tommy Hall of the 13th Floor Elevators used the electric jug, evoking a sense of disorientating cosmic motion with the undulating drone that underpins almost everything the band recorded. When we consider the time-morphing potential of LSD or mushrooms, whereby you may get stuck completely in the present, unable to conceive of a time when you *weren't* tripping — it is easy to see why the sitar or tanpura, say, which pivot on a constant drone — becomes so compelling. The drone of these instruments is intrinsically tied to the psychedelic experience because they, also, play with the fabric of our perceptual mechanism — namely our reading of time itself.

Dr James Giordano — one of the world's foremost experts on hallucinogens and neurology — explained to me the neurological effect of LSD on our auditory processing system and the way that even previously 'staid' or 'solid' sounds — such as the drums — become stretched and elongated and drone-like when acid enters the equation.

'LSD changes the network properties of the brain,' he said. 'That becomes important not only in processing visual information, but in processing perceptual and sensory information. Your perception of time shifts. Time is what we call an "event per unit" experience. We say "time flies when you're having fun": that is, if you're having a good time, you're not paying attention to the perception of the unit of which you're metering. Music is very interesting because if you dissect music into its component parts two things are often fundamental — beat and tone.

'In rhythm we "keep time",' he continues. 'A drummer will talk about "keeping time". On LSD, our perception of the sensory input of those rhythmic beats changes and our perception of the temporal qualities also changes. Rhythmic tones therefore change their characteristics. You get an *elongation* of the rhythmic tones which then give an elongation of the rhythmic underline of the music itself! One of the things many people report on LSD — and, to a lesser extent, psilocybin — is that it is synaesthetic: you're "seeing" tones or "tasting" colours and the reason for that is that LSD causes a disinhibition of the isolated network properties. As a consequence of that, you move into a change in the *default* network, so you're processing information differently — somewhat more holistically!'

Enter the Bardo!

From the mid sixties, Shankar records increasingly accompanied psychedelic journeying in bedsits, squats and student digs all over the world. His music was particularly beloved by the loose psychedelic network instigated by Michael Hollingshead in west London. A key figure in the counterculture, Hollingshead boasted psychedelic credentials of *absurd* potency: he'd been a close friend of Aldous Huxley and was the man responsible for turning Timothy Leary on to LSD. In 1965 he'd converted his Chelsea flat into the World Psychedelic Centre — a meeting place for like-minded heads looking for a suitable setting to open the doors of perception in comfortable surroundings. Indian drapes hung from the walls, joss sticks billowed and chillums of strong Nepalese hash did the rounds before the mercurial Hollingshead dosed his guests up after midnight: 300 milligrams of pure LSD placed, ceremoniously, inside a red grape. Attendees included Paul McCartney, William S. Burroughs, Donovan and Alexander Trocchi, and the musical accompaniment and light projections were taken seriously, with Indian classical music and iconography featuring heavily. Hollingshead recalled the detailed procedure in his autobiography *The Man Who Turned on the World*:

Shortly after dropping the acid, I played a tape of Buddhist *Cakra* music, followed by *Concert Percussion* by the American composer, John Cage. Next I played some music by Ravi Shankar and some bossanova. Interval of fifteen minutes. Then some music by Scriabin and part of a Bach cello suite. Interval. Some Debussy, and Indian flute music by Ghosh. Interval. Bach organ music and some John Cage 'space' music. Interval. The Ali Brothers and Japanese flute music. We also looked at slides projected on to the ceiling: Tantric yantras, Vedic Gods, the Buddha, Tibetan mandalas.[6]

Hollingshead was — like his counterpart Timothy Leary in the States — an acid evangelist. To him, LSD wasn't about recreation or intoxication, it was sacrament. Aside from the music, he harboured a keen interest in Vedic spirituality. It was all part and parcel of the quest he espoused: acid as a *ritual* experience, the spiritual aspect drawn from a vague hotchpotch of Eastern and esoteric texts. This was a common feature of the time: half-digested Eastern philosophy twisted like so much malleable modelling clay to fit any number of woolly, acid-inflected hypotheses. He explained his views on 'LSD methodology' in a letter to Alexander Trocchi in 1965.

I felt the time had come for us to share some of the things we had discovered about the methodology of taking LSD in positive settings. I wanted to rid people of their inhibitions about mystical writings, and demonstrate to them that the *Tibetan Book of the Dead*, the *Tao Te Ching* and the *I Ching* were really basic manuals with fundamental instructions about taking LSD . . . From what I had heard in letters and conversations, the psychedelic movement was small and badly informed. It appeared that those who took LSD did so as a consciously defiant anti-authoritarian gesture. The spiritual content of the psychedelic experience was being overlooked.[7]

Acid as a means to spiritual awakening, Eastern mysticism encouraged by self-appointed Svengali figures — these tropes were borne out by the alternative publishing scene. By the mid sixties the texts named by Hollingshead were de rigueur reading for any self-respecting head, and the nascent network of underground bookshops that sprang up in sixties London stocked (alongside the usual Burroughs, Hesse, Ginsberg, *International Times* and vegetarian cookbooks) a cornucopia of Eastern texts.

In America the conflation of Eastern spirituality with LSD was equally manifest. In *The Psychedelic Experience* Timothy Leary co-opted the *Tibetan Book of the Dead* as psychedelic manual. The original — a thirteenth-century Buddhist text — describes the journey of the conscious spirit in the *bardo*, the hinterland between this life and reincarnation in the next. In his reimagining, Leary took the journey between life and death as an analogue of the ultimate endgame of the acid experience: ego death. *The Psychedelic Experience* was intended as a handbook for guiding or inducting others through the experience. In Leary's view, acid needed stewardship: a steadying hand on the tiller. The last section of the text — 'Instructions for Use During A Psychedelic Session' — provided a 'script' for the guide to read aloud at pivotal points, like some *Dungeons & Dragons* gamemaster describing the action in a role-playing game.

Reading it today, it's debatable — to say the very least — whether Leary's text would have had the desired calming, transcendent effect on someone tripping balls in some musty bedsit. In the 'Second Method: Meditation on Good Games', for example, the 'guide' is to proceed along the following — utterly terrifying — lines, using a *mirror*, of all things, as prop:

(Name): You are now wandering in the Third Bardo! . . . look into a mirror and you will not see your usual self (***show the wonderer a mirror***) . . . think not of evil actions which might turn the course of your mind . . . persevere with ***good games*** . . .[8]

Like Hollingshead, Leary was also a staunch believer in providing a suitable musical accompaniment for his 'good games', with Shankar his favoured audio correlate. Indeed, when a (barefooted, white-gowned, lotus-positioned) Leary debated Professor Dr Jerome Lettvin at MIT — 'LSD: Lettvin vs Leary' — it was a Ravi Shankar record that provided the musical backing. The correlation between Shankar's musical influence and Leary's wild, Tibetan-influenced script from the void was soon to reach a spectacular sonic apex in the hands of the Beatles.

Innocent Victims of a Wicked Dentist

By 1965 the Beatles were kicking at the doors of perception with gleeful enthusiasm. *Revolver* (1966) was *steeped* in acid, although the band's introduction had been an unnerving affair. After a dinner party in April 1965, Lennon and Harrison became, in their words, the 'innocent victims of a wicked dentist'[9] — one John Riley — who put acid-laced sugar cubes in their coffee in the hope, thought George Harrison, of instigating an orgy. Harrison and Lennon were furious. Leaving via the lift, they were drawn to *the red button*, became convinced it was 'a fire' and started screaming. On calming down they went to the Ad Lib club in Leicester Square where Harrison had an epiphany, describing to *Rolling Stone* 'an overwhelming feeling of well-being, that there was a God, and I could see him in every blade of grass. It was like gaining hundreds of years of experience in 12 hours.' Ending the night at Harrison's house, Lennon remarked that 'it was just terrifying, but it was fantastic, George's house seemed to be just like a big submarine.'[10]

The acid test was reconvened on an American tour a few months later at a party in LA, also attended by the Byrds and Peter Fonda. Fonda, describing a childhood near-death experience in which he was shot in the stomach, kept whispering to Lennon — who was on a heroic dose himself at the time — 'I know what it's like to be dead!' This understandably irked Lennon who didn't, at that precise moment in time, want to know what it was 'like to be dead'.

Famously retorting, 'You know what it's like to be dead? Who put all that shit in your head? You're making me feel like I've never been born,' the incident inspired 'She Said She Said' on *Revolver* (1966) — one of the three overtly Indian-influenced songs on the album. The lyric was culled verbatim from the exchange with Fonda, while Harrison's fuzz-laden guitar evokes a sitar drone.

By 1966 George Harrison had forged a firm friendship with Ravi Shankar and was receiving regular sitar tuition from him in London. Harrison's playing — clumsy on 'Norwegian Wood' just a year previously — was now deployed to majestic effect on 'Tomorrow Never Knows'. A scattershot psychedelic masterpiece, it closed *Revolver* and captured the acid awakening with rare lucidity.

Sitar and tanpura drones provide the bedrock, atop which a collage of chaos magic unfolds. Tape loops were overdubbed live onto the rhythm track — a stumbling looped beat — and Lennon's vocals were treated with distortion in order to sonically mirror the 'melting' sound hallucinations that so frequently occur on acid — he'd asked studio engineer Geoff Emerick to make him sound like the 'Dalai Lama shouting from a mountain top' and to capture the feeling of 'one thousand Buddhist monks chanting'[11] — while a single E chord churned out another drone. Touching on Indian classicism, *musique concrète* and the joy of staunch noise, 'Tomorrow Never Knows' was the drone in *action* — transcendent magic captured on tape. Neither some blessed-out peace and love trip nor the black acid nightmare later evoked by Hawkwind at their most incandescent, the song was, rather, a call to *submission*. The seismic cranial shift the Beatles underwent on *Revolver*, from the lightweight pop of 'Please Please Me' just three years earlier, was truly remarkable; a testament to both tireless studio experimentation and the cranial power of the successful — and repeated — acid test.

Lyrically, the song was directly influenced by Leary's *Psychedelic Experience* which Lennon was reading at the time. The first line is a direct quote from the text. 'Turn off your mind relax and float down stream / It is not dying, it is not dying.'

Harrison described the song as a paean to transcendence, an escape from the tyranny of a mind in constant flux.

From birth to death all we ever do is think . . . but you can turn off your mind, and go to a part which Maharishi described as 'Where was your last thought before you thought it?' The whole point is that we are the song. The self is coming from a state of pure awareness, from the state of being . . . Indian music doesn't modulate, it just stays. You pick what key you're in, and it stays in that key. I think 'Tomorrow Never Knows' was the first one that stayed there, the whole song was on one chord . . . the basic sound all hangs on the drone.[12]

Transcendental meditation — as espoused by the Maharishi Mahesh Yogi — soon became an important practice in the Beatles' camp. It hinges on the idea of the silent mantra. Using the TM method, a personal mantra — to be kept secret — is repeated in the head for twenty minutes with eyes closed. While rooted in Hindu tradition, the practice is not considered religious per se. Rather it's used to clear the mind: an unprescriptive ritual. Earlier we explored how chant is used as a vehicle for transcendent experience, removing one incrementally away from the *meaning* of words in order to achieve a transcendent state. Harrison described the effect of the silent mantra in similar terms: 'the whole idea is to transcend to the subtlest level of thought. And the mantra becomes more and more subtle until finally you transcend even the mantra. Then you find yourself at this level of pure consciousness.'[13]

The Drone Omnipotent

By 1967, sitar drones were omnipresent. Countless bands fell under the influence in the Beatles' wake. Such was the number that *Crawdaddy* magazine ran a feature in 1967 exploring 'raga rock' — the first use of the term — where Sandy Pearlman (who later produced the Clash and Blue Öyster Cult) fretted over whether the rapid assimilation of Indian music was anything other than novelty:

> One of the problems raised by an eclectic influence — like Indian music — is its assimilation . . . For the most part, the appropriation of the 'Indian' sound represents a self-conscious attempt to introduce novelty into rock.[14]

Certain records — cod raga, if you will — bore out Pearlman's novelty claim. Legendary session guitarist Big Jim Sullivan, for example, recorded a full album of high-camp sitar-based rock covers (*Sitar Beat*) in 1967. Novelty or not, however, rock 'n' roll has always been a mongrel form. There *is* no 'established framework': from day dot it's assimilated influence from anywhere and everywhere. Nothing exists in a vacuum. Whether or not bands fully understood the spiritual background — and most didn't — the effect was seismic. Sitar and tanpura drones were soon found in everything from brutal south London acid blues (the Pretty Things) to wide-open psychedelic folk (Incredible String Band), American primitive rumblings (Sandy Bull and John Fahey) and bombastic hard rock (Led Zeppelin). What follows shouldn't be taken as an exhaustive exploration — it would take a book this length to cover the full gamut — but, rather, a taste of the breadth of influence.

The Yardbirds were early adopters. They took a scuzzy blues-rock template and amped it up with abundant feedback, fuzzy tones and raga-inflected riffs. Both 'Heart Full of Soul' (1965) and 'Still I'm Sad' (1965) had a distinctive Eastern undercurrent gleaned from using an open D string as a drone. The Rolling Stones, of course, added a sinister undertow to 'Paint it Black' (1966), that creeped-out whinnying sitar drone and tremulously picked lick evoking an atmosphere of terminal descent.

The Pretty Things' masterful *S.F. Sorrow* (1968) meanwhile — one of the earliest concept albums — was darker still, navigating the lonely life of one 'Sebastian F. Sorrow'. The centrepiece was the powerful 'Defecting Grey'. A raging psychedelic storm, it captured many of the audio hallmarks of the era — fuzzed-out guitars, backwards tape noise, a sitar on loan from George Harrison — in a head-on descent into negative space. Opening with a deep sub-drone, atop which a plinky waltz unfolds, Phil May's jaunty music hall-esque delivery belies the bleakness of the lyrics, finding Sebastian 'Sitting alone on a bench with you / Mirrored above in the sky'. A brief sitar drone signals a switch to a frenetic, distorted, proto-punk thrash, lifting the curtain on a scene shifting, both literally and metaphorically, to black: 'Night sky hangs in blackness / Night threads, patterns weaving'. Here the sitar acts as audio signalling device — depression to full-on psychosis, pastoral waltz prefiguring jarring distortion.

Singer Phil May described the source of Sebastian's despair as a struggle with his sexuality:

this was somebody who suddenly realised that everything they'd lived for, and were brought up to believe in, wasn't right . . . his homosexual side was coming out . . . it's 'sitting alone on a bench with you, the brush of your hand, chasing shadows away', that's the story.

The heavy-duty sonics mirrored the oppressive lyrical vibes. Guitarist Dick Taylor's tone was — bar Blue Cheer — about as sludgy as it got in 1968, a tar-thick churn. The Pretty Things carried an air of seedy menace: they had the ashen pallor of men who'd spent too many nights thrashing out a racket in the less salubrious boozers of darkest south London. They were also completely open about their love for LSD: no concealed metaphors here, it was brilliantly lumpen and literal (one of their songs was called 'LSD' another 'Tripping'). That Electric Wizard — Dorset doom overlords, who we'll fully explore later in the book — personally chose them to play the album at their 'Electric Acid Orgy' curated stage at Roadburn 2012 says it all. The Pretty Things brought a scuzzy misanthropic bearing to the prevailing good-time vibes of the era: tweaked-out, acid-fried rhythm and blues for heinous speed comedowns, the Camberwell rain turning an electric hue.

The folksier end of the spectrum was equally entranced by India. Edinburgh's Incredible String Band were one of the most unique bands of the sixties, stirring up a bewitching alchemical brew on instruments gleaned from near and far.

They took in everything from acid-inflected jamborees to ballads and raucous bar-room stomps. Their fantastical, psychedelic bearing put them somewhat at odds with the puritanical 'beer and kippers' vibes prevalent in the purist folk clubs. Keen travellers, they'd spent serious time in both India and Morocco and brought a questing, cross-cultural bearing to their sound, felt particularly intensely on their 1968 masterpiece *The Hangman's Beautiful Daughter*.

Fusing a roaming, wyrd pastoral edge to the outer reaches of folk, the album riffed on tarot imagery and esoteric themes over surreal music hall ('The Minotaur's Song' on which the narrator cries for 'Porridge for my Porridge Bowl! Porridge for my Porridge Bowl!') to poppier fare ('Mercy I Cry City') and tripped-out laments ('Three Is a Green Crown'). A grab bag of instruments were assembled for the sessions — sitar, gimbri, pan pipes, water harp, oud, dulcimer, harpsichord — the drone steadying the rapturous chaos like a barnacled anchor dropped into a roiling sea. 'Three Is a Green Crown' hums with hypnotic majesty. Sitar, bouzouki and gimbri provide a viscous drone while vocalist Robin Williamson performs some Qawwali-esque vocal acrobatics in a lyric that explores that genesis of 'the Empress' — the tarot card that symbolises fertility, rebirth and nurture.

Pentangle were equally tuned into mystic, hypnotic territory. Fusing trad folk roots with early music and baroque atmospheres, guitarist John Renbourn was a skilled sitar player who played it to haunting effect on songs like 'Once I Had a Sweetheart' and 'Cruel Sister'. Donovan, meanwhile, traversed a more winsome take on pop folk that skirted the terminally twee but, for the most part, came off charmingly innocent rather than gratingly earnest. Having accompanied the Beatles on their Rishikesh sojourn, he'd experimented with drones on his 1968 album *The Hurdy Gurdy Man*. Recounting the tale of a travelling troubadour 'singing the songs of love', the title track retains a shambolic charm, Donovan's understated vocal delivery offset against the stumbling beat and warm sitar drone. As he described in a recent interview, the song was intended to act as 'a mantra. In the Celtic music that I come from, they have drones, one-chord drones. In the meditation you can chant, and it centres you. It can take you into an inner world. That's why drones and chanting have always been part of tribal shaman music. "The Hurdy Gurdy Man" had the sound of a drone — *aaaahhh* — it was meditational. But in the words, I wanted to remind us — at the height of the violence of wars and unrest and student protest all over the world — that there was an inner world.'[15]

Primitive Fantasias

Aside from the more acid-fried corners of the British folk scene, the American roots axis of the sixties was equally wide roaming in influence. Guitarist Sandy Bull, for example, predated the Beatles by some three years in incorporating Indian rhythms and drone elements on his magical *Fantasias for Guitar and Banjo* (1963). Drawing on folk, jazz and classical techniques, Bull was a virtuoso guitarist who also played the oud, banjo, pedal steel guitar and sarod. His relative obscurity belied an extraordinary talent. Coming up through the Cambridge Massachusetts folk scene — where he regularly performed alongside Joan Baez — Bull loved Ravi Shankar and Ali Akbar Khan, leading him to incorporate drone tunings in his playing, which he described as carrying 'something eternal about it, sort of a foundation of music. I find it — and the kind of undulating rhythms which go with it — very moving.'[16]

On a darker tip, John Fahey assimilated raga influences alongside (in a discography which stretched from the late 1950s to his death in 2001) everything from tape hiss collage and mournful acoustic suicide ballads to full-on noise. A thorny character with a wicked sense of humour, Fahey was, though a passionate blues scholar and voracious record collector, somewhat at odds with the earnest archivist collectors tracking down impossibly obscure 78s in the early sixties.

He released a single — 'Paint Brush Blues' (1959) — under the name Blind Thomas before setting up the Takoma imprint to release his *Blind Joe Death* album the same year. Such was Fahey's command of form that many collectors were convinced that 'Blind Joe Death' was, in fact, some long-lost, ancient Delta bluesman (a notion Fahey, ever the prankster, did absolutely nothing to disavow). His future liner notes would be riddled with deliberate half-truths, invented mythologies and jokes — often written in pompous purple prose — designed to poke fun at the self-appointed blues establishment, while his idiosyncratic picking style evoked bleak, eerie vistas. Fahey used dissonance to build tension and repetition to mesmerise. His woozy tone conjures images of oddball Americana — a flickering half-light of empty motel lobbies, unfiltered Camels, eerie truck stops and moonshine blindness.

Though steeped in blues, country, bluegrass and gospel, Fahey's Indian influence was equally manifest. 'A Raga Called Pat' (1967) — a four-part odyssey — is a case in point, a staunch celestial trip of trance-inducing drone picking, echo effects, thunderstorm field recordings and crowing roosters. It's a proper head twister, a widescreen rendering of raga tonality grounded in roughshod American roots — Sam Peckinpah lost in the Calcutta backstreets.

Fahey occasionally put out records by like-minded players on Takoma. Max Ochs had a foot in both trad blues and Indian music, fusing the two to hauntingly majestic effect. The 2008 *Hooray for Another Day* compiled long out-of-print pieces like 'Ain't Nobody High Raga' and 'Raga Puti'. Both bore the hallmarks of the American primitive take on Indian technique: bendy drone on the bass notes, countrified finger picking underneath.

One of the more eccentric Takoma artists was Robbie Basho (born Daniel Robinson Jr), said to have consumed a heinous dose of peyote and climbed to the top of a mountain where he 'received' the name Basho, after seventeenth-century Japanese poet Matsuo Basho. A great bear of a man, Basho was an ex-bouncer who dressed in thigh-high moccasins and a dashiki. His formidable physicality belied a devout appreciation for Indian classicism, however: if Fahey skirted the edges, Basho dived into the Ganges. A former blues head who had, like so many others of the time, become obsessed with Ravi Shankar in the early sixties, Basho soaked up the music in his student digs before coming up with his own raga tuning for twelve-string steel guitar.

With its open-stringed drones and intricate finger picking *The Falconer's Arm I* and *II* (1967) (the sleeve has Basho standing next to a stream, resplendent in moccasins, falconer's sleeve and multicoloured smock, glazed eyes fixed dead ahead) is imbued with the soul of the windswept journeyman. It's majestic stuff: haunting, innocent, (unintentionally) hilarious. In the pantheon of Eastern-influenced, psych-addled, acoustic gear, Basho stands shoulder to shoulder with Bull and Fahey, although he was untethered to the gnarled roots that bound the latter two. His playing was sheer cosmic majesty: sky music. The blues, country and folk traditions are all discernible in his steel-string motifs but they come as a haunting satellite echo rather than a grounding. His guitar playing hinges, rather, on fleet movement, effortless and hypnotic. Studying with sarod master Ali Akbar Khan, Basho's playing was also connected — on an alchemical level — to Indian classicism. On 'Pavan Hindustan' cascades of gossamer-light notes tumble around angular chord patterns anchored by the formidable drone of his bass notes, evoking the shimmering flux of the sitar.

Basho's music speaks of the vast plains of pre-colonialist America, rather than Fahey's surrealist railroad chug. This is music shorn entirely of the urban; while Bull and Fahey's primitivism was characterised by steely grit, the hard-won chops of the terminal roots fanatic, Basho was more earnest. His vocals are imbued with such *deep* vehemence and commitment that you wonder whether he may be playing an elaborate joke. But no. As with dramatic metal titan Dio, say, Basho means every righteous word. And — as with Dio — there is joy in the unrestrained *commitment* to such gloriously overblown delivery. His deranged spoken-word section on 'A North American Raga' is a thing of glory: 'Deep into the night, near dark mountain, there is a white tipi, pitched against a purple sky / In it, the princess of the silver waters sings to her lover' et cetera.

The absurdity of delivery was often missed by certain po-faced sections of the music press: it was every bit as pompous and overblown as a Yes triple LP, but therein lies its charm.

White Rabbit Holes

In San Francisco, the Bay Area folk scene birthed two bands — the Grateful Dead and Jefferson Airplane — who represented psychedelia as full-on lifestyle, as opposed to musical colouring. For the Dead, Indian music was in the psychic mix from the very start — a key catalyst to Jerry Garcia's awakening. When he first dropped acid in 1965, it was a Ravi Shankar record that provided accompaniment, as described in a *Rolling Stone* interview with guitarist Robert Hunter: 'Jerry took it and he and Sarah [Ruppenthal, Garcia's first wife] came over to my house. They were on acid and said, "What do we do now?" I said, "Go home, put on a Ravi Shankar record, just listen to the music." It worked.'

The effect was cataclysmic. The Dead were soon *steeped* in acid — human blotters, essentially — attracting a moveable camp of freaks, purveyors of fine herbs and chemicals, vegetable burrito salesmen and addled acoustic bards wherever they played: less tour, more dysfunctional travelling circus.

The travelling camp that followed the Dead resembled a spiritual analogue of the English free festival scene: a ragtag community sustained — both spiritually and practically — by the coast-to-coast tours undertaken by the band. The band were wise to the fact that they were playing to people who'd be watching them night after night. Improvisation — always part of the Dead's DNA — was therefore key, the set list shuffled consistently to keep the diehards satisfied with jams drawn out over hours. A fearsome chemical intake by band and audience alike ensured that the drone was present, albeit more in the alchemical collective consciousness — some warping jamboree — than in the blues-infused jams that were *actually* emanating from the speakers of whatever Midwest enormodome they happened to be playing. Because for all the glorious maelstrom of psychedelic iconography associated with the Dead — the tie die, skulls, bandanas, aviators, painted wagons et al. — it's something of an irony that the music itself was so often a plodding pedestrian boogie (Garcia even had a sticker on his guitar that read 'boogie' to remind him to do exactly that).

By contrast, Jefferson Airplane pursued a tighter psych vision. The imposing voice of Grace Slick propelled their *Surrealistic Pillow* (1967) into a space entirely evocative of late-sixties San Francisco: jangling guitars, mildly foreboding whimsy, churning Moogs. Her vocals took the role usually reserved for lead guitar, acrobatic Moorish and Indian-inflected choral runs that cut right through the mix. 'White Rabbit' was a glorious statement of intent, Jorma Kaukonen's lead mirroring a sitar, Slick's vocal transposing *Alice in Wonderland* imagery to the acid age.

The End

The US scene unfolded to the backdrop of the Vietnam War — a nightmarish, futile conflict. Between 1964 and 1973 the United States drafted over two million young men — often poor, alienated and demoralised — to fight the fabled Communist 'domino effect' in North Vietnam (itself a direct hang-up of McCarthyite paranoia).

Apart from being the most serious war America had fought since the Second World War, it had the distinction of being the first fuelled by psychedelics. The use of heroin, by 1973 endemic among American troops, and widespread weed smoking, have been well documented. Less discussed was the use of LSD and magic mushrooms. A 1971 report commissioned by the US Department of Defense indicated that 51 per cent of troops had smoked marijuana, 28 per cent heroin and 31 per cent had taken LSD[17] during their tour of duty. This aspect of the war has been long immortalised in film, from Charlie Sheen's young GI huffing blowbacks down a rifle barrel in *Platoon* to the hallucinatory languor of *Apocalypse Now*. The latter perfectly evoked the humidity, terror, mental discombobulation and nightmarishly trippy aspect of Vietnam, both visually and via the soundtrack. The Doors' raga-inflected dronal masterpiece 'The End' (1967) — accompanying Martin Sheen as he undertakes his doomed downriver ascent to the heart of darkness and Brando's lair — was a masterstroke of a soundtrack choice. It's the ultimate slow burner, Robbie Krieger's shimmering lick mirroring the sitar, conjuring the steaming vegetation, mission creep, battle fatigue and sense of insurmountable doom that personified the war. The song was directly influenced by the band's tuition with Ravi Shankar — as recalled here by drummer John Densmore to *Rolling Stone* — another key example of the seismic influence of Shankar on the myriad intersections of Indian classicism and psychedelia:

Rob so brilliantly tuned his guitar into an East Indian tuning, so it had a trance thing going. We tried to hypnotise everybody. We could see people looking like they just got a drink or some herb, and they'd be swooning. It was like, 'Oh, wow, this is work- ing. They're out of it. They're hypnotised. Let's stay with it.' It's fashioned exactly like ragas, which go on for 10 or 15 minutes with droning and a climax. Robby and I went to Ravi Shankar's school of Indian music. He took a sitar and I took tablas. And Ravi Shankar said, 'You need to be patient, you Americans. With Indian music, you take time before you have an orgasm.'[18]

Rock may have been inundated with the (literal) buzz of India but Shankar had quickly become disillusioned with the combination of cultural appropri- ation and hedonism, what he saw as a fundamental lack of respect shown by bands and audience towards the tradition. He had a genuine fondness and respect for artists like Harrison and Donovan — who'd studied and took their learning seriously — but not for those who took it flippantly.

On 18 June 1967, Shankar performed a four-hour concert to a crowd of 90,000 at the Monterey Festival. Headlined by Jefferson Airplane and the Grateful Dead and featuring (literally) incendiary performances from Jimi Hendrix and the Who, it was Shankar's first appearance on a rock bill. Heralded as a pivotal performance, it was released as a double album the following year and was responsible — along with his Woodstock performance in 1969 — for solidifying his immense countercultural stature. The crowd were enraptured, if somewhat confused. Notoriously, he received rapturous applause as he was tuning up, the audience completely unaware that he hadn't actually started playing.

The gig was later immortalised by Eric Burdon in 'Down in Monterey' — an earnest, deeply *Tap*-esque hymnal to the weekend that name checked Shankar, Hendrix and the Who. But while Burden loved Townshend et al. at their auto-destructive best, Shankar was horrified by the idea of musicians smashing up gear and watched the Who with incredulity. More than that — and despite his ever growing mainstream recognition — he was offended by the idea of Indian music, a sacred tradition based on years of intense disci- pline, being appropriated in service of sensory oblivion. For Shankar, a deeply conservative Brahmin, it amounted to heresy. In a 1968 *Rolling Stone* interview he laid his feelings bare.

Unfortunately, the whole mix-up of sex and spiritual exercise all became one. All of a sudden I saw it was more like a pagan ritual . . . And it makes me sad because I happen to be a Hindu, a Brahmin . . . it is absolutely gross, a distortion of facts.

Mantra Rock Dance

The 'whole mix-up of sex and spiritual exercise' reached an apex during the late 1960s. Various sinister cults attached themselves to the West Coast scene. Some had direct links to the counterculture, twisting the ideals of 'free love' to ever more exploitative extremes. The Manson Family were, of course, the most infamous example here — the lyrics of the Beatles' 'Helter Skelter' notoriously appropriated as codified justification for an apocalyptic race war in which the Family would, supposedly, rise from Death Valley, the rightful rulers of Earth. The hideous and tragic outcome, culminating in the murder of five people, including the pregnant actress Sharon Tate, has been well documented. The Children of God, meanwhile, were run by David Berg — 'Moses David' — and preyed on young acid casualties in Haight-Ashbury, many of whom Berg exploited through prostitution.

The Hare Krishna movement also attracted thousands throughout the closing years of the sixties. Many former members remain adamant that it is, to all intents and purposes, a cult[19] itself, with all the restrictive hallmarks — coercive control, separation of members from family and friends, rejection of the wicked 'material' world — that the word entails. In the 1960s, however, the Krishna movement was widely viewed as benign. As such, many leading countercultural figures took up the chant.

On 29 January 1967 the Mantra-Rock Dance was organised by Krishna followers in San Francisco, featuring the Grateful Dead, Janis Joplin and Allan Ginsberg alongside a talk by founder of ISKON (International Society for Krishna Consciousness) A.C. Bhaktivedanta Swami Prabhupada. Though vehemently anti-drugs, ISKON was clearly keen to galvanise the growing interest in Eastern philosophy. On arrival on the West Coast, Swami was interviewed by the *San Francisco Chronicle* and claimed that the organisation welcomed 'everyone, in any condition of life . . . everyone, whatever you are — what you call an acid head or hippie or whatever. What you are doesn't matter. Once you are accepted for training you will change.'[20]

On the night, the hall was wreathed in clouds of weed smoke and filled with people in various states of chemically induced discombobulation. The extension of a welcome for 'everyone' was no idle boast: the Hells Angels provided security. Ginsberg was a devoted chanter of the Krishna mantra. He was also a fully paid-up psychedelic adventurer, some distance from the austere devotee. Like many at the time, he drew comfort from the *act* of chant rather than the discipline of a monastic lifestyle — he had zero interest in renouncing sex, drugs and literature. From the stage, he espoused the power of the mantra as an overtly psychedelic enabler. The Krishna mantra, he said, was a vehicle for 'mind deliverance' and those on a bad trip could use it to 'stabilise themselves'. They should, he continued, simply 'sink into the vibration and think of peace'. To a cheering crowd Swami and Ginsberg then led the chant. Even the Hells Angels joined in.

It was a potent scene, but there was a transactional element at play. ISKON were keen to infiltrate the hippy movement despite their misgivings on drugs and sex; figures like Ginsberg were looking to spiritually validate their overwhelming psychedelic experiences. It laid bare an uneasy contrast. Wealthy celebrity adherents were able to pick and choose at will from a smorgasbord of teachings while holding on to the materialistic, artistic and narcotic 'trappings' (the very act of making music, art or literature that doesn't directly venerate Krishna is, after all, strictly *verboten* to followers) denied true adherents. More vulnerable members couldn't command the same agency. Violent power struggles and myriad stories of abuse emerged throughout the 1980s and 1990s, many of which make deeply harrowing reading.[21]

George Harrison remained a vocal champion of the movement until his death. He bankrolled the sprawling Bhaktivedanta Manor headquarters outside Watford and recorded and produced devotional songs throughout the late sixties and seventies — 'Hare Krishna Mantra' (1969) and 'My Sweet Lord' (1970) being the most well known, the act of chant remaining his anchor, to sometimes extreme ends . . .

Once I chanted the Hare Krishna mantra all the way from France to Portugal, nonstop . . . It gets you feeling a bit invincible. The funny thing was that I didn't even know where I was going . . . once you get chanting, then things start to happen transcendentally.[22]

Ascension

In the 1960s a deep friendship blossomed between Ravi Shankar and John
Coltrane. Coltrane was about wild discordance, serious physical chops,
dissatisfaction with traditional jazz structures and — above all — transcendence. Beyond jazz, beyond himself, beyond music: from 1966 it sounded
as if he was attempting to blow his alto sax clean through the space-time
barrier. Acoustically, Coltrane at his wildest shared little with the grounding
bedrock of Indian modal structure or raga discipline. His music broke free
of almost *any* boundary, bar the inescapable wager between the human soul
and the physical limitations of an instrument. Indian music nonetheless
influenced his radical harmonic approach — his wild solos were frequently
layered over a drone note, as opposed to the rapid scattershot chord changes
typical of hard bop.

On 'India' (1961) Coltrane made explicit his newfound respect. He'd
already experimented with droning basslines on 'My Favourite Things' (1960)
but this was, as he described, a 'more or less subconscious'[23] influence. 'India'
was different; here Coltrane spoke directly to the Shankar records he'd been
playing since the early sixties. He was fascinated by Indian scales and would
copy out pages of them in his notebooks. Stasis was by no means front and
centre — his was a music of ceaseless movement — rather, it served to *anchor*
his ferociously untethered playing. Shankar once recalled how Coltrane took
particular interest in 'the drone, which is an essential part of our music. He
said that he had been experimenting with the drone effect in some of his
compositions after hearing me play, and that the effect had been very calming
and soothing.' Shankar also turned him on to the concept of *rasa* — the idea
that each individual raga corresponds to an emotion, season or mood — and
Coltrane kept detailed notes on their conversations, linking Shankar's music to
a universal continuum.

I like Ravi Shankar very much. When I hear his music, I want to
copy it — not note for note of course, but in his spirit. What brings
me closest to Ravi is the modal aspect of his art . . . I seem to be
going through a modal phase . . . it's particularly evident in Africa,
but if you look at Spain or Scotland, India or China, you'll discover
this again and again . . . take away their purely ethnic characteristics — that is, their folkloric aspect — and you'll discover the
presence of the same pentatonic sonority, comparable modal

structures. It's this universal aspect of music that interests me and attracts me; that's what I'm aiming for.[24]

Coltrane was a deeply spiritual man — a universalist at heart — and it was this, alongside a depth-charge interrogation into the fabric of jazz that drove his late-period work. He was passionate about science, Indian mysticism, Christianity, vegetarianism, astrology. Most of all he was driven by a dissatisfaction with the hard bop orthodoxies that had emerged by the late 1950s and committed to pushing the outer limits. Playing in Thelonious Monk's quartet in 1957, his dizzying cascades of rapid notes were memorably described by Ira Gitler in *DownBeat* magazine as becoming great 'sheets of sound'; Coltrane played with Miles Davis later that year, recording on *Milestones* and *Kind of Blue*, while suffering a debilitating heroin addiction. After testing the boundaries throughout the late fifties, however, he found himself at the forefront of the emergent free jazz movement — the fire music that stormed the ramparts of tradition.

The music made by Albert Ayler, Ornette Coleman, Cecil Taylor and John Coltrane during the 1960s was transcendent, joyous — sometimes brutal — sonic architecture freed from the shackles of expectation and conformity. Free jazz was fundamentally playful. It asked questions of musician and listener alike without expecting anything approaching a concrete answer in return. To say that people weren't ready would be something of an understatement. Early reviews veered from incomprehension to mockery to outright hostility. But while critics and audiences were waylaid by the shock of the new, the core artists were steadfast in pushing forward with a sonic disembowelment of traditionalism.

Albert Ayler — the pioneering free jazz saxophonist whose wonky noise attack evoked some warped, acid-blasted marching band fuelled by mescaline soup — equated his music with 'the blues of all of America all over again, but a different kind of blues. This is the real blues, the new blues, and the people must listen to this music . . . This is the only way that's left for musicians to play. All the other ways have been explored.'[25] Coltrane *adored* Ayler, describing his playing as 'beyond notes'. Ornette Coleman, who had unwittingly given name to the nascent movement on 1961's *Free Jazz*, was another seismic inspiration on Coltrane. His sax playing wasn't so much 'sheets of sound' as monolithic slabs of irrepressible pressure. His delivery was sheer vehemence — vein-throbbing, cheek-expanding, lung-buffering *force*. Coleman had abandoned the chord system altogether in favour of complete improvisational freedom. It was this that struck the biggest chord with Coltrane, writing in a letter to Benoit Quersin, 'I love him. I'm following his lead. He's done a lot to open my eyes to what can be done . . . I feel indebted to him . . . I don't know if I would have thought about just abandoning the chord system or not. And he came along doing it and I heard it and thought "well, that must be the answer".'[26]

The drone was deployed time and again by free jazz's first guard. On Ornette Coleman's 'Lonely Woman' (1959), for example, a frolicking, folksy melody is underpinned by Charlie Hedon's bass thrum while *Dancing in Your Head* (1977) was recorded with the Master Musicians of Joujouka in Morocco. The result was spectacular, goblin music of *incessant* hypnotic power, a warped fractal dementicon of upwards motion underlined by the shrieking drone of the rhaita pipes.

Likewise, Ayler marshalled drone power in his discordant bagpipe-beasting 'Masonic Inborn' (1969), a *Sturm und Drang* thunder voyage in which Ayler doesn't so much blast as *squall* the pipes in evocation of mystic symbolism and lost rites.

It wasn't just the free jazz heads who were into the Eastern vibe. A world away from the wild frontiers of Coltrane, Ayler, Coleman et al., Joe Harriott and John Mayer released two smooth Indo-fusion records — *Indo Jazz Suite* (1966) and *Indo Jazz Fusion* (1968) — with a polite coffee-table vibe. Likewise Tony Scott's *Music for Yoga Meditation and Other Joys* (1968) — a collaboration between Italian American clarinettist Tony Scott and sitarist Collin Walcott, an ex-pupil of Ravi Shankar — was a humdrum affair. Walcott's sitar lacked density while Scott parped away inconsequentially.

Indeed, Walcott's sitar is heard to much more powerful effect alongside Don Cherry and Naná Vasconcelos on *Codona* (1979), a foreboding take on Indian and North African traditions, sitar and polyphonic vocals from the trio shimmering with eerie luminescence. Don Cherry was also strongly influenced by Indian music elsewhere, most notably on the masterful *Brown Rice* (1975). Inflected with Cherry's globetrotting sensibility, it featured takes on traditional Indian ragas including the sinister 'Malkauns' (the midnight raga) and was one of the more successful 'fusion' records in a crowded mid-seventies market, drawing on Arabic, African and pan-Asian vibes.

A freewheeling atmosphere predominates, with Cherry — who'd spent the sixties collaborating with everyone from Coltrane to Coleman and Ayler, as well as spending time in Joujouka village and studying with Indian master Pandit Pran Nath (more on whom later) — putting the questing improvisational spirit of free jazz to work with consummate ease. Searching for what he termed 'organic music' (the cover bears the words, alongside '*om mani padne hum*'), Cherry embraced the role of shamanic guide, his whispered vocal throughout guiding the listener through borderless lands.

The dawn of the psychedelic age; Vietnam War protests; civil rights freedom marches; radical student activism — though free jazz was not always blatantly 'political', the portent of awakening brewing in urban America's unstable cauldron found its ultimate soundtrack therein. Drab suburbanite conformity was widely challenged, the swivel-eyed paranoia of McCarthyite militarism had been rejected and 'the man' — that amorphous greyscale block of humourless authoritarianism — became a figure of equal parts mockery and dread.

While the 1960s are often said to have ushered in an age of hippified 'togetherness', the reality was an age of individualism on a scale never before seen. Established thinking on the direct and indirect rules of societal cohesion — be they familial, religious, political, social — were all thrown up in the air. Free jazz was, in turn, the music of the *individual*. Anything was permitted — bum notes, discordant key changes, missed beats — just as long as the spirit essence of the player broke through. As Coltrane had it, every note must be a 'whole expression of one's being'. There is a thrilling dichotomy at play in Coltrane's music. He was getting to the absolute core of *himself* but in service of something far bigger: it was non-denominational godhead music, music in service of an absolute belief that there *is* a higher power reached — not via slavish, meek and mild unquestioning churchy devotion — but, rather, by stretching towards the light; sweating, clawing, fighting with every breath, towards the fulfilment of artistic potential.

His most critically storied — and, in an age where the word is much abused, *iconic* — record, *A Love Supreme,* was a case in point. The spiritual uplift is overwhelming, to the extent you feel you're trespassing on hallowed ground. Though not as wild as what was still to come, it's the most emotionally resonant record he made — certainly his most personal. Recorded on a single day — 9 December 1964 — *A Love Supreme* pivots on a mantra, repeated throughout in Coltrane's booming baritone — 'a LOVE su-PREME, a LOVE su-PREME, a LOVE su-PREME, a LOVE su-PREME' — rising above the shimmer, thunder and squall like a call from on high.

Religious iconography threads the album, from the opening breakthrough gong chime to the fourth movement — 'Psalm' — which saw Coltrane riffing on a poem he'd written of the same name, placing it on the music stand and 'playing' it. His wife — Alice Coltrane — described the album's genesis in religious terms, Coltrane taking to his room and emerging five days later 'like Moses coming down from the mountain. It was so beautiful . . . the gifts God gave him . . . he said "this is the first time that I have received all of the music for what I want to record, in a suite, the first time I have everything ready." Every part, every passage, every movement, from beginning to end, even the prayer, everything! *Everything*.'[27]

While *A Love Supreme* was cerebral, *Om* — recorded in 1965, released posthumously in 1968 — was no holds barred. Described in the album's liner notes by Coltrane as being devoted to the 'first vibration — that sound, that spirit, which set everything else into being', it starts and closes with Coltrane and Pharaoh Sanders reciting 'The Yoga of Mysticism' from the Bhagavadgita[28] and remains one of the most mind-blowingly psychedelic albums ever made.

Over a twenty-eight-minute wall of sound, *Om* ignites anarchy, Coltrane and Sander's double sax attack blasting into hyperspace. This is all about awe: an ultimate reckoning, sound in motion. *Om* doesn't so much move as *flail*, a spectral dance that channels the entirety of Coltrane's spiritual being into a form unconcerned with melodic structure or rhythmic cohesion in exchange for sheer *ejaculation*. It's a serious fucking trip, one widely held to have either been informed by his later-life experiments with LSD or, indeed, recorded while under the influence.

Ascension (1965) was equally wild but, unlike the unfairly derided *Om*, is widely regarded as a masterpiece. Music, noise, sex, death, life, *everything* is there — it's a brutal expurgation of rigidity, a free-jazz milestone, an exhilarating power trip into the ether. Coltrane and Sanders[29] are *screaming*: an apocalyptic cacophony, blowing harder, wilder, up up up. The title is perfect: music without ceiling. It sounds as if every player is attempting not only to break the limits of the instrument but also their bodily foundation, their very lungs, reaching towards the godhead, spinning the music out of the realm of physical control and into celestial heights. Both *Om* and *Ascension* are the sound of Coltrane — who made frequent allusions to the idea of a 'force' that he was trying to reach through music — harnessing exactly that.

'Once you become aware of this force for unity in life . . . you can't ever forget it. It becomes part of everything you do . . . my conception of that force keeps changing shape. My goal in meditating on this through music, however, remains the same. And that is to uplift people, as much as I can. To inspire them to realise more and more of their capacities for living meaningful lives. Because there certainly is meaning to life.'[30]

Late-period Coltrane is a storm, a singularity, an audio ecosystem all its own. Break on through to the other side? Try break on through to the event horizon. You could spend a lifetime listening to these records: it wouldn't be enough. As Alice Coltrane once said: 'The use of the term "jazz", I feel, is inadequate in its description of the music created through John. A higher principle is involved here. Some of his latest works aren't musical compositions. I mean they aren't based entirely on music. A lot of it has to do with mathematics, some of it on rhythmic structure and the power of repetition, some on elementals. He always felt that sound was the first manifestation in creation before music.'[31]

Transcendence

If John Coltrane's music spoke of the journey — the will to transcend physical boundaries and propel the notes somewhere west of the stars — Alice Coltrane made the heavenly music heard on *arrival*, the sound of celestial spheres. Her music was inexorably bound to both the jazz and gospel of her Detroit childhood, but it was Indian music that would become her overriding muse. Her music approaches a synaesthesia, a lush aural landscape — languid riverbanks, overhanging trees, shimmering lakes, humid nights — that you can almost reach out and *touch*: dappled audio sunshine pushing through wooden slats.

Born in 1937, Alice Coltrane was raised in boomtown Detroit. A far cry from the decayed husk of today, the city she grew up in was the epicentre of the automotive factory production line. It was also a musical *powerhouse.* Most Detroit musicians gained their early chops in the spiritual fervour of the Baptist Church. It was the musical discipline that drove Motown, and Alice Coltrane was no different, singing and playing piano and organ to a virtuoso standard in various combos around town before her stepbrother, the bassist Ernie Farrow, introduced her to bebop.

Moving to Paris in the 1950s, she played piano with Bud Powell before joining the Terry Gibbs quartet. Meeting John Coltrane at the Birdland club in New York in 1963, the pair bonded immediately and were married in 1966. The same year, she joined John Coltrane's late-period band as a pianist, playing alongside saxophonist Pharaoh Sanders, bassist Jimmy Garrison and drummer Rashied Ali. After her husband's death in 1967, Alice Coltrane recorded her debut solo LP *A Monastic Trio*. Dedicated on the sleeve to the memory of 'the mystic Ohnedaruth, known as John Coltrane, during the period from September 23, 1926 to July 17, 1967', it combined blues- and gospel-tinged atmospherics with Eastern dronal elements, her piano swinging throughout. The second side, however, showcased the harp. It was the sound that was to become her indelible sonic hallmark. Michelle Coltrane — daughter of Alice — recalled its importance when we spoke:

'I remember my mom would play it and have blisters on her fingers,' she said. 'She wasn't trained in the instrument, but when musicians go to other instruments they approach it with a musician's ear . . . she knew the sound she was searching for and she knew what she wanted to hear. She did it in her own style. Indian music was a *huge* influence. My brother is named Ravi, after Ravi Shankar (*laughs*). My father was a huge fan. When they heard Ravi Shankar on the sitar, it had a profound influence on my parents.'

Despite the clear brilliance and originality of her playing and composition, Alice Coltrane was not always taken seriously by the pompous self-appointed jazz 'purists' or equally snobbish critics. They derided her decision to posthumously overdub harp and string arrangements onto unreleased John Coltrane recordings during the early 1970s, the resulting album — *Infinity* (1972) — seen by some as an 'insult' to his legacy, this despite the fact that the couple had made detailed written plans together for the inclusion of other instruments on the album before he died.

This absurd critical attitude was indicative of how her work was sometimes perceived at the time, and, occasionally, now — as an 'appendage' to John Coltrane's legacy, rather than an idiosyncratic catalogue that stands shoulder to shoulder on its own merit. In their review of *A Monastic Trio*, the magazine *DownBeat*, for example, stated that the piano and harp were 'unsuitable instruments for transmitting John Coltrane's passionate utterance' while Richard Cook wrote in the *Jazz Encyclopedia* that her records 'often come across as soft-headed and incoherent . . . one wonders if she would have enjoyed any attention at all if she had remained plain Alice McCleod.'[32]

'It is something that she never really spoke of,' Michelle Coltrane explains. 'But then, I think back to her being in some television station interview, and the conversation would *always* turn. It would flip to "so John did this, John said this". And she would graciously talk about him. She'd never say "well, actually my record's coming out!" I don't know if she knew that she had such a super talent that was every bit as deserving of accolades. She had such a distinct style, such a unique style. It's like my father, too — as soon as you hear the saxophone, as soon as you hear the reed, the sound of the horn, you know who it is. And it's everybody's *dream* as an artist to have that identity, that instantly recognisable quality. Talk about being ahead of the time! What she went through — as a widow at twenty-nine, with a man who was at a pinnacle — and then she didn't want to do bebop any more! She was always on to the next thing. She followed the artist's way: "what am I going to do now?" And her lifestyle reflected that — the spirituality of being able to play devotional music and chant and follow God's wisdom. It was a divine order.'

Alice Coltrane's interest in Vedic spirituality — cultivated with John during the 1960s — burgeoned to a full-scale calling during the decade's closing years. In 1969 she met her spiritual guru, Swami Satchidananda. Born in 1914, and inducted into the Divine Life Society — a Hindu ashram — Satchidananda travelled the length and breadth of India preaching. After serving his own guru throughout the 1950s, he gained US citizenship. A sizeable countercultural following ensued, galvanised by his opening speech at Woodstock in 1969 where he preached sound vibration to a crowd of 400,000. To say he was on 'home turf' would be something of an understatement. He drew on the concept of Nadha Brahma as he intoned that '*music is the celestial sound. And it is *sound* that controls the whole universe, not atomic vibrations. Sound energy, sound power, is much greater than any other power in this world.'

Satchidananda followed the Advaita Vedanta philosophical school whose central idea is the inseperability of the soul from god. It was an accepting doctrine; other faiths were welcomed, harmony gained via a focus on daily life, as opposed to prescriptive dogma: 'I feel we don't really need scriptures,' he wrote. 'The entire life is an open book, a scripture. Read it. Learn while digging a pit or chopping some wood or cooking some food. If you can't learn from your daily activities, how are you going to understand the scriptures?'[33]

Recording, grieving, composing and performing while bringing up four young children took its toll on Coltrane, however, and she entered a breakdown period she later described as her *tapas* (a Sanskrit word that translates as 'trial'), a gruelling time of mental and physical torment in which she hallucinated, lost weight, suffered debilitating insomnia and was admitted to hospital after burning herself. Satchidananda's influence was immeasurable on her music and philosophy throughout this period and beyond (she took the name Turiyasangitananda after travelling with him to India) and the albums she released during the 1970s remain unparalleled in beatific atmosphere and spiritual uplift.

Journey in Satchidananda (1971) was a case in point. The title track's shimmering harp is offset against the deep buzz of Tulsi's tanpura and

Cecil McBee's droning bassline. Evoking the presence of palpable *good*, the record transcends gospel, jazz and Indian traditions while drawing on the influence of all three. This is the sound of non-denominational humanism, music in service of a higher power. Coltrane was, clearly, on a profound personal journey. However, her lightness of touch, given her mental state, is extraordinary. The joyfulness stops far short of twee self-congratulation or hectoring religious fervour. She removed any trace of the musician's egotistical morass in favour of a fundamentally *useful* music, a functionality that could be applied — much like a personal mantra — to all comers. Likewise, *Transcendence* (1977) reflected the pivotal role Indian spirituality had taken in her life, group chants moving atop a funky backdrop. As she wrote in the liner notes, this was *her* take on devotional music, open to everybody, regardless of faith (or, indeed, lack thereof).

Divine music is a curative virtue; it is a gift from God that brings healing and comfort to the soul. This music can uplift one's spirit to a higher dimension of being that is filled with peace and joy.[34]

In 1976, she opened her ashram — the Vedantic Center — in the Santa Monica mountains. A spiritual sanctuary open to all, she continued to perform and record while devoting herself to ashram life, chant and the spiritual counselling of others.

'Chanting became a huge part of her life,' says Michelle Coltrane. 'She would help us write personal mantras that would help with spiritual development. She'd be awake in the morning hours — she loved the dawn — I'd see her sitting up from the very early morning. I asked her why and she said "all my kids are asleep, everything is safe, it's the quietest part of the day and there is such beauty and tranquillity." Sometimes she'd play her harp then. A lot of musicians like that time, but usually they'll be at the after-party (*laughs*).'

'She grew up with a Baptist background,' she continues, 'but when she was older she wanted to have a lifestyle beyond the weekly worship. She was drawn to the Vedantic philosophy because it wasn't just on Sunday — where you go to church, and then after church there is a BBQ, people playing cards and drinking beer. She began seeking elsewhere.'

During the ashram years Alice Coltrane continued to make music, albeit with differing methods of dissemination. Throughout the 1980s she increasingly focused on self-produced, lo-fi Vedantic chant cassettes, usually accompanied by low-key strings or synthesiser backing. These tapes — the most well known are *Turiya Sings* (1982), *Divine Songs* (1987) and *Infinite Chants* (1990) — are a separate entity from her 1970s canon. They were never commercially released (they were mainly distributed among friends, family and visitors to the ashram), featured gospel-style backing from the ashram singers and, although underpinned by her virtuoso synth playing, lack the transcendent majesty of her 1970s albums. In a sense these remain the most personal of Coltrane's recordings: this was the sound of her relaxed and in her element, unencumbered by any major label or critical expectation, playing for the joy of it among friends and family. Her Oberheim synth gave an idiosyncratic tone — that familiar, slightly tinny, 1980s sheen (the Oberheim was a mainstay of bands like Depeche Mode and Duran Duran) that sounded slightly incongruous among the layers of choral chant.

Coltrane remained a cult figure for much of the 1980s and '90s, operating outside of jazz circles and the music industry and devoting herself to ashram life. She underwent a more serious critical reappraisal in the noughties, however — particularly after her death in 2007 — with everyone from Sunn O))) to the Bug, Flying Lotus to Björk vocal in their appreciation. It's bizarre that it's taken so long for her discography to be accepted on its own terms. For me and many others, particularly during times of stress her music remains a sonic tonic: a dose of sanity in a world gone mad. Certain music exudes such positive spirit that the simple ritual of putting the record on the turntable feels like a small act of service to the universe itself, like spinning a prayer wheel out into the ether. It is, of course, easy to dismiss such sentiments as hippy nonsense. But to do so misses the point. Because Alice Coltrane's music was about true belief, regardless of the eye of the beholder: harnessing those fleeting moments of universal awe.

Chapter 4

THE DRONE OF
THE HOLY NUMBERS

Aside from the small sticker reading 'Dream House' next to the third-floor intercom, 275 Church Street, Manhattan looks like a typical downtown, late nineteenth-century tenement. I ring the intercom and wait to be buzzed in. As soon as the door closes I hear a sub-laden drone. It gets louder with every step up the stairs. On the third-floor landing a volunteer sits at a table with a donation jar. A sign on the wall instructs visitors to avoid making any unnecessary noise and a shoe rack lines the wall. I put $10 in the jar, take my shoes off and walk down a carpeted white corridor towards the source of the sound, a side door opening onto a windowless, incense-scented room, bathed in magenta light.

I feel like I've entered a strange portal. Sub heavy drones judder out of two speakers at the back, shaking the walls. Wisps of incense shimmy through the air. A light projector sits at the front of the room, a sheet in front of it perforated by thousands of tiny holes forming shifting images, light passing through the holes in a slow spectral dance. A couple sit lotus style in front of the projector. Others are asleep, either curled into the foetal position or sitting with their backs to the walls, eyes closed. A small shrine to Hindustani master singer Pandit Pran Nath sits on a table at the back of the room.

I put a cushion against the wall, cross my legs and close my eyes.

The drone manifests as a near physical presence in the room. It reaches into the crevices of my skull, shimmers down my spine, wipes out residual jet lag and caffeine jitters. The psychic hum of the New York streets fades. It feels like a return to warm stasis, to the womb. I enter a dream state propped against that wall, drifting in and out of sleep, enveloped by the juddering drone and soothing magenta lights. After a while I awake. I slowly turn my head in a circular motion. It induces a Doppler effect, the drone seemingly juddering down a couple of octaves.

After an hour or so, I move to the back of the room. The vibration is soothing, great swathes of fibrous sound placing me in a zone of beatific discombobulation. I settle back and watch the projection, entranced by the slow shifting light, neurone-like connections appearing before fading into the ether. I check my phone for the first time since arrival: I've been in there for four hours.

Less 'instillation', more living, breathing sound, the Dream House has been 'playing' — continuously — since 1993. The brainchild of drone lifer La Monte Young and light artist Marian Zazeela, it was conceived as a work that would, in Young's words, 'exist as a living organism with a life and tradition of its own'. It is never 'closed', per se. Outside opening hours the music 'sleeps' rather than stops: the amps remain powered, sliders on the mixing board lowered. An incense-scented drone portal, a shrine to sustain, it's a seriously intense experience. The windowless room feels like a sealed sonic vector. I was expecting some kind of chilled, cerebral, white box installation space. It's nothing of the sort: The Dream House is loud, visceral, hot. It's like the endgame of the drone playing out in real time: a stern, eternal, oracle buzz.

Widely considered the father of minimalism — as Brian Eno famously had it 'the daddy of us all' — Young was bewitched by the drone from the start. It became his lifelong obsession, fuelling his quest to create an 'eternal music' and defining both his philosophy of micro-detailed tonal obsession and his quasi-mystic personal bearing. He's long cut a controversial figure in the avant-garde, however. His eccentricities — and titanic ego — are notorious. At eighty-four years old he's still clad in black denims, wraparound shades and a cut-off biker jacket, metal trinkets dangling from his hearing aids, long pleated beard and open shirt suggesting a wizened piratical adventurer. His 'safeguarding' of his archive is the stuff of legend; in over sixty years, activity he's released a tiny handful of records, rarely performed live, seldom grants interviews and keeps — alongside his wife, the light artist Marian Zazeela — to an idiosyncratic twenty-seven-hour day. He's given to grandiose statements,[1] is convinced of his irrefutable genius and carries himself with a mystic bearing that can veer towards a comic level of self-importance. He's frequently been the subject of as much controversy as praise.

Regardless of controversy, however, his music remains revolutionary. While Indian classical musicians used sustain to support the raga, they seldom focused on the *naked* drone. This changed with Young. From pieces that started before they were 'played' and continued after they 'stopped' to twelve-day blues, sine wave rumbles and his six-hour epic *The Well-Tuned Piano* (still considered a 'work in progress' over three decades after its debut performance), Young's music hinges on the power of hypnosis. More than that: it's an attempt to harness eternity itself.

A Drone State of Mind

The drone axis ran deep in New York throughout the sixties. The most hyperactive city in the world gave birth to a music that hinged on stasis. Minimalism was the music of the listener. It demanded total presence, drew attention to the micro detail and eschewed classical notions of virtuosity and slavish adherence to an accepted canon in favour of obsessive textural and tonal interplay.

It remains a contentious term, however. It was coined some distance after the fact,[2] and there has been much discussion as to what it denotes, and who falls under the banner. Generally, though, we're talking music that followed in the revolutionary vanguard of John Cage and Karlheinz Stockhausen, is often of long duration and contains — in the classical sense — minimal melodic 'progression'. Too often it's used to describe the canon of four composers and four composers alone — La Monte Young, Terry Riley, Philip Glass and Steve Reich — all of whom, to greater and lesser degrees, have played with stasis and repetition and circular melodic progression. Terry Riley dislikes the term, however, and doesn't — despite hundreds of articles describing him as such — consider himself a 'minimalist' at all.

We'll forsake such hair-splitting here, however and focus on those emerging from the minimalist oeuvre who pushed the drone to the outer limits. From the nexus that formed around Young and his improvisational drone supergroup the Theatre of Eternal Music (which launched both future Velvet Underground members John Cale and Angus MacLise, as well as underground agitator Tony Conrad) to Deep Listening pioneer Pauline Oliveros, as well as the enduring legacy of the band who emerged, via John Cale, from minimalism to take the drone into the rock sphere and in the process change everything, for ever: the Velvet Underground.

In many respects — and certainly in regard to people like La Monte Young, Terry Riley, Pauline Oliveros, Tony Conrad and Angus MacLise — 'minimalism' is really the story of mid-twentieth-century American *mysticism*: a loose grouping of composers with shared influences — John Cage, Zen Buddhism, Fluxus, altered states, mathematics — who ruminated on the spiritualism of repetition. Like so much of the music they went on to influence, they were concerned with the visceral *grain* of sound. Stasis was celebrated, hypnotism cast as a liberatory device, the drone an end in itself.

Indeed, the drone was hard-wired into La Monte Young's DNA from day dot. Born in 1935, he was raised in a log cabin in the tiny Mormon hamlet of Bern, Idaho. His first memory was the sound of the wind lashing through the wooden eaves in a winter blizzard. As a boy he'd stand in a field mesmerised by gales whipping eerily over the plain, by the buzz of crickets in the summer and the hypnotic static buzz of the telegraph poles.

Later, in teenage years he'd lay on the roof of his grandfather's petrol station, inhaling rising diesel fumes, transfixed by the hum of the electrical transformers next door. A few years later, he'd be similarly transfixed by the hypnotic drone of legendary Hindustani musician Ali Akbar Khan, playing his record over and over until his grandmother was compelled to write 'opium music!' on the cover.

Moving to Los Angeles in the early 1950s, Young immersed himself in jazz. He played alto sax with future radicals like Don Cherry and Ornette Coleman, led various combos and developed an idiosyncratic mode for blues, emphasising lengthy periods for each chord change to best express 'the modal drone aspects of the music'. At the University of California he was exposed to a plethora of new sounds, many of which hinged on sustain. *Gagaku* — the ancient imperial court music of Japan, based on the harmonic interplay between oboe, flute and extended notes via the sho (a type of mouth organ) — made a particular impression, likewise trips to an abbey in Berkley to listen to the Dominican monks chanting.

It was Indian music that had the greatest influence on changing his path from jazz to no-holds-barred radical composition, however — the aforementioned recording by Ali Akbar Khan (sarod) and Chatur Lal (tabla) of *Raga Sindhu Bhairavi* in particular. The sound of the tanpura during the slow introductory (*alap*) section of the raga — where elements of the melody are introduced with no rhythmic accompaniment — particularly enraptured Young, and the drone, which had mesmerised him so viscerally as a boy, was calling ever stronger as he described in a rare 2002 interview.

We have the sound of the wind, the sound of the telephone poles, the sound of resonance, outdoor canyons, and crickets . . . in other words, I had begun to tune into them when I was a child, but I didn't really begin to make physical manifestations of them until around 1958 when I wrote the *Trio for Strings*.[3]

Trio for Strings drew on what Young termed 'sustenance' — i.e. the drone at the core of the piece, as opposed to a background to melodic progression. Only when working with sustained tones, believed Young, could one fully appreciate the intricacies of individual harmonics. Although his earlier compositions *For Brass* (1957) and the following year's *For Guitar* had both worked with sustained tones, *Trio for Strings* was more extreme than either. It was the first classical composition to pivot entirely on the drone. While Indian classical musicians had long used drones as sonic bedrock, Young made it the fundamental. Melody — in the Western classical sense of a series of notes relaying a recognisable 'tune' or motif — was eschewed entirely, allowing harmonics — the pure overtones — to occupy the foreground.

Studying at Berkley in 1958, Young premiered *Trio for Strings* at the home of his professor, Seymour Shifrin. All his peers (including a young Pauline Oliveros) were in attendance. Bewildered, most thought he'd 'gone off at the deep end' while Shifrin told him that if he continued in a similar vein he wouldn't make the grade. Undeterred, the following year he enrolled in Karlheinz Stockhausen's composition class at the Darmstadt Summer School where he discovered the work of John Cage, whose conceptual ideas — particularly the use of 'unmusical' sound sources — made a deep impression. Back in California, Young dived into the conceptual fray with abandon. *Poem* (1960) was inspired by the drone of wooden benches dragged across the floor of a Berkley laundromat. The piece involved furniture being dragged around an 'engaging surface' and was part of a wider set of what Young dubbed his 'live friction experiments'. 'I vividly remember trying out the large, heavy wooden benches,' he wrote, 'which when pulled or pushed across the cement floor produced unimaginably beautiful sustained tones.'

West Coast academia contained a number of like-minded souls — not least Terry Riley, Pauline Oliveros and the San Francisco Tape Music Center axis (which we'll explore later in this chapter) — but for anybody serious about the avant-garde in the early 1960s, most roads led to New York.

For Young the chaotic, mischievous world of Fluxus beckoned.

Chance Operations

Moving to the city in 1960, Young cut an eccentric figure. Resplendent in black velvet suit and cape, he was caught up in the radical nucleus of the nascent Fluxus scene. Fluxus was, primarily, about the *experience* — namely smashing the art/life barrier — as opposed to classical notions of artistic virtuosity, formal canonisation or hierarchy. Essentially an 'anti-art' movement, it aimed to remove art from the perceived tyranny of hushed spaces and sober academic discourse, and set it to *action*: experimentation, multimedia bombast, inclusivity — a fundamental burning of both the gatekeepers and the gates.

Centred around Lithuanian American artist George Maciunas, the movement incorporated visual artists, film-makers, writers and performance artists — Yoko Ono, Nam June Paik, George Brecht and Alison Knowles were all key instigators — and was based on the premise that art needed 'purging' of petit bourgeois preciousness and exclusivity. It was, above all, a clarion call to the *moment*, as Maciunas wrote in his bombastic *Fluxus Manifesto* (1963):

Purge the world of dead art, imitation, artificial art, abstract art, illusionistic art, mathematical art — PURGE THE WORLD OF 'EUROPANISM'. PROMOTE A REVOLUTIONARY TIDE AND FLOOD IN ART, promote living art, anti-art, promote NON ART REALITY, to be grasped by all peoples, not only critics, dilettantes and professionals.[4]

Like the Dadaists before them who, revolted by the senseless butchery of Flanders fields, devoted themselves to a surreal art that laughed bitterly in the face of a 'society' that could allow such brutality, Fluxus artists were confrontational. The boundaries between life and art were amorphous as so much shifting silt. The 'audience' were no longer passive bystanders, but often cast as co-conspirators. In 'Cut' (1964) Yoko Ono infamously sat motionless on stage and invited audience members to 'cut' away her clothes and hair with a pair of scissors while 'Total Art Matchbox' (1966) saw Ben Vautier produce a box of matches with specific instructions to: 'use these matches to destroy all art — museums art library's — ready mades — pop art and as I Ben signed everything work of art — burn — anything — keep last match for this match'.

Modernist patriarch John Cage was a key inspiration to the movement, particularly his fondness for harnessing chance as a creative catalyst. Best known in the collective subconscious for *4 33* — a rumination on the impossibility of 'silence' in which the musicians are instructed to play nothing for four minutes and thirty-three seconds (the piece, of course, being entirely different wherever and whenever it is performed depending on what is happening in the room at the time) — Cage was fascinated by Eastern religion, particularly Zen Buddhism and Taoism.

In the 1950s he'd adopted the *I Ching* (The Book of Changes) — an ancient Chinese system of practical divination — as a compositional tool. *I Ching* divination works on the premise of building a numerical hexagram. Usually this is done by throwing coins, although in ancient times stalks were more commonly used. The process works as follows: you toss three coins in the air at once; each coin is given a value of two or three, depending on whether it lands heads or tails; you then take the result and consult the book which contains a total of sixty-four hexagrams, a commentary — advice for action — given on each. Cage used this method to compose *Music of Changes* (1951), consulting the oracle book to make decisions on tempo, melody and timings, itself a subversion of the classical obsession with order and control. Cage's obsession with chance fed back to an early epiphany he'd had with the bodily drone: in the late 1940s he'd spent time in Harvard's famous anechoic chamber (often cited as the most acoustically 'dead' space in the world) and was fascinated by the visceral sonics emanating from his own body.

I went into an anechoic chamber not expecting in that silent room to hear two sounds: one high, my nervous system in operation, one low, my blood in circulation. The reason I did not expect to hear those two sounds was that they were set into vibration without any intention on my part. That experience gave my life direction, the exploration of non-intention. No one else was doing that. I would do it for us . . . I gave up making choices. In their place I put the asking of questions. The answers come from the mechanism, not the wisdom of the *I Ching*.[5]

These ideas resonated with Fluxus. The game of chance speaks strongly to the 'anti-art' aesthetic. Chance, after all, adds an anarchic frisson — a universal intervention — to the creative process, removing agency from artist as omnipotent 'creator'. The Cageian influence was solidified with the publication of *An Anthology of Chance Operations*, a Fluxus text edited by La Monte Young in 1963. The book was a manual for creative action, a series of sparks to help ignite ideas or confront preconceived notions on the nature of art and music.

Young offered a selection of surreal compositions. His 'Piano Piece for Terry Riley #1' involved pushing a piano into — or, perhaps, *through* — a wall: 'if the piano goes through the wall, keep pushing in the same direction regardless of new obstacles and continue to push as hard as you can whether the piano is stopped against an obstacle or moving'.

Another — 'Piano Piece for David Tudor' — gave instructions to bring a bale of hay and a pitcher of water onto the stage for the piano to eat and drink. The performer was instructed to either 'feed the piano, or leave it to eat by itself.'

Ostensibly, it made sense that Young — radically challenging preconceived notions of musical theory and form — would gravitate towards a shake-up movement like Fluxus. It soon proved grating to him, however. He was a classically trained musician who'd spent years at the coalface, hacking away at countless hours of painstaking solitary practice. The adage 'you have to know the rules in order to break them' may as well have been invented for him. He was a radical, yes. But he was also fastidious, a stickler for detail. Never mind that the movement was breaking the frame — for Young the frame itself was still, clearly, of some import. Worst of all, though, was the suspicion that some of the Fluxus crew were simply having a laugh. And herein lies the rub. Young's Fluxus 'compositions' were — on paper — in keeping with the playfully anarchic core of the scene. But, to him, there was nothing playful about them. He was deadly serious. When asked by Yoko Ono to curate a series of events in her loft in the early sixties, he stuck up a poster loftily reading: 'THE PURPOSE OF THIS SERIES IS NOT ENTERTAINMENT' on the door (as if anyone needed ask . . .)

'Fluxus people are like tenth-grade artists. They had no ability. They are hacks that rode on my coattails and then made a name for this movement doing humour. They never understood what I was doing . . . as soon as I understood what Fluxus was, I didn't want to be a part of it.'[6]

During the Fluxus years, his conceptual art was augmented by a burgeoning drone obsession. Pieces such as *The Second Dream of the High-Tension Line Stepdown Transformer* (part of his *Four Dreams of China* quartet) were *pure* drones, constructed from specific pitches and frequency ratios that track back to Young's childhood, imbuing the drone of the American power grid with metaphysical spiritual significance. There was an obsessional, ritualistic element at play, painstaking charts drawn up on precise frequency ratios and the interrelation between the pitches. Biographer Jeremy Grimshaw described the ritualistic atmosphere of an early performance of the piece at George Brecht's YAM Festival in May 1963, musicians positioning themselves in 'the middle of a meadow in a symmetrical figuration of intersecting diamond shapes' — Young was soon to take the ritual higher.

Dream Music

The Theatre of Eternal Music — or Dream Syndicate — made the most extreme psychedelic music of the 1960s. Forget the twee jangle of a thousand paisley-shirted soundalikes, *this* was true psychedelia. Deploying screeching electric violas, amplified sine wave drones, nasal whines and all manner of other warped frequency oscillations — usually at a tumultuous, hellish volume — they sought sensory oblivion through 120 decibels of drone power. As Lou Reed once quipped when asked about the (supposed) extremity of his 1975 feedback fest *Metal Machine Music*, 'you should have heard the Dream Syndicate'.

As ever with La Monte Young, *time* was of the essence, an attempt to tune into the vast and unknowable cosmic infinitude the overarching goal. In 1962 he was playing soprano saxophone in New York, accompanied by a young poet — Angus MacLise — on percussion. Marian Zazeela and Terry Jennings provided a vocal drone alongside the pair, and the group put on a few gigs over the summer at the 10-4 Gallery. Tony Conrad — a Harvard maths graduate and accomplished violinist with a keen interest in the New York avant-garde and Fluxus — came to some of the gigs and, fascinated by the hypnotic vibe, asked to join on violin. The band was completed by John Cale, a young viola player from the Welsh valleys. Cale had studied classical music at Goldsmiths College in early sixties London and, like Young and Conrad, was into Fluxus and Cage. Before leaving Goldsmiths, he'd shocked classmates with a concert in a Fluxus vein that saw him frantically chopping up a table with an axe.

The Theatre holed up in Young and Zazeela's Church Street loft space in Manhattan, devoting themselves to hours of daily practice amid a thick fog of hash smoke. For six hours a day they essentially lived inside the drone. Throughout 1963 they worked mainly around Young's *Dorian Blues* series, each member holding a different pitch for as long as possible while Young blew soprano sax fast and wild, cascades of notes blasting in circular motifs above the dense dronal bedrock. The sound soon became more pared down, however. Young ditched the saxophone and MacLise left the group in 1964, allowing the group to work with pure drones, unadorned by any rhythmic accompaniment.

Here was New York's hidden reverse. The audio buzz of a city in a state of neurotic, nervy energy birthed a music, not of constant flux, but dense electrified *stasis*. This was extreme music by today's standards, let alone the mid sixties. In the heart of New York City, the Theatre's music was defined, on one level, by absence — namely of melody and progression — but on another by the physical *presence* of sound. I imagine them sitting in their loft space amid clouds of pungent Nepalese temple ball, multilayered electrified drones ringing out, sweltering NY summer outside, sprinklers on, the sound as thick as the humid air.

On some level their music was an act of negation: a sonic barrier against the psychic morass of the city, a womb impervious to the outside world. Young may have been obsessed with form and theory, but Cale and Conrad brought the audio ruckus. It was *electric* — far removed from the frigid preciousness of the hushed 'spaces' that much early minimal music occupied. The Theatre of Eternal Music worshipped at the altar of *extreme* volume. Young and Zazeela hummed into powerful condenser mikes, Tony Conrad operated a side chain of effects for his violin, driving it through a pre-amp and various oscillators. All of this was then connected to a mixing desk via a third amplifier which fed a further ten speakers.[7] Conrad, meanwhile, had introduced contact mikes into the mix, painstakingly amplifying every element of the sound while Cale's bastardised electric viola — he'd installed a flattened bridge, so that he could play several strings at once, and strung it with electric guitar, rather than viola, strings — pushed them deep into the red.

Aside from all this they'd run the drone of Young and Zazeela's tortoise aquarium motor through the amps too, its 60Hz hum — the frequency of the power grid — underpinning the whole lot. By galvanising this hum their music became folded into the 'background of life' as Cale explained in 2001:

'There was this whole theory of hypnosis and alpha rhythms . . . we were tuning to a 60-cycle hum. The third harmonic was 60 cycle tuned to the refrigerator, or to the hum of the amplifier system . . . That meant the key we were really in was ten cycles: alpha rhythm. Which is what the brain experiences in a dream state.'[8]

The tortoise — slow and wise, outliving its owner — became a perfect visual analogue of the drone. Young was obsessed with tortoise imagery, concocting a dream-world mythology around the animal. *The Tortoise, His Dreams and Journeys* was an improvisational framework — a selection of frequency ratios — that enabled the band to move from one tone to the next. This was the 'eternal music' concept in action. Young included silences of 'indeterminate length' as part of the 'piece', the idea being that the silence could last minutes, days, weeks, years, decades, centuries, millennia — indeed, any time at all — between performances, which would then always start on the same tone. When performed, *Tortoise* was billed under wonderfully evocative names that indicated the singularly gnostic aesthetic at play. Its first performance took place at a seedy old burlesque theatre at 100 Third Avenue on Thirteenth Street over a couple of weekends in October 1964. There it was dubbed *The Tortoise Droning Selected Pitches from the Holy Numbers for the Two Black Tigers, the Green Tiger and the Hermit.* At the same theatre in December, it was billed as *The Tortoise Recalling The Drone of the Holy Numbers as they were Revealed in the Dreams of the Whirlwind and the Obsidian Gong and Illuminated by the Sawmill, the Green Sawtooth Ocelot and the High-Tension Line Stepdown Transformer.*

Performances were lengthy ritualistic wig-outs, band sitting cross-legged, audience boggling at Marian Zazeela's mind-bending magenta lights, while the titanic drones — capable of inspiring beatific bliss or clammy nausea — flowed from the stacks. Though the psychedelic revolution was — in 1964 — two years off, the Theatre of Eternal Music foresaw it all, the triptych of disorientating sound, mind-bending lights and altered states preceding the West Coast happenings by some distance.

Drugs, of course, played their role. Strong hash enabled the band to get into the required mindset, and the audience to stay put for the ensuing barrage. Rhys Chatham — who played in the later 1970s incarnation of the Theatre — recalled to me the rigours of desperately trying to stay in tune at one practice, unaccustomed to the fearsome strength of Young's stash.

'We'd have to sing with sine waves and it was very hard . . . there is nothing in nature that approaches a sine wave, the stability of a sine wave. So what happens is this: when my ear is attempting to latch onto the sine wave, the sine wave appears to drift — except it is not drifting physically, it's the synapses in the *ear* that are drifting (*laughs*). So the only way to tune to that mofo is to listen to beat phenomenon, and you should try doing that for three hours . . . La Monte would take hashish, melt it, put it in honey and heat it up and eat it. He gave me some, but I only did it that way with him once. He could do it because he had the tolerance, but I was *totally* stoned and trying to get to these pitches. It was quite the experience.'

Indeed, the Theatre of Eternal Music — for anyone who encountered them live — was a visceral, full-body experience. Reviews of the time point to them preceding the Sunn O)))-style maximal volume totality by some decades, their brutal 120-decibel barrage leading *Village Voice* critic John Perreault to describe it as an 'almost unbearably loud, low-pitched electronic hum . . . at first even to enter the auditorium seemed too dangerous to risk, for the sound was painfully loud even with the doors closed.'[9]

Scant documents of the band remain. No official recordings of the original Theatre line-up were ever issued. American avant-garde revivalist label Table of the Elements issued a fascinating bootleg recording in 2000 entitled *Day of Niagra: Inside the Dream Syndicate* which collated a recording of the original

Theatre, although it was unsanctioned by Young. Though lo-fi in the extreme, it captures a heavy, discordant vibe: La Monte Young's whinnying nasal vocals, Conrad's brittle metallic violin scrapes and Cale's dominant — often punishingly bright — viola. It lacks the essential sub-bass of the sine waves, however: the mind has to fill in the blanks. Aside from the Theatre, the wider Young discography is also remarkably slim. Most vital is what has become known as 'The Black Album' — an untitled LP by Young and Zazeela released in a tiny run in 1969 (copies regularly change hands for upwards of £500). Comprising one pure sine wave drone piece (a section of the piece *Map Of 49's Dream The Two Systems of Eleven Sets of Galactic Intervals Ornamental Lightyears Tracery*) alongside a dual gong piece (with a typically exacting instruction to 'be played back at any slower constant speed down to 8 1/3 rpm, i.e. 16 2/3 rpm which is available on some turntables') 'The Black Album' was a slow-burning rumble that hummed with an otherworldly power.

Beyond the Dream Syndicate

The Theatre of Eternal Music were — ostensibly — a freewheeling improvisatory unit who existed far outside the machinations of the music industry. But tensions emerged in 1965, particularly between Young, Conrad and Cale.

The ensuing acrimonious split has coloured the critical perception of La Monte Young to this day. As is often the case with band tensions, it boiled down to the issue of creative ownership. In Young's view, having written down frequency ratios and imposed improvisatory boundaries he — and he alone — was the 'composer', the setting of dronal boundaries (disputed by Conrad and Cale) constituting creative 'ownership'.[10] Conrad and Cale thought differently. The 'Dream Music', as they termed it, was in their view a collaborative effort. Even when working around specific frequencies, it remained a group improvisation — a collective alchemical reaction. The idea that Young could lay claim to the music was — to Conrad and Cale — akin to a blues guitarist calling out 'this one's in E' and then claiming ownership of the three-hour jam that ensued. More hurtful for the pair, though, was the issue of the Theatre's recordings. *Hundreds* of hours are filed away in Young's private Church Street archive but — aside from that unofficial Table of the Elements release — nothing has been issued.

Young had wanted Cale and Conrad to sign a contract that stipulated he was the sole overall composer in order to grant them access. Both refused. Conrad, in particular, remained bitterly opposed to what he saw as an aggressive commandeering of the collective's legacy until he died in 2016. Particularly galling to the ever radical Conrad (who had wanted to 'end composing! Get rid of it! I wanted it to die out!'[11]) was the idea that Young was treating the legacy of the Theatre as a precious commodity or, worse, a dainty art fetish object. In Conrad's view, 'the hundred or so recordings of Dream Music emblematically deny "composition" its authoritarian function as a modern activity' and Young's siphoning of a legacy of such open-ended collaboration was a betrayal of the spirit of the work itself. Ironically — for a band who spent so long conjuring dream sonics — the Theatre of Eternal Music exist more in the collective imagination than codified recorded 'reality'. Music conceptualised as eternal was doomed by Young to exist only as fading memories.

As Conrad wrote in the sleeve notes of his 1997 *Early Minimalism* compilation:

By 1987, I realised that La Monte Young wanted me to die without hearing my music . . . on the one hand, it had entered the American musical tradition, somewhere near its core, and influenced many people in many ways. On the other hand, it existed privately.[12]

Despite being — through the presence of Cale and MacLise — *the* fundamental influence on the Velvet Underground and, therefore, one of *the* fundamental influences on the history of rock 'n' roll, the Theatre of Eternal Music continue to exist, for now, in a hermetically sealed memory tomb.

Whether that will ever be broken remains to be seen, but recent decades have uncovered reams of tape recordings made by Conrad, Cale and MacLise sans Young — a cache of gloriously anarchic drone, noise and tape music that has gone some distance to rewriting the established narrative of early minimal music.

Slapping Pythagoras

Playful, self-deprecating and mischievous, Tony Conrad was, in many regards, the polar opposite of the mercurial Young. A thorn in the side of the anally retentive avant-garde from day dot, Conrad was more concerned with the possibilities of the *moment* than conceptualising eternity. He loathed pomposity, particularly the reverent Eurocentric world view many in the modern arts world held. In 1964 he'd picketed Karlheinz Stockhausen's New York premiere of *Originale* with a clapperboard reading 'Action Against Cultural Imperialism'. The previous year he'd been involved in Fluxus actions at the Metropolitan Museum of Art to 'Fight the Snob Art of the Social Climbers!'[13] Later — livid with the tape situation — he used similar direct action on Young, standing outside his Buffalo Arts Center show in 1990, handing out leaflets and walking round in circles chanting: 'Young out of Buffalo!'

His post-Theatre work — in both sound and image — frequently intersected with the tonal obsessions of the band but, while systematic (Conrad was a mathematician and had a long-standing interest in 'just intonation', the natural tuning system closely associated with the Theatre of Eternal Music), was never bogged down in Young's obsessional rhetoric: the preciousness, finickiness and grandiosity. He had a near permanent wry smile on his face, a keen appreciatioin of the absurd. The idea that musical scales were to be pored over — bent to the genius will of an all-powerful creator — was, to Tony Conrad, anathema. Until his death in 2016, he railed against what he described as the 'neo Pythagorean' world view of Western culture which 'announces great heroes and re-inscribes the dominance of an aristocratic cultural strategy'. For Conrad, the Theatre of Eternal Music represented a state of mind; as he told the *Wire* in 1998, it was 'a world to inhabit. I never left. I always occupied that space, virtually or otherwise.'

After the Theatre of Eternal Music, the drone continued to reverberate through Conrad's art. He cast his violin not so much as instrument but psychoacoustic dream machine, its amplified scrape a means of surveying the lay of strange lands. His experimental films, meanwhile, mirrored the textures of his sound — the drone on film, essentially. A pioneer of 'structural' film-making, Conrad navigated the sensory shifting possibilities of light, sound and static. His 1966 film *The Flicker* consisted of rapidly moving black and white images, strobe like — nothing more, other than a warning for epileptics, and a schlocky 1950s B movie-esque caveat that a 'doctor should be in the house' whenever it was shown. It hinged on intoxication, disorientation: brutal film that took you by the collar with feral intent. Conrad was a modern primitive. Forget plot, character, progression, all that jazz. This was film that reduced the viewer to a base state — sitting in a dark room cranially bombarded by flickering light to the point of submission.

Conrad's films were often concerned with time, both the present moment and its inescapable passing. His *Yellow Movies* series, for example, took the idea of watching paint dry literally. He painted black frames to mirror the same proportion as movie frames. He then filled in the frames with a cheap white house paint that would yellow over time. These were, in Conrad's view, not paintings at all, but movies that — even when not on 'display' at a gallery — continue playing to this day. Just as the Fluxus artists had wanted to cast off the silken skin of European institutionalism, Conrad's films were free of cinematic convention, texturally brutal, fundamentally hallucinatory.

He described the effect of *The Flicker* in suitably visceral physical terms:

Certain things engage directly with your perceptual processes and force themselves on you. These include such things as secondary sexual characteristics, like, our eyes naturally follow lines — the secondary sexual characteristics of a figure. Your eyes just do that. You look at people's eyes. Or in the case of the flicker or certain musical effects, things happen in your ear or eye or brain, which are not something you choose to have happen, but happen as products of the transitivity of the material. The contestation between these modes of receptivity has always fascinated and intrigued me.[14]

This idea — the mind filling in blanks in the static, conjuring visions independent of the source material — is a potent form of magic. Consider techno. When dancing for hours at a time to sparse loops you'll often hear things that aren't there: weird little sweeps, off-kilter hi-hat patterns, motifs, the hallucinatory synergy between body movement, chemical intake and minimal sound enabling the mind to focus on minuscule sonic details, which are then bent slightly off grid — like trying to focus on a magic eye picture. Minimal music invites ambiguity. It breaks the frame of commonalty, facilitates *unique* experience, unleashes the cranial goblin.

And the goblin was alive and well in Conrad; it was there in the amped cat-scratch drone of his violin; the nauseating physical frisson of *The Flicker*; his commitment to getting right to the centre of a sound. When Conrad joined the Theatre of Eternal Music in 1962 he came with a bold spirit and radical ear. If La Monte Young approached the drone with a mathematician's eye for detail — seeking to harness it, control it to the nth degree, make it *his* — Conrad was more about *submission*; letting the music take *him* west. No ending or beginning, no climactic wave, no bridge to recognition or epiphany, just being present in the sound, deep in the sonic ether. In Conrad's mind, the Theatre's music was an evocation of the moment, a clarion call — not an attempt to harness eternity, as Young had sometimes spoken of doing — but to inhabit sound, to walk among it. 'There wasn't a reliance on cadence . . . just being there . . . part of the reason was that we were able to hone in on the drone as a way of getting into, and remaining in the middle of a single sound for a longer time.'

Though often criminally overlooked, Conrad's music is therefore among the most compelling of the twentieth-century avant-garde. His was *maximalist* minimalism — sparse elements pushed to the outer limits of their own possibilities. His 1997 *Early Minimalism* compilation comprised both reclaimed sixties recordings and 'reimagined' recreations of older pieces. The record went some way to reclaiming his vital stake in the history of minimal music. 'Four Violins' (1964) was an exercise in brute economy — quadruple overdubbed violin scratching against itself in weird atonal micro strokes, early tape splicing affording terse movement, startling in lo-fi intensity.

A deep dive into the grain of Conrad's amplified violin, layers were recorded individually, Conrad bouncing them back and forth on his reel-to-reel tape recorder and layering them together afterwards. The sound comes from all sides, tough and fibrous, the scrape and crawl both sombre and strangely energising. Likewise his many hypnotic collaborations, which hinge — like the best dub or techno, say — on the spaces *between* the notes. We'll fully discuss Conrad and Faust's 1972 hypno masterwork — *Outside the Dream Syndicate* — later on, but equally compelling was his recording with Laurie Spiegel and Rhys Chatham, *Ten Years Alive on the Infinite Plain*, a long-lost 1972 New York live recording that was finally released by Superior Viaduct in 2017. It's one long, funereal trudge groove: an unrelenting chug that doesn't let up or change for the best part of an hour and a half. If you're in the mood for hypnotism, it's an unbeatable trip. Meanwhile 1995's *Slapping Pythagoras* was a seriously abrasive wall of sound produced by Steve Albini, layers of microtonal violin forming a wall of sound, the incessant drone of Conrad's violin enhanced by the feedback-drenched scrape of Jim O'Rourke's guitar (the title was a thinly veiled dig at Young).

Other ex-Theatre members were equally industrious during the mid sixties. John Cale's sprawling three-disc retrospective *New York in the 1960s* shone a light on a long-forgotten cache of DIY tape recordings, showcasing a hallucinatory welter of solo pieces that had lain untouched in Tony Conrad's attic until 2000, when Cale started the arduous task of listening to them, cataloguing and restoring them. Most startling was the epic 'Sun Blindness Music', a forty-minute Vox organ excursion into alien soundscapes that hinges on a single chord around which a wall of noise of indeterminate source orbits in constant motion. It's like being sucked into a black hole in some seedy outpost of the far galaxy: disjointed stabs, churning distortion and disorientating panning utterly fucking your perception of time and instilling a sense of rapidly rising panic. Working in clear contrast to the static of the Theatre of Eternal Music, 'Sun Blindness Music' is the sound of multifarious malfunction, an exorcism of theoretical fustiness: Cale sounds like he's been gripped by the sensual joy of noise.

Cale's hermetic solo experiments with found sound, amplified viola and swathes of white noise — recorded in his Lower East Side loft — prefigure noise, no wave and ambient all at once. Crucially, they also point towards what he (and Angus MacLise) were about to bring to the Velvet Underground: dissonance, abrasive texture and a predisposition for hypnotism mainlined into the rock 'n' roll, rather than conceptual avant-garde, underground. As we'll see, through Cale and MacLise's influence, the drone moved into rock, through punk, into metal, post-rock, techno and beyond — they were *the* galvanising figures in its dissemination *outwards*, away from the cloistered arts and avant-garde worlds and onto the streets (you need only listen to the two Velvet Underground records made *without* Cale to understand his seismic influence on everything that made that band what they were).

Thunderbolt Pagoda

Angus MacLise also recorded extensively during the sixties, sometimes alongside Cale and Conrad, though often alone. His remains the strangest and most criminally overlooked discography of any of the ex-Theatre alumni. A true bohemian spirit, even before joining the Theatre, MacLise was a known face among the Lower East Side underground flotsam who shared each other's loft space, beds, exhibitions, scant food, gut-rot wine and dope among the crumbling low-rent ex-tenement blocks.

A drummer, poet, artist, publisher and occultist with a life story straight out of a Kerouac novel, MacLise had lived in Paris during the early sixties where he founded the underground Dead Language Press and moved through the beatnik underground fuelled by a voracious amphetamine habit and passion for the esoteric. He contributed beguiling soundtracks to underground movies and wrote poetry. His mystic calendar — *Year* (1961) — was a cryptic reworking of the calendar year, each day distilled to its alchemical essence by MacLise. Reading it instils a peculiar trance state, as if glimpsing some peculiar hidden — and perhaps terrible — truth through a foggy porthole window: 'Day of the Waste Arena', 'Day of the

White Glare', 'Day of Slack Reins', 'Trumpet Lung', 'Day of Bessie Smith'. It's a stunningly evocative work — a shamanic subversion of time and order. Indeed, the activities of MacLise represented something of an underground *within* an underground — what filmmaker Ira Cohen presciently described as 'electronic multimedia shamanism':

There was something happening in those years that has never been taken into consideration, which is electronic multimedia shamanism . . . people like Angus . . . people like Jack Smith . . . Brion Gysin was a fantastic calligrapher, writer. We were all friends and we all influenced each other on a personal level.[15]

Like Conrad, MacLise was tapped into the underground Lower East Side film scene. He collaborated with experimental film-makers Jonas Mekas, Jack Smith, Jerry Jofen and Ira Cohen with haunting, noise-saturated soundtracks. His soundtrack to Ira Cohen's hallucinatory *The Invasion of Thunderbolt Pagoda* was particularly evocative, a tripped-out descent into some dank netherworld of wet cave sonics. Hinging on disembodied voices, flutes, processed field recordings, tanpura drones, distant tribal drums and ethereal harmonics, MacLise mangles everything with delay, echo and primitive dubbing to disorientating effect.

Equally thrilling was his Indonesian-influenced soundtrack to Ron Rice's *Chumlum* (1964) where layers of echoing gamelan-style strings move against a rising swell of disquieting dream music. MacLise's sound was unique in its subterranean *density*. His patchwork approach — splicing found sound into white noise into heavy drones into distorted melody — was eerie and elemental: the hiss of the reel to reel covers the mix like jungle mist, and his drums — understated at the best of times — sound like they've been recorded from some far-off forest clearing.

MacLise also put on infamous underground parties in New York throughout the mid sixties which he dubbed the Rites of the Dream Weapon. The idea of the Dream Weapon fed back to the hypnotic, narcotic sound induced by the Theatre of Eternal Music, the drone cast as a tool for transcendence, albeit wilfully imbued with a dose of New York scuzz. Hand-drawn flyers of the time are adorned — grindhouse movie style — with salacious promises: 'Coma' 'Delirium' 'Frenzy' 'Dark Rituals of the New York Underground' — while the all-night sessions fused film, hallucinatory light

shows, ear-busting volume and foolhardy chemical consumption in a bacchanalian feast of sensorial oblivion.

A lifelong interest in esoteric spirituality and occultism soon led MacLise
down the rabbit hole to Kathmandu in the early seventies. There he found
himself among the countercultural nucleus that had settled around the
infamous Freak Street — a warren of legal hash shops, run-down hostels and
acid-fried street prophets — throughout the sixties. He continued publishing
in the city, setting up the Bardo Matrix press alongside Ira Cohen. Specialising
in beautifully ornate rice-paper editions, they published pamphlets, posters
and books, both by themselves and kindred Beat spirits including Paul
Bowles, Gregory Corso and Diane di Prima. MacLise's approach to publishing
mirrored the layered physicality of his music: he'd use rice paper, woodblocks,
letterpress and handmade paper to create beautiful limited editions — anything from a dozen to a few hundred — which were sold in the Freak Street
co-operative bookshop to travelling heads. A voracious lifelong drug user,
MacLise died in Kathmandu in 1979 from hypoglycaemia and malnutrition
and was cremated on a traditional Buddhist funeral pyre. Despite recording
during much of the sixties and seventies — both solo and alongside Conrad
and Cale — most of his New York music, like that of his ex-Dream Syndicate
collaborators, didn't surface until the late nineties/early noughties, much of it
compiled on *The Cloud Doctrine* (1999) compilation released by Sub Rosa and
featuring a tapestry of spoken-word exhortations, the whistling wind of the
Himalayas, gong chimes and ghostly tape crackle. MacLise's music remains a
ramshackle channelling of deep mystery and foreboding. His paintings of the
time — which frequently used an improvised Tibetan and Arabic influenced
calligraphy — mirrored the woozy magic of his music.

Ghosts in the Machine

Lower Manhattan — with its cheap rents and ample loft space — was a
natural hub for the American avant-garde throughout the sixties, but equally
visceral underground vibrations were stirring on the West Coast. The San
Francisco Tape Center became a vital nucleus for experimental electronic
sound of wildly vivid hues, the drone alive amid the crackle of mysterious
tape loops and the idiosyncratic wiring of nascent music technologies bent
into strange new forms. During the early sixties Terry Riley, Pauline Oliveros,
Morton Subotnick, Ramon Sender and others twisted the boundaries of
tape machines, tone generators and mixing desks any which way. The tape

machine — long a key part of the sonic arsenal of the original *musique concrète* composers in France — was particularly prized, enabling West Coast radicals to loop, edit and layer sounds to startling psychedelic effect.

Ramon Sander was a classical music student at the San Francisco Observatory of Music who'd started experimenting with a two-track Ampex tape recorder in 1961 on the Indian-influenced piece *Four Sanskrit Hymns*. The following year he collaborated with fellow composer Pauline Oliveros on the tape music concert series *Sonics*, which also featured Terry Riley and Philip Windsor. In 1962, Sender invited fellow composer Morton Subotnick to set up the San Francisco Tape Center. Quickly gaining a reputation for radical arts happenings, and seeding collaborations with musicians, actors, artists and like-minded souls, the Center acted as a launch point for the West Coast underground.

A rotating cast of characters made use of the third-floor studio, including countercultural journeyman Terry Riley, whose early tape piece *Mescaline Mix* — a ghostly piece inspired by psychedelic experiences with the namesake plant — was composed by him physically feeding the tape spool out of a window and running it onto a spindle set up around wine bottles in his garden. Tape music enabled Riley to take recognisable source material — found sound, live recordings, radio samples, whatever he fancied — and malleably twist it to unexpected areas, shear it of its surface meaning. He'd chop tape at random intervals, then splice it back together intuitively, often surprising himself on playback. *Birds of Paradise* (1964) was constructed entirely at random, using tape the contents of which Riley was unaware, while *Shoeshine* (1964) saw him record a Hammond organ blues solo from Jimmy Smith from the radio, chop it to pieces and reassemble it in different order. This was primitive sampling in action — new sound from old — composer, player, technology and the giddy dance of chance moving together in mystic motion. The parallels here with the sampling techniques enabled by technology like the Akai MPC sampler during the 1980s, whereby sampled drum breaks could be chopped and reassembled, then physically punched in on the fly — are manifest.

What, I wondered, attracted Riley to the medium of tape during the early sixties? Was there some 'ghost in the machine' element at play?

'The ghost in the machine is a very good description of tape music, I like that (*laughs*). When I first started working with tape I was still a student at UC Berkley and I only had a very primitive modified machine to work with. And I started hearing things in these loops which caused an awakening in me. The first piece I made was *Mescaline Mix* — I started working on that in the early sixties. It was *absolutely* the ghost in the machine! All these spirits that I was hearing as I mixed together loops that I'd recorded. And I started hearing all kinds of strange voices coming through the textures that you'd never be able to create in instrumental music or in any other way.

'I became fascinated with tape and its ability to create another world of sound,' he continues. 'The whole culmination of that time was when I went to France and worked with Chet Baker and I got to work with an engineer who created a time- like accumulator, stretching the tape across the machines. This was in 1963 — way before Frith[16] or anybody else did this kind of tape music — nobody had ever heard of this before. That was a revelation, a turning point — really the prelude to writing a piece like *In C*.'

Like La Monte Young, Riley was strongly influenced by John Cage and the creative potential of chance actions. On tape machines, Riley was setting up audio snapshots, allowing events to unfold without a road map. On *In C*, however — one of *the* early minimal benchmarks — he went further into the game of chance. One of the most open-ended and truly collaborative pieces ever 'scored', *In C* proved revolutionary. Extending free rein to musicians over fifty-three separate musical modules, the score is wide open. Any number, of any kind, of musical instrument is allowed, with a constant pulse performed on the high C's of a piano or a mallet instrument grounding the piece. The fifty-three short phrases can then be repeated any number of times — a new pattern started at any time, by any musician. The only condition specified by Riley is that performers can't move 'backwards' once a pattern is started. Riley's notes offered advice on the importance of active listening when performing it.

Sometimes it is best to just listen and not to play. It is important to fit into the group sound and understand how what you decide to play affects everybody around you . . . always listen to the pulse.[17]

In C can be read as a state of mind — faith in chaos — rather than score, per se. For it to work as a cohesive piece, individual players need to temper their journey through the modules with a keen ear and open temperament. It is not a piece for the untapped ego to run amok in, lest the whole thing come tumbling down. *In C* also differs from much minimal music in that it actually *grooves* as it hypnotises — the ceaseless chink of the piano evokes the 4/4 of techno as the modes unfold like separate locked grooves all around.

'A lot of my interest in chance is due to my relationship to John

Cage, who was a philosophical mentor to me,' Riley explained. 'John had discovered Zen Buddhism which is, essentially, a surrendering of the ego to whatever is going to happen: the idea that *everything* is equally valuable — you don't make a judgement that one thing is better than another. John was very accepting of all that happened, and that was influential on *In C*. If you leave things completely open, then you set up the opportunity for very surprising things to happen; you set up ecstasy and great moments. And it's been a way for me to work in general, throughout my life. I start with chaos and then filter out and I'm left with what I like. But for me chaos is where all the real, fertile, good stuff is.'

Throughout the sixties Riley embraced the chaos of the dawning psychedelic age. The avant-garde may be (wrongly) held in the collective subconscious to be psychically at odds with the counterculture — the former generally held to be turtlenecked, sober, frigid, humourless; the latter free-wheeling, hairy, loose — but Riley ably straddled both worlds. Visually, he was the archetypal West Coast hippy: flowing hair, abundant beard, kaftan, clouds of weed. He was an enthusiastic psychedelic experimenter. His was no dalliance: psychedelics were an essential part of Riley's early musical reckoning, a pass key that opened musical doors that may otherwise have remained bolted (an enthusiasm he shared with his old friend La Monte Young, who'd introduced him to marijuana in the late 1950s when the pair were studying at Berkley). Riley went on to experiment enthusiastically with peyote, psilocybin mushrooms and LSD during the mid sixties.

Psychedelic experiences and the drone were, to Riley, fundamentally connected: both enabled a state where the ego was knocked down a peg or two, where space-time was blurred, where you could get *lost*.

'There was a renaissance driven by psychedelics,' he tells me. 'People were beginning to take these substances and beginning to have these experiences with realities other than normal life. Musicians were experimenting . . . Marijuana has always been a drug of choice for musicians, because it elevates the senses and perception and slows things down so that you can look more deeply into them. So there was a consciousness revolution in the sixties that was very transformative for the culture and for music. Especially for me personally. It changed the way that I decided to put music together. Especially if you look at Beethoven and Bach — traditional classical composers that were more tied to ego, expressions of power and ego. With the drone you want the self to disappear into the music.'

Despite the success of *In C*, Riley was reticent to join the traditional avant-garde pathway of grant applications, lecturing and residencies. Ever the journeyman, he went to Mexico for three months and spent time in Morocco before travelling the length and breadth of the United States. Eventually settling in New York, he joined his old friend La Monte Young in the Theatre of Eternal Music in 1965, playing a few shows on improvised vocals, taking up soprano saxophone and studying just intonation tuning with Tony Conrad.[18] Around this time Riley also came to major label attention via composer David Behrman, who had been given free rein by CBS Records to curate a series of experimental records for the label's Columbia imprint. It was on CBS that Riley unleashed the swirling, hypnotic *A Rainbow in Curved Air* in 1969, one of few avant-garde crossovers of the period.

The title track rolls out multi-tracked layers of electric harpsichord and electric organ — bending, sideways motifs that duck over and under like some frolicking autumnal faerie, grounded with undulating electric drones while 'Poppy Nogood and the Phantom Band' hinged on Riley's saxophone stabs amid a dense swathe of humid drone. Riley's playing throughout exudes a deftness of touch that belies the busyness of the material. Grounded by the warmth of the drone, it's immersive rather than scattershot, albeit some way off what most would describe as 'minimal'.

This spectral dance — a warm, buzzing energy — has long been Riley's audio hallmark. It makes sense, then, that Riley's music has long been so enthusiastically championed by the electronic underground. Indeed, although a scant forty minutes, *Rainbow* was regularly presented in elongated form during Riley's all-night happenings during the late sixties. Bringing sleeping bags, hammocks, beers, acid and hash pipes, people would settle in for the duration, drifting in and out of sleep as Riley played for eight hours at a time. A direct line can be drawn from these sessions to the chill-out rooms (now, sadly, a rarity) that proliferated throughout the rave scene in the early 1990s, providing gurning ravers a space in which to retreat. Riley records — *A Rainbow in Curved Air*, in particular — were regularly played during the era: the tinkle of his harpsichord sending chemically-induced chills down spines everywhere from Megadog to the Orbit. As JD Twitch of Optimo put it in a recent interview:

In the early nineties *A Rainbow in Curved Air* resurfaced in lots of ambient sets and I started to delve deeper into his catalogue which I swear has healing properties. Try it. Next time you feel under the weather, listen to a few hours of Terry Riley and I bet you will feel at the very least a bit better.[19]

Deep Listening

Music that cleaves to the micro detail and draws attention to near imperceptible changes demands an audience willing to fully immerse. Arguably nobody did more to challenge perceived ideas about the differences between listening and merely 'hearing' than Pauline Oliveros. A contemporary of both La Monte Young and Terry Riley, Oliveros was a sound artist and composer whose life work was a commitment to enhancing sensory perception via the philosophy of deep listening. She defined it as follows:

Deep Listening is expanding to take in and listen to everything that is around you; inside of you. When we do this we can expand almost infinitely to include everything that is possible to listen to. Most of the time we are discarding what's going on as not important, but in order to do what I call Deep Listening we have to include everything.[20]

The genesis for deep listening was laid in the late 1950s, when Oliveros conducted a tape experiment. Placing a contact mike outside her window and recording what was happening, she later played it back and realised that — despite having been present — she hadn't remotely taken in all the sounds. Listening back, she found that she needed to focus actively, rather than passively hearing.

A meditative practice that ran contrary to regular meditation — where you're often instructed to 'allow' background sounds their space, rather than specifically focusing on them — deep listening practice aimed to develop a sense of wonder and appreciation, giving the acoustic world equal precedent to the visual. Not confined to music, deep listening doesn't place any inherent system of value on individual sounds: rather, everything is interesting, everything valid.

Oliveros believed immersion in slow-moving sound aided perception in every aspect of life. In the late 1960s, traumatised by the escalating Vietnam War and the fatal self-immolation of a protesting student at USCD (where she was teaching at the time), she used the drone as a healing mechanism. For a full year she experimented with a single note on her accordion while developing *Sonic Meditations* — radical text compositions that gave instructions, or 'recipes' — as suited to the curious participant as the classically trained musician. She was adamant that none of her meditations required any kind of musical training whatsoever: they were, rather, about inclusivity and developing the inner ear.

One meditation — *Native* — reads:

Take a walk at night. Walk so silently that the bottom of your feet become ears.[21]

At the San Francisco Tape Music Center Oliveros created hours of brain-mashing electronics that navigated alien sonic territory. Many of them sound fresh today — pings, bleeps and reverb come from all angles, sound sources indeterminate, a palpable sense of glee at the lack of boundaries. Recent compilation *Four Electronic Pieces 1959–1964* included her very first tape piece, the twenty-minute epic 'Time Perspectives', a journey through discordance and disorientation. Oliveros was wildly inventive in this period. This was turbo-charged DIY — like Terry Riley, she experimented with new methods ceaselessly. She explained some of her methods in a lecture shortly before her death in 2016:

These [early pieces] were improvised sounds using found objects of various kinds and voice. For filters, I used cardboard tubes . . . I didn't do a lot of cutting and splicing of tape. I thought that was too labor intensive (*laughs*). I would improvise very long sections of the piece and then put them together as a continuity. This was a time where there were no mixers, so I had to use a patch bay to put sounds together . . .[22]

The drone was also central to much of Oliveros's work. She discussed the 'sensuality of sustained tone' with artists Aura Satz and Laurie Spiegel in the 2015 installation *Dial Tone Drone* — a piece that used the electronic dial tone of telephones as a starting point for a conversation.

Working with sustained tones allowed me to work inside a sound . . . You can put direct sensuality inside a note . . . A drone isn't ever really static; the changes that happen are within our perceptual mechanisms.[23]

Across a sprawling discography Oliveros explored the drone time and again with questing intent. If her early picks hinged on electronics and cranky lo-fi tinkering, her later records were organic, focusing on her beloved accordion, voice and the spaces between the two. Key junctions include her masterful *Accordion and Voice* (1978) and its follow-up *The Wonderer* LP (1984). Pieces like 'Horse Sings from Cloud' are forensic in detail and focus and belie her past electronic work: the precision of the overlapping tones builds to soaring epiphany, sonics so precise as to sound practically quantised, accordion drones providing a mesmeric sonic blanket over which her vocal improvisations soar.

Equally vital was *Deep Listening* (1989). Recorded with trombonist Stuart Dempster and vocalist Panaiotis (as the Deep Listening Band) it was an investigation into the Fort Worden cistern in Washington State — one of the most resonant spaces in the world. Boasting a reverberation time of forty-five seconds, Fort Worden is an immense decommissioned underground concrete reservoir that was once capable of holding 200 million gallons of water. *Deep Listening* used the incredible natural resonance of the cistern — an omnipresent rumble — for a series of imposing drone-based pieces, drawing on Oliveros's haunting accordion melodies and Dempster's sustained trombone. The instruments were tuned to just intonation — that is, natural pitch — to enable a seamless melding with the contours of the cistern. The result is a masterpiece of site-specific atmosphere, the stone reverb coming through on an alchemical level. As Oliveros put it in the sleeve notes to the record: 'The Cistern space, in effect, is an instrument being played simultaneously by all three composers.'[24]

Silver Apples of the Moon

While both Riley and Oliveros were interested in the spiritual aspects of sound, fellow Tape Center innovator Morton Subotnick was fascinated by the raw mechanics. For Subotnick — a classically trained musician — electronic music represented an opportunity to break with the past and forge new frontiers of sound, unencumbered by the weight of melodic expectation or formalised theory.

At eighty-six years of age, he still bristles with excitement at its limitless possibilities. What was the initial excitement of working with tape and electronic sound?

'When I started working with tape I had a strong sense that everything was going to be changing,' he says. 'My sense of it was that we were moving into a period where music would undergo the same change — socially, culturally — as what the printing press did for language. It would become something not just for the elite — a very small part of the population — but something that everybody could have. The technology would allow people to do it cheaply . . . I thought of it as the ground zero of music.'

Closely associated with electronic instrument designer Don Buchla, Subotnick produced most of his key works on the Buchla 100 modular synthesiser — a beautifully chaotic and unwieldy beast of a synth, originally commissioned by Subotnick and Ramon Sender at the Tape Center. Combining envelope generators, oscillators, filters, voltage-controlled amps and analogue sequencer modules, the Buchla 100 led to Subotnick's key late-1960s/early-1970s trio: *Silver Apples of the Moon* (1967), *The Wild Bull* (1968) and *Sidewinder* (1971).

Silver Apples of the Moon was an extraterrestrial tableau of bleeps, pings, drones and a tense, ever-building pulse. It's a stark listen: chilly, seemingly removed from any kind of lineage. If Riley was interested in the ghost in the machine, Subotnick was obsessed with the machine itself: he's loath to attribute any spiritual element to what he does, rather describing the process as one of constant invention, bewitched by possibilities. Subotnick brought the album to life in multimedia performances that married sound and visuals at the Electric Circus in New York — Andy Warhol's notoriously acid-fried disco. A bacchanalian feast that married circus performance, warped visuals, serious volume and chemical excess, the Electric Circus was the perfect venue for Subotnick's spooked sound.

'The technology should be offering you new vistas or sparks. I envisaged it as a performance piece 100 years in the future: it had lights and musicians and electronics, but it was a multimedia piece. I didn't know people were starting to take LSD and all this stuff! I was offering them this hallucinatory experience: it was a futuristic piece that was highly technological. I wanted to integrate the senses through technology. This was going to be new music based on a democratised world — not music that was based on what had evolved from the past 100,000 years. It was the beginnings of a music that wasn't dependent on you having played a musical instrument all your life. There's nothing wrong with that — I love doing it — but I sacrificed the clarinet by 1966 so I could immerse myself in this thing that I wanted to do. I wanted a piece that involved all the senses.

'I spent time with La Monte Young every time I went back to New York, although I had a very different background to Terry and La Monte,' he continues. 'My whole thing was quite different to what they were doing. I had a whole studio garage before the Tape Center and I was making one-or

two-minute pieces. I brought some of my one-minute pieces back when I
met with La Monte and we'd share what we were doing. I played him a few.
He said, "I'll play you a portion of what I'm working on." So he turns on
the loudspeakers and it sounds like they're completely broken, they're just
rattling and he didn't seem to notice. And I'm looking at my watch and
thirty minutes goes by, forty minutes and I said, "La Monte you were going
to show me a part," and he said, "It is a part" and I said, "Well, how long
is it?!" and he said, "Oh, the full piece is five weeks long" (*laughs*). We were
going in different directions.'

Pran Nath and the American Underground

Technology aside, the most enduring influence on the American drone axis
throughout the 1970s was that of master Hindustani vocalist Pran Nath.
From the late 1960s onwards myriad artists came under his tutelage. Some —
Terry Riley and La Monte Young and Marian Zazeela — became his disciples. Nath lived in a cave in Tapkeshwar, India during the 1930s. He spoke to
nobody. He practised his morning raga at dawn and his evening raga beneath
the stars. His voice — as strong as oak, as mesmeric as a spellbinding incantation — was palpably *ancient*, imbued with a stern mystic power. He stayed in
the cave for five years until his guru — Abdul Wahid Khan — ordered him
to renounce his ascetic life, and rejoin society to teach.

Nath was a hard-core devotee of the austere Kirana vocal tradition. Born
in Lahore in 1918, he left home at thirteen, travelled to India and studied
under vocal master Khan for many years, following a rigorous programme of
practice and solitary retreat — often for years at a time. This was the Gharana
system: guru and disciples living together in a disciplined environment, guru
bestowing traditional knowledge, disciples practising ceaselessly and serving
the guru in household tasks. It was a tough life. Disciples were duty bound to
follow instructions to the *letter*, be it a command to perform solitary retreat,
housework or to leave the Gharana altogether.

Khan became a prominent figure in the Kirana Gharana. Widely regarded as the most foreboding and uncompromising vocal tradition in the Indian
classical oeuvre, the Kirana style emphasised the perfection of individual notes
and the slowly unfurling introductory *alap* section of each raga, drawn out to a
crawl pace, each note introduced in a hypnotic, improvisatory fashion.

For Nath, a Hindu without family connections or money, to gain acceptance from Khan — a devout Muslim and master of his trade — was no easy

task. He had to work for eight years as his cook before gaining admittance to the Gharana proper and, once admitted to study, found himself in a rigorously, sometimes brutally disciplined environment. Khan wouldn't allow his students to practise within earshot. The young Nath would instead retreat to the jungle before dawn to practise for hours at a time. Later — on retreat in Tapkeshwar — he'd stand submerged up to the waist in a stream, the nearby waterfall taking the role of the traditional tanpura drone. During lessons, wrong notes were sometimes punished by beating.[25] Khan was wedded to music to an intense degree, and was notoriously lost in the hypnotic swirl of the raga. When giving performances he was sometimes known to stay on for up to twenty hours after a show had ended, eyes closed, still immersed in the raga.

For the young Nath, this was a serious apprenticeship. On leaving the Gharana, he joined All India Radio in 1937 as a resident singer. However, his rigorously traditional rendering of ragas proved no more suited to mainstream Indian tastes than Miles Davis's *Bitches Brew* or Ornette Coleman's *Science Fiction* would be to a smooth FM jazz station. He taught advanced classes in Hindustani music at Delhi University during the 1950s where he was known for his forensic knowledge of hundreds of individual ragas and his commitment to traditional vocal craft: resolutely uncommercial and uncompromising.

Nath entered the orbit of La Monte Young in the late sixties. Bewitched by the roughshod majesty of his *Earth Groove: Voice of Cosmic India* (1967) album — a raw recording of ragas 'Boophali' and 'Asavari', complete with throat clearing, coughs and plenty of background noise — Young invited him over to New York where he quickly became immersed in the avant-garde world, teaching numerous figures from the scene and setting up the New York Kirana Centre for Indian Classical Music in the city in 1972. Nath's influence on Young, Riley and Marian Zazeela during this period was incalculable. They were bewitched by his voice and presence, and became immersed in the discipline of his vocal teaching, practising ceaselessly.

More than mere influence, for the three of them this was a calling — a wholesale awakening — they became his disciples, devoting decades of study to Kirana vocal music, spending serious time in India and, eventually, teaching the music themselves, a practice all three continue to the present day. Indeed, go to the Dream House today and look to the back of the main room: you'll see a permanent shrine to Nath and Abdul Wahid Khan. Speaking to Terry Riley about his influence today, it's clear that Nath's voice exerted a primal alchemical pull.

'The quality of his voice is something that I'd never experienced before,' he explains. 'The velocity of it and the amazing melodic intention and the variation that he would use as he was expounding a raga. It really did reso-nate with me. When I heard what he was doing I realised there was a whole tradition that I wasn't aware of and needed to learn in order to advance my own improvisational skills. I studied with him for twenty-six years — from 1970 until his passing in 1996. I was with him a great deal for that time, both in India and the United States — he was living in my house for long periods of time, I lived in his house in India for a long time. We had a very close relationship . . . hardly any musicians in India let disciples train with them for that long, that much time. He was very kind in letting me listen to him practise at all hours of the day and night, and get exposed to the music in a very intimate way.'

Nath's voice was a remarkable instrument. His 1971 recording of *Ragas* ('Yaman Kaly' and 'Punjabi Berva') — featuring La Monte Young on tanpura (Nath pioneered his own specially built tanpura with an accentuated bass drone) — is imbued with an *ancient* bearing, the grain of his voice portentous and otherworldly, all offset against the eternal thrum of the tanpura. Listening to Nath is an exercise in extreme hypnosis; time doesn't stand still so much as warp around his voice, captured in an event horizon, surrounded by a granular audio density. While Ravi Shankar was a more user-friendly introduction to Indian classicism, the warp of the sitar offset against strong tabla rhythms, the raga played with clear moments of tension and release, Nath was a very different proposition. His music was as hard core as it got, and offered zero compromise to the Kirana vision. Either strap in and commit for the duration or leave it until you're ready (and don't even think about mentioning 'fusion'). It carried a sense of inevitability, like some distant meteor travelling through the freezing depths of space: it just *was*. His voice contained pain, struggle, the unbearable lightness of being. Listening to an hour of Nath is a serious cranial commitment. There is weight, beauty, oppressive portent — most of all, the feeling of a shadow just behind you.

His music — based on intense disciplined focus and microtonal repetition — was far removed from the lackadaisical hippy signifiers that personified many of the raga rock 'fusion' experiments of the sixties that we explored in the previous chapter. However, his influence on the avant-garde represented the *same* sea change that occurred in rock — the symbiosis of Indian music with a psychedelic awakening. Figures like Nath and Ali Akbar Khan, whose *Music of India* (1956) is repeatedly name-checked — offered the same kind of primal inspiration to the underground as Ravi Shankar did to the rock mainstream, as Terry Riley explained.

'During the sixties we had Ali Akbar Khan coming to America from a very deep Indian tradition — a very old tradition — and Ravi Shankar, of course. And Ravi, in my view, connected more with his virtuosity and showmanship. Ali Akbar Khan brought the deeper, older India to his performances. And this was all happening while musicians in the West were starting to search for new ways to approach music, too. Not all musicians, but a lot of them were attracted to this. So, it's like an opening up in time. You don't know why these things happen but they all simultaneously come together. It was a time for the Western world to be awakened to something that had been in the East for millennia.'

Nath's assimilation into the New York underground — as teacher and guru — represented a crossroads. An entire generation of underground musicians came into his orbit. The drone, honed to mathematical exactitude by La Monte Young, to the whirling spectral dance of Terry Riley, was set into motion yet again by Nath's presence. Aside from Young, Riley and Zazeela, pivotal figures like Henry Flynt, Charlemagne Palestine, Rhys Chatham and Christine Helix all undertook tuition with Pandit Pran Nath. For a full, depth-charge session check La Monte Young and Marian Zazeela's *The Tanpuras of Pandit Pran Nath* (1982), which showcases the (specially built) Nath-style tanpura, which resonated with an extra-deep bass drone: it's a thrumming, mesmeric wall of sound. It's strange to think of early 1970s New York — with its grime, Vietnam vets and homeless prophets; the peepshows, burnt-out tenements and tense, humid nights; its ceaseless energy — reverberating to his voice. But for a fair chunk of the underground, it provided an anchor amid the madness.

For others, though, it was the neurotic buzz of the city itself — it's dankest, darkest corners — that provided the ultimate muse.

Chapter 5

DO THE OSTRICH

If the avant-garde world that Young, Riley et al. inhabited was seriously underground, their ideas nonetheless changed the rock 'n' roll landscape for ever. The drone ran through the Velvet Underground like a black vein. Just as La Monte Young had stood listening to power transformers in rural Idaho, the Velvets' drone was also electric: theirs, however, was that of the bare light bulb flickering in a dilapidated Alphabet City apartment, NYPD helicopter buzzing low outside. Aligned to the hinterland of narcotic psychosis, the music they made was enveloping and — in its own peculiar way — psychedelic, albeit far removed from the winsome hippy definition: no shared 'togetherness' here, other than the spoon — 'Venus in Furs', 'Heroin', 'Waiting for the Man', 'Sister Ray' — this was New York made (rotten) flesh, underpinned by the scratchy sense of physical neediness and mental detachment that makes up the headspace of severe opioid abuse; the negatively charged, nihilistic underbelly of the city.

The Velvets weren't interested in hippy idealism or blues-based 'authenticity'. John Cale hated folk music. Their sound was hazy, submerged. The first record they put out was a thorny statement of intent. An experiment in feedback recorded by Cale in 1964 — a locked groove, essentially — it was called 'Loop' and given away on the cover of experimental magazine *Aspen*, answering a question Andy Warhol had once asked Lou Reed: 'Why does the record ever have to end?'[1]

Well, now it didn't.

Like the minimalists before them, the Velvets favoured raw texture above technical proficiency. The drone ley line that ran through the New York avant-garde was mainlined directly to the Velvets, of course, via John Cale and original drummer Angus MacLise who had, as we've seen, already spent two solid years holding down single chords with La Monte Young in the Theatre of

Eternal Music. The Velvets therefore represented the perfect synergy between bleakly romantic rock 'n' roll rebellion and avant-garde experimentation.

Lou Reed — born in 1942 — was from suburban Long Island and obsessed with rock 'n' roll from the start. His parents didn't understand it at all. His father, an accountant, sent him for therapy aged eighteen. It was more than a sit-down counselling session, though: like the Ramones, we're talking shock treatment: 'I didn't have the bad ones where they don't put you to sleep first,' he later recounted. 'I had the fun ones where they put you to sleep first. You count backwards and then you're out. It was shocking, but that's when I was getting interested in electricity anyway.'[2]

At Syracuse University, Reed was close to Beat poet Delmore Schwartz and future Velvets guitarist Sterling Morrison. Schwartz lived a life straight out of one of Reed's lyrics: a street prophet, raconteur, poet and paranoid hedonist. He once told Reed that if he ever sold out, and if there was a 'heaven from which you can be haunted, I'll haunt you.'

By early 1964, Reed was working as a jobbing musician for a Long Island imprint called Pickwick Records, bussing in every morning and recording godawful schlock before leaving, exhausted and demoralised. Essentially a one-stop shop, Pickwick constituted a warehouse, rudimentary recording studio and distribution company. They specialised in novelty rip-offs. The label would make cheap records that were sold on a radio 'name' of the time, only to include one original song by the artist, filling in the remainder with cover versions recorded cheaply by the Pickwick in-house team. It was a dismal affair.

But while Pickwick represented an often unreported nadir in an otherwise critically storied, trailblazing creative life, it served the purpose of gaining the young Reed his *chops*. The Pickwick period also fits neatly — with its sleazy old record industry execs, warehouse setting, sling 'em down and turn 'em out approach — to Reed's endless obsession with the gritty underbelly of New York. This was the pulp fiction branch of songwriting. A few years ago I wrote a feature on the New English Library — the cult London pulp publisher made (in)famous by Richard Allen's lecherously grotesque *Skinhead* series. The following quote, from editor and publisher Mark Howell, seems apposite here.

That damn delivery schedule was the most driving force I've ever met in publishing. You just had to get it out there — it was break-neck, insane. I started a series called 'Deathlands', and the first writer I gave it to had done a wonderful first story and was given the green light — and spent his entire advance on heroin, which, back in those days, was not unknown. It was crippling for some, but most of our writers were addicts of the typewriter, and one of the glories of this was that it was a conveyer belt — we thoroughly addicted our readers.[3]

So it was with Reed at Pickwick. The pace was relentless. Speed was king. Songs were recorded as they were written. Four songwriters sat in a room churning out songs like short-order cooks. Reed once explained that the studio would ask for 'ten California songs, ten Detroit songs' then the assembled team would decamp to the studio where they'd have to cut three or four albums at the gallop.[4]

While most of the records produced by the studio were eminently forgettable, they afforded the young Reed the chance to get to know his way around a studio and, occasionally, work on his own songs. In 1964 he'd been working on a strange one-string tuning that he dubbed the 'Ostrich'. Writing and recording 'The Ostrich' in 1964, Reed had an eye on the teenage novelty dance craze market, as did the (no doubt Brylcreemed and polyester suited) Pickwick executives. Sending the record around to various radio and television stations, the label got a call from a station eager to film the band. The trouble was that there *was* no band, not in any sense that a radio station would understand — just Reed and a few session musicians. This was soon to change, however.

Having met John Cale and Tony Conrad at a party, Pickwick executive Terry Phillips invited them to the studio to rehearse with Reed the next day. The pair — as bohemian as it got and both recently exiled from the Theatre of Eternal Music — were completely at odds with the seedy cut and thrust of the bargain basement end of the music industry. They were offered the gig although it was not, artistically speaking, of any serious interest. On assembling at the studio the following morning, however, both were floored to hear Reed explain that they wouldn't need to spend much time learning the song as it was all, much like the drone of the Theatre, tuned to a single string. 'The Ostrich' was a strange record: a caveman stomp featuring a rough-voiced Reed bellowing 'dance' instructions — 'everybody get down on your basement!' — while a down-tuned garage racket clattered around him.

It was noisy, abrasive, derivative. The tuning, however — alongside Reed's bull-headed, sardonic presence — was enough to gain John Cale's interest. Like Tony Conrad, he'd grown increasingly disillusioned with La Monte Young and found himself at a loose end in a city of boundless possibility. Offered the opportunity by Pickwick to tour East Coast schools, radio stations and clubs under the banner of 'The Primitives', Cale and Conrad got in the van. The band spent a miserable few weeks trudging their cranky novelty song around to resounding apathy. Two weeks later, that was that. Reed — disillusioned with the crummy grind — left the band and returned to Pickwick while Cale and Conrad returned to the dilapidated Lower East Side.

The Primitives' record and tour was disillusioning, a faintly ludicrous situation for all involved. It did, however, serve to pique Reed and Cale's curiosity about each other's respective musical worlds. Reed knew nothing of the avant-garde scene Cale was steeped in; Cale didn't have a rock 'n' roll bone in his body. The pair stayed in touch, Reed becoming a frequent visitor to the squalid Ludlow Street apartment Cale shared with Conrad and, eventually, moving in when Tony Conrad moved out. It was a *Withnail and I*-esque scene of bohemian austerity: no heat or running water, a rotating cast of addicts and starving artists dropping in and out, wooden pallets smashed and burnt for heat, everyone surviving on festering pots of porridge that would sit on the stove for days on end.

Also at Ludlow Street was one of Reed's old university friends — Sterling Morrison — and Angus MacLise, the rambling mystic drummer who published esoteric poetry and mainlined meth amphetamine. MacLise and Cale were still playing, intermittently, while Reed was hanging on at Pickwick — albeit falling more heavily under the hazy influence of the Lower East Side street scene that surrounded him.

Ludlow Street was a far cry from any hippy scene. The area was gravely dilapidated and attracted a flotsam of artists and drifters who had been priced out of safer, folksier Greenwich Village. This was a tough, individual, street-smart scene. The drugs were hard: speed and smack. The New York climate — humid skin-crawl summers and cataclysmically freezing winters — equally so. The street life that surrounded him famously became Reed's muse; inspiration was everywhere, in every dilapidated tenement that hummed with a malevolence straight out of a Hubert Selby Jr. novel.

It was a bewitching scene charged with the kind of jittery energy that could flip at any moment. For the young Reed — suburban, completely misunderstood by his uber-square parents — NYC was *everything*. His studiously cultivated image of savvy, sardonic street prince, king of the pithy putdown, black book of nefarious contacts ever at the ready, was primed here. It was a complete invention, of course, but New York facilitated rebirth like nowhere else. He and Cale dabbled in smack, although speed was king; everyone staying up for days on end, grinding out whatever they happened to be working on — painting, poem or song — while taking frequent blasts of pharmaceutical-grade amphetamine.

In the dank Ludlow Street apartment, the Velvets — initially called 'The Warlocks' — began to take shambolic shape. Angus MacLise on drums; Sterling Morrison on guitar; Reed singing and Cale scraping his deathly, dronal viola over the top like a pneumonic vulture. 'The blues' was out. Good time rock 'n' roll was also out. Folk music was out. A Stalinist year zero was imposed on any form of rootsy nostalgia. Just as James Brown had docked the pay of band members skipping beats, the nascent Velvets — at Reed's behest — imposed a fine system on anyone found noodling the blues. He and MacLise worked up an essay which, in fine amphetamine-fried overdriven Beat prose, set out their unique stall and ongoing obsessions: death, sex, drugs, darkness.

Western music is based on death, sex, violence and the pursuit of progress. The root of universal music is sex. Western music is as violent as western sex. Our band is the western equivalent to the cosmic dance of Shiva. Playing as Babylon goes up in flames.[5]

The seismic influence of Angus MacLise, though he never recorded with the band, should in no way be underestimated here. MacLise was a chaotic operator. Both he and Cale were locked into the drone, completely outside the rock 'n' roll sphere. Crucially, MacLise was a drummer for whom the concept of *time* was absolutely fluid. Indeed, the reason he left the band was because he couldn't understand that being booked for a gig meant showing up on, well, time. On hearing the schedule for a gig in Summit High School in New Jersey in 1965, MacLise reportedly exclaimed: 'You mean we have to start when they tell us to and we have to end when they tell us to? I can't work that way.'[6]

The Velvets were propelled by musical tension from the start, not least between Reed and Cale. Lou Reed was schooled in rock 'n' roll and folk. Early versions of 'Waiting for the Man' are imbued with a Dylanesque twang all elongated nasal delivery and acoustic shamble. Cale, by contrast, *loathed* folk music. His viola drone buzzed over the mix like a bare light bulb. If the Theatre of Eternal Music was about sitting amid the sound, shutting out the city, creating an autonomous audio zone in which to swaddle yourself, the drone of the Velvets was a *refraction* of the city. Far beyond muse, NYC might as well have been the fifth member. The electrified scratch of Cale's viola was thus a caustic echo of the streets; sickly, haunted, unlike

145

anything else of the time. It evoked cramped stress, humidity, the 'sick, venal' New York immortalised in *Taxi Driver* some years later.

'Venus in Furs' was the first fully formed song. Tony Conrad had named the band through happenstance after finding a copy of a lurid pulp novel of the same name on the street in the Bowery and bringing it to Ludlow Street. The cover featured a leather boot, whip and cat mask. The band had a name, the song referencing the S and M imagery on the cover, the famed 'shiny, shiny boots of leather'. A funereal death tramp that hinged on the elongated crow of Cale's viola and a clinking cymbal keeping time, it was sheer *doom*: high camp imagery offset against a disquieting aural death toll. As statements of intent go, it couldn't have been more visceral, the lifting of a moth-bitten curtain to reveal some sickly house band.

This was *speed* music rather than smack, however. While the Velvets are associated in the collective subconscious with a negative opiated vibe they ran — like so many involved in the New York underground — on speed; theirs, however, was the sound of the *third day* awake. Speed is often woefully misconstrued by those who have not experienced it first-hand. While the initial buzz is, indeed, characterised by a burst of intense energy and euphoria, by the second day that's gone, to be replaced by a gritty — and, in its own unpleasant way, deeply psychedelic bent. Unlike other stimulants such as cocaine or ecstasy, sleep is simply impossible on speed. This creates a palpable shift in reality: a strange waking dream state, bursts of energy tempered by jittery melancholy or clammy dread. Deprived of sleep the brain shifts into a gear whereby internal dream imagery is assimilated into waking reality — not (generally) via intense visual hallucinations, but a more insidious gear shift: familiar surroundings take on a surreal sickliness, certain sounds are distorted or amplified, repetitive tasks performed compulsively.

The speed experience — chilly, individual, accentuating the weird, grim edges of the everyday — ran contrary to the countercultural obsession with LSD and its bendy, warped warmth. Speed was egalitarian, industrial, functional. As Lemmy once had it, it 'got you there on time'. Nowhere in the world was this more apparent than at the Factory, the fifth-floor studio at 231 East Forty-seventh Street run by Andy Warhol. A parallel universe inhabited by a glamorous, frequently deranged, coterie of androgynous artists, actors, film-makers and bohemian drifters of all stripes, the Factory was a twenty-four-hour happening orchestrated by the whippet-thin Warhol.

It was an assembly line, a space of ceaseless amphetamine-fuelled activity. The Warhol prints were produced as if on a Detroit conveyor belt — churned out by a speed-blitzed team who had the detail down pat. The space also functioned as a studio. Warhol churned out hundreds of experimental films, many of which involved a cast gleaned from those who spent time in the Factory — his 'Factory Superstars'. Using a 16mm Bolex camera, from 1963 Warhol set to work in typically frenetic fashion although his experimental films riffed on similar ideas of static and inertia being explored by the minimalists elsewhere in Manhattan at the same time. New York City, both its transient nighthawk population and its uniquely feral urban atmosphere, provided his palette, and the same amphetamine-fuelled energy and commitment to repetitive tasks that personified his printmaking (he'd finished his iconic Campbell's Soup can series the year before) was applied to film-making. Like Tony Conrad, the *grain* of the image often took precedence over any linear narrative.

In *Sleep* (1963), for example, he filmed the poet John Giorno sleeping naked for five hours. *Empire* (1964) was eight hours of the Empire State Building shot through the late afternoon gloom. His screen test series involved a sitting cast of whoever happened to be passing through the Factory, seated and instructed to neither speak nor blink. Inspired by police mugshots, there were no introductions or speech and the subject was shot from the neck up. It provided an interesting juxtaposition: famous figures who passed through — Salvador Dalí, Bob Dylan, Susan Sontag, Donovan — alongside the regular Factory faces.

Everybody who came through the door had their fifteen minutes. The 'Warhol Superstars' — the razor tonged crew of artists and bohemian faces who featured in his films, helped make the prints and instigated the endless parties were the (icy) soul of the place, however, and it was through a Factory superstar — the actor Gerard Malanga — that Warhol connected with the Velvet Underground for the first time. In January 1966, Malanga had gone to the Café Bizarre for an early gig where he'd donned black leather and performed a dance to 'Venus in Furs' while wielding a giant bullwhip. The band looked half starved. Lou Reed was implacable, coiled, stripped of fat, hooded black eyes; John Cale gangling and vampiric; drummer Moe Tucker (who had, by this stage, replaced the increasingly unreliable Angus MacLise) elfin and androgynous, Sterling Morrison standing at the back, impassive amid the lights. The next night Malanga took Warhol to see them. He loved them. Here were a band who embodied *his* New York — the New York of the Factory — a place of street-level mythology and (re)invention. The Velvets offered a gritty elevation of what was happening when you stepped out of the door, albeit imbued with dark pulp romance.

There was a Svengali aspect to Andy Warhol. The Factory was every bit the bohemian court, Warhol the medieval king surrounded by his courtiers, jesters, sycophants, tumblers and trusted advisors. To Warhol, however, the Velvets represented not only a wildly different take on rock 'n' roll, but a commercial opportunity. Factory regular, the film-maker Paul Morrissey, explained in an interview the idea was that 'Andy could make money not only from underground films but from putting the movies in some sort of rock 'n' roll context. Discovering the Velvets, bringing them up to the Factory and working with them was done for purely commercial reasons.'[7]

For somebody so tuned into the twisted world of fame and artifice, however, the star factor was missing. Lou Reed — short, rambunctious, scowling — was fascinating. But he wasn't *magnetic*. Warhol offered to manage them, but only on the proviso that they put Nico in the band. A formidable presence — tall, blonde, German — Nico was an actress who'd shown up at the Factory just a week previously. For a band fuelled by tension and amphetamines, the uniquely febrile atmosphere of the Factory felt like home. Here, surrounded by the equally chemically unbalanced flotsam of the arts scene, the Velvets could rehearse, get high and argue to their hearts' content.

The relationship with Warhol was complex. He wasn't a manager in any meaningful sense of the word, more loose artistic 'advisor' and — crucially — occasional benefactor. He bought new amps and guitars and set about fusing the band's nihilistic sound to his static films, instigating the infamous travelling 'happening' — the Exploding Plastic Inevitable — which acted as a New York-centric precursor to the acid-drenched happenings that were, as of mid 1966, yet to start occurring regularly over on the West Coast. It's something of an irony that Warhol and the Velvets — with their chilly demeanour, sharp clothes, love of speed rather than acid and disavowal of hippy guff — should have got there first. And, in typically bombastic Warhol fashion, it was Hollywood, rather than Manhattan, that was the first port of call. A full page advertisement in *Beat* magazine caught the vibe:

A Happening! What is it? It's Andy Warhol, it's The Plastic Inevitable, it's the Velvet Underground, it's Nico, it's a pair of dancers, a candle, two whips, a candy bar, a violin, a pop bottle and movies. It's from New York and it's on the West Coast for the first time at the trip in Hollywood. It's going to other parts of the nation soon. It's drawing crowds of curious celebrities and it's confusing crowds of the curious. It's happening. No questions allowed.[8]

Was The Exploding Plastic Inevitable a psychedelic experience? Absolutely. Was it a hippy vibe? Absolutely not. It had far more in common with the 'drone state of mind' espoused by La Monte Young — albeit amped to 11 — than some lysergic, isle of the lotus-eaters mind palace for the beautiful people to immerse themselves in. It was a descent into sensorial oblivion, presided over by the twitching Warhol, a wild show where the Velvets played at extreme volume, backs to the audience, feedback droning while Warhol projected movies like *Blow Job*, *Sleep* and *Eat* onto the backdrop. In essence a before-the-fact multimedia experience, the Exploding Plastic Inevitable utilised five film projectors, mirror balls, lights, interpretative dance from various 'Warhol superstars', a set from the Velvets and incessant strobes. Most of the attendees were on speed, acid, Quaaludes or a combination of all three.

The show proved troublesome, however. It was expensive to keep on the road. Many disliked the barrage and reviews of the time point to a confused reception. Those expecting hippy vibes were shocked, none more than notorious West Coast promoter-impresario Bill Graham who put them on at the Fillmore East in San Francisco where he was disgusted by the whole vibe. Graham was wound up by Paul Morrison who had cornered him and delivered a gibbering sermon on the joys of smack while dropping tangerine peel all over the floor. Graham snapped and started screaming a diatribe worthy of some deranged Midwestern sheriff from the conference at the end of *Fear and Loathing in Las Vegas*: 'You disgusting germs from New York! Here we are, trying to clean up everything, and you come out here with your disgusting minds and *whips!*'[9]

If the sixties psychedelic explosion was kaleidoscopic — an auditory attempt to capture the synaptic explosion of the acid experience — the Velvets were monocular. All the queasy undercurrents of psychic excess were laid bare. Four days awake, no food, dive bars, tramping the cold streets of the Lower East Side in pursuit of chemicals: it was channelled unflinchingly. What they were doing was diametrically opposed to the West Coast scene. If the psychedelic experience was an exercise in amplified sonic *ascent*, the acid experience given cosmic flight by the drone of the sitar and all manner of discordant musical trickery, the Velvets were concerned with *descent*, reduction — not of an experience too cranially complex to musically encapsulate — but of a city. New York's shadowlands were reduced like a sticky red-wine jus. Reed, in particular, loathed the West Coast vibes.

We had vast objections to the whole San Francisco scene. It's just tedious, a lie and untalented . . . you know, people like Jefferson Airplane, Grateful Dead are just the most untalented bores who ever came up . . . it's a joke! The kids are being hyped.[10]

By 1966, Warhol was keen to put something down on tape. A former Columbia Records executive called Norman Dolph put up $2,500 for three days' studio time. The band cut *The Velvet Underground and Nico* in a day. The drone defined the record: it was there in Reed's notorious 'ostrich tuning', the imposing Teutonic contralto of Nico, the hexed scrape of Cale's viola and the overriding hiss and buzz of the lo-fi production. Norman Dolph was not an experienced producer. Cale and Reed did most of the work without the input of an engineer. This is important. *The Velvet Underground and Nico* sounds street-level *nasty*. Indeed, Andy Warhol was famously credited as producer but his studio input was zero: he was more akin an enthusiastic cheerleader.

The Velvet Underground and Nico is defined by a gnawing discombobulation. Bleaker dronal elements are deployed between straighter, more harmonious songs. The record opens with the twinkling winsome melody of 'Sunday Morning' — Reed's thin vocals evoking the waking of a city when you've been up all night. It makes the jarring chug of 'I'm Waiting for the Man' all the more abrasive. The action moves to Harlem, Reed feeling more 'dead than alive' as he stands with his 'twenty-six dollars' in hand on the corner of Lexington 125. The feeling of stark need is accentuated by the droning two-chord chug of Sterling Morrison's guitar, Reed framing himself in the crosshairs of a habit. However, the genius is that it captures the *excitement* of buying drugs; the bloodhound thrill of the chase which is, in many ways, as potent and enjoyable as the end product, a ritual game with an erotic frisson of danger. There is an element of puckish *fun* at play. This isn't the sound of deathly endgame addiction, rather the adrenal rush of desire soon to be satisfied. The dronal chug doesn't let up, two chords — DGDGDGDGDGDGDGDG — on it goes, the heartbeat of anticipation.

Indeed, the Velvets' beat was unique. Moe Tucker was a fiercely idiosyncratic drummer, every bit as vital a cog as Cale and Reed. She held a mallet in her right hand, stick in the left, the bass drum mounted sideways. Tucker stood while playing and hardly ever struck a cymbal. Her beat — or, in drummer parlance, her 'pocket' — was a trance-inducing sub-aquatic thud that matched the austerity of the songs. Listen to the 4/4 on 'Waiting for the Man' — low down in the mix, matching the ceaseless thrum of Morrison and Reed's scratchy rhythm. It was also Tucker who told Reed to only play the down stroke on the song, resulting in that ceaseless cat-scratch vibe. She was a true minimalist, eschewing egotistical flash (her style was completely at odds with that of her predecessor Angus MacLise, who had a folksier style involving bongos and fills).

Tucker's chops acted as pneumatic anchor on songs like 'Heroin' and, in particular, 'European Son'. The latter was sheer searing noise, a tribute to Reed's friend and mentor Delmore Schwartz, who had died a few months previous to recording. Starting with a chicken-scratch garage chug before descending into a wall of noise, it represented a brilliant mind in turmoil. 'The Black Angel's Death Song' was equally abrasive. Never had Cale's viola sounded so caustically twisted. Three minutes of viola squall while Reed recounts a ghostly tale of cruel twists of fate. Although Cale may have loathed folk music, this was dissonant folk music par excellence.

The Velvets parted ways with Warhol and Nico in the spring of 1967. Their next album was, for many, their definitive statement. *White Light/White Heat* removed most of the moments of respite in favour of a heat-seeking howl. Overdriven, obtuse, raging — often ears-shreddingly atonal — *White Light/White Heat* was post-punk before punk. A visceral reaction to both the summer of love and a band experiencing serious personal friction — not least between John Cale and Lou Reed — Cale described it as a record defined by 'anti beauty'. A direct line can also be drawn from Cale's noise experiments — 'Sun Blindness Music' and the like — and *White Light/White Heat*: it's very much Cale's record.

The title track was a straight-up, Bo Diddley-style garage rocker extolling the virtues of meth amphetamine. The fuzz is amped to oblivion (the result of a sponsorship deal from Vox Guitars which led to Reed using multiple fuzz boxes while boosting the mid range on his amp[11]), the whole mix subsumed by hiss and dirt. Tucker's thud is omnipresent but somewhere far in the middle distance, Cale's bass near inaudible, the song disintegrating into shards of noise and feedback towards the end. 'The Gift' took its lyric from one of Reed's short stories, John Cale recounting the tale of one 'Waldo Jeffers' — who mails himself in the post to his lover only to be sliced to ribbons on opening. 'I Heard Her Call My Name' was a cranky garage thrasher that belted along on Tucker's primitive thwack while Reed dives in on one of the most atonal, squalling guitar solos he ever put on tape. Reportedly a tribute to free jazz sax master Ornette Coleman, it resulted in a blazing row between Cale and Reed due to the fact that Reed — unbeknownst, and much to the chagrin to the others — went down to the studio and cranked up his tracks on the mixing desk.

Most vital was 'Sister Ray'. The ultimate expression of what the Velvets represented — oddball pulp fiction, discordant noise, dronal undertow, laconic street smarts — it was a seventeen-minute gutter trawl. Reed recounted a story of a group of smack-dealing drag queens who take a bunch of sailors home for an orgy and who — right in the midst of 'searching for my mainline' and 'sucking on the ding dong' — are interrupted by police. Cale augments the sleazy tale with a jaunty backing of Vox Continental organ while Morrison and Reed weave a two-chord riff.

The first half of the song carries a demented, chicken-scratch energy — a primitive Hasil Adkins-style rockabilly vibe — but the mania steadily builds and builds: by the ten-minute breakdown, which leaves just Cale's organ and Tucker's unrelenting snare, you can practically smell the room, the acrid amphetamine sweat, hot overdriven amps and stale cigarette reek. It's an overwhelming rock 'n' roll spirit: the audio equivalent of Austin Osman Spare's automatic writing or painting, the hidden hand of chance guiding the band.

The band made a pact before recording that whatever happened during the session would stay, warts and all. As the song builds, Morrison's guitar lead becomes increasingly atonal while Reed's gurning rhythm strokes become ever more erratic. Cale drones a single nightmarish note on the organ and even Tucker — austere, steadfast Tucker — begins to deviate from her trademark opioid thud with fills (practically unheard of from Moe Tucker) and, even, cymbals. It's a loose-limbed freak-out. The tape hiss and overdriven white noise provides a surrogate bass element (there was no bass guitar on the song). albeit a muffled and toppy one, while the move towards climactic epiphany — a speedy chugging sprint — signals the end of the party, the sailors turfed out to the cruel morning on shore leave, the drag queens calling for a last-minute bail bond. Reed recounted the song's chaotic genesis in a 1994 interview:

> They asked us what we were going to do. We said, 'We're going to start' . . . They asked us when it ends. We didn't know . . . if 'Sister Ray' is not an example of heavy metal, then nothing is.[12]

It was, to all intents and purposes, the beginning of the end for the Velvets. Such intensity was hard to follow. Cale and Reed's relationship was at breaking point. Cale wanted to continue the maelstrom. Reed wanted to sell some records. Like their debut, *White Light/White Heat* had stalled commercially. It was pretty much banned on the radio due to its supposedly 'obscene' lyrics and obtuse, noisy vibe. A cursory look at the big records released in 1968: the Rolling Stones' *Beggars Banquet*; the Beatles' White Album; Van Morrison's *Astral Weeks*; the Kinks' *Village Green Preservation Society* — reveal not so much gap, as chasm between the Velvets and almost everybody else. The band lumbered on without Cale, releasing the middling *The Velvet Underground* in 1969. A markedly more commercial venture than anything the band had released, it was a pedestrian affair in comparison. They remained a dynamic live unit without Cale, however, as borne out by their incendiary *1969: Live* LP. However, 1970's *Loaded* was equally uninspiring, trading on lumpen workaday rock (the title was related to the fact that MGM had told Reed that they wanted the band to deliver a record that was 'loaded with hits' — they didn't) and lacked Moe Tucker, whose absence was felt every bit as strongly as Cale's: her no-frills drumming was a vital audio hallmark.

Ultimately, the key dynamic for the Velvets was the tension between Reed and Cale. Cale's drone, while grindingly obtuse, was an anchor. Removed, the ship ended up smashed on algae-encrusted rocks.

While late-period Velvets were traversing increasingly conventional territory, Nico — with John Cale producing — was channelling magical and mysterious realms. On parting ways with the Velvets she'd made a record — *Chelsea Girl* (1967) — which, mainly due to an overly busy production by Tom Wilson, left her unhappy. She was disillusioned, too, with the bullshit that surrounded the Warhol scene — the sour, posey artifice that inevitably came with spending too much time hanging around the Factory. Her next album *The Marble Index* (1968) was, therefore, a line in the sand, a serious statement of artistic intent.

Produced by Cale, it was a deathly masterpiece that hung on her trademark harmonium drone — she played a portable, Indian-style hand-operated version — and stark, foreboding arrangements. There was a gothic hymnal aspect to her voice that was completely unmistakable, too often underestimated. While frequently described simply with adjectives like 'icy' or 'Teutonic' it was, in fact, a malleable, deeply expressive instrument. While slightly off-key and staid on the first Velvets record, here she harnessed the majesty and tragedy of Mittel Europe, condensed it to a sonic essence: it was like taking a solitary walk through the Black Forest at dusk, haunted by flashes of past lives and the foreboding shadow of future horrors. There was a sense of portent — of happenstance — whenever Nico sang. On *The Marble Index*, her intonation was precise, she'd undulate the volume within a single line of a lyric, vibrato ending her phrasing. Though some dwell on the sense of sadness she evoked, the feeling of *inevitability*, of acceptance in the face of life's cruel twists of fate, was stronger. There was a fierceness in her delivery: a stern oracle vibe.

If she was typecast in the Velvets — the eponymous 'Femme Fatale' of legend — any vestige of the Warhollian celluloid character was gone by the time she made *The Marble Index*. Indeed, given the majesty of what she produced afterwards it seems ludicrous — cruel, in fact — that she should be forever associated with three songs recorded on that album. Because *The Marble Index* is imbued with the otherworldly atmosphere of a disquieting lucid dream. It evokes a similar bodement later conjured by Neil Jordan in his dark gothic fantasy *The Company of Wolves* — some opulent fantasy that shimmers with eerie luminescence, an ever-present sense of dread.

A childlike glockenspiel melody opens the 'Prelude', leading straight into the harmonium drone of 'Lawns of Dawn' — all sinister hall of mirrors carnival atmospherics, Nico singing of the morning 'filling my nights with fear'. The sparse string arrangement of 'No One Is There' continues the sinister vibe, Nico singing of a 'demon, dancing'. Album closer 'Evening of Light' is *pure* doom — a creepy, sepulchral rumination on the journey's end: 'Dungeon's sinking to a slumber at the end of time'. Her use of harmonium — a pedal-operated reed organ used in Sikh and Hindu devotional music (Nico used a portable version) — throughout *The Marble Index* was equally idiosyncratic. In Nico's untrained hands it became an abyssal drone, an unceasing carnival churn. Rather than Western chord progressions, she developed a modal style that carried an ancient bearing — both Ornette Coleman and Terry Riley were influences on her vibe.

'Ornette Coleman said that it would sound like a saxophone if I played inversed. Because I didn't know how to play at all! I used to improvise with the Velvet Underground, but without knowing music. I took Terry Riley as my example. That repetitive way of playing, I think that's a good way . . . Just chords are boring.'[13]

1970's *Desertshore* was Nico's most mystical record. Channelling neoclassical elements — her harmonium again dominates the mix — alongside an ascetic, near monastic, sensibility, it opens with her greatest vocal performance. 'Janitor of Lunacy' is a hymnal to deathly forces, a mind in turmoil (the lyric is about Brian Jones and his mental descent). It's a chilling song, her harmonium droning *way* up in the mix, world-weary vocal conveying certain doom.

'My Only Child' features Cale harmonising with Nico, while Nico's son Ari (then five years old) sings the haunting 'Le Petit Chevalier'. She sings in her native German on 'Abschied', another paean to the passage of death ('his body does not move'), Cale accompanying with mournful viola scrapes. As statements of intent go, *Desertshore* is the complete, concise, picture: it fixes you in a stark white glare and doesn't let the tension drop for a moment. Finishing with the Iberian-inflected (check those opening horns) 'All That Is My Own', *Desertshore* stays with you long after playing, in a way that few records do.

Despite her genius, Nico was broadly disregarded by the mainstream rock press during her lifetime. Reading interviews with her from the early 1970s is a deeply depressing exercise. Hardly any writers mention her music in any meaningful sense — if they do, it is in a mocking, condescending tone focusing instead on her 'cheekbones' and drug use. Invariably described as a 'chanteuse' she is painted as nothing more than an appendage to the Velvets' story, as opposed to an artist with a discography that was every bit as compelling as the band she was associated with for a scant two years.

The latter half of her life was indeed difficult. She spent the 1970s and most of the 1980s — until her death in 1988 — addicted to heroin. She spent much of the 1980s living, somewhat incongruously, in Manchester. She liked the atmosphere, the faded grandeur of the city's industrial past, the Prestwich pubs where she could play pool, score smack and remain anonymous.

A friend from the time, Nigel Bagley, recalled interesting scenes in an interview with the *Guardian* about her Manchester days:

> She didn't really socialise with the Manchester glitterati or hang out in clubs . . . She once asked me round for dinner, and there was this bizarre scene of Nico cooking couscous with one hand and cooking up heroin with the other. I was thinking, 'I hope she doesn't mix them up'. . . I once asked her why she took heroin, she said: 'Well, if I was a drunk I'd be fat.'

Although life in Manchester could be hard, Nico kept working throughout the 1980s. Undertaking notoriously gruelling world tours in a cramped van with a revolving entourage that sometimes included her son Ari, himself a heroin addict (she had introduced him), alongside her band and manager, her later albums included the excellent *Drama of Exile*, which saw her explore synth-infused post-punk territory. She died in 1988 after a bike accident in Ibiza.

Nico created arguably the most compelling body of work to emerge from the entire Velvets scene, and that includes the Velvets themselves. Her music stands alone in the space-time continuum: an eternal long dark night of the soul. Indeed, Wordsworth's poem *The Prelude* — from which *The Marble Index* took its title — serves as a fitting epitaph: 'The marble index of a mind for ever voyaging through strange seas of thought, alone.'

After the Velvets finally split in 1973, and after launching his storied solo career, Lou Reed did an about-turn and looked back to John Cale's interrogation of extreme drones and noise for inspiration. Despite the shocked critical reception at the time, and the painting of the album as revolutionary since, there was nothing remotely original about *Metal Machine Music* (1975) — it was karaoke Cale, a direct result of the influence of the Theatre of Eternal Music. There were no vocals, riffs or drums — just sixty-five minutes of screaming sound, a numbing cacophony of strip-light noise created by layering and looping guitar feedback. Rumour surrounded the record — that it was a joke; a revenge fantasy cooked up by Reed in order to free himself from his RCA contract; that it could trigger epilepsy.

In reality, it was none of those things. As Reed stated in 2013, the record was born — like that of the Theatre — of a simple desire to 'have a sound in which to surround yourself and intoxicate yourself. I made it out of a love for guitar-driven feedback and the squall of the metal machine.'[14] To some it was inexplicable and offensive. To others it was highly original — and to this day, it's often erroneously posited as the precursor to sub genres like noise, industrial and power electronics. To anyone familiar with Conrad, MacLise, Young et al. however, it was essentially karaoke rushed out ten years after the fact. Many were completely blindsided. The Theatre of Eternal Music were always a deeply underground concern; Tony Conrad operated at the fringes and La Monte Young wasn't anywhere near as well known as, say, Philip Glass. There was no reason that a rock audience would get the reference points (by this stage Reed had launched his successful solo career and released *Transformer* [1972] — a record that, commercially at least, had eclipsed his modest cult following in the Velvets) and, for a long time, it was seen as an unlistenable aberration.

There is another element at play, however. Like the music made by the Theatre of Eternal Music, *Metal Machine Music* can be read as a paean to tonal intoxication with layered distortion, reverb and feedback in wild combination — cosmic reach tempered by city grime. For a musician so deeply schooled — from his Pickwick days onwards — in the discipline and mythology of rock 'n' roll, this was fundamentally 'un-American' music: no quick fixes, the antithesis to convenience culture and the three-minute radio single. This was, after all, music that played with time, that most valuable of capitalist commodities. But it also bears remembering that — for both the Theatre of Eternal Music and for Reed after them — while the music played with ideas of stasis, the conceptual ambitions were beyond lofty and often skated perilously close to prog rock's later overdrive mode: as pompous and grandiose as Rick Wakeman performing *King Arthur on Ice*. Sometimes the 'squall of the metal machine' can be taken as a simple exercise in life-affirming catharsis.

Chapter 6

KOMMUNE

'There is a word in German: *Lebenskünstler*! Do you know it? There are two ways to look at it,' explains Faust's Jean-Hervé Péron, 'one is "artist of life" — the person who makes his *own life* a piece of art. But it could also mean an artist who is having a hard time making ends meet. For us, it was the first option. Everything we did was art — we had nothing else to do! As the years have passed I've reflected on this because I've since discovered Fluxus — which states that "art is everything and everything is art" — and I realised "well hey, I've been an adopter of Fluxus my entire life" (*laughs*).'

Faust were the most anarchic band — in a very crowded field — to emerge from the radical nucleus of late-1960s Germany. Stitching improvised jams, rudimentary sampling and garage thrashings to an 'organic' performance aesthetic — making coffee on stage, say, or stopping mid song to skin up if the vibe wasn't there — they were a force of nature. Like so much of the music coming out of West Germany at the time, they were relentlessly inventive. Alongside bands like CAN, Ash Ra Tempel, NEU!, Amon Düül II and Cluster they had zero interest in reductive transatlantic aping. Rather the artistic freedom afforded by unfettered psychedelic exploration, radical politics and communal living provided Faust — and numerous others in Krautrock's first guard — with a unique inspirational bent: this was the music of the hive mind.

Accepted radio-friendly structures (verse, chorus, verse; easy hooks; big riffs; short songs) were largely shunned while alternative methods — tape loops, surreal chants, found sound, idiosyncratic tunings, improvisation — emphasised textural physicality over commerciality. Egotistical preening was out — although there were plenty of phenomenally talented musicians involved — the boundaries between art and life were consistently challenged. Studios, though often modestly equipped, were also pushed to the outer limits, maverick producers like Conny Plank taking a proto-dub approach and tweaking with alchemical instinct. The drone — whether via synth, ring modulator, white noise, flute, vocal or lord knows what else — was deployed both as a means of challenging plodding blues-rock orthodoxy and as the ultimate hypno-device; in combination with repetitive grooves, obtuse riffs, electronic collage and metronomic rhythms it was one of *the* signifiers of Krautrock.

Here was the ultimate head music. Krautrock was psychedelic in the truest possible sense: not some West Coast cartoon, but a swirling maelstrom that was frequently as gritty and noisy as it was loose and woozy. It reflected not only a turbulent political present but also a wholesale rejection of the (all too recent) past: the shadow of Nazism. The children of the Second World War — including many thousands of orphans who'd been through the harsh, post-war care system — were entering adulthood in the sixties. Many were furious with a system reintegrating ex-Nazis into the upper echelons of public life while simultaneously maintaining a grotesque amnesia about the war; middle-class Germany essentially operated a self-regulating 'don't ask, don't tell' social policy. Add to this anti-Vietnam War protests — which had an enthusiastic support base in urban West Germany — and the radical student movement, and you have a roiling social brew.

After a post-war economic boom, West Germany was in a state of flux. The inner cities — dilapidated and pockmarked with the scars of war — were emptying as the middle classes moved out to newly built suburbs. There was a literal, as well as cultural, vacuum and industrial spaces in West Berlin and other urban centres were ripe for the picking. Groups of squatters moved in and established a tough, radical counterpoint to the West Coast counterculture vibes. The West German communes of the late sixties sprang from the anti-war and student protest movements and represented a break from the patriarchal family unit: the original, so the thinking went, oppressive structure from which all other systems of destructive social and political control emanate.

Kommune 1 opened in Berlin in 1967. It flipped the script on prevailing domestic attitudes. Children were raised by the group, not individual family units; possessions were communal; meals and household tasks were shared; free love was practised amid clouds of hash smoke and hefty doses of acid. As always with utopian living experiments, the reality was somewhat different from the ideal. Kommune members were on the receiving end of hassle and violence from the police, bikers and right-wing gangs and, just as J. Alfred Prufrock measured out his life in coffee spoons, the residents of Kommune 1 might well have measured theirs in cleaning rotas, petty squabbles and bitter political debates.

Musically, however, communal living touched Krautrock in a big way: the free-form approach to sound sprung from the dissolution of the divisions between day-to-day life and music. Living was cheap, the countercultural hustle — be it DIY, selling hash, gardening or amateur electronics — honed to a fine art. While only Amon Düül came through the hard-core political scene associated with the original kommunes, many of the key players were in communal digs, working up sonic storms, hermetically sealed from the outside world. CAN had their old cinema outside Cologne; Cluster were out in the woods at Forst; Kraftwerk had the Kling Klang studio in Dusseldorf; Faust, meanwhile, were in an old schoolhouse in Wümme, outside Hamburg, where they'd formed in 1968.

Musically, Hamburg remains associated with the gritty hardship of early Beatles lore: a famished band sweating out R & B in grimy dockside bars, living on fags and beer, getting into fights with drunken German sailors and reeking of sweat and smoke as they tumbled, exhausted, into lice-ridden bunk beds after the umpteenth matinée show of the week.

Faust were a band principally defined by their lack of interest in rock 'n' roll canonisation or convention, however. They were adrift on their own space-time continuum. The German mainstream of the time was drowning in sentimental schlock: the deathly forced jollity of *Schlager* — a kitsch, beer-drenched, sentimental pap designed to anaesthetise the deep-seated shame of a nation only two decades away from the horrors of the Second World War. Rock 'n' roll had its adherents in West Germany — not least due to the myriad American army bases that remained in the country, whose radio stations belted out the latest imports — but the domestic scene was a small, underground affair. The commercial market was centred around *Schlager* and lightweight pop.

An enterprising journalist called Uwe Nettelbeck — smart, sympathetic to the radical left, business-savvy and plugged into the underground — saw an opening. Why, he wondered, were there no German bands on the international rock stage? Commissioned by Polydor Records, he set about creating a band with the intention of giving them the same financial backing afforded more commercial fare. Trawling the small Hamburg scene, he got in touch with Jean-Hervé Péron, a Frenchman then playing with a beat combo called Nukleus — alongside a group of more avant-garde leaning musicians including Werner 'Zappi' Diermaier and Hans Joachim Irmler. The hastily assembled together group began rehearsing. A noisy demo tape emerged from early sessions and — despite its wild and deeply uncommercial sound — the band signed to Polydor, with all the financial clout such a deal entailed.

Faust had little interest in playing the commercial game, however. The music they were making was experimental and raw, a hypnotic hodgepodge of field recordings, fuzz guitars, electronic drones and chanted vocals. Others of a similarly experimental bent had to beg, borrow and steal. Faust found themselves in an unlikely and enviable position: Polydor, at Nettelbeck's behest, generously availed them of funds and facilities, but left them to it artistically, undisturbed to do as they pleased. Faust holed up in an ex-schoolhouse in Wümme in 1971. They had money, beer and weed. They were supplied with an in-house engineer — Kurt Graupner — to record whatever they wanted, whenever they wanted. It was halcyon-days stuff. Speaking today, Péron retains a sense of palpable glee at the band's early good fortune.

'The deal was that we got a place where we could live and work — in peace and quiet with no production stress — for one whole year. It was *amazing*! And we would also have at our disposal a recording engineer. Somehow Uwe managed to get that out of Polydor (*laughs*). So we were in a situation where life became art, because we had nothing else to do. We were there, we had no financial problems any more, we had the basic recording material. We grew our own pot, so that wasn't an issue either, although it was very cheap at the time anyway. Everything we did was dedicated to art.'

In Wümme, Faust eschewed the outside world in favour of the hermetic existence of the terminal aesthete. It was a 'year zero' vibe. No TV, no radio, no newspapers. Nothing to infringe on the music. The band did as they pleased. They smoked weed, wandered around naked, drank beer with the local farmers in a nearby barn, and experimented ceaselessly.

Pivotal to the early Faust sound were what became known as 'the black boxes'. Engineer Kurt Graupner was a tinkerer by nature — a dab hand at rudimentary electronics — and delighted in rewiring equipment, disassembling circuit boards and building his own kit. He furnished each member with a sound-processing unit housed in a meter-long box that enabled primitive dubbing and effects chains — echo, distortion, ring modulation and phasing — to happen in real time. The boxes allowed Faust to layer and mangle sounds on the fly. It was an approach that resulted in the chaotic maelstrom of their self-titled debut LP in 1971. Deadline looming, Polydor getting itchy, the band had a single night to record the album. They decided on the only sensible course of action: drop acid and work through the night. The result was spectacular, clod-hopping, disorientating. Strange waltzing pianos drift in and out of the mix, fuzzed-out guitars ride roughshod over the top, disembodied voices, choral song, bizarre childlike chants: it evokes a peyote-addled walk through the Reeperbahn at night, all Hogarthian revelry, leering red faces melting before your eyes, vast beer steins clinking the hallucinatory acoustic residue of a city stirred into a bizarre electric soup.

Faust were unsung sampling pioneers. They set about it with a feverish intent. Almost any sound was fair game: footsteps plodding about the school-house corridors, phone conversations, industrial noise. The use of established musical forms in Faust's anarchic tundra — waltzes, samples of the Beatles and the Stones, random radio snippets — was confrontational, rather than know-ingly kitsch. Unlike the misty-eyed, beer-burping *Schlager* singers, they weren't looking back towards a sentimental past. They were fully aware of the horror of WW2 drawing a line in the sand, the future unwritten. Faust was thus a feast of wild contrast, a heavy-duty channelling of a country in social flux. And although they were in their own world, Péron is keen to emphasise the connec-tion between the Faust sound and what was happening on the streets:

'Nineteen seventy-one — there were so many riots in the streets. The sounds of the people marching! *Thump! thump! thump!* — it reminded us of the sound of drumming. There were so many *actions*: actions in industry, actions in our lives, sounds that we had heard before that would fit so beau-tifully. This is how we got into what they now call "field recordings". The sounds around us might be classified as noise — in a building site for example or, say, a printer: all these machines! The old Heidelberger — the cement mixer. For me, that is like the sound of the sea. And the more I play it, the more I discover very strong symbols in it. Symbols of being humble, being eternal, being fertile . . . When I remember the sound of a printing machine I love the never-ending, never-tired rhythm.

'For me this was the first beat machine,' he continues. 'Nowadays they have fancy beat machines that you can program, but of course you could not program a printing machine. It sounded good the way it was. Or the sound of horses running! Or the sound of the wind in the trees. These are fascinating things: the sound of squeaking doors, the sound of seagulls, the sound of a plane. All of these things, if you take the time — and we *had* the time — inspire. We were never told it had been done before.'

The 'anything goes' approach to sound design had its precursors, of course — Fluxus, *musique concrète*, Stockhausen, Cage — but where Faust differed was in the application. The American Fluxus artists may have talked a good game but they were often preaching to the converted and showing in the museums and galleries they purported to despise; making applications, draw-ing down grants, cannily working the machinery of a well-oiled arts scene. By proxy, Faust were working through what Péron describes as the 'vacuum' of post-war Germany.

'We were fed up with the emptiness! The cultural vacuum; the European vacuum. The vacuum after the Second World War was not sunny *at all*. There was rock 'n' roll and so on, but it was not our culture . . . we wanted to *fill* a vacuum. And we all had the inspiration of using electronics. Not just using guitars anymore, but thinking what can you do when you plug it into a ring modulator? We were ready to experiment.'

Life in the Faust camp was not a hard-line political scene. They were hedonists with a surreal sense of humour. However, their idiosyncratic mode of being was — in and of itself — political. With the formation of leftist terrorist groups like Baader-Meinhof and the Red Army Faction, anybody displaying countercultural signifiers could find themselves under serious police scrutiny. Faust were no exception: the schoolhouse was raided in 1971 by machine-gun toting police, a result of Diermaier's girlfriend of the time bearing a passing resemblance to Baader-Meinhof founder Andreas Baader's girlfriend.

By the time Faust recorded *So Far* in 1972, the band were under pressure from Polydor to bring in some return on investment. The resulting sound was still untethered, but tempered by a less wilfully chaotic approach, with more traditional song structures — ostensibly, at least — brought to the fore. Opener 'It's a Rainy Day, Sunshine Girl' starts with Zappi's pneumatic drums before a plinking piano joins the mix. This, in combination with the background vocals — all Presley-esque 'uh-huh's — point to a rock 'n' roll stomp-along. But it never develops. Instead, a gnawing tension builds, like the queasy building promise of a pill slightly stronger than you were expecting: anticipation that could go down the path of total euphoria or clammy panic. Piano gives way to a two-chord strum, the drums pound along with intent and the title lyric — 'it's a rainy day, sunshine girl' vamps incessantly, a hint of American intonation in Péron's accent, electronic drones swooshing under the mix like a murky chemical undertow. As statements of intent go, it's dramatic: if you *must* have your basic rock 'n' roll, Faust seem to be saying, you will have it droning, you will have it unrelenting and you will have it bent sinister.

Elsewhere, *So Far* veers from whacked-out 1970s chase scene fuzz — 'No Harm' — to the title track, a steady groove that plods along in polite pedestrian fashion while uncanny noises swish beneath. 'Mamie was Blue' is a nightmarish noise excursion that hinges on swathes of mechanistic noise — oscillators that sound like revving engines, disembodied guitars that veer wildly off key, layers of growling, droning bass. It's fearsome stuff: indeed, one can draw a *direct* line from Faust at their most incandescent to the likes of Throbbing

Gristle, or the brittle clank of Einstürzende Neubauten. Even in their darkest moments, however, Faust are playful, resolutely human. Did they, I wonder, seek to provoke a primal, hypnotic response in listeners? Was their music, on some level, trance inducing?

'If you repeat something for a long time you will transcend the situation,' says Péron. 'Like a mantra: you repeat something and then you repeat and you repeat and you repeat and then you forget about yourself. Forget about everything. Get into a dream. Why do people do this? Maybe to reach a certain state of mind — maybe to reach out to their gods — maybe to forget what is around them at that moment: I do not know why they do this. But I know for sure that it *works*. If you repeat something — a sound, or a rhythm, or a word — you will get into another state of mind. We love it when we get into a groove. That is why it is so great to play with Zappi — our drummer. Sometimes he gets into a, uh, a funny state of mind. And then he goes on with the same rhythm with only slight changes, and that keeps you going so that you can hear colours in the music — very slowly; very subtly. Of course, we don't always play like this. Sometimes we are brutal and not subtle at all.'

Faust curbed their noisier instincts and distilled their hypnotic rhythm to an unrelenting chug on their Tony Conrad collaboration *Outside the Dream Syndicate* (1973), a monochrome exploration into the hypnotic power of repetition, the album a symbiosis of two differing sonic worlds. Faust's wild frontiers — their druidic approach to chaos noise, their black boxes, their magpie approach to sound — was tamed to a flinty groove, while Conrad's wildcat violin was honed to a restrained, mournful scrape. It was a symbiotic pairing. Faust loved the Velvet Underground and, through Conrad, connected to the New York ley line that had initially inspired the dronal bedrock of their sound. The resulting album was an exercise in restraint and reduction for both Faust (represented only by the rhythm section of Zappi and Péron) and Conrad. Each honed their more jagged contours in service of a deathly groove, the drone of Conrad's violin offset against the chink of Zappi's drums, Péron holding down a single bass note tuned to the tonic of Conrad's violin.

The first track — the twenty-seven-minute 'From The Side of Man and Womankind' carries a funereal aspect, a dead set trudge through a still-smoking battlefield, desolation all around as Conrad's violin caws crow-like from above at the bloodied limbs below. 'From the Side of the Machine' is looser (again a full half-hour in length) but warmer and less unrelenting in execution. Here, Conrad's violin is back in Dream Syndicate mode, circling above Péron's loose walking bassline, a languid flip to the menace of the first half. Today, Péron emphasises the influence Conrad had on both his playing and philosophy.

'Tony had a huge impact on my way of thinking and getting about in life; it was like crossing the Sahara. My memories are very vivid: Tony was ten years older than us. And when you're twenty, the age difference seems bigger. What he was asking was very precise. It was: "Why don't we repeat for one hour?" And as soon as we started to change anything — even a *little* bit — he'd shout: "No! No! No! No! One tone! One beat!" (*laughs*) . . . Zappi and I did a few recording sessions. Our sound engineer would say "rolling" and there goes Tony on the violin — "Bwwwwwwhhhhhhaaaaaaaaaaaaaaaaa" — one note on his violin, and there goes Zappi on the drums, "boom-cha, boom-cha, boom-cha". Once you'd done that a couple of times you'd forget about yourself; forget about your fingers; forget about the key; you'd travel into the strings of Tony Conrad, into the skins of Zappi's drums. And you'd look at the clock and two hours has passed! And some of the time — because we did quite a few sessions — we'd notice "Hey, we are well past one hour." So time would expand and reduce. It was amazing, although very painful. Striking the same strings for one hour can cause bleeding in the fingers.

'We played with him again in 2017, in Berlin,' he continues. 'It was the last concert Tony did before he died. The venue was beautiful. It was an industrial plant where they used to produce electricity — it was huge, I mean *really* huge. It had been "good vibed" by Tibetan monks before the concert, chanting their mantras to tune the place. The light was perfect, the sound was perfect, although Tony was very, very ill. It was amazing that he was standing on his feet, but he was in a great mood and so were we . . . Faust fans who contacted me said that they went sober — no LSD — but they started to see colours and say: "Hey, what is happening?" It was really strong.'

Perhaps inevitably, *Outside the Dream Syndicate* — a record with even less commercial potential than the first two Faust records — sank without trace soon after release, though it has been rediscovered in recent years. Finally realising that they weren't going to get their *Sgt. Pepper*, Polydor finally let Faust go, and the band returned the favour by comprehensively stripping out the Wümme studio on departure. Signing with Richard Branson at Virgin — a label yet to hit pay-dirt with Mike Oldfield's *Tubular Bells* — Faust found themselves, again, on an imprint that let them get on with minimal fuss and maximal funds.

Their first release with Virgin was the cut-price *Faust Tapes* released in 1973 for forty-nine pence. Designed as an introduction, it's a confusing — and often lacklustre — listen: a tapestry of out-takes, untitled skits and ponderous jams, the mystic fire of their first two records largely absent. By contrast, *Faust IV* was magisterial. The first material made away from the creative hot bed of Wümme, it was recorded in the Oxfordshire countryside at Manor Studios. An expensive set-up with state-of-the-art mixing desks and in-house engineers, Faust were initially reticent at the more restrictive, professional vibe they found at the Manor, but *Faust IV* remains a proper trip, arguably the most cohesive (if that word isn't anathema, in this context) record they made. Opening with 'Krautrock' — eleven minutes of circular drones, electronic noise, and driving hi hats — it comes on like a narcotised drive down the autobahn, at once poking fun at the (deeply contentious) genre term, while celebrating its most recognisable musical trope: the gnostic chug. 'The Sad Skinhead', meanwhile, is a disconcertingly jaunty-sounding tale of a skinhead unable to move on from a monochrome existence of 'going places / smashing faces' while 'Jennifer' was a mangled take on dreamy pop.

Faust were no more of a fit for a fledgling major like Virgin than an established big hitter such as Polydor, however. The recording sessions were fraught from the outset. Tensions ran high. Away from the 'world within a world' of Wümme, lost amid the possibilities afforded by a professional multi-track studio, Faust were productive but unhappy. In the end, Uwe Nettelbeck took it upon himself to compile the final track list himself from the masters — unbeknownst to Hans Joachim Irmler or Rudolf Sosna, who quit in furious protest, leaving the remaining members to hastily assemble replacements and organise a ramshackle tour at the last minute.

It was typical Faust chaos. The regular music industry followed a cyclical work cycle that mirrored the verse, chorus, verse structure: rehearse, record, tour — ad infinitum. Faust — with their Fluxian approach to work and life — were unable to submit to that kind of set-up. They simply weren't suited to long tours or, indeed, grindingly repetitive mechanisations of any sort other than of their own making. Their way of life mirrored their music: freewheeling, with the occasional dramatic noisy interlude. After racking up huge bills in various hotels, the court jesters of Krautrock were unceremoniously dumped from Virgin's roster and ceased activities until various mid-nineties reformations. Indeed, Péron makes the final point that — though a vital cog in the German underground — Faust were 'always alone! There was Amon Düül II in Munich and CAN and Kraftwerk but we never had contact — even decades afterwards we still don't have contact.'

Yeti Talks to Yogi

Communal life for Faust — jovial, hedonistic, freewheeling — was markedly different from the heavier scene that surrounded Amon Düül. The band most closely associated with the radical commune world, Amon Düül was equal parts band and community. Formed in 1967 at drummer Peter Leopold's Munich flat with brother Ulrich and guitarist Chris Karrer, they were initially free-jazz heads who'd been turned on to Hendrix, Zappa and the Velvets. At the German student protests in Munich, they'd turn up, hand out instruments and encourage others to make some noise.

This approach was central to the band's ethos: right from the start, sound was ergonomic, anybody's. Amon Düül was a commune as well as band, the community centred around a crumbling, tumbledown house outside Munich where anybody — including the children — could (indeed, were expected) get up and play. Band 'membership' was amorphous, freedom of expression prized above all else. The early sound was woodblock primitive, demented Neanderthal sonics. *Psychedelic Underground* (1969) was culled from a forty-eight-hour freak-out and is far west of lo-fi: proto-blues metallic chugs; wailing, howling vocals, layers of fuzz — it's sub-basement knockabout stuff, primal, scuffed and — taken in large doses — rather tiring. Singer Renate Knaup had joined the commune but — alongside guitarist Chris Karrer — had quickly wearied of the ragtag approach to sound, not to mention the increasingly nit-picky aspects of day-to-day commune life.

'There were certain rules you had to obey,' she explained in 1996, 'and if you broke any you had to go in front of this tribunal and explain your actions to these fuckers! Even when I wanted to buy a new pair of stockings I had to ask the cashier for money. This is why we split from Amon Düül I, they were too involved with this political shit.'[1] Tensions came to a head at the Essener Sonntag Festival in October 1968. Half the band were at one end of the stage stoned out of their gourds, repeating the same riff ad infinitum while the more musical heads — John Weinzierl and Chris Karrer — were attempting to instigate something more interesting at the other.

It was the end: Amon Düül II rose from this chaotic scene like a dervish, making one of Krautrock's defining albums — *Phallus Dei* — in 1969. By turns apocalyptic, eerie and bucolically evocative, *Phallus Dei* — 'God's Cock' — was a serious statement of intent that blew anything the previous incarnation had done clean out of the water. This was heavy-duty freak-out gear, but imbued with a grandiose — near gothic — tempestuousness. The title track is the centrepiece: twenty minutes of staunch psychedelic power thrum. Renate Knaup's vocals come in great operatic crests, Leopold's drums are a free-jazz inspired maelstrom of rhythm — alternately locked down tight or veering into choppier waters — while Karrer's rhythm guitar rides disconcertingly high in the mix, off-key jazz chords chugging away like proto-metal without the pedals. It's a welter of stylistic changes, ducking and weaving through jazz, oddball folk, pomp and ceremony.

Nothing sits still — *Phallus Dei* is shot through with high-camp ritual drama. 'Kanaan' hinges on Indian-inflected riffs, pounding tribal drums and a spoken-word vocal cut through with whoops and shrieks. It treads the sublime-to-ridiculous ratio perfectly: a stoned exotica that pounds along at a barely contained gallop, Renate's operatic wail evoking some Hammer Horror forest vista. The pacing is extraordinary. No band has captured the spectral acid dance — exhilaration to imminent mental collapse — better. A pronounced Indian influence is heard on 'TouchMaPhal' where sinister sitar drones intertwine with Renate's breathy vocal, shimmering harps underpinned by a woodblock — like Faust, Amon Düül use the drone as gear stick, as well as texturiser: a pivot to never stop moving.

After such tumultuous and anarchic majesty, Amon Düül II were in the ascendency and their next album — *Yeti* (1971) — was another seminal document of the period, a sprawling double that married the tempestuousness of *Phallus Dei* to (slightly) straighter structures. With a cleaner production and tighter songs, *Yeti* is still batshit intense but tempered by self-confident musicianship and an (even) wider sphere of influence. Opening with head twister in four parts 'Soap Shop Rock', it veers from jaunty to sludgy to freak-out noodling and back again, the lyrics full-on bleak, a righteously psychedelic portal of doom in which John Weinzierl intones in heavy Teutonic tones about the 'assassin training his soul'. Echoes of John Fahey can be heard on the primitive acoustic picking that opens 'Cerberus' before the whole thing descends into a flurry of fuzz. 'Archangel Thunderbird', meanwhile — the band's most recognisable song — saw Renate Knaup's vocals come to the fore around a hymnal melody she used to sing in her local church, haunting tones adding a gothic portent to the storm raging around it. The flip side is entirely improvisational, and brings the dronal element simmering right to the top. The first movement is an eighteen-minute howl into the ether, Peter Leopold's ride cymbal lashing out time like a drunken captain lacerating a syphilitic sailor's pock-marked back with the cat-o'-nine-tails, John Weinzierl and Chris Karrer noodling away with fevered intent and the steady burr of Falk Rogner's organ underneath it all.

The band never reached the heights of *Phallus Dei* or *Yeti* again, though they continued to release strong records through the early 1970s. The slightly ponderous double *Tanz Der Lemminge* (1971) didn't match the giddy dance of the aforementioned but contained thrilling moments nonetheless; by contrast *Wolf City* (1972) was something else altogether: a concise, punchy half-hour that saw them strip back to rockier fare, albeit shot through with their trademark bizarre pomp. There was always an epic, fantastical bearing to Amon Düül II. Check the closing improvisation on *Yeti* — 'Sandoz in the Rain'. Flutes, bongos, violins, twanging acoustic guitars — it's all there, but rendered without any hint of twee folksy jangle. It's *bucolic* music, mysterious music. They may have emerged from the protest scene — cramped smoky digs, tense city streets, a revolving door of new faces, relationships, fall-outs, collaborations — but their music is imbued with the great outdoors: *Phallus Dei* and *Yeti* evoke the scent of decaying vegetation on the forest floor, mulch underfoot, ancient Teutonic fairy tales: gnarled-earth music.

Others were looking to the stars, however.

Amboss of the Gods

'I grew up in West Berlin which was surrounded by the wall and the territory of the East German Democratic Republic,' explains Ash Ra Tempel's Manuel Göttsching. 'Every time I wanted to go out, I'd have to go past it. It was like living on a small island. I thought: don't look at the surface, look up at the sky. Instead of looking at the horizontal, look vertical — up at the cosmos.'

Founded in 1971 by Manuel Göttsching with drummer Klaus Schulze and bassist Hartmut Enke, Ash Ra Tempel navigated the outer edges of the galaxy with swirling, largely instrumental soundscapes that alternated between pummelling cosmic freak-out — all barrelling percussion and bluesy guitar squalls — and lysergic electronic drones. As a teenager in early sixties Berlin, he'd be up in the early hours spellbound by the American Forces Radio stations blasting out import R & B, soul and rock 'n' roll. The Four Tops and the Temptations in particular provided a thrilling antidote to the lightweight *Schlager* of the time, although Göttsching was soon seeking out more hypnotic sounds.

'As a guitar player, it's always interesting to find out how to play long notes or sustained notes,' he explains, 'because the guitar produces only short notes — so you might use feedback or delay boxes . . . I was twelve, thirteen at the beginning of the sixties. I became fascinated with longer pieces. There was *Schlager* — careful music, stupid lyrics — it wouldn't have touched anybody! (*laughs*) A little bit of domestic rock 'n' roll, a few German singers but not very interesting. But then I remember the Rolling Stones' "I'm Going Home". That was eight or nine minutes long! And they started to *improvise* at the end: they broke out of the radio time limit of three minutes. It wasn't radio controlled. I also loved the long concert recordings from Cream, the live recordings from Jimi Hendrix: the experimental side, the live atmosphere.'

During the late sixties Göttsching fused these influences — Cream, in particular — in a blues combo called the Steeple Chase Blues Band while Enke and Schulze played in the earlier — harsher — incarnation of Tangerine Dream, marrying greyscale semi-industrial electronics made via ring modulator and tape splicing to jagged, droning strings, ominous tribal percussion and distorted guitar interjections. Both bands shared a rehearsal space at avant-garde composer Thomas Kessler's Beat Studio — a hub for the experimental scene in Berlin at the time.

By the time they linked up and formed Ash Ra Tempel, decent equipment was scarce in West Germany. Enke went over to London and came back with four heavy-duty WEM speaker cabinets that he'd picked up from a Pink Floyd roadie on the Charing Cross Road. This was a pivotal moment. WEM cabinets were serious kit. They'd powered the Isle of Wight festival and the Rolling Stones in Hyde Park. On returning, Ash Ra Tempel were — overnight — the loudest band in West Germany and their eponymous debut LP (1971) found them in full, righteous form — a thrumming wall of sound.

Produced by Conny Plank — who mixed down live, riding the faders as the band played — *Ash Ra Tempel* was a lesson in equilibrium: equal parts tumultuous whirlwind and settled dust, dervish motion tempered by stasis. However, *Ash Ra Tempel* was unique in that the blues influence was clearly audible. While bands like Tangerine Dream, Faust, Cluster and NEU! had — like the Velvets before them — rejected the blues outright, Göttsching put it through an acid mangler. Unlike the guitarists he was listening to — namely Hendrix and Clapton — he hadn't spent years studying the source material, pouring over Delta blues records: rather he came at it *through* them — guitarists who were already at the wild frontier — and kept pushing on, to thrillingly unhinged results.

The first side — 'Amboss' — was as heavy as the title ('anvil') suggested. Portentous synth drones hang heavy for a few minutes before pounding drums signal action. The propulsive swirl of Göttsching's guitar is giddying, Conny Plank's idiosyncratic mix-down adding thrilling drama — the drums are right up in the mix, bright and loud, while muffling and distortion on Göttsching's guitar mean his increasingly frenetic bluesy squalls come on like a piston sporadically powering up under the bonnet, only to be submerged by churning power chords and ringing feedback. His playing is busy, but a far cry from gratuitous axe hero wankery. He uses repetition cleverly, returning throughout to Eastern-inflected licks that circle like vultures above a sickly sky. There's a gnostic quality to his playing: guitar cast as dowsing rod probing the spongy surface of a peculiar planet. On the twenty-five-minute 'Traummaschine', however, his guitar is largely absent. Bleak, wintery echo box pads are layered against synth tones. Disembodied voices dip in and out of the mix, strings mournfully scraping along. The imagery conjured is otherworldly, dilapidated — some hulking ghost craft orbiting a decayed outpost of a distant galaxy.

Ash Ra Tempel was a remarkably assured debut album — certainly the most dynamic of their early records — a result of the near telepathic synergy between the players. Improvisation was key, as Göttsching explains: 'We'd sometimes use blues structures and themes as a start, and then improvise. But when we made *Ash Ra Tempel* in 1970 we left the themes alone — we were only improvising. Our idea was to make free music, no rules. We didn't talk about music when we met, we just sat down and started playing. We didn't talk about any key or any melody, we just started playing and every one of us played what he liked: instead of talking, playing!'

The music may have been flowing, but the business remained a mystery. Like so many bands of the period, Ash Ra Tempel learnt as they went, employing a DIY ethos as they felt their way in the dark: 'There wasn't a business structure for this type of music,' laughs Göttsching. 'We were not dependent on management or agencies — it was *much* more experimental in those years. Everything was very unprofessional compared to English or American standards. People just played, things just happened . . . there was nobody who said "Oh stop, you cannot do it!" There were experimental labels. The most famous label was Ohr Records and a lot of bands — Popol Vuh, Ash Ra Tempel, early CAN, came through Ohr. Everybody was doing it for themselves. Eighty per cent was rubbish. But the twenty per cent that was interesting was *really* interesting.'

Ohr Records was the brainchild of Rolf-Ulrich Kaiser, one of Krautrock's great Svengali figures. Like Uwe Nettelbeck, Kaiser was a former rock journalist. He was also a promoter (he put on the legendary Essen Festival), a 'businessman' of dubious credentials and a die-hard acid freak who pushed the German underground as far as he could. He dubbed the music he released on Ohr '*kosmische*' — cosmic — both in the hope of broadening the appeal of what could be staggeringly uncommercial sounds, but also as a way of distancing it from the controversial and loathed Krautrock tag that had originated from the British music press. There wasn't a unified Ohr sound. Aside from Ash Ra Tempel, Kaiser signed everything from the grinding, Neanderthal chug of Guru Guru to the frostily magisterial soundtracks of Popol Vuh and ambitious electronics of mid-period Tangerine Dream.

One of the weirder moments of happenstance arose when he put out Ash Ra Tempel's *Seven Up* (1973) — a collaboration with countercultural guru Timothy Leary. One of the more peculiar sonic artefacts of the era, Leary was on the run at the time of recording. In 1968, the American authorities had sentenced him to a ludicrously harsh ten-year prison sentence for possession of two roaches — a clear warning shot to countercultural agitators. Sent to a low-security prison, he was given a series of psychological profiling tests. However, there was a snag: the tests Leary was given had, in fact, been written by Leary himself — a former psychotherapist — some years previously. He was thus able to suitably 'game' the results, knowing precisely the multiple-choice answers to give to appear docile and obedient. Duly sent to a low-security gardening assignment in the prison grounds, he escaped by jumping off a roof and scaling a wall. Absconding to Algeria on a false passport, Leary hooked up with exiled Black Panther leader Eldridge Cleaver before making his way to Switzerland. There — moving among his usual coterie of freaks, academics, acid casualties and bohemian sycophants — he was introduced to Tempel bassist Hartmut Enke who invited him to record a session with the band. Göttsching remembers him more as easy-going bon viveur than the lofty, self-important guru of popular legend.

'He enjoyed driving. He liked good food, good wine. He was very good at communicating with the band. I didn't know much about Timothy Leary when we did the album. It was the idea of Enke and also of Kaiser — the owner of Ohr. We wanted to make something with lyrics. We thought of trying to meet with Allen Ginsberg, but he was nowhere to be found (*laughs*). Our producer said: "Timothy Leary is in Switzerland, maybe you want to meet him?" I'd never heard of him before! I didn't know much about LSD, but Enke was really enthusiastic about these things. Leary had made some records where he was talking — speeches — he did a few records and he had a good voice. He liked the idea of getting involved and making lyrics about this book that he was writing at the time — *Seven Levels of Consciousness*. That is how the idea came up. We prepared it and went to Switzerland because he was on the run — he had the possibility to stay in Switzerland without being extradited, but he couldn't leave Switzerland. We recorded there and mixed it in Cologne. He was a nice guy. I expected some kind of spiritual guru, but he was the contrary.'

The resulting album encompassed two side-long pieces — 'Time' and 'Space'. The former features bluesy noodling, electronic drones and an altogether subdued vibe. The second side is livelier, shot through with Leary's spectacularly creepy vocal style, alternating between rock 'n' roll clichés about 'downtown!' and 'my new Cadillac' and hollering about being a 'right-hand lover, with a hinge on my thumb!' while Göttsching blasts out the boogie. As soon as things get going, however, the entire mix is subsumed by swathes of rushing synth drones, all-consuming, like the 'swooshing' auditory hallucinations that you get after huffing a nitrous oxide balloon. It's a strange document, but novelty and great genesis story aside, not one of the band's more memorable records.

Ash Ra Tempel recorded two further albums — the heavy groove of *Join Inn* (1973) and the poppier *Starring Rosi* (1974) — before Göttsching went solo for the spectacular *Inventions for Electric Guitar* (1975). Drenched in echo and reverb, his guitar playing shifted from the wild, blues-inflected howl of Ash Ra Tempel to a refined, steely groove machine. Influenced by Terry Riley, the record was a starkly minimal exercise in reduction, Göttsching reining in his chops in favour of tight focus. 'Echo Waves' came on like proto-minimal techno — a twenty-minute groove that bounced along the edge of Göttsching's brittle funk lick, his muted strings mirroring the insistent vamp of Riley's *In C*, while the haunting 'Pluralis' plays with echo in such a way to make his guitar sound like lush synth pads. That Göttsching recorded the entire thing on a TEAC four-track with nothing but an echo box, wah-wah pedal and primitive effects box is extraordinary given the slickly soporific vibe that he slowly builds: indeed, despite such basic gear, it's sometimes difficult to discern a guitar at all, just a rhythmic thrum.

'I was fascinated by how Terry Riley played,' Göttsching tells me. 'He'd perform just with a synth or tape recorder and play incredible sounds and melodies at the same time. He's a *fantastic* keyboard player. I experimented with delay and reverb with Ash Ra Tempel, but just with effects — not so much composition. The idea came up to make a real set. I thought, "Well I'm a guitar player, so maybe I can try something on guitar like Terry Riley did with keyboards." I got a four-track recorder and started experimenting with my own studio. *Adventures With Electric Guitar* was minimalism — both the composition and the sound: one guitar run through effects units.'

Göttsching's minimalist bent was, later, to reach an apex with *E2-E4* (1984). An hour-long improvisation, a deceptively simple two-chords vamp incessantly meeting subtle dub echoes, flanging effects and a drum machine beat. Recorded one afternoon in 1981, it was intended simply as a knockabout piece to accompany Göttsching on his Walkman on a flight to Hamburg. His playing is funkily brittle: he chugs between the chords, applying a hand bridge dampener, propulsive and confident yet dreamlike and ethereal: cocaine and Quaaludes, essentially.

Playing it back, he realised he had something special and decided to release it. It soon became a cult favourite at the Paradise Garage in New York, much to Göttsching's bemusement. Unlike the disco rollers, Italo wobblers, cranky early Chicago house and Frankie Goes to Hollywood extended 12-inches that usually rocked the sweaty, amyl-scented, peak-time floor, it lacked anything approaching a pounding beat. Nonetheless, DJs like Larry Levan appreciated its pliability. On the weighty rig, bewitching tapestries unfolded, Göttsching's humble two-chord dronal chug underpinning sounds of all persuasions. *E2-E4* was to attain talisman-like status in the techno world, too, Göttsching's mechanical guitar — tight and robotic — the perfect foil for the cavernously deep dub techno stylings of Basic Channel, whose 1995 'Basic Reshape' was a gloriously hypnotic remix of the piece.

'I played live with sequences and synthesisers and I worked with this for maybe four or five years. *E2-E4* was another step — really a last step — in this way of working,' he explains. 'Everything worked. It was a kind of magic moment — the preparation took maybe four, five, six years: the recording just one hour (*laughs*). I feel honoured that it has influenced so many people. It's probably because it's very simple: it attracts people to do something with it or to make something with it — remixes and so on — or to play something on top of it or to mix it — you can listen to it entirely or listen to it in the background.'

Bunker Sonics

Others were to embrace electronic experimentation with a similar enthusiasm to Göttsching, albeit to more abrasive ends. Kluster (as they were known until 1971, when they became Cluster) used a motley selection of malfunctioning ring modulators, old echo boxes, tape recorders and rewired guitar pedals to evoke a dissonant proto-industrial sound, alien and often frighteningly bleak.

Formed by the late iconoclast Conrad Schnitzler, alongside Dieter Moebius and Hans-Joachim Roedelius, the first incarnation of Kluster pre-figured early industrial music by some decade, their music standing in stark contrast to the psychedelic extremes of what was happening around them in West Germany. This was *cold* music, bunker sonics: clanking, brittle, improvised noise made with the intention of breaking free of any form of melodic or progressive expectation whatsoever. Bands like Faust and Amon Düül II were similarly keen on breaking with established form and theory, but did so with an inclusive spirit. Music was there for everybody, all sounds were valid and the tyranny of exclusivity — in the form of the precious virtuoso — to be taken down a peg. Kluster were at odds with all of this. Conrad Schnitzler also had little time for musical perfectionism, but even less for hippy idealism. He believed in noise as an engine of antagonism. Intention was everything, classical training counted for nothing, melody was anathema. He loathed hippies and dreamy complacency. He disliked most rock music, too. He was, rather, into free jazz and Stockhausen and disruption. As he told the writer David Stubbs, he hated the prevailing commune vibe: 'All these people making music with the drums and flutes and melodies that were like worms in your head.²'

Kluster sprung from Berlin's infamous Zodiak Free Arts Lab. Founded by Schnitzler and Roedelius in 1968, the Zodiak was an austere black room underneath a theatre. They painted all the windows black and knocked up a bar at the back. Hot boxed with hash smoke, free jazz and psychedelic noise of every persuasion blasted out into the early hours. There was no clear demarcation between bands or staff. Impromptu sessions would last into the night and bands would help out behind the bar or in the kitchen. Though short lived, the Zodiak was a key station for the cross-cultural pollination associated with Berlin. Radical jazz heads like Peter Brötzmann were there, as were future members of Ash Ra Tempel, Tangerine Dream, writers, artists and bohemians of all persuasions: it was a lo-fi, scruffily anarchic vibe, born out of a deep-seated need to make a clean break from the black shadow of what was then (very) recent history.

Indeed, Kluster were — more than any of their peers — a product of the horrors of the Second World War. They were a decade older than most other Krautrock bands. Conrad Schnitzler was born in 1937 in Dusseldorf and experienced the ravages of war first-hand in early childhood. Allied bombing raids hit the city throughout the later stages of the war, the infamous 'firestorms' devastating, huge chunks of the city decimated. Schnitzler saw it all. Later, he worked in a textile factory amid the clanks, drones and judders of industrial sewing machines and looms. Abrasive, pitiless noise was hard-wired into his DNA. Roedelius was also a child of war: he was conscripted into the Hitler Youth as a boy. If much of the Krautrock oeuvre was joyously wild and propulsive, looking, as Manuel Göttsching had it, 'to the sky', Kluster channelled something else entirely: blank-eyed inertia, shadow play, industrial hinterlands. Their first three records — recorded by Conny Plank and improvised over the course of a few nights in 1970 — are *chilling*. Every bit as disturbing as anything Throbbing Gristle or Whitehouse put out, theirs wasn't the sound of arch transgression or morbid obsessions: it was born of first-hand experience. Their two 1971 records — *Klopfzeichen* and *Zwei-Osterie* — were defined by naked dread. Taking guitar, cello and percussion and mangling them through sound processing units until they were shorn of almost any semblance of recognisability, Kluster conjured an alien sound world. They rigged their boxes together and started recording: everything was improvised, the modest run of 300 bizarrely sponsored by a nearby church after Schnitzler read in the local paper that the organist had a fascination with avant-garde music. It was thus agreed that the church would help pay for studio time, but only on the proviso that the band include spoken word biblical text on the first track of each album. The result was a clipped Teutonic voice robotically reading liturgy behind a droning swell of echo-treated noise. Needless to say, it sounded *exceptionally* sinister.

After a third, similarly oppressive, album — *Eruption* — Conrad Schnitzler left to pursue a prolific and wildly inventive solo career while Moebius and Roedelius continued under the name Cluster, alongside producer Conny Plank. Pursuing a (marginally) less austere, more cinematic sound, their first record — *Cluster* (1971) — was still imbued with the ominous portent of old, albeit to slightly less fearsome ends. Comprising three drone pieces named only by their running times, the first ('15:33') starts with the sound of a train coming down the tracks before rolling out a cacophony: drone atop drone, menacing echoes, metallic pangs, juddering synth noise, intermittent cymbal crashes like doors slamming shut in a sinister underground training facility. '7:38' carries a sub-aqua vibe, plinks evoking a submarine homing device while '21:17' is a more spacious affair, a vestige of melody appearing under the gritty tape fuzz in the form of an occasional parping horn or the scrape of a cello. Cluster are channelling rather than sculpting, however: this is the sound of electricity running its own course.

The following year's *Cluster II* was notably cleaner and more cerebral. Less oppressively dense and with clear instrumentation for the first time, 'Im Süden' is built around a haunting guitar line while organ and ominous bassline build around it — windswept atmospherics that foresee the dusty Sam Peckinpah soundtrack aspect of late-period Earth, while on 'Live in der Fabrik' analogue tone generators add a richness and clarity of sound previously absent, the atmosphere less industrial, more verdant.

While the music of Kluster was a product of the harsh, brutalist vibe of post-war Berlin, and the sparse black box of the Zodiak Arts Lab, the Cluster sound was influenced by the duo's relocation to the village of Forst in Lower Saxony in 1971. Escaping the city and setting up a studio in bucolic isolation, they collaborated with various heads, not least Brian Eno and Michael Rother from NEU! The Rother sessions resulted in the two Harmonia albums *Musik von Harmonia* (1974) and *Deluxe* (1975). Markedly different to the dark vistas of Cluster, listening today, one can draw a direct line from *Musik von Harmonia* both to the ambient records Eno was putting out in the late 1970s but also to the more wistful areas of ambient techno — the Orb, KLF et cetera (which we'll explore later). This was music of a soaring, druggy, melodic bent that hinged on the sky-bound oscillations of Roedelius and Moebius alongside the lightly insistent guitar of Rother. No exercise in bare-bones minimalist reduction, it was trance inducing but luxuriously rich.

The NEU! connection was absolutely key to the Harmonia records. While Cluster were essentially beatless, NEU! guitarist Michael Rother had spent years standing in front of drummer Klaus Dinger, the architect of the motorik beat. One of the key Krautrock sonic signifiers, the motorik was an insistent 4/4 chug that was powerfully propulsive without being overtly rockist or aggressive: it was, rather, an exercise in reduction and discipline. No garish fills, no needless cymbal splashes, just a relentless, steady (but somehow very human) metronome that provided a bedrock for any number of wild experiments. Perfectly capturing the lonely speed and drama of a night-time autobahn drive, it was heard to best effect on NEU!'s first album — 'Hallogallo' and 'Negativland' specifically — but also appears on the first Harmonia record on 'Dino', a track that could easily have been a NEU! tune. Indeed, the Cluster influence is difficult to ascertain here: it belts along at pace, while Rother's artful chug adds to the sense of forward motion. By contrast 'Ohrwurm' is *pure* Cluster, an ominous exercise in electronic doom. Brian Eno was a big fan of Harmonia (in 1975 he'd described them as 'the most important band in the world') and their influence on his ambient records was manifest. He worked with Roedelius and Moebius on a number of occasions, most notably on the superlative *Cluster and Eno* (1977) on which Eno's disciplined peace and command of wistful melody is married to the Germans' outré experimentation, expansive drones offset against innocent piano melodies and sweeping ambient atmospherics.

Indeed, it's somewhat ironic that the electronic music coming out of 1970s Germany was so often suffused with a spiritual, earthy power at the exact same time that electronic music was — in Britain and America, at least — becoming mistrusted as a somehow inferior or fake form, or an insult to 'real music', by the mainstream rock press. The 'Disco Sucks' era — a sinister, fascistic nadir in popular music history that saw a mass record burning in Chicago's Comiskey Park baseball stadium in 1979 organised by an irate radio DJ — wasn't far off, and attitudes to electronic music were frequently luddite, with a strong undercurrent of misogyny. Guitars were macho, phallic; synths were soulless, anaemic, effeminate. Nascent disco culture — where the *dancers* were the stars, the club an alternative nocturnal world in which records were utilitarian, functional, repetitive — flew in the face of musician as omnipotent controller, ultimate focus. It was, of course, the anonymous aspect that made it so exciting: here was a world where one could reinvent oneself and get lost. In Germany, attitudes to electronics were somewhat more accepting. Krautrock had, after all, done away with the histrionics and idolatry from the start. In rejecting the bloated rockist ego it reinstated wonder and mystery. The best of the electronic music made in Germany contained as much soul, humanity and mystery as anything on the rock spectrum. And nobody went further into the realms of arcane spiritualism than Florian Fricke.

Garden of the Pharaohs

Florian Fricke was a mystic at heart. A deeply idiosyncratic composer, the music he made as Popol Vuh — which he described as a 'mass from the heart' — was informed by spiritualism and esoteric myth. Early Popol Vuh records were magic and mystery personified: verdant, transcendent, tempered by a restraint not generally associated with the wilder frontiers of the wider Krautrock continuum. Named after the ancient Mayan religious text, Popol Vuh was, to all intents and purpose, Florian Fricke's solo project (although he collaborated with various musicians, over three decades and numerous albums, he was the sole member). He loved free jazz, John Coltrane in particular, and — like Coltrane — was fascinated by religion, particularly Christian mysticism and Eastern texts.

The early Popol Vuh sound was driven by Fricke's cranky and unpredictable Moog synthesiser. In the late 1960s Fricke had got hold of this giant machine, one of only two in circulation in West Germany at the time, and was instantly enthralled. It was an unwieldy beast: a four-module heavy-duty machine that enabled Fricke to actualise sounds that would have been otherwise impossible. Having no manual, he dedicated himself to teasing out strange sounds for weeks on end.

Debut album *Affenstunde* (1970) was a haunting instrumental set built around the spooked drone of Fricke's Moog: indeed, *Affenstunde* was the first album that was based almost entirely around the machine. However, the cosmic drones and evocative windswept chords are only a part of the story: it's the combination of the electronic with the *organic* — the tribal percussion of Holger Trülzsch — that provides fascinating contrast, linking the modern and ancient. Like the music of Angus MacLise, say, *Affenstunde* exists in its own space-time continuum.

The cover — a magical-looking wooden door, with a glowing orange light coming from beyond the threshold — was, in fact, a photograph of the Roter Pfarrhof ('Red Parsonage') in Wasserberg. The building had once been was the home of Gottliebe von Lehndorff, a German bohemian whose husband had been executed for his role in an unsuccessful plot to assassinate Adolf Hitler in the later stages of the Second World War. It later became a philosophical school where the young Fricke studied, calling it a 'monastery for art and philosophy'. To Fricke it represented tapping the interior, in an exterior world that didn't make any spiritual sense: the same place he was attempting to reach with Popol Vuh. Opening with the twenty-one-minute 'Ich mache einen Spiegel' ('I Make a Mirror') — an epic split into three movements — Fricke unfurls layers of droning Moog that draw you in gently before Trülzsch's earthy percussion comes in — a dense thicket of jangling handheld drums. There is practically nothing in the way of traditional melody or progression on *Affenstunde*: like Tangerine Dream's dark cosmic master-piece *Zeit*, say (itself heavily influenced by Fricke, who guested on the album), it's concerned with textural layering, space and density. This is *deeply* trippy music: too disquieting and shot through with tension to work as ambient, but a definite head journey nonetheless. There is nothing quite like it in the wider Fricke discography, although the next Popol Vuh record — *In den Gärten Pharaos* (1972) — is generally held in higher critical regard.

Carrying a more regal, neoclassical bearing than the lo-fi oscillations of *Affenstunde*, *In den Gärten Pharaos* was imbued with glorious pomp, an almost medieval bearing. Fricke's Moog is, again, the driving force but here he has confident control over its previously wayward pitch. He no longer sounds as if he is tinkering, rather heading towards a solid vision — a non-denominational mass. The Moog tones are clearer and cleaner, field recordings of rippling rivers adding an aquiline ambience to the title track and, again, the powerful handheld drums of Trülzsch powering the drones. More powerful still was the transcendent 'Vuh', an eighteen-minute dronal epiphany that saw Fricke adding the foreboding sound of the cathedral organ to the mix.

Indeed, Popol Vuh was largely defined by the feeling of wonder in the face of the unknown and unknowable: Fricke's music is not the sound of reverent worship or spiritual certainty but, rather, the sound of *awe*. It makes sense that the most abiding creative partnership in Fricke's career was with the film-maker Werner Herzog. Herzog's celluloid beat was the idea of the quest: often against incalculable odds, or in foolish, damned circumstances. The sheer *folly* of man, insufferable situations brought on by the rashness of the vainglorious ego, was an overriding obsession for Herzog. In Fricke, he found an artistic spirit who could add a grave, hypnotic sonic rendering to action which so often straddled the fertile boundary between the ritualistic and the masochistic.

The first collaboration between Herzog and Fricke was *Aguirre, the Wrath of God* (1972). Set in the sixteenth century, the film examined the inherent violence and destruction of empire building, following a group of violent conquistadors on the search for the mythical South American city of El Dorado. Starring frequent Herzog collaborator Klaus Kinski — a notoriously maniacal and abusive (though nonetheless absolutely magnetic) figure — the film introduced both cast and crew to Herzog's cruel cabaret. Herzog was a notoriously harsh taskmaster. He put them through their paces to an absurdly visceral degree. On location; sweating it out; lugging heavy equipment through impenetrable jungle; battling insects, sickness, fatigue and a sense of mission creep that mirrored the doomed venture of the narrative, Herzog deliberately set up intense situations, drawing on the creative potential of stress and pain. He wanted films that became more than fiction, that were imbued with the sweat and cortisone of the subject. By beasting his actors and crew, so his thinking went, he'd end up with something powered by a genuine emotional strain that mirrored the fictional material: method acting applied to the entire film-making process, essentially.

Fricke's soundtrack to *Aguirre* was powered by the otherworldly drone of the 'choir organ'. A unique handmade instrument that had been put together by an eccentric Austrian named Herbert Prasch, the instrument was a kind of primitive sampler/organ hybrid. First used by Amon Düül II on *Tanz der Lemminge* (1971), it was an ingeniously bastardised Mellotron. For every key on the Mellotron, Prasch had recorded the corresponding note sung by an actual choir. He then rigged up the keyboard to a cache of tape reels — four huge boxes underneath the keys — and the corresponding note would trigger the sound of the choir singing the note instead of the keyboard note: primitive MIDI, essentially. The result was spectacular. Florian Fricke could now 'play' his own choir and — because each note could loop indefinitely — he could drone any individual note as long as he wanted. It had a magnificently creepy, hyperreal, effect, somewhere between human and machine, as Herzog explained in 1979:

This instrument has inside it three dozen different tapes running parallel to each other in loops. The first of these tapes has the pitch in fifths, and the next has the whole scale. All these tapes are running at the same time, and there is a keyboard on which you can play them like on an organ so that, when you push one particular key, a certain loop will go on for ever and sound just like a human choir but yet, at the same time, very artificial and really quite eerie.[3]

Fricke soon moved from electronic music into baroque instrumentation, delving further into his obsession with religious imagery. He offered the operatic, harpsichord-driven *Hosianna Mantra* in 1972, and recorded various records based around sacred texts throughout the late 1970s. His later records were something of a mixed bag, to say the least, 1990s recordings like *City Raga* (1995) veering perilously close to woo-woo new age territory, lacking entirely the nocturnal mystery of early Popol Vuh. Echoes of Fricke's early records can still be heard today, however. Stereolab were huge Krautrock fans and contributed to the 2011 *Popol Vuh Remixed and Revisited* album, as did producers like Tim Hecker and Russell Haswell. Perhaps the strongest parallel, however — in terms of ancient vibe rendered via modern technology — is drawn with former dubstep pioneer Shackleton — ex-Skull Disco boss — who now works (right) on the edges of techno and bass, ploughing a powerfully hypnotic and epiphanic furrow. Fricke's echo is there in the complex splicing of organic percussion, the feeling of transcendent veneration, the predilection for arcane instrumentation (in Shackleton's case the Italian drawbridge organ, which he plays, samples and reconfigures extensively). Ultimately, Fricke remains one of Krautrock's great outliers. His reverential sound sits outside the wider canon, lacking the rootsy psych-infused looseness of his peers. While the likes of Faust, Amon Düül II and Ash Ra Tempel were pushing the boundaries of rock in service of outer-stellar exploration, Fricke was attempting to navigate inner space.

In London, however, the trip was scuzzier and darker — and space was deep.

In Search of Space

If Krautrock thrived on communal creativity, there were strong parallels in early 1970s west London. In Ladbroke Grove and Notting Hill, the freak scene was serious. A far cry from the gentrified streets of today, the area was a decrepit vista of seedy bedsits, crumbling squats, breaker's yards, lock-ups and industrial lots. Aside from long-standing Caribbean and Irish communities, there were students, penniless bohemians, squatters, jazz heads and drifters of all stripes, while the social landscape — middle-class exodus from the inner city, housing surplus, tolerant socialist-led council, widespread dereliction — provided the perfect conditions for subcultural fermentation and counter-cultural infrastructure.

Underground papers like *International Times* and *Frendz* — which covered music, arts, drugs, politics and legal advice on the various 'hassles' that may befall the average head — had headquarters in Ladbroke Grove, alongside street markets, head shops, and a serious drugs scene. Key squat-lands were Freston Road — where in the late 1970s squatters had declared independence and formed a micro state, replete with passports ('Frestonia') — and the area around Portobello Road. The Grove also had a long history of blues parties and shebeens, stretching back to the fifties-basement bars set up in terraced houses where ramshackle sound systems would blast out calypso and, later, reggae and dub.

Throughout the late sixties and early seventies myriad bands called the Grove home, from the Edgar Broughton Band — who played hard acid blues — alongside raga rock favourites Quintessence, the Pretty Things and proto-punk scuzzers the Pink Fairies. Then there were the writers and pub-lishers — J.G. Ballard, Barney Bubbles (who designed most of the Hawkwind covers) and underground SF overlord Michael Moorcock. Myriad dodgy boozers — the Elgin, the Apollo, the Kensington Park Hotel — catered to the ever-growing coterie of heads, and you could get anything you wanted on the streets — Afghan hash, speed, acid and Mandrax being the order of the day.

Sitting atop this fusty, patchouli-scented scene were Hawkwind. Their black cosmic chug was the very soul of the grittier end of early seventies London counterculture, marrying epic sci-fi conceptualism to a street-level sensibility. While closely associated in the collective subconscious with the free festival scene, they were, however, a fundamentally *urban* band. Theirs was a modern-day Hogarthian dreamscape: decrepit digs, greasy spoons, bro-ken-down transit vans, oil-slicked underpasses, dingy backstreets, gaffer-taped windows, astral bedsit flying. If the likes of Pink Floyd and Soft Machine were imbued with whimsy, Hawkwind were full throttle: a chugging black tar liner, proto-punk primitives. It's no coincidence that they were particularly beloved of a young John Lydon and count Jello Biafra and Henry Rollins among their fans. Hawkwind were the perennial outsiders, punk before punk.

Formed in 1969 by Dave Brock — a Ladbroke Grove busker — on guitar and vocals, the original line up also featured Nik Turner on saxophone, Terry Ollis drumming (often naked; often on fistfuls of downers), Dik Mik twisting his rudimentary ring modulator, and a head-bending light show blasting a chemically twisted audience into submission with blinding strobes. They weren't idealists: they were chaos incarnate. There was something medieval about Hawkwind — an anarchic rabble howling at the cosmos, setting up camp wherever would have them. Gigging around west London, they soon attracted the attention of Universal Artists who signed them for a multi-album deal. Their eponymous 1970 debut (produced by Pretty Things guitarist Dick Taylor) was underwhelming, however, serving as a mere hint of things to come. Featuring an acoustic song from Brock's busking repertoire — 'Hurry on Sundown' — *Hawkwind* introduced their trademark space chug on 'Seeing It as You Really Are', although the record was a cleaner, more sedate affair than what they're known for.

The following year's *X In Search of Space* (1971) was the real thing, both musically and conceptually. As we saw earlier in this chapter, the German '*kosmiche*' tag was a simple marketing invention of Rolf Ulrich Kaiser: most of the Ohr bands didn't obsess over space or SF. Hawkwind, meanwhile, were the full ticket: space was the place and *X In Search of Space* introduced their musical and sartorial hallmarks in fully realised form. The underground artist Barney Bubbles started his long association with the band here, his sleeve perfectly representing the music: flashing thunderbolts, black space, Amazonian acid priestess, stars and a militaristic badge motif somehow caught the twisted cosmic chug, while poet Robert Calvert — later to join the band as vocalist — contributed the fabled Hawkwind 'logbook', a demented vision of the band as ancient time-travelling cosmonauts backtracking through space and time to save the human race from itself.

Lyrically, all the Hawkwind themes were present and correct — the grandiose space-traveller narrative ('Master of the Universe'); the perils of pollution and overconsumption ('We Took the Wrong Step Years Ago'); the punky anti-authoritarian polemic ('You Shouldn't Do That') — while musically, the swirling chaos chugged along at a rollicking pace. This wasn't motorik precision barrelling down the autobahn, more a battered transit van wheeling around the M25 with a dodgy clutch and a can of cider spilling on your lap: full throttle, but loose as you like. Terry Ollis's pounding drums were shot through with a drunken jazzer's swing which, in combination with Dave Anderson's two-note bass, imbued the sound with an unrelenting, queasy motion. Dave Brock's three-chord rhythm guitar was equally aggressive, and carried a proto-punk bearing. Hawkwind's dual electronic tinkerers Del Dettmar and Dik Mik, meanwhile, added warped oscillations over the top of it all. Neither were remotely trained in synths. In the BBC 4 documentary

Hawkwind: Do Not Panic, Lemmy recalled Dik Mik sitting and reading the manual for his ring modulator 'on stage, while he was playing'.

Their freewheeling approach to electronics added both a frisson of danger (rumours abounded that Dik Mik could make some poor unfortunate in the crowd soil themselves at his will by dint of the bowel-quaking power of his strange black boxes — a targeted sonic attack) and, crucially, added a dronal texture that both bedded down the sound and evoked the infinite expanse of space referenced in the lyrics. Speaking to Dave Brock a few years back, he explained to me the vital — though, sadly, still unsung — contribution that the pair made to the wider history of electronic music.

> Not a lot of people have ever picked up on it or written about it but Del and Dick never got the acclaim they deserve, they were pioneers. They were completely revolutionary, doing what they did with electronic music. Dik used to go off down Portobello Road to get hold of this mad rudimentary gear. He'd be setting up echo units, audio generators on a card table, wires everywhere. I think Del eventually got an EMS synthesiser that could do a lot more. But the pair of them were quite revolutionary in their electronic gadgetry and what they were doing at the time. We supplied the rhythm and they supplied the electronics that went over the top of it: there were not many other bands in the early Seventies doing that. The essence of Hawkwind is that combination; the weird psychedelic stuff with the echo units and all the electronics.[4]

Hawkwind were uniquely suited — in their hypnotic, driving, muddy chug — to the acid-fuelled chaos of the free festival scene and, by the mid 1970s a ramshackle network was established with regular free events around the country. The first Glastonbury had taken place on Worthy Farm in 1971 (it was preceded by Phun City in Worthing the previous year), and, throughout the decade, the festival circuit did away with the increasingly corporate structures of the mainstream rock industry in favour of temporary autonomous zones. Favouring an anarchic approach to entertainment (everything from free jazz to theatre and modern dance), readily available drugs and a DIY approach to the festival infrastructure, events were self-policing and became a way of life for many. By the middle of the decade it was possible to spend a fair chunk of the summer travelling, and an increasing number lived on the road during these months. Hawkwind were true believers in the cause and — despite being signed to a major label and touring the regular gig circuit constantly — would always make time to play and help out on the free circuit. Hawkwind would often play benefits alongside other like-minded bands (the Pink Fairies were an even more primitive proposition and frequently gigged with Hawkwind) and a freak scene quickly emerged with emphasis on community and mutual support.

The music reflected the heady times. *Doremi Fasol Latido* (1972) was a rawer vibe than *In Search of Space.* By far the nastiest album the band made, it was recorded at Rockfield Studio when the facility was in a state of spartan infancy. The (very) lo-fi production job was a step down from *In Search of Space* but it crackles with atmosphere, evoking a feeling of cosmic dilapidation out in the arse end of space. The bass sound — by this point handled by Dave Anderson's replacement Lemmy — is a far-off rumble, while the electronics sound like they're being picked up on satellite from a distant galaxy. It's magnificently seedy. Opening with the grinding drone of 'Brainstorm' — a chugger that hinges on Brock's Neanderthal thrum, new drummer Simon King's frenetic drum fills and the queasy ring modulator drone of Dettmar — Nik Turner's lyric sets a scene of Burroughsian cosmic dread about the 'paranoia police' who've 'sussed out my potion', a need to get out of the void and escape transformation into android stasis. As Lemmy so memorably had it, Hawkwind were 'a fucking black nightmare, not Pink Floyd' and *Doremi Fasol Latido* was a doom-laden trip. 'Time We Left (This World Today)' is a case in point. A four-part, droning psych beast that draws on Brock's recurring obsession with planetary collapse, all the early seventies Hawkwind audio hallmarks are there: Nik Turner's parping sax squalls; off-key call-and-response vocals, dense electronic noise and a lyric that foretells the end times. *Doremi* itself may (wrongly) not be regarded as an essential Hawkwind record, but its tour was the springboard for the most storied chapter — and album — in Hawklore: *Space Ritual.*

First, though, came 'Silver Machine'. The band's only bona fide hit single, it was an ode to Robert Calvert's bicycle, sung by bassist Lemmy — the only band member who could nail the (really not very) high note in the chorus. Though underwhelming and atypical in sound — a staid rocker lacking the transcendent flight of their album cuts — it nonetheless changed everything for Hawkwind. Reaching number 3 in June 1972, the profits were funnelled into the infamous *Space Ritual* live show, a multimedia bombast involving strobes, disorientating lights, surround-sound PA, dancers and props.

Every element was honed for maximal cranial overload. Hawkwind live was always about the ritual immersive experience rather than ego-driven histrionics. Dave Brock has never been a 'frontman' as such (for one thing, he often stands at the back) and — other than parping Nik Turner, who used to annoy the rest of the band by playing his saxophone very loudly at inappropriate junctures — the lights and smoke and volume were key.

The *Space Ritual* set was largely culled from *Doremi Fasol Latido* and it's these cuts that remain definitive, bassier and more hypnotically driving than the studio versions. The ten-minute opener of 'Born to Go' was particularly majestic: the driving rhythms of drummer Simon King make a huge difference to the sound (he was a far more precise operator than Terry Ollis), his furious fills adding a sense of pitiless forward motion entirely befitting of a band obsessed with outer-galactic travel. Add to this Lemmy's idiosyncratic bass — a toppy tone; bass chords strummed like a surrogate rhythm guitar, as opposed to regular bass runs — and you have a rhythm section that doesn't so much bed down the pocket as gallop over it roughshod. This was the closest any British band ever got to the motorik vibe (indeed, Dave Brock was an early champion of NEU!, penning the sleeve notes for the UK run of their first album) but looser, woozier. *Space Ritual* was lead-weight heavy. Ads in the music press at the time promoted it as '88 minutes of brain damage' and the dampened chug of 'Upside Down' — near Sabbathian in downer attack — alongside the fearsome version of 'Brainstorm', merit the description. Hawkwind had a rare talent for vamping songs without tearing off into tedious solos or superfluous breakdowns: rather, they extended songs to keep the chug alive and facilitate a mental zone of glorious discombobulation.

Given the theatrical vibes, *Space Ritual* could potentially have gone west into Pete Townshend-esque yawn territory. That it stayed raw was testament to their refusal to compromise their sooty essence. Hawkwind were that rare beast: a band who could flirt with the grandiose and conceptual while retaining true grit. Which isn't to say that *Space Ritual* didn't have its share of high camp: the Michael Moorcock-penned spoken-word 'Sonic Attack', for example, saw Robert Calvert deliver the iconic 'Do Not Panic!' speech amid a churning maelstrom of electronic drones and squalls and has been a vital part of the live show ever since. Proper music-hall greasepaint, it's a gloriously OTT spectacle. Indeed, spoken-word passages (which frequently appear on Hawkwind records) also served to connect the band to the sci-fi counterculture that provided them with their unique lyrical bent.

Wildly prolific underground sage Michael Moorcock was a key instigator. He churned out books at a fearsome pace (check his essay 'How to Write a Novel in Three Days' for detailed discussion of his frenetic method) and collaborated with writer Michael Butterworth on two deeply eccentric Hawkwind-themed novels — *Time of the Hawklords* — and its sequel *The Queens of Deliria* (in which Hawkwind have to save the world from the music of Elton John). Live, the spoken word — alongside the lights, dancers and oscillators — added a theatrical element. Dave Brock was always adamant that Hawkwind should offer an escape from the everyday, that the live show should be more immersive experience than the regular gig. As Robert Calvert explained to the *NME* in 1972:

> I suppose if the underground has any meaning at all, we're part of it, simply because we don't see ourselves as part of the music industry . . . Gigs seem to get into a very ritualistic, tribal thing where people come to lose their personal identity and expand their consciousness collectively.[5]

Calvert also contributed to the band's wider fictive universe, penning the detailed space log that was included in *X In Search of Space* and contributing the lyrics and vocal to the controversial 'Urban Guerrilla' single in 1973. Directly inspired by the febrile political atmosphere of early 1970s Europe — IRA bombings, Baader-Meinhof, the Angry Brigade et al. — the lyrics pointed to a clean break from the late 1960s hippy idealism ('let's not talk of flowers and things that don't explode') but quickly caught the ire of the BBC due to the British mainland bombing campaign being waged by the IRA at the time. Despite reaching number 39 in the singles chart in July 1973 it was withdrawn after three weeks.

Both *Hall of the Mountain Grill* (1974) and *Warrior on the Edge of Time* (1975) were more progressive than anything the band had attempted before. The narcotic chug and cosmic grot were still present, but the addition of Simon House on violin and Mellotron brought a newly found melodic complexity. *Hall of the Mountain Grill* — named after the Ladbroke Grove greasy spoon that sustained the band on those rare occasions they deigned to actually eat — opened with 'The Psychedelic Warlords'. A call to arms for all those 'sick of politicians, harassment and laws' it decried the disaffection of modern life — a common Hawkwind theme. The pace was slightly less frenetic, the vibe less tripped out — Robert Calvert's trademark spoken-word interludes are notable for their absence — and the instrumentation clearer. *Warrior on the Edge of Time* signalled a return to the feeling of the early records: SF themes, portentous spoken-word passages, Dave Brock's brittle rhythmic, monotone thrum and great swathes of space echo covering everything, albeit underpinned by a cleaner production and the continuing melodic chops of Simon House. From the darkly driving 'Magnu' to the grand conceptual majesty of the title track, it's arguably their most fully realised studio album, perfectly straddling the more considered sound of their preceding album and the wilder, rougher early vibes. Coming in the heyday of progressive and conceptual rock — Pink Floyd, Yes, late-period Zeppelin, Jethro Tull et cetera — *Warrior on the Edge of Time* spoke to prog while remaining resolutely Hawkwind.

Perhaps in a parallel universe Hawkwind are as big as Pink Floyd. Here, though, they were never given their true dues. The festival circuit they'd long helped nurture, while affording moments of glorious freedom, could be unforgiving. The band were expected to play everything going, often paying for rigs and generators out of their own pocket, and all while maintaining a regular touring and recording schedule. If they couldn't make a benefit or festival slot they were, of course, accused of being 'sell-outs' while their association with festivals led to their being unfairly maligned in the UK press as a hippy band. Regardless, the first six Hawkwind records are the *absolute* equal of anything that came out of Germany during the same period: their combination of driving rhythms, oscillating drones, apocalyptic themes and spacey textures a uniquely satisfying brew that belonged equally to the outer reaches and urban west London. *Warrior on the Edge of Time* was the last in the band's classic run, although the band — who went through almost as many line-up changes as the Fall throughout the 1980s and 1990s (for some time Dave Brock has been the sole original member) — have released plenty of strong albums since, ploughing a singular furrow and, in their strange way, connecting dots through punk, the free festival scene and on into rave.

Throughout the 1980s and into the early 1990s — before the Criminal Justice Act of 1994 decimated the free scene — Hawkwind could be found playing on festival line-ups with, say, Ozric Tentacles, Misty in Roots, Levellers, Killing Joke, Crass, Gong and any number of banging techno systems. At its best, the free festival scene was a genuinely free and anarchic vibe that segued the way, organisationally and spiritually, for the rave scene. For many, Hawkwind remain associated with that indelible freedom of spirit — the same freedom that drove Krautrock and the same freedom that was to seep into dance music — although it eventually soured, as Brock explained to me in 2015:

The scene was very much a community organised thing and was good motivation for a lot of people but it became corrupted eventually; dealers came into the scene with heavy drugs, bad drugs . . . It was like a rose that flowered and then withered away and died, that's the way I see it. People saw it as a way of making money. Free festivals only used to have about 100 people; it got bigger and bigger until there were about 60,000 people at the Stonehenge events in the eighties. We played thousands of them, but then the rave scene took over from it in the late eighties, people going into the warehouses and stuff. It was a similar thing with the rave scene because people could just freak out and be themselves and that is the objective, isn't it? To (*shouts*) BE YOURSELF (*laughs*) but in the end the whole thing, unless you keep it wired together, becomes corrupt . . . The thing about Hawkwind is that we were always fond of repetitive riffs, really chugging fast stuff and I think that's why the punks didn't mind what we did. In a sense it was early dance music. Driving, highly repetitive rhythms — we've always had that strong foundation.

One Chord Best

Few matched Hawkwind for droning repetition and sheer hypnotic density. Spacemen 3 were one of the few bands who came close, however — albeit to very different stylistic ends. Informed by no-fi production, and worshipping at the church of the Velvets, the Stooges, Krautrock, the 13th Floor Elevators and the Cramps, they were dirt-box minimalists who'd happily vamp the same chord for hours in a fugue of hash.

Coming out of Rugby in 1982 they were formed by vocalist/guitarist Jason Pierce and bassist/guitarist Pete Kember (aka Sonic Boom) and were completely at odds with both the angular post-punk and more melodic jangling indie of the time, preferring, rather, to fold into a lysergic drift of two chords — even one chord — for hours at a time, channelling the transcendent joy of sheer primal repetition.

A product of the Thatcher years — specifically a drive to escape the dead-eyed aspirational viscousness that personified the decade and made towns like Rugby violent and dispiriting places — Spacemen 3 were steeped in chemical escapism, spiritual mythology and Americana. Pierce sang in a lackadaisical drawl that belied the building, transcendent, quasi-religious awe he sung of.

Kember, meanwhile, often vamped single notes, having been obsessed — La Monte Young-style — with the drone since he was a kid, explaining in 2002 that he was always

> very impressed by droning washing machines, heard through the floor on those sick days in bed off school, and the symphony of summer mowers in suburbia . . . I was always particularly fond of simple music, ideally featuring a drone or common note through-out the music. Basically one chord best, two chords cool, three chords OK, four chords average. Much of my sound in Space-men 3 was textural. Simple drone chords of texture, slow cre-scendo and dynamic — being able to take one chord from the proverbial whisper to a scream.[6]

A demo tape — *For All The Fucked Up Children Of The World We Give You Spacemen 3* — was recorded in 1984 and contained future single 'Walking with Jesus' while debut LP *The Sound of Confusion* (1986) distilled the Spacemen sound to a heavier, dronal essence through the application of ragged overdrive and a distortion tone at once brittle and warm. Pierce had got himself a vintage 1970s RR amp while Kember had a 1960s Vox Conqueror amp, both tweaked to play off each other with lashings of fuzz. They'd sit down while playing; the volume was heinous and there was a gritty, lo-fi visual backing to gigs — cranky repurposed disco lights set to strobe. This was a raw, antagonistic vibe: they were adamant that they only wanted proper heads at their shows and made no concessions to melody, focusing on head-spinning repetition. Songs like 'O.D. Catastrophe' were based around a single chord while their infamous seventeen-minute cover of the 13th Floor Elevators' 'Rollercoaster' was sheer nightmarish mesmeric descent that evoked melting Texan asphalt and bending walls.

Second album *The Perfect Prescription* was markedly more laid back, softening the band's sound somewhat with more melody. However, the drone remained core to the bands ethos. Kember had, by the late 1980s, got into the Turkish *saz* — a stringed instrument similar to the lute that produces a strong drone — and 1989's largely beatless *Playing with Fire* was a chilled affair that carried Eastern and gospel influences (a mood Pierce would fully explore later with Spiritualized). The chemical mood was shifting too. Aside from their beloved acid and hash, they'd started to experiment with MDMA and a distinct — if somewhat uneasy — warmth enveloped songs like 'Come Down Softly to My Soul' and 'Ecstasy Symphony'.

Most hard core, however, was an infamous gig — later immortalised as the live album *Dreamweapon: an Evening of Contemporary Sitar Music* (named after the Angus MacLise sessions of the 1960s) — that took place in 1988 at the Watermans Art Centre in Brentford. Attempting a Theatre of Eternal Music-esque drone session, it was a legendarily chaotic affair. It involved no sitar, for starters: rather Kember droned a single E chord, atop which Pierce improvised. Will Carruthers thought he was playing too, although, as he recalled in his memoir *Playing the Bass with Three Left Hands*, when he went to switch off his bass he found 'that it was impossible to switch it off.'

It was impossible to switch it off because I had never switched it on in the first place. This was quite confusing and embarrassing until I realised that nobody, not even me, who had been sitting on my amplifier, had actually noticed that it wasn't switched on . . .
To this day, I'm not sure if it was art or not.[7]

Chapter 7

REVERSE HARDCORE

The drone was part of the (proto-) punk DNA coding from the start. While Hawkwind were thrashing out the astral judders in west London squat lands, the Stooges tapped a similarly hypnotic rhythmic vein in Michigan. A seedy pummel with brute repetition and lithe physicality at its core, the Stooges' sound was sheer unrelenting hypnosis; a goof-eyed, droning jig for the wastrels and terminal acid casualties of the dilapidated rust belt. Repetition, repetition, repetition: their whole shtick was the glory of primal repetition — bare-bones rock 'n' roll with an avant-noise bent ground out with feral intensity. A base distillation of the increasingly jaded spirit of a dying decade in all its seedy, decrepit confusion, the Stooges offered the perfect soundtrack to the post-Altamont blues, from the dissolution of the summer of love into the ongoing horror of Vietnam, Manson, civil disturbance and narcotised suburban boredom.

A product of the Ann Arbor underground, the Stooges were formed in 1967 by Iggy Pop, the Asheton brothers (Ron on guitar, Scott on drums) and bassist Dave Alexander. Situated forty miles from Detroit, mid-sixties Ann Arbor was a bastion of bohemian rebellion. Regular anti-war protests at the city's University of Michigan campus were frequent, with faculty staff and students organising strikes and teach-ins. The *Ann Arbor Daily*, meanwhile, attracted consternation for an editorial agitating for cannabis legalisation in 1967 and the city became the established stop for those travelling from the East Coast to San Francisco, itinerant heads passing through constantly, communes springing up and the city sustaining a thriving underground scene. Detroit had a harsher vibe altogether. The former automotive power-house was crumbling, most of the major car factories having closed during the fifties, with hundreds of thousands moving out of the inner city to the suburbs. Detroit was left to rot with depressingly familiar tinderbox conditions

— extreme urban poverty, bankrupt local government, widespread racism and police brutality — leading to the 1967 riots in which forty-three people died.

A world away from Ann Arbor's laid-back atmosphere, Detroit none-theless played a major role in the genesis of the Stooges, as it was home to political primitives the MC5. As hard as it got in 1967, the MC5 knocked out hard two-chord, proto-punk R & B with spattering off-key solos courtesy of Wayne Kramer — a free jazz head who looked not to fellow rock 'n' rollers, but to the wild sax of late-period John Coltrane and Albert Ayler for inspira-tion. Famed for their cathartic, brutally loud gigs, the MC5 were managed/propelled by John Sinclair. A Beat poet, passionate jazz fan and revolutionary firebrand who'd founded the White Panther party (in solidarity with the Black Panthers) in 1967, Sinclair saw the MC5 as a state of mind: a means of shaking up the underground consciousness by way of full-body sonic attack. A full-throttle, working-class antidote to West Coast hippy guff, the MC5 gigged relentlessly and left a sweaty mess everywhere they played, garnering both a rabid live following and — due to their revolutionary politics — major-league police harassment.

Among their biggest fans was a teenage Iggy Pop — then plain James Osterberg. He'd done stints playing the drums in gawky high-school bands (he once set out to build himself the 'highest drum riser in Ann Arbor' and sat up there, thwacking away at barn dances), before meeting guitarist Ron Asheton — an aficionado of British beat groups and Nazi memorabilia. Joined by his brother Scott Asheton on drums and bassist Dave Alexander, the Stooges — initially 'The Psychedelic Stooges' — made a primitive racket that threw mutant blues and noise into oddball sludgy rock 'n' roll. It was a strong-ly astringent brew — murky and potent — and, like the Velvets, completely at odds with the prevailing times.

But for a twist of fate the Asheton brothers could have ended up in some Beatles soundalike combo. The brothers were heavily into the British scene, so much so that they flew to London on a fact-finding pilgrimage in 1965. Naively expecting to gain instant access to the main players, Asheton explained in the Jim Jarmusch *Gimme Danger* documentary that he thought he'd be able to get off the plane and meet the Beatles. Quickly disabused of such conceits in London (they'd apparently wandered the streets asking people, in all seriousness, 'Where's Ringo?'), they made their way to Liverpool to visit the Cavern Club. The Beatles were, of course, nowhere to be found. Instead they saw the Who. Astounded by the sweat, feedback and volume, they went home changed.

Unlike the MC5, the Stooges weren't overtly political: they set out to make rock 'n' roll with a similarly animalistic spirit. They did so with an inquiring mind, however. Iggy Pop had worked at Discount Records in Ann Arbor and soaked up sounds from Sun Ra and John Coltrane to Bo Diddley and the Velvet Underground. Avant-garde noisemonger Harry Partch was a particular favourite. A proponent of cranky home-spun DIY electronics, Partch experimented with microtonal scales and bizarre home-made instruments, many of which had names straight out of a Michael Moorcock novel: 'the Chromelodeon', 'the Zymo-Xyl', 'the Quadrangularis Reversum'. A reclusive iconoclast who'd burnt all of his early Eurocentric compositions in a (literal) bonfire of conformity, Partch had dedicated his life to the wild frontiers of experimental sound, alternating between lecturing and periods of homelessness.

'One thing we'd do is get really stoned on marijuana or LSD and we'd turn off all the lights and put on Harry Partch,' explained Iggy in 2016. 'Harry Partch was huge for me. I'd be making instruments while we'd be playing primitive riffs. We'd find a simple theme and play it over and over.'[1] Much taken with Partch's commandeering of household items as noise machines, Iggy started stoned experiments of his own, cranking up juice blenders and vacuum cleaners while Ron Asheton cranked out dunderheaded two-chord riffs, brother Scott thwacking oil drums with mallets. Sometimes, Iggy would stand there with a funnel and attempt to 'bottle' the feedback, playing it up and down the scales while Asheton would mangle and distort a cheap Hawaiian guitar in an attempt to recreate a sitar.

Disorientation, abrasion, noise — the drone was intrinsic to the Stooges from the start. Living in a tumbledown farmhouse on the city limits of Ann Arbor, they subsisted on strong hash, cheap wine and bad acid. They pursued their sound relentlessly. Billed as 'The Psychedelic Stooges' they made their live debut on Halloween 1967 at the Grande Ballroom in Detroit supporting the MC5. It was here that Iggy Pop honed his torso-flexing live chops, his bodice-ripping style inspired by reading books about Ancient Egypt in the library and sagely noting that the pharaohs 'never wore shirts'. The Michigan scene was gaining traction; the MC5 could fill venues of a few thousand capacity without a deal. Soon the majors were interested and in 1968 Elektra signed both the MC5 and the Stooges on the same day.

The Stooges' eponymous debut was recorded in 1969 by former Theatre of Eternal Music and Velvets man John Cale. Cale had been a vital thread of the drone continuum since the early sixties and the Stooges had been inspired by the Velvets, Iggy Pop liking the fact that they were 'simple — the droning and some of the moods had a big influence on us. So when they suggested John Cale we thought it was perfect. That record wouldn't have felt the same if we hadn't of brought it to New York and played it to John Cale. I remember he wore a big black cape like Z Man in *Beyond the Valley of the Dolls.*'[2]

The Stooges was a raw beast, and suitably fraught in execution. Entering the studio with only four songs — 'I Wanna Be Your Dog', 'No Fun', '1969' and 'Ann' — they cut an early version of the album by extending each of the tracks with improvised jam sections on the end of each song. On playback it was deemed too meandering, however, so the band — holed up at the Chelsea Hotel — went back in, writing and recording 'Cool Time', 'Little Doll' and 'Not Right' at the double. Opening with the sucker punch of '1969' and 'I Wanna Be Your Dog', the tone of *The Stooges* was driving, down-tuned and sinister from the start, a white-glare riposte to the prevailing loved-up vibes of the time. The former was a basic dunderheaded chug, a two-chord celebration of blank-eyed teenage apathy; the latter riffed on submission and sadism. A droning slug to the slobber chops, '. . . Dog' was grindhouse nihilism, a paean to sadomasochism that hinged on a bluesy call-and-response drawl, doom-laden descending riff and drums that dragged just behind the pocket. To this, John Cale added a genius touch of sheer sleaze: tinkling handheld bells and an out-of-tune piano vamping a solitary note like a saloon drunk in a spaghetti western.

Strangest of all was the drug-blitzed inertia of 'We Will Fall'. Ten minutes of narcotised drone that hinged on Iggy's Om chant — sounding like a negative inversion of the mantra — that hummed with dark ritualistic intensity, it connected the Stooges on an alchemical level to the ancient — but also straight to the New York underground via producer John Cale's viola drone dragging through the mix. To include such a muddy dirge on the *first* side — among material of such urgency — was an audacious, even foolhardy move. The song was derided on release. *Rolling Stone* described it, for example, as a 'ten-minute exercise in boredom that ruins the first side of the record.'[3]

Recording their debut over five days in a tiny studio above a peep show theatre in Time Square, the Stooges were mainlined into the sleazy energy of New York. But while *The Stooges* was a tight set of songs, it didn't *quite* capture the animalistic essence of the band. Cale's production was slightly anaemic, a little top-heavy. Having played in both the Theatre of Eternal Music and the Velvet Underground, as well as untold hours recording viola drones and feedback on his own in his loft, he was well versed in serious volume.

Even he wasn't prepared for the chaotic onslaught the Stooges brought into that tiny studio, however. He urged the band — who were used to cranking it all the way to oblivion in Ann Arbor — to turn down their battered Marshalls. The Stooges refused, staging an impromptu *Tap*-esque 'strike' in the studio, as recounted by late guitarist Ron Asheton in 2006: 'He said, "This is a studio, you don't use a stack on *10*",' says Ron. 'I said: "Yeah we do, I don't know how to play any other way." So we went into the vocal room, got some cushions out and kept smoking hashish until John Cale goes, "OK, we'll compromise." The compromise was nine!'[4] The Asheron brothers found the transition to the studio particularly tricky. Used to playing as Iggy writhed and juddered in front of them, like some demented pied piper, they found they couldn't get a decent backing track unless he danced around the control room while they were playing.

If *The Stooges* hinted at the power source, *Fun House* (1970) was a runaway train to the mainline. Bringing a flailing psychedelic noisenik vibe, *Fun House* was maximal carnage: a carnal *furnace* of a record. The songs were more aggressive but also funkier and looser. The beats were harder, a sheet of sound aesthetic brought on by saxophonist Steve Mackay who was instructed by Iggy Pop to 'play like Maceo Parker on acid'.

'Loose' laid down their infernal stall. A down-home garage rocker that hinges on Asheton's chugging rhythm, it sets up the amphetamine rhino charge of 'TV Eye' perfectly, the tension ramping as Iggy drawls and yelps before the raw thrash is taken down a notch on 'Dirt'. Simultaneously paying homage to the blues while foreseeing the wide-open spaces of post-rock, 'Dirt' is driven by the vamping groove of David Alexander's funky bassline while Ron Asheton adds a lurching tapestry of creepy reverb-laden notes over the top. '1970' riffs on the previous album's '1969', albeit ramping up the energy with the gloriously reckless parping of Steve Mackay starting up at the three-minute mark. This is the precise moment that *Fun House* passes garage righteousness and enters transcendent spiritualism: grinding blue-collar swing. Ending on the demented wreckage of 'L.A. Blues' — a song that channels the energy of free jazz, Mackay blowing like Coleman — and grinding hardcore. Nihilistic, driven and darkly surreal *Fun House* is the greatest Stooges album by some distance: if their debut gloried in depression, this was the sound of strutting court jesters inverting negative energy, tapping the bizarro river of Americana and using it to their alchemical advantage, rather than wallowing in self-pity. Yes, there is a blank-eyed intransigence but the body is moving, spinning, *wheeling*: this is music of gaucheness and sex, a life force so potent it threatens to overwhelm. On *Fun House* the repetition — the hypno-thrum — is alchemically powerful: a charnel-house drone.

I spoke to Henry Rollins — ex-Black Flag and Rollins Band singer and die-hard Stooges authority — about the mystic power of the band.

'I think the Stooges understood the power of energy being found in the *centre* of the music, and that you had to go deep in to tap it, as they do so perfectly on *Fun House*,' he said. 'Ron's guitar playing is amazing but — for me, at least — the power of the Stooges came from the pocket that Scott Asheton found so instinctively on every song. The Stooges' understanding of drone and its power potential on "We Will Fall" showed a band navigated by a collective instinct, like a pack of hyenas on the Serengeti. Their chops were natural. What they did, you can't learn — you have it or you don't.

'Ron understood tone and sustain. A drone sounds — to the untrained ear — as one sound: but it's dynamic, a blizzard of intervals. You hear Ron harness this power in the opening chords of "I Wanna Be Your Dog". I think it's fair to say that a few of those Michigan guitar players from that time understood the power of sustain and drone — from Fred Sonic Smith to Ted Nugent. But the Stooges — at their core — were a blues band. All those Michigan groups had an ear for it. "Dirt" sounds like a repurposing of "Born Under a Bad Sign", a lot of Iggy's phrasing is blues based. There's intensity and power found in that repeating, unrelentingly urgent style — that in *itself* is a drone. The Stooges mainlined into something dangerously powerful, that's why they eventually had to stop. The music had broken them. That's how close they got to the source. Most musicians can rest assured they'll never get within one hundred miles of that. Good. They'll live longer.'

Guitar Trio

In their own idiosyncratic way, the Ramones were bare-bones minimalists. Drawing on the Stooges and the MC5's primal noise twinned with a goofball rock 'n' roll sensibility, in their white T-shirts, ripped jeans and battered trainers they looked like some mutant fifties street gang while their songs — tough, fast, buzz-saw — were equally uniform. They lacked the sex and sinew of the Stooges, the righteous firebrand rage of the MC5 or the wasted glamour of the New York Dolls. Instead they had a thrilling *fragility*, a tragicomic vibe: the bowl cuts, the gangling limbs, the obsession with mental disarray, dodgy medication, heartbreak. They chronicled outer-borough New York in all its weird day-glo glory, providing a sharp riposte to the bloated stadium rock of the mid seventies.

For minimalist punk pioneer Rhys Chatham — soon to marry punk energy with minimalist drone power on his groundbreaking *Guitar Trio*

— they provided a particularly visceral inspiration to get out of the lofts and into the streets. It was Chatham, alongside like-minded composers like Glenn Branca, who successfully melded the conceptual avant-garde to the gut-punch feeling and swagger of rock 'n' roll, as he explained to me:

'My friend Peter Gordon said to me "Rhys, have you ever in your entire life been to a rock concert?" and I said "no" (*laughs*). I'd heard records — I loved the Velvet Underground — but Peter just laughed and said, "Well, there's this group playing tonight in this nice club nearby. Why don't we go together?" Well, the place was CBGB's and the band was the Ramones! Oh, man — it was just so *romantic*. The image of the four skinny guys with the leather jackets? I'd never seen anything like it in my life. This was May of 1976 — by that time they really had their act together, they were seasoned performers. I thought, you know what? This music is not dissimilar to what I'm doing, stylistically. They might be using two more chords than I normally use (*laughs*). They might be a little more complex, but it's not dissimilar to the music that I was doing. A logical evolution of three chords. I thought I can really get into this. I was so excited by it. I wanted to make barre-chord music. I got together with this guitarist in Peter's band — Scott Johnson — and he had this beautiful Gibson and he showed me how to play barre chords and a basic blues scale and the rest is history — that's how I got into it. I found what I wanted to do — integrate this wonderful rock music, make it my own.'

Feeling the drone was — in its own strange way — intrinsic to punk rock from the start. Chatham eventually set about amalgamating the urgency that energised him that night into his minimal compositions. Born in Manhattan in 1952, he had originally trained in classical flute before studying composition with Morton Subotnick at New York University. An early encounter with Terry Riley's *A Rainbow in Curved Air* at the Electric Circus left him conflicted, but ultimately thrilled — and set him on the path to minimalist composition.

'I went to the concert and there was this long-haired hippy guy and he started playing this thing and I was completely disgusted! (*laughs*) Because — at that time — I was a young composer into atonality and complex music, and here was this guy playing *tonal* music. I went downstairs and I asked for my money back but they wouldn't give it to me and it was kind of expensive. So I went back and thought, "Hey, you know what? This stuff isn't so bad" and I ended up doing it (*laughs*). The first piece was *A Rainbow in Curved Air*. And it changed my life. I walked into that concert a post-serialist composer and came out a confirmed minimalist: not that we used that term back then.'

Working and studying with avant-garde figures including Maryanne Amacher, Charlemagne Palestine and Éliane Radigue, Chatham eventually snagged a gig tuning La Monte Young's piano in exchange for piano and vocal tuition. Singing in the hash-fuelled early 1970s iteration of the Theatre of Eternal Music, he immersed himself in New York's avant-garde underground. His early minimalist pieces from the period were strongly influenced by his teachers (his best-known piece from the period — 1971's *Two Gongs* — was a psychedelic affair that saw Chatham layering deep tones from two Chinese gongs, the idea being to keep the tones ringing loud for as long as humanly possible); however, they soon left him unsatisfied. 'They were student pieces,' he explains. 'I'd hear La Monte and think "OK — I can do something like that" but after 1976, I thought, "I've got to break away from my teachers."'

The Ramones provided Chatham's second epiphany. He immediately set about galvanising the energy and sweat and grime that he experienced that night in CBGB's and marrying it to the overtone drone of multiple electric guitars. *Guitar Trio* (1977) was the spectacular result: a powerfully hypnotic twenty-minute piece, originally for three guitars (although sometimes performed with many more), it was comprised of layered, ringing overtones from a single chord. The result is a transcendent wave building towards epiphany. The rock element, however, is front and centre. And, unlike a majority of minimalist pieces, drums are pivotal, busy fills adding dramatic movement. It's uplifting, joyous, *loud*. If La Monte Young and Éliane Radigue were harnessing eternity through stasis — and, in the case of Young, negating the psychic stress of the city — Chatham was about *energy*. His take on minimalism was soaring, a constantly building crest, and *Guitar Trio* would prefigure his later 'guitar army' ensemble pieces that would see him leading upwards of one hundred players in overtone overdrive.[5]

Chatham took minimalism out of the art spaces, galleries and lofts and into downtown dives like CBGB's and Max's Kansas City. This was the drone of New York amplified as much as the city itself: unapologetic, in your face: resolutely *maximal*. That it was happening at the exact same time as no wave — music that prized abrasive textures and jagged noise — made sense, although the vibe was markedly different. Chatham's massed guitar pieces were imbued with widescreen drama — sonics of the city but also the sky: it was awestruck. By proxy, no wave was urban ergonomics, the sound of a city in a death rattle: frayed nerves, flickering subway light, burnt-out tenements, fires burning in oil drums, heinous chemical intake and the ever-present threat of violence and insanity, set to a jittery, propulsive soundtrack that took in mutant funk, one-chord sandpaper chops and trigger-finger tension.

New York was a mess. Declared bankrupt in 1975, it had endured woeful financial mismanagement for over a decade. Much like Thatcher and the 'managed decline' of Liverpool, the city was left to rot when various bailout plans were rejected by President Ford, and an *extreme* recession ensued. Manhattan's Lower East Side — today gentrified, sanitised, expensive — was one of the worst-hit areas. Documentary footage shows a panorama of decay: piles of rubble, rats running free, entire blocks demolished, frequent blackouts. Martin Scorsese's *Taxi Driver* (1976), of course, caught the vibe: boiling-point tension. Downtown Manhattan was a free for all: there was a huge surplus of crumbling, dilapidated housing, as artist Maripol had it in the 2012 documentary *Blank City:* 'all the straight people were trying to get out. But all the freaks? We were trying to get in.'

Rent was dirt cheap and a coterie of artists, addicts and film-makers piled in, creating an alternative universe among the derelict tenements and brownstones. Experimental film-makers like Jim Jarmusch, Vivienne Dick, Amos Poe and Vincent Gallo slung movies together quickly — Factory style — on black and white Super 8, documenting the city in its gritty decrepitude, mucking in on each other's films and pooling resources. Likewise, bands like Mars, DNA, Suicide, Teenage Jesus and the Jerks, James Chance and the Contortions and — later — Sonic Youth and Swans, brought the dystopic daily grind to life with feral intensity. There was no script, no limits. The Velvets, the Stooges, the Cramps, the Ramones, Blondie, Talking Heads et al. may have paved the way but no wave took a different path. It denied rock 'n' roll itself as the immovable foundation stone. Instead funk, free jazz, grindhouse movies, noise, sex, the tooth-loosening grind of amphetamines, gut-rot wine, the sheer *hustle* of daily survival in a city gone to the wall were the drivers.

No wave burned hard and fast. Most of the key records were made in a scant two years between 1979 and 1980, and Brian Eno produced the scene's definitive document — *No New York* — in 1979. Focusing on four bands — the Contortions, Teenage Jesus and the Jerks, Mars and DNA — the compilation pivoted on scraping sheets of metallic guitar, shouted call-and-response vocals, drums devoid of superfluous fills or cymbals, unusual, twitchy time signatures, repetitive grooves and feedback. There was an urgent funk at play: a jitterbug energy. The Contortions' 'Dish it Out' was a case in point: parping saxophone atop howled vocals, atonal Rhodes keys evoking traffic noise. Free jazz, funk, avant-garde, drones and tribal rhythms, mutant disco — all shoved into the meat blender.

From the Ramones — steeped as they were in the iconography and musical language of 1950s rock 'n' roll — to bands like DNA and Mars in the space of four years? New York moved *fast*. Lydia Lunch famously stated that 'punk was just Chuck Berry riffs sped up'. Some pointed to the Velvet Underground at their most dissonant as a no wave precursor but, as we've seen, Lou Reed was a romantic at heart. He chronicled New York with a rheumy eye. If you're looking for precedents, the Stooges' *Fun House* — with its demented free-jazz parping, dronal underbelly and atmosphere of off-key nihilism — was more on the money.

Teenage Jesus and the Jerks' eponymous 1979 EP veered between a twenty-second wall-o-noise thrashing ('Red Alert') and a nightmarish crawl space of distortion ('Baby Doll') at once foreseeing both the frenetic violence of grindcore and the weird humidity of sludge metal. As always, the music mirrored the drugs: amphetamine pulse offset by the elephantine thwack of long discontinued barbiturates. Here was the perfect evocation of a peculiarly late-1970s brand of chemical intake: the peak and trough of the midnight cowboy.

'You're living in a shitty apartment between two abandoned buildings,' remembered Lydia Lunch in 2012. 'On a nightly basis you're taking your life into your own hands just by walking home. At night you might need a little something to ease the burden of reality . . . There were better drugs in the late seventies, too — Tuinal, Seconal, Quaaludes, all kinds of barbiturates.'[6]

Suicide tapped New York chaos energy like few others. I moderated a discussion with the pair — Marty Rev and Alan Vega — alongside Henry Rollins in 2015, shortly before Vega's death. Before the panel, Rollins described their music as being akin to the 'indigenous music of New York'. That's the core of it. Proto-punk, post-punk, no wave? Call it what you will, Suicide were punker than *anyone* and they'd been at it since the early 1970s, emerging from the performance art scene in the Lower East Side. Hungry and wired, they did it without a guitar, Marty Rev standing implacable in wraparound shades hammering his battered Farfisa keyboard, Alan Vega snarling into the mike and cracking a bullwhip. *Suicide* (1977) was like nothing else: tinny 1950s rock 'n' roll transposed to the lunatic streets and tethered by Rev's crackling power-line drones and weird, childlike melodies. 'Ghost Rider' was demented acceleration — a gnawing, nagging, proto-8-bit squall while 'Frankie Teardrop' is the most harrowing, saddest song ever written — a ten-minute descent into violent desperation and murder-suicide, Vega inhabiting the eponymous 'Frankie' who loses his job and decides on the most drastic action — killing his entire family — in the face of despair. Not many understood Suicide during their initial phase however — they were despised by plastic punks who couldn't fathom the lack of guitar and reacted with ever increasing violence. A disastrous tour supporting the

Clash was a typically chaotic affair, with the Glasgow gig a particular near miss, as the pair recounted to me in 2015:

> They said 'if you can survive Glasgow, you can survive anything' and then we found it embedded in a bass drum. A hatchet. A fucking axe head! . . . See, they started with the Specials. Two bands opened for the Clash on that tour . . . then out comes Suicide and it was 'BOOO!! BOOOOOO!!!' We had to work our way up from there . . . upwards or sideways or downwards, I don't even know . . . you saw all kinds of shit. Glasgow was hard core. Very serious.[7]

Suicide thrived on chaos. They absorbed it all — the humidity, stress, the freezing winters, the radio static, the cigarettes, speed, black coffee. New York endless: no band got under the skin of a city like Suicide. For Rhys Chatham and countless others, however, the frenetic energy of no wave was a life spring, a wonder.

'Things happened very, very fast,' he tells me. 'The rhythm of things happening is much faster in rock than in other forms of music. Groups like DNA, Lydia Lunch, Mars — the people on the no wave compilation album . . . that was my generation. It was so exciting because it was people who couldn't play, but had figured out their own way of playing. I loved Arto Lindsay from DNA, his guitar playing; it was like listening to Steve Lacy or somebody! He was doing these highly asymmetric things. Or Lydia Lunch: when I heard her for the first time I was tearing my hair out with ecstasy (*laughs*). Because I was making guitar pieces that were carefully out of tune and Lydia was doing this DERDEDERDERDER stuff — it was just great. By that time, it felt like the entire art scene was in the rock world.'

The Ascension

Another key figure in the intersection between the art and rock worlds was the late Glenn Branca. Moving to New York from Boston to work in experimental theatre troupe the Bastard Theatre, Branca played in both Chatham's Guitar Trio and with obscure no wave outfit Theoretical Girls, before striking out with his own massed electric-guitar orchestra pieces. A notoriously cranky character who worshipped at the altar of extreme volume and windswept melancholy,

Branca was somebody who — like Rhys Chatham — inhabited the more maximal end of the minimalist oeuvre. No wave had energised Branca as it did Chatham. For him it represented freedom, energy — a move away from both the staid confines of generic rock and what he termed the 'dead' visual arts.

If you want to know why you've even heard of no wave, why anyone even bothered to give it a name, it was because there was this whole new scene of young visual artists who had grown up listening to rock music, who had come to New York to do visual arts, to do painting, to do conceptual art. And when they heard these bands that were clearly coming from the same kind of sensibility that they were coming from, all they could do was imagine themselves up on that stage playing this fucking music.[8]

Reaching epiphany after debuting an overtone piece for multiple guitars at Max's Kansas City in 1980, Branca split Theoretical Girls to focus on the sound that he'd been looking for, breaking down in tears in the rehearsal studio. Realising immediately that his former band was redundant, Branca committed himself to ensemble pieces for electric guitar, writing — and conducting, with hulking physical presence — great walls of dissonant, droning electric guitars. Building his own guitars with closer fret alignment in order to maximise the harmonics, Branca was an evangelist who honed his sound *relentlessly*. And he loved volume. Guitarist Elliott Sharp — one of Branca's ensemble guitarists who performed early gigs — remembered the sound in near synaesthetic terms.

The band was bone-crushingly loud. It was not hi-fi loud or disco loud; it was *factory* loud . . . the guitars mashed and clashed, producing a throbbing drone and bright ringing. Suddenly, they would clarify into a two-chord stomp, like the Stooges' heavier moments. As the music neared its extended climax, a startling physical manifestation to the sound was revealed . . . guitars flailed and overtones rang . . . one could *see* the sound shake.[9]

Where no wave was brittle, disjointed, shorn of sentiment, Branca's guitar pieces were devastatingly emotive. *The Ascension* (1981) was a ceaseless build of cacophonous rhythm guitar alongside pounding drums, walls of feedback and harmonic overtone. It's dense and dronal but transiently beautiful. Check the sweaty-palmed, chase scene-esque build of 'The Spectacular Commodity' — the way Branca amps the tension to unbearable levels before breaking out the high-end overtones at around the nine-minute mark, signalling resolution. It's devastating. In both Branca and Chatham we foresee the obsession with textural *vastness*, great plains of sound that evoke cinematic grandeur, that bands like My Bloody Valentine, Loop and Mogwai — the whole shoegaze and post-rock continuum, essentially — would soon make their beat. First, however, a new generation of NYC guitarists were galvanised in the most visceral of terms.

Bad Moon Rising

For many musicians in early 1980s New York, performing in either Branca or Chatham's multi-guitar ensembles was a rite of passage. Due to the collaborative nature of the pieces both were instigating there was a steady stream of players, usually with links to the avant-garde or no wave undergrounds, droning out the feedback in Lower East Side dive bars. Sonic Youth's Lee Ranaldo — one of the most innovative guitarists of all time — was one such player. Having played with Branca in the early 1980s, he'd also been transfixed by experiencing Chatham's *Guitar Trio* live at Max's Kansas City in 1979. Speaking today, he recalls a sonic experience of near psychedelic potency:

'When I first moved to New York some of the first music I saw was Rhys Chatham and Glenn Branca,' he tells me. 'It was right at the time of no wave . . . people were doing radical music in this city that was washed up and dirt poor. *Nobody* gave a shit what you were trying to do: it wasn't like there was any money to be made (*laughs*). We went along to Max's one night and it was Rhys playing *Guitar Trio* with Glenn. I remember being astounded by this half-hour piece that was, basically, built around one droning note. When the piece was over, the audience were stunned. When it had finished Rhys said "We're going to play another number" and they just played it again! It was no less thrilling the second time. It seemed to activate some psychoacoustic phenomena . . . I remember coming away from that evening feeling like I'd heard something in actuality that had previously only been heard in my head — like you've heard something you've never heard before, but you've always known. And that's the experience of the drone: people tie it back to the heartbeat in the womb — sometimes it's rhythmic, sometimes it's tonal.'

The individual members of Sonic Youth were — from before their formation in 1981 — deeply embedded in the New York underground. Ranaldo had played with Branca; singer and guitarist Thurston Moore had played in various hardcore bands; bassist Kim Gordon had also played in hardcore bands, and was equally tuned into the DIY art scene. All three were swept up in the visceral energy of no wave, as Kim Gordon put it in a recent interview: 'It was expressionistic but also nihilistic. Punk rock was tongue in cheek, saying "Yeah, we're destroying rock." No-wave was more like "No, we're *really* destroying rock." It was very dissonant.'[10]

Sonic Youth referenced everything from hardcore to free jazz to full-scale noise while remaining, broadly, in the rock 'n' roll sphere. New York — in all its crumbling, anarchic glory — fed into everything they did. Theirs was a fundamentally mongrel sound. Dissonant tunings, doctored guitars, songs that segued into each other on a wave of feedback, primitive garage thrashings, structural dynamics that favoured abstraction and abrasion — they were a mass of energy and contradiction, assimilating every bastard underground form and twisting it to oblivion while keeping the bare-bones structure of guitar, bass, vocals and drums. They were pushing the arrangements as hard as the music; traditional structures were often eschewed in favour of dizzying, queasy stumbles. Crucially, it's hard to think of another (rock) band who held a greater command of *space* than Sonic Youth and — as Ranaldo explains — the drone was a key component of his playing from the early days.

'Some musicians tap into the idea of drone from the very start, like "What does it sound like if you just hold the sustain pedal down and just bang the keys and let them go on as long as they can?" Or lean the guitar against the amp, and one string starts to feedback out at you? You're immediately immersed in the idea of droning . . . I was in a band playing rock 'n' roll covers; we were playing punk covers and Velvet Underground and Stooges songs and I became aware that the Velvets were experimenting with guitars tuned all to one note, and with the viola of John Cale there was this strong dronal element. Even the Beatles — a lot of George Harrison's songs carry a heavy droning element. It's a part of *all* music so there's no reason that it wouldn't be a part of rock 'n' roll as well. At a certain point I started to become aware of people who were working with it formally, like Glenn and Rhys or people like Steve Reich or Philip Glass or La Monte Young and Tony Conrad and Terry Riley. And the Velvet Underground were a great link between the Theatre of Eternal Music and John Cale.

'New York was an island off the coast of America, almost,' he continues. 'Isolated in the way that, say, West Berlin was isolated. The audiences here were not coming with any expectations that there would be a specific sound. New York was a hermetic scene at that time: there was no real outside influence. There was no internet, there were no magazines covering it or anything like that. If you lived downtown you were able to witness these people doing experimental things but, after a number of years, there was no way that anybody else understood it, but within New York people were accepting of just about every experimental test that you could make.'

Slow-building tension, dissonance and drone were at the core of the early Sonic Youth sound. Their debut album — *Confusion is Sex* (1983) — released on Glenn Branca's Neutral Records — hung on Moore and Ranaldo's jagged guitar weave, moving like a serpent over hot cracked concrete. It's a disquieting listen. An atmosphere of sepulchral dread prevails. '(She's in A) Bad Mood' sees the guitars scraping, plinking and buffering against one another in a loose, downer stumble while the funereal trudge of 'Protect Me You' offsets Kim Gordon's matter-of-fact vocal (a harrowing story of sexual abuse) with a menacing three-note bassline anchoring the mix. Moore and Ranaldo's guitars have a tactile quality, like layers of colour on a Jackson Pollock painting: check the plinking twine on 'The World Looks Red' — gangling sound coming from all angles — or the atonal discomfort of 'Confusion is Next': these are guitars that drone, judder and plink *all at once*. There is a subtly nightmarish quality to *Confusion is Sex*, a hall of mirrors aspect: all the recognisable components of rock 'n' roll morphing and refracting at unpredictable junctures. Ranaldo and Moore bring an *alien* approach to their playing — a hacking of the sensory potential of the instrument that evokes a Burroughsian cut-up, the familiar rendered uncanny. Ranaldo recalls Glenn Branca as one of the galvanising influences in his own experimental approach towards the instrument.

'In my early period of working with Glenn he was starting to get more expansive and build his own instruments. He created a few instruments that were made from a two-by-four of wood with some pick-ups and strings — very primitive. He was experimenting with multiple bridges on the strings and he discovered this technique where you divide a string in half, you divide a string in thirds, and you end up with these different overtones . . . I had a few experiences performing with this instrument and I was looking to do something similar with an electric guitar. If you slip a screwdriver under the strings, there are certain frets . . . if you put a screwdriver underneath the ninth fret you get a chiming, bell-like sound. It wasn't a punk rock move, like (*shouts*) "stick something under the strings!" (*laughs*) — more trying to get this alternate bridge to change the sound of the strings. With an electric guitar it made this angelic kind of chiming sound and that's what you hear on "The World Looks Red" from the first album.'

Sonic Youth not only disassembled the fabric of rock but the means of production. Screwdrivers jammed between the strings; tape loops; guitars turned on to bizarre tunings; amps EQ'd to an inch of the their lives — they were channellers of accidental electricity and peculiar happenstance.

Bad Moon Rising (1985) ruminated on warped Americana, sex, death and the end of sixties innocence — one of the bands recurring themes — placing hippy idealism as a putrid, rotting albatross around the neck of a sickly urban America. The dissolution of shared togetherness, the rot beneath the painted surface of the white picket fence: an atmosphere of oppressive, sepulchral claustrophobia prevails. The cover — a hulking pumpkin-faced scarecrow standing over a dark, crumbling New York City — might have been comic book horror, but the music was imbued with a genuine menace. 'Death Valley '69' was a case in point; a duet between Thurston Moore and Lydia Lunch, it lurches along like a drugged greyhound stumbling out of the traps, Ranaldo vamping the droning lick while Lydia Lunch and Moore embark on a hallu-cinatory trawl through a desert murder scene. It's a master class in dynamic tension, evoking a febrile dream landscape: the psychic residue of a thousand bad trips converging in the pitiless desert sun. 'Ghost Bitch' is swaddled by the drone of reverb-laden guitars, field recordings and jagged industrial clangs before breaking into an unremitting tribal pound while Kim Gordon rumi-nates on the violence at the core of the formation of America. 'I'm Insane', meanwhile, was (lyrically) assembled from fragments of pulp novels collected by Moore, the hand of chance casting a sinister shadow.

For all its dark imagery, *Bad Moon Rising* isn't devoid of light, however: the sickly glare of the sun beats down oppressively — New York humidity, musty apartments with the blinds drawn, sunlight streaming through the cracks — day unfolding amid narcotic sleep. Songs roll into one another, stitched together by minimal judders, noise, dreamlike radio static. As Ranaldo recalled, 'It's was us working out what we were getting at compositionally. On the more dronal pieces like "I'm Insane" and some of the other things, we were using tape loops live on stage with tape decks. There were recordings of the Stooges and we were incorporating a lot of other different elements. The song "Ghost Bitch" from that record has me feeding back from an acoustic guitar, long droning tones like a fog horn or something (*laughs*).'

EVOL (1986) built on the dank vibe set up by its predecessor (*EVOL* being 'love' spelt backwards) but here the dissonance was tempered by a more considered melodic bent. New drummer Steve Shelley had an ability to slink around the haunted leads, powering up to tsunami volume when need be and holding back to the merest brush when the time called. His sense of dynamics changed the band significantly, as did the new-found melodic sensibility. Check Kim Gordon's whispered vocal on 'Shadow of a Doubt', the tension between the plinky lead and threat of rhythmic explosion held back time and again, or how the warped countrified twang on 'Madonna, Sean and Me' gives way to a face-blasting noise. The searing dissonance doesn't work against the melody, rather accentuates it. Sonic Youth were, of course, soon to change the course of alternative rock for ever with the more polished stylings of *Daydream Nation* (1988) — one of the most storied and influential records of the era, and arguably *the* vital catalyst for the grunge explosion a year or two later — but it's those first three records that are imbued with such eerie luminescence; more than any others in their sprawling discography they show the haunting and dronal, rather than judderingly abrasive, legacy of no wave: the city that never sleeps in fitful slumber.

Filth

Swans traded on breeze block slabs of sound that didn't so much evoke New York as sound like the inner scream of the city *itself*: the walls expurgating a thousand sickening sights. If early Sonic Youth represented a flight out of no wave's nihilistic ghetto, early Swans records did the precise opposite: they distilled the grot and anger and brittle funk and seething monotony into a vial of venomous potency. They were an exercise in brutality, in endurance. This was end-times music: Swans were the band who actually made good on no wave's promise of bug-eyed annihilation. They sounded like they were channelling something that existed outside of them, something hideous and exhausting and true.

First album *Filth* (1983) was released on Glenn Branca's Neutral Records and welded clattering rhythms, barked vocals, atonal guitars and swung grooves in a sonic rhino charge. Where no wave bands like Mars or DNA were all jittery amphetamine-charged energy and jangling top end, Swans were sheer physicality. They were propelled by a stilted, dubwise approach to bass weight: the sub-frequencies were bowel quaking, the rhythms industrial. They were known for their volume — people would vomit; venues would complain, all that jazz — while atmospherically, Swans were akin to the movie *Falling Down* (which saw a white-collar worker played by Michael Douglas undergoing a violent mental disintegration triggered by the myriad daily absurdities and micro humiliations of modern life) made flesh. Like that movie, *Filth* casts urban life as endurance test: a nightmarish trawl through banality and pain and shit and tension and futility. Lyrics — repetitive sloganeering alluding to violence and submission and sex — are barked out like a drill instructor, while the rhythmic churn clangs and reverberates with a brittle intensity. There is no vestige of melody or let-up. Even when not working with sustained tones — and they often are — the repetitive grind ossifies into a drone: Swans are *über* drone. It's pointless dissecting individual tracks on *Filth* — the whole is the point. The ossification of hope. The infinite grind — so much so that it can be a spiritually *deadening* experience to be taken with extreme caution — a world away from the soaring transcendent majesty of later-period records like *The Seer* or *The Glowing Man*, imbued as they are with a far more hopeful, widescreen sense of spiritual uplift and sonic awe.

Swans were unparalleled — indeed, remain unparalleled — in terms of claustrophobia. Others were traversing similar ground, however. Big Black, Steve Albini's Chicago noise-rock crew were using industrial inflected rhythms — namely a battered Roland drum machine — scattershot bastardised funk guitars, brittle sheets of noise and echo box drones in staccato two-minute blasts that shone a light on the absurdity, hypocrisy and grotesque aspects of humanity. Their 1987 LP *Songs About Fucking* was their most fully realised record, an abrasive trawl through murder, revenge and humiliation — mostly gleaned from real-life news stories — and rendered in Steve Albini's quivering snarl.

From the cover (gleaned from a Japanese pornographic comic) to song titles like 'Columbian Necktie' — taking inspiration from the legendarily horrific method of cartel gangland execution in 1980s Bogota — to the sludge and drawl of 'Kitty Empire' and the frenetic motorised pound of 'Fish Fry', everything was rage and sour breath and slamming doors and palpitating tension. The rhythms call to mind the rabid pulse of mid-period Ministry/Revolting Cocks — the beats can push upwards of 180 bpm at times — while the guitars, ducking and weaving between Albini and Santiago Durango were a strange and powerful animal. The pair went to great pains to ensure that their riffs were as alien as possible: unusual tunings were favoured, while Albini was notorious for using metal, as opposed to plastic, picks. He dubbed his custom-built guitar 'Black Sled' and made heavy use of a motley collection of distortion pedals.

Big Black are hard work — not in the elemental way of Swans, say, but more in a *needling*, deliberately irritating sense; like some sadistic micromanager in a polyester suit hovering over your shoulder. Albini was a past master at assuming roles; he'd inhabit these flawed, violent, sad people and throw them into your face. His vocal delivery — ranting, raving, staccato — predates the spittle-flecked delivery of Consumer Electronics or Sleaford Mods; indeed, the emotional drivers are very similar — a fury at entitlement and idiocy and latent sadism. On 'Steelworker' from *Lungs* (1982), for example, he assumes the pathetic bravado of the insecure macho man — 'I'm a steelworker! I kill what I eat! I'm a hunter gatherer!' And this is the very core of Big Black: the subversion of impotent anger.

Others took a yet more warped approach. Butthole Surfers were the most demented band of the 1980s. Here was all the hallucinatory slush of backstreets Texas — meat sweats, drunken afternoons, granular speed, blotter acid, bathtub moonshine, prison tats, biker gang law, flickering, late-night grindhouse movies — condensed into a greasy, screwy, ribald whole. They took the anarchic rebel spirit of fellow Texan acid freak overlords the 13th Floor Elevators and pumped it chock full of bovine growth serum: this was music that positively *groaned* with the mondo bizarre excess of the Lone Star State. Famed for their incendiary live show — and their heroically addled following — their music was a hotchpotch of electric blues, psych rock, the weirder edges of hardcore and no wave, chaotic sampling, chants, found sound, dronal guitars and shrieking, gibbering, drooling vocals.

Emerging from the San Antonio underground in 1981, Butthole Surfers gigged relentlessly before signing to Touch and Go in 1985 and reaching a frothing, incandescent crescendo in 1987 with *Locust Abortion Technician*. An electric gumbo that packs more into its scant thirty-two minutes than most bands would manage in the same number of years, *Locust Abortion Technician* is hallucinatory in the extreme; however, it conjures neither transcendent majesty nor black horror. No: *Locust Abortion Technician* calls forth the *mischievous* aspect of psychedelics, the goblin dance, the melting jester, the feeling of insurmountable incomprehension   that feeling that some aspect of the acid itself, deep in your neural pathways — is *enjoying* your discombobulation and playing with you: it's the most troll-like music it is possible to imagine, a waltz of insanity. Taking a Bomb Squad approach to plundertronics, everything from bastardised blues to Thai pop music to electronic noise and gibbering scat vocals are thrown into a blender set to 11 and pulped to a fine, viscous grain. Indeed, the whole thing was recorded at the band's home studio in Austin onto an eight-track — extraordinary given the sheer density of the sound.

Opening with the tumbling, muted blues of 'Sweet Loaf', a Black Sabbath through the mincer vibe prevails, with guitarist Paul Leary's acidic blues tone vamping ad infinitum while Gibby Haines howls unintelligibly and disembodied voices laugh and gibber in the background. It's proper hellbilly gear: 'Graveyard' is a droning slab of tramadol-slow sludge guitars and down-tuned vocals that trudge along at a crawl pace, 'Pittsburgh to Lebanon' is an old-school blues howler shot through with genuine venom. They capture the wet blanket humidity of the Deep South, the apocalyptic grey skies, parking lots, prescription drugs and violence. The drone covers the whole mix but it's the drone of chaos and overload. Although recorded in 1986, *Locust Abortion Technician* foresees the ADHD aspect of the internet age in sharp focus: it's like listening to a hundred radios tuned to different stations occasionally coming into focus in peculiar synchronicity. 'Kuntz' samples distorted Thai pop; 'USSA' uses the scrape of vinyl scratch as a percussive element alongside indefinable metallic churn; 'The O-Men' is completely demented, frontman Gibby Haines channelling a Pentecostal preacher 'speaking in tongues': guttural, grotesque, rabid, disgusting.

No one — not least Butthole Surfers themselves — came close to *Locust Abortion Technician*'s rabid churn. It's one of those rare albums — like the Melvins' *Lysol*, say, or *Earth 2* (more on these later) — that occupies a hermetically sealed vacuum. A few others tapped a similarly obtuse vein to the Surfers, mining the rich vein of the American grotesque. Touch and Go label mates Killdozer made a tar-thick bluesy grind, while the Jesus Lizard were also, at heart, a blues band — albeit an obtuse, screamingly loud and thrillingly debased one. Their singer David Yow was one of the most idiosyncratic front men of the era, writhing and leaping and generally ploughing his own punch-drunk furrow. Both Killdozer's *Twelve Point Buck* (1989) and the Jesus Lizard's *Goat* (1991) share certain elements: namely guttural vocals, a predilection for feedback, grindingly primitive blues riffs, guitars as churning drone generators, and a dark atmosphere of debasement.

In Seattle at the same time, of course, grunge was about to blow. In the next chapter we'll discuss the Melvins — America's most prolific purveyors of surreal heavyocity and the vital role they played — but, aside from them — of the Seattle bands — it was Tad who were closest in spirit to the dronier, noisier Touch and Go axis. Displaying a predilection for sledgehammer groove and a twisted sense of humour, albums like *God's Balls* (1989) and *Inhaler* (1993) were lumped in with grunge but were actually far heavier than most of the bands associated with that world. Tad also lacked that movement's mawkish tendency towards angsty introspection and irritating self-pity. Like the Jesus Lizard, theirs was a sound based on barrelling riffs, repetition and a maniacal, red-eyed delivery. They toured with Nirvana and Soundgarden but never quite broke out of the cult bracket, lacking the hooks of the former or the dynamics of the latter.

Indeed, the first Nirvana record — *Bleach* (1989) — traversed similarly muddy waters. A far heavier beast than their breakthrough *Nevermind* (1991), *Bleach* hinged on the murderously overdriven ('Floyd the Barber') alongside melancholy, poppier gear ('About a Girl'), and it was this very tension — between Beatles-inflected ear-worm melodies and detuned, flailing rock — that would (in slightly more polished form, courtesy of Butch Vig) come to define them, their music soundtracking the lives of millions and changing the course of mainstream rock for ever, sounding the death knell for the stadium histrionics of the 1980s.

The sludgy, dronal, detuned tone that defined grunge had its origins in the early 1980s West Coast punk scene, rather than in Seattle, however, where bands like Flipper, Chrome and Black Flag were subverting the fleetness of punk rock and allowing the drone to run wild through it.

Nothing Left Inside

If punk rock was, in the popular imagination at least, defined by speed — the brittle three-chord race; the hollow-cheeked amphetamine gurn — by the early 1980s, the burgeoning American hardcore scene (alongside UK bands like Discharge) had amped everything to warp-speed velocity.

A movement that thrived on aggression, political agitation, self-discipline and a hard-line DIY ethic, hardcore was never going to dent the mainstream. Bands like Dead Kennedys, DOA and Minor Threat were sheer rhino charge: all tinny buzz-saw guitars, straight-up blasts and no-fi production values. Borders between bands and audience were, by and large, dissolved. Everyone did everything — roadying, fanzine -making, playing, running labels — and a loose network of squats and underground venues was established across the US that supported this passionate grassroots scene.

California quickly became a vital hub. Southern California harboured a network of bands like Circle Jerks, Fear and Black Flag while the Bay Area and San Francisco was home to Crime, Negative Trend and the Dead Kennedys (who came to define the California scene with their firebrand political stance) as well as being the headquarters of notoriously hard-line, genre-defining fanzine *Maximumrocknroll*. Indeed, by the early 1980s, San Francisco was a world apart from the hippy clichés of a decade ago. Nowhere was the souring of the dream more stark than in its former bedrock. Heroin had run rampant in Haight-Ashbury; Jim Jones ran his Peoples Temple from Geary Boulevard before decamping to Guyana and persuading 800 of his followers to drink the Kool-Aid; the Zodiac killer was on the loose and Harvey Milk — the first openly gay politician in America — was assassinated in 1977. Add to this simmering racial tensions, out-and-out gang warfare and some of the starkest urban poverty on the West Coast and it was easy to see why many in the Bay Area had ditched the acid in favour of music that reflected the reality of the daily grind. The Dead Kennedys summed up the feral atmosphere in their frenetic 1980 debut *Fresh Fruit for Rotting Vegetables.*

While most on the hardcore scene were pushing harder and faster, a few notable exceptions were slowing down. Chrome made some of the weirdest music to emerge from the punk diaspora and marshalled electronic bleeps and pings, brittle guitars, hellish oscillations, humid drones, vocals that alternated between harsh barks and opulent warbles and no-fi production values. Their second album *Alien Soundtracks* (1977) was a queasy electric soup that married the energy of punk to a warped Beefheartian open-ended approach, particularly guitarist Helios Creed, who once stated that he wanted Chrome to reflect what he heard when he listened to Black Sabbath on acid. *Alien Soundtracks* is psychically aligned to the blue-collar SF imaginings of Philip K. Dick — like the Stooges put through a time-warping device — the sound of a gritty parallel universe slightly off centre but still recognisable.

San Francisco's Flipper, meanwhile, dealt in loose, fetid groove and an atmosphere of seedy debasement. They sounded like a punch-drunk stumble through the Tenderloin on a bottle of Thunderbird and a clammy fistful of rapidly melting barbiturates; a cough-syrup crawl that hinged on punishingly distorted guitar tone and turgid bass drones. Emerging from the same Bay Area scene that birthed Dead Kennedys, Flipper were a deeply antagonistic proposition who flew in the face of both speed (they played at a funereal trudge) and political agitation, preferring nihilistic paeans to despair and apathy over concern about social injustice.

Predating both Black Flag and the Melvins in reversing punk's tendency towards escape velocity tempos, Flipper would extend their set into sludgy jams (venues would often have to pull the plug), distorted, beer-soaked trance-inducing mantras that led to their infamous 'Grateful Dead of punk' tag. Best known in the underground consciousness for their vital influence on Nirvana (Kurt Cobain was often photographed in a Flipper shirt while Nirvana bassist Krist Novoselic briefly joined a reformed Flipper in the late noughties) they were formed by Vietnam vet Ted Falconi, with bassist Will Shatter, singer Ricky Williams and drummer DePace in 1979. Debut LP — *Album Generic Flipper* (1982) — was primal. The genesis of sludge metal is writ large on the doom-laden eight-minute trudge of '(I Saw You) Shine', which pivots on a slow-creeping bassline over which Ted Falconi's guitar atonally drones while Ricky Williams wails about 'lights going out' and 'flesh stripping from bones'. An atmosphere of mental disarray prevails. 'Way of the World' riffs on eternal doom while 'Life is Cheap' brings a mournful atmosphere, almost gothic in portentous dread, as Williams offers a dirge-like mantra on the futility of existence. Shards of angular noise, off-beat, jazz-inflected rhythms and angst-ridden screams — taken at volume it becomes a power dirge that threatens to overwhelm.

It's also dirtbox psychedelic. *Fun House*-era Stooges is writ large over album closer 'Sex Bomb', for example, a squalling, free-jazz infused stomp that layers sickly sax atop a greasy stomp, distilling the demented spirit of rock 'n' roll into a glorious droning gumbo and offering some respite from the airless vibe that seals *Generic Flipper* in a tomb of despair. It's weird boogie for the apocalypse. As critic Jim Sullivan noted in an early 1980s live review for the *Boston Globe*, the 'tempo may seem leaden, but don't be deceived. The mixture is volatile. Rock n roll doesn't boil over much more than this.'[11]

Following up with the more avant-leaning *Gone Fishin'* (1984), Flipper beefed up the sound with a (marginally) clearer production. Grounded by the insistent plod of Will Shatter's bass, cutting through the noise way up in the mix (Flipper were always driven by the bass rather than guitar) alongside Ted Falconi's angular guitar, shelling down dissonance at irregular intervals, they added a plethora of wonky elements — sax, tribal drums and drunken, atonal piano — in service of their schlocky, doom-laden vision of B-movie apocalypse. Songs like 'Survivors of the Plague' and 'One by One' were imbued with a caustic desperation and oddball psychedelic density: like being stuck inside the *Das Boot* submarine with nothing but the first two Stooges records and a massive bag of Mexican weed. Flipper comprehensively flipped the script on San Francisco's hippy legacy, instead offering up the city as a festering, petulant hellscape simmering in malevolence and wreathed in sickly green fog. Breaking from the straitjacket of early-eighties punk orthodoxy — which could be every bit as conservative, in its way, as mainstream rock — there was a greasy, carnal element at play amid the dereliction. This wasn't sexless political posturing: Flipper swung hard; as Henry Rollins had it, they were 'just heavy. Heavier than you. Heavier than anything.'

Black Flag played a similarly pivotal role in inverting hardcore's abrasive fleetness with sludgy tone and slow tempos, particularly on their hugely influential *My War* (1984) LP. Emerging from the hyper-violent early 1980s Californian hardcore scene, they were defined by discipline and a fearsome American work ethic. They toured constantly, revelling in a masochistically spartan life: theirs was a world of bloody noses, hostile cops, freezing concrete bunkers, crowds baying for blood, broken-down vans, scant food, no money, press-ups, no time off.

A well-drilled unit who — like Flipper — weren't afraid to plumb the depths of human misery and despair for inspiration, they were formed by guitarist Greg Ginn in Southern California in the late seventies and were largely a product of Ginn's obsessive, one-tracked focus. Aside from the relentless tour schedule, rehearsals were equally ceaseless, often running for over six hours (in the 2006 US punk documentary *American Hardcore* ex-Black Flag drummer Bill Stevenson recalled his first rehearsal with the band: reporting for duty at 8 a.m. on Christmas Day). There were no off days. They personified the DIY ethos of the hardcore scene: design was in-house; their records were put out on Ginn's own SST label — an epoch-defining independent that was the home of Hüsker Dü, Minutemen, Meat Puppets and doom metal overlords Saint Vitus, among many others — while a loose network of bands, fans and promoters the length and breadth of the States provided floors to crash on while touring. It was a gruelling scene, physically and mentally exhausting, frequently confrontational. Initially influenced by the Stooges and the Ramones, Black Flag quickly garnered a fearsome reputation on the hardcore circuit with a speedy, abrasive, buzz-saw sound. Fronted in the early years by Dez Cadena, they settled into a well-drilled unit when a twenty-year-old Henry Rollins — then managing a branch of Häagan-Dazs in Washington DC — joined in 1981. Debut LP *Damaged* (1981) was an incendiary statement of intent that spat bloody venom at consumerism, complacency and brainless hedonism: themes that would recur throughout their discography. The cover — showing a skin-headed Rollins smashing his fist into a mirror — the only Black Flag record not to feature cartoon imagery on the sleeve — defined the music succinctly.

There was a howling atonality to Ginn's playing that set Black Flag aside from the outset and, unusually for a hardcore band, guitar solos were integral to their sound, Ginn's flailing, off-key solos completely idiosyncratic. Has any guitarist before or since evoked a mind about to break with such visceral intensity? The closest comparison is some demented Albert Ayler sax break: cascades of notes that seem to double back on themselves, bend sinister, boil over in clouds of steam. There was often a gallows humour at play in Black Flag, too. From their brilliantly grotesque 1950s-style cartoon covers to their exploration of bad sex ('Slip It In') and aimlessness ('TV Party'), humanity — specifically young, alienated, urban America — was held up to the flickering bulb and found severely lacking. Rollins's voice — often stereotyped as a gruff drill-sergeant bark — was, in fact, a multifaceted instrument. Menacing spoken-word sections, high-pitched whoops, guttural screams, terrace chants; he *inhabited* the songs with a ferocious energy.

Second LP *My War* (1984) featured a more pronounced dissonant, free-jazz influence in Ginn's playing — brought to the fore on his bizarre, bendy, chase-scene evoking solo on 'The Swinging Man' — alongside a notable Sabbathian influence, most keenly felt on side 2. Indeed, *My War* was defined by its second side. Featuring three songs — 'Nothing Left Inside', 'Three Nights' and 'Scream' — that lasted six minutes each (epic in comparison to the usual two-minute hardcore blastoff), *My War* side 2 traversed a negative crawl space of extreme mental disarray. Shorn of the usual hardcore tropes — furious political polemic, acidic dart aimed at Middle American suburbia — instead it offered a vibe that was despairing, raw, deeply personal. The three songs displayed something not readily associated with punk rock: naked vulnerability. 'Nothing Left Inside' sees Ginn riffing on a down-tuned blues riff slowed down to a crawl pace, while Rollins dredges up simple epithets of despair and depression. You can *hear* the room, so much space in the mix that you hear breathing: it feels like you're intruding on a private moment of reckoning. Likewise, 'Three Nights' a disturbing paean to bodily abuse that stretches out amid bluesy squalls and drones, Rollins singing of making his 'body scream!' It's bracing and despairing and heavy as fuck. 'Scream' is bleakest of all, a vanishingly sparse arrangement that opens with a slow 4/4 beat, three-note baseline and Rollins sounding closer to the edge than ever before.

Indeed, this was year zero for sludge-leaning sonics, an immeasurably influential side of vinyl. One can draw a direct line from *My War* side 2 to the Melvins, to Neurosis, to Eyehategod, to Nirvana and Soundgarden and myriad others. They weren't the first punk band to play slow and low, but the sheer emotional intensity was disarming.

'One of the things I think people liked about the songs was that they were incredibly intense,' remembers Rollins. 'It was like getting mugged in slow motion; it didn't seem to end. Those songs were hard to play physically and emotionally — for me, at least; I was into it but there was a price to be paid. The slow songs definitely seemed to be different than what bands around us were playing — besides the great Saint Vitus. I think once audiences heard the songs the second time, or after the album came out, they were more prepared and they went down pretty well. There were other intense songs in the set like "My War", so overall the set was pretty ferocious. I'm not exactly sure what the direct impact of the slower material was on any band or musician, but over the years I've been told by people in bands of note, if you will, that the *My War* album resonated.'

Like many others in the hardcore scene, however, Black Flag came to loathe the straitjacket of the scene they'd helped to define. The violence was an increasing problem. Racist skinheads would turn up at shows baying for blood, the police would line the walls outside hoping to crack a few skulls, people would attend Black Flag shows and expect *violence*. By the mid-1980s hardcore was, often, a scene defined by a leaden conformity — a toxic machismo every bit as deadening as the Mohawked plastic punks in England spitting and pogoing to bands like the Exploited or GBH. *My War* — with its fragile emotion, droning slow tempos and spacious arrangements — was a rebuke to hardcore conformity and lumpen expectations. The band even grew their hair around this time — anathema to most in the scene — and were vocal in their love of Black Sabbath (Greg Ginn also playing a pivotal role in the genesis of doom metal by releasing the first few records by raw doom lifers Saint Vitus on SST and inviting them to tour with Black Flag). As Rollins put it in 2017, 'the slow crushing heaviness of Black Sabbath is beyond satisfying . . . I have always searched for music that sought to either smash the earth or turn its back to it and plunge deep into the human/alien experience. And bands like Earth, Electric Wizard and Sunn O))) make some of the best records ever.'[12]

Chapter 8

BEYOND THE ELECTRIC CARAVAN

Much has been made of the intro to 'Black Sabbath' down the years — the Hammer-inspired thunder crack; the sinister vibe; Ozzy's mournful wail. But it was the sustain used by Tony Iommi on those opening chords — that hang-dog tone, held long past comfort — that evoked realms of squalid darkness hitherto unimagined in 1969, setting out Sabbath's bleak stall.

The drone was thus intrinsic to Sabbath from the start, Iommi time-stretching notes with doom-laden vibrato, their namesake song based — albeit unwittingly, according to Iommi — around the sustained tritone scale ('the devil's interval') once banned by medieval religious scholars as corrupting and satanic. And though the lyrics could veer towards the schlocky camp — bassist and lyricist Geezer Butler was a fan of both Hammer Horror and popular occult novelist, Dennis Wheatley — the music never was. Offering a greyscale flip side to late-sixties hippy idealism, Sabbath made music of brute industrial swing born of grinding poverty — the bastard son of Birmingham.

In his autobiography *I Am Ozzy*, Osbourne describes his early life in Aston. It's a panorama of brutalising, at times near Victorian, hardship. Scraping shit off a sex offender's back in prison with a wire scrubbing brush; owning no shoes; decapitating sheep in an abattoir; being deafened testing car horns in a factory. This was the social context that gave rise to Black Sabbath: true British blues. It's the music of the underdog, the howl of men who knew the foul taste of 1960s prison food, the ever-present threat of a life of pitiless grind in the factories just around the corner. Sabbath resonated with people for whom lackadaisical West Coast hippy bullshit may as well have been a parallel universe; they appealed, rather, to provincial, early-seventies stoners, the shift workers, the heads who wanted to get *numb*.

Apart from their vital influence on hard rock and heavy metal through-out the 1970s, the first six Sabbath records (before 1976's *Never Say Die* saw them lose touch in a blizzard of cocaine) laid *the* blueprint — monolithic riffs, elephantine swing, themes of madness, drugs and despair — that gave rise to the doom metal subculture that took root in the 1980s, and emerged as an underground force in the early 1990s. And, though widely derided by the mainstream press during their heyday ('like Cream . . . but worse'[1] was a typical early assessment from Lester Bangs), Sabbath's subsequent influence on doom, sludge, stoner rock, drone metal — the whole sub low metal spectrum — is impossible to overstate. They laid immovable foundations. As Rise Above label boss and ex-Cathedral frontman Lee Dorrian put it when I interviewed him some years back, 'Sabbath *are* doom.'[2]

Formed in 1968 under the name Earth, Tony Iommi, Geezer Butler, Ozzy Osbourne and Bill Ward initially played the circuit — Midlands and Cumbrian working men's clubs — when blues rock was getting brasher and weightier. Bands like the Yardbirds played loud, raw, aggressively maximal blues, heavy on distorted repetitive riffing courtesy of Jeff Beck and Jimmy Page. Cream also had their share of pile-driving moments, driven by the rhino charge rhythmic chops of Ginger Baker, while Stateside, Blue Cheer were one of the heaviest of the proto-metal crop. Named in tribute to the band's favoured type of LSD, they were a gloriously sloppy unit whose cult 1968 debut *Vincebus Eruptum* was foundational gear on the level of the MC5 and the Stooges in terms of flailing dunderheaded heviosity. Wilder still were Brooklyn's Sir Lord Baltimore. Fronted by singing drummer John Garner, they were a ludicrously energetic band who fused frantic clusters of riffs with Garner's demented, vein-popping vocals. Myriad other bands — Bang, Leaf Hound, Bulletproof, Trapeze, Atomic Rooster and Budgie, to name a few — also amped the blues with feral intensity, down-tuning and providing a bong-water scented portal to fuzzy oblivion. Indeed, in recent years 'proto-metal' — as it has been termed — has become something of a digger's paradise with labels like Riding Easy Records doing sterling work digging up a welter of impossibly obscure 7-inches, demos and ancient practice tapes of long-forgotten bands for their sprawling *Brown Acid* compilations.

Nobody approached Sabbath for heaviness, however. Deep Purple and Led Zeppelin were flashier, camper. Zeppelin's heaviness was also tempered by folksiness, Robert Plant's lyrics imbued with whimsical visions, Tolkienesque dreamscapes of stone circles wreathed in mist, wizards, trolls and the like. Purple were more classically theatrical, having a strong whiff of greasepaint about them, driven as much by Jon Lord's raunchy Hammond organ as Richie Blackmore's relentless riffing. Sabbath, then, were heavy in a different way to either Purple or Zeppelin. They lacked the theatrical bent of the former or the sexual energy of the latter but were *elementally* weighty. Zeppelin may have sung *of* hermits, but Sabbath made music *for* hermits and hash-lung miscreants: theirs was a resolutely gritty and urban sound. Bill Ward recalled Birmingham as a city of 'constant steam and smoke, a very drab looking landscape . . . I felt compelled to want to play harder and louder. I would go past the factories and put rhythms in my head to different machine sounds.'[3]

Sabbath evoked hallucinatory scrumpy and Afghan hash; shadows lurking in backstreet Aston pubs; oil-slicked canals, sickly yellow light and stale chip fat; two-bar electric fires and peeling wallpaper; bad acid; sitting in musty bedsits skinning up on a battered Groundhogs LP; grainy yellow speed and festering pints of Watney's Red Barrel. They tapped the dream subconscious of early 1970s England, the dark corners of the everyday. Madness — or, more specifically, the *fear* of madness — was Sabbath's idiosyncratic beat. As Mark E. Smith once said of late-nineteenth-century supernaturalist Arthur Machen, 'he lives in this alternative world: the real occult's not in Egypt, but in the pubs of the East End and the stinking boats of the Thames — on your doorstep basically.'[4]

Black Sabbath understood this implicitly: for Butler, the occult was sitting at the end of his bed, the band's namesake song inspired by a terrifying sleep-paralysis visitation he had experienced as a young man, waking to find the 'figure in black' of the song sitting at the end of his bed staring at him. The occult was everywhere in the early seventies. Novelist Colin Wilson had published his best-selling *The Occult: A History* in 1971; folk horror master-pieces such as *Witchfinder General*, *The Wicker Man* and *The Blood on Satan's Claw* all found large audiences, as did magazines like *Man, Myth & Magic*. There were even children's shows — *Children of the Stones* — based on pagan folklore. Black Sabbath were a product of the age, in that respect. Indeed, they were prefigured in their use of occult imagery by US rockers Coven, who made melodic rock with a distinctly diabolical flavour, releasing their debut *Witchcraft Destroys Minds and Reaps Souls* in 1969; Arthur Brown had also, of course, declared himself god of hellfire a year previously, while Midlanders Black Widow released the occult-themed *Sacrifice* in 1971, to say nothing of Jimmy Page's infamous Aleister Crowley obsession. But if Sabbath's namesake song teeters thrillingly on the edge of absurdity, it's saved from camp pastiche by the sheer *intensity* of delivery.

Osbourne's vocal is imbued with a genuine slack-jawed terror while Bill Ward's busy jazz fills propel the bottom end, alongside Butler's galloping bass runs, underlining Iommi's diabolic tritone riff. Sabbath were as much defined by their sense of *swing* as their chugging heaviness. Ward's drumming was unique. He hit like Obelix — his drum tech used to have to physically nail his bass drum to the stage before shows — but kept the rhythm moving with the unpredictable flair of the seasoned jazzman. Jazz and blues were thus writ large on *Black Sabbath* (1970): 'The Wizard', 'Wicked World' and 'Behind the Wall of Sleep', while heavy, display a peculiar *jauntiness* that — title track aside — defines Sabbath's debut. Even the weightier moments — 'N.I.B', say — are imbued with a jazzy fleetness that belies the doomy subject matter (Satan falling in love, in this case) and cavernously heavy riffing.

As for Iommi's guitar, that monstrous fuzz tone wasn't the result of a distortion box but the Dallas Rangemaster treble-boosting pedal (also used by Hendrix and Marc Bolan) that — in combination with thin strings and an enthusiastic overdriving of the mids and treble on his amp, a habit he picked up while playing in Earth in an attempt to cut through the crowd noise of working men's clubs — gave him a unique tone. More significant though, was a pre-Sabbath industrial accident he suffered at a Birmingham sheet metal factory. Put on an unfamiliar machine one shift, Iommi accidentally trapped his fingers, losing the tips of the middle and ring fingers on his right hand. Despite the bloodied tips being retrieved from the floor and sent to hospital in a matchbox by the factory foreman, he was told by doctors that he'd never play again. Severely depressed at home, he was visited by a colleague who told him about famed Belgian gypsy jazz guitarist Django Reinhardt who had himself lost the tips of his fingers in a fire in the 1920s, but taught himself to play again using just his left index and middle fingers.

Buoyed by the story, Iommi went through a period of disciplined — if idiosyncratic — rehabilitation: he melted down a bottle of washing-up liquid and fashioned 'little plastic balls' that he used as surrogate fingertips. He tried to play, but couldn't feel the strings. He persevered, restringing his guitar with light-gauge banjo strings, and taught himself to play again, modifying his amp set-up to arrive at his idiosyncratic Sabbathian rumble.

'I had to make whatever I could sound big, because of my disability. I came up with another sound by tuning the guitar down . . . losing my fingertips was devastating but in hindsight it created something, it made me invent a new sound.'⁵

Iommi's bludgeoning tone was felt to serious effect on Sabbath's follow up *Paranoid* (1970). Released just six months after their debut — which had sold surprisingly well in both England and America — Sabbath had six whole days to record *Paranoid* (they did the first in twelve hours). Musically it featured everything from sub-aquatic stoner lounge, replete with flute and bongos ('Planet Caravan') to the frenetic energy of 'Paranoid' (recorded as a filler in a couple of hours) and the lumbering majesty of 'Iron Man' and 'War Pigs'. *Paranoid* was at its most thrilling when it ventured into slower, doom-filled territory, however. 'Electric Funeral' and 'Hand of Doom' were both anti-war songs — a common Sabbathian trope — the former warning against nuclear holocaust, the latter telling the story of a Vietnam veteran returning home to a life of heroin addiction. This was doom metal before the fact, all the (future) genre's tropes — slow-building riff, atmosphere of narcotised despair, bass rumble — playing out over seven oppressive minutes.

Where *Black Sabbath* carried a woozy bluesy vibe, *Paranoid* was more urgent. If the genesis for traditional heavy metal is found in *Black Sabbath* and *Paranoid* — the frenetic chug of the title song foreseeing the brittle energy of the new wave of British heavy metal (NWOBHM) explosion of the late 1970s — then Sabbath's next record *Master of Reality* (1971) remains *the* blueprint for doom to this day. Continuing the themes of madness, drugs and war, augmented by monolithic riffs and Bill Ward's wet-cave thwack, *Master of Reality* also marked the moment Iommi started seriously down-tuning, dropping three semitones beneath a standard E, resulting in a ludicrously weighty, swampy tone.

A statement of intent that marked Sabbath out as the heaviest band in the world, the onslaught of *Master of Reality* was partly a reaction to their new-found legions of teenage fans who had come to the band through the 'Paranoid' single. Indeed, one can draw a direct line from *Master of Reality* to Saint Vitus, the Melvins, Nirvana, Soundgarden, Eyehategod and Neurosis. It's all in the tone. The drone was ever present in Iommi's playing, a burring, silt-like density. Starting with a hacking cough, 'Sweet Leaf' is a paean to the glories of weed. Osbourne drops some gloriously of-the-time seventies head lore, alongside one of the most elephantine riffs in Iommi's groaning repertoire.

Master of Reality is head music, weighty and urgent — the sound of a band distilling their essence like a toothless farmer making a batch of bathtub poteen. It also contains two of Sabbath's three heaviest songs[6] — firstly, the droning thrash of 'Children of the Grave' — driven by Bill Ward's double bass drum pattern and left-hand timbale ricochet alongside one of Tony Iommi's finest riffs, and the doomy trudge of 'Into the Void' which lumbers like a wounded Cyclops. Listening to 'Children of the Grave' for the first time in 1971 must have been like being hit by a truck, its brutally primitive groove compounded by Osbourne's mournful voice soaring way above the mix, the sludgier tone emphasising the upper end of his range all the more (he never gets the credit he deserves as a vocalist: he's a belting soul singer, wrestling for redemption).

Sabbath followed *Master of Reality* with a strong trio: *Vol. 4* (1972) was a more polished set, recorded in LA and fuelled by heinous quantities of cocaine; *Sabbath Bloody Sabbath* (1973) saw them experimenting with synths and strings while *Sabotage* (1975) was an angry record driven by legal hassles. All went to make up the 'classic six' — Sabbath's fabled unbroken run of quality — before they lost their way in a blurry miasma of roadburn, personal animosity and coke bloat. *Technical Ecstasy* (1976) was forgettable. Sabbath sounded tired. Punk was blowing up, and metal responded in turn with the raw attack of the NWOBHM, bands like Iron Maiden, Saxon and Angel Witch combining raw chops with in-your-face adolescent energy: speed was king and Sabbath were out of puff.

Forever Doomed

By the time the ponderous *Never Say Die* (1978) sounded the death knell for the original line-up, the raw dread and lumbering groove of their early records was entirely absent — not only from Sabbath, but from the wider musical landscape. It was precisely this absence, however, that paved the way for a new generation of bands hungry for that missing sound. The first wave of doom metal was defined by a devotion to the church of Iommi, placing primacy on lumbering groove rather than dazzling histrionics. In the mid 1980s, while thrash and hair metal raged to greater commercial success, bands like Saint Vitus, Pentagram, Trouble, Witchfinder General and Candlemass hunkered down, making bizarre records charged with negative energy; succubus talisman to eclipsed hope that fitted nowhere and were all the more powerful for it.

Cleaving to the primal bludgeon of the first six Sabbath records, doom replaced traditional rockist tropes of macho posturing, brash confidence and virtuoso performance with a celebration of melancholy, altered states, misanthropy and womb-like immersion in viscous sound. Where traditional heavy metal tended towards overblown fantasy, preening machismo and frenetic speed, doom played with gothic lyrical fatalism and slow tempos. It was *physically* heavier than traditional metal: while thrash was all pimply aggression and thrusting velocity, its principal documents — Metallica's *Master of Puppets*, say — were thin and trebly. Doom pushes the sub frequencies. It's physical in a similar way to dub — the bass hits you in the chest and pushes the air around the room. Haunting minor-key melodies, blues scales, muted groove, themes of dread, madness and despair — doom is the most personal and introverted form of metal, the drone subverting its extrovert tendencies in service of a lonely sonic mass.

A proudly retro-focused genre, doom inhabits its own aesthetic universe, hermetically sealed from the outside world. As Electric Wizard's Jus Oborn once put it to me, 'we create our own little world . . . and it's the early seventies for ever.' Wreathed in weed smoke, obsessing over esoteric literature, occult themes, long-forgotten horror movies and a tight canon of records, doom wallows in self-referential iconography with Black Sabbath frequently cast as *deities* rather than band (see Japanese stoner crew Church of Misery and their *Master of Brutality* cover art, which lifts the *Master of Reality* bendy letting wholesale, for example; or the lyrical references to the 'Iomisphere' by Sleep; or the sheer number of 'Worship Iommi' patches at Roadburn). It isn't only the riffs that are repetitive — themes, riffs, lyrical obsessions, cultural touchpoints — they all circle, too. To complain about a lack of originality in doom metal would be to miss the point entirely. One might as well say the same about the Delta blues or roots reggae. Authenticity of *intent* is what distinguishes the best stuff: the last decade has seen a surfeit of occult-referencing, bell-bottom-sporting soundalikes but much of it is too clean and polished. Doom should be made by people who've seen trouble: like the blues, it demands an intensity of lived experience, being, as it is, a form of wretched soul music, a channelling of the wounded spirit animal.

There were, however, few bands going for the down-tuned early-seventies vibe in the NWOBHM era. Witchfinder General were something of an anomaly among their frenetically paced brethren. Largely ignored during their obscure original existence (1979–83), they emerged from Stourbridge blatantly influenced by *Master of Reality*-era Sabbath, and have since become cult favourites, name-checked by everyone from Electric Wizard and Cathedral to Metallica. Both debut LP *Death Penalty* (1981) and follow-up *Friends of Hell* (1983) are highly collectable, though crude, affairs. Their album artwork featured page-three models awaiting sacrifice in churchyards, guitarist Phil Cope's riffs were sludgy as tar while singer Zeeb Parkes could carry off mournful Ozzy-esque cries with aplomb. Lyrically, they were straight out of the Geezer Butler playbook: war, drugs, mental illness. Pagan Altar were a similarly Sabbathian NWOBHM proposition, and featured the unusual combination of a father and son — Terry and Alan Jones — in the band, on vocals and guitar respectively. Sweden's Candlemass, meanwhile, pioneered epic doom with their aptly titled *Epicus Doomicus Metallicus* (1986) doing precisely what it said on the tin: a foundational record that hinged on technical prowess, operatic vocals and dynamic peaks.

It was a trio of underground American bands, however — Saint Vitus, Pentagram and Trouble — who came to define the nascent doom sound in the early 1980s, some time before the genre was fully codified. Pentagram had formed in 1971 in Alexandria, Virginia by vocalist Bobby Liebling and guitarist Geof O'Keefe, bonding over a shared love of Sabbath, Sir Lord Baltimore and Uriah Heep. They were plagued by black luck — 2012's *Last Days Here* documentary, following Liebling from the throes of crippling crack and heroin addiction to recovery and tour, is one of the most harrowing music documentaries ever made — and line-up changes from the start, their story one of strife, missed opportunities, drugs and despair.

Gigging sporadically throughout the 1970s, they didn't release an album until 1985. An acknowledged genre classic, *Pentagram* (1985) fused satanic themes with a sleazy hard-rock edge: blackened, dangerously unhinged rock 'n' roll. Trouble was the most 'classicist' of the three, first LP *Psalm 9* providing down-tuned riffs and foreboding atmospherics alongside a technical tightness often lacking in doom. They were also unusual in that singer Eric Wagner was a practising Roman Catholic, a fact that informed much of his god-fearing lyrical output. Saint Vitus were a far rawer proposition — roughshod and charged with a nihilistic undercurrent — gigging as extensively in the hardcore scene as in metal. Saint Vitus vocalist Scott 'Wino' Weinrich recalled the pressures of playing doom in the hardcore punk world when we spoke in 2012:

> We were the only metal band on SST. When we started out we were really caught in a tough place. A lot of the metalheads in America at the time were big into the thrash sound, either that or the more radio-friendly stuff, but not what we were doing . . . We'd play in Hollywood and get 50 people — 60 on a good night . . . we toured with Agnostic Front, which was really tough. We were outsiders: we were playing the punk rock shows, rather than metal. What we were doing was obviously *way* slower; a totally different thing. In fact, our first singer took a full cup of piss in the face at a Black Flag support show — for 25 years he told us it was a coke! (*laughs*) As far as 'doom' goes, to me, if I had to sum it up, it's all in the infernal progression, the Devil's scale that Iommi was into, you know — *that's* doom.[7]

Saint Vitus evoked nihilistic urban vibes — the aural equivalent of chugging malt liquor and smoking meth in a Southern Californian parking lot under the pitiless glare of the afternoon sun. Others revelled in fatalism, dark romance and maudlin atmospherics. Cathedral's seminal *Forest of Equilibrium* (1991) was a lyrically opulent case in point. Taking the dour atmosphere of Vitus and Trouble but amping up the drama and atmosphere, Cathedral added a crunchier and more extreme tone, themes of isolation clutched as proud baroque talisman rather than pivots for adolescent rage. *Forest of Equilibrium* was a purist statement of intent that exists, as the best doom metal often does, in a strange vacuum, a state of stasis: eternity's feedback loop. Singer Lee Dorrian was a true believer from the start. Playing a pivotal role in the passage of doom from the most obscure subgenre in metal to the dedicated worldwide force of today, he'd grown up in early 1980s Coventry immersed in punk and hardcore.

Obsessing over Crass, Discharge, G.I.S.M. and Swans, Dorrian was originally the singer in grindcore overlords (and John Peel favourites) Napalm Death. Reducing hardcore to a flailing, roiling essence, albums like *Scum* (1987) and *From Enslavement to Obliteration* were an exercise in wild speed and aggressive extremity. Dorrian soon found the spittle-flecked velocity a creative dead end, however, and quit the band in 1988, forming Cathedral shortly afterwards alongside Mark Griffiths (bass) and Garry Jennings (guitar).

Based around a shared obsession with Trouble, Saint Vitus, early Black Sabbath and Witchfinder General, Cathedral spearheaded an epic, slow, crushingly heavy brand of doom. *Forest of Equilibrium* — though released on underground metal mainstay Earache, who had Cathedral touring with the bigger death metal bands of the day — flew in the face of the speedier styles of the time, hinging instead on lumbering cyclopean groove. Their funereal trudge evoked dark fantastical imagery, helped by the idiosyncratic artwork of Dave Patchett, who placed as strong a visual stamp on the band's identity as Derek Biggs had done for Iron Maiden (morning mist, crumbling cathedrals looming in the distance, gurning gargoyles, frolicking nymphs, mud-splattered simpletons, brutal knaves, inbred monks and the like).

Musically, Cathedral revelled in velvet gloom. Dorrian's lyrics sometimes teetered on the very edge of absurdity but were all the more compelling for their Byronic poetic drama. Indeed, *Forest of Equilibrium*'s gruelling melancholy is every bit as intense as the feral grind of Napalm Death. The atmosphere of doleful depression is *crucifyingly* bleak, but pleasurable nonetheless: this is music to wallow in, Dorrian's mournful growl offset by Gary Jennings's wringing emotive sustain out of every last note. (Indeed, one of doom's key sonic signifiers is the droning and the bending of the last note at the end of a riff. Iommi was the past master of this technique but Jennings slowed it down *way* past comfort.)

Forest of Equilibrium was an exercise in doom purism: it pushed the sound to greater extremes than it had ever been before. Dorrian was also responsible for the underground dissemination of the sound via his Rise Above imprint — without question the most important label in the genre's history, releasing epoch-defining LPs from the likes of Sleep, Electric Wizard, Sunn O))) and Orange Goblin. Cathedral displayed a more eclectic bent elsewhere, however. Over twenty-three years together and a dozen albums they experimented with acoustic folk, psychedelia and prog, their thanks lists indicating a breadth of influence often missing in the trenches of extreme metal. Alongside Sabbath et al., they'd name-check acid folksters Comus, occult acoustic duo Mellow Candle and obscure proto-metallers like Bang and Curved Air. Cathedral — Dorrian, in particular — were tireless crate-diggers at heart. Delving into groovier, more psychedelic territory, second album *The Ethereal Mirror* (1993) was a markedly less extreme proposition than their debut. Signing to Columbia for an ill-fated year (they were soon dropped and returned to Earache), *The Ethereal Mirror* was nonetheless a rollicking trip. No longer tethered to the morose crawl space of their debut, songs like 'Ride', 'Grim Luxuria' and 'Midnight Mountain' were pitched somewhere between classical doom and maximal early-seventies hard rock. *The Carnival Bizarre* (1995) was groovier still, including a cameo from Tony Iommi on the ludicrously propulsive 'Utopian Blaster' while 'Hopkins (Witchfinder General)' was an outrageously camp paean to the murderous fervour of the song's namesake seventeenth-century zealot, a monstrous smoking groove.

Dopesmoker

Indeed, during the mid 1990s weed became something approaching sacrament for a certain section of the metal underground. Running parallel to doom was stoner rock, a loosely defined movement that encompassed everything from the peyote- and mescal-scented desert hypno-thrum of Kyuss to the motorised diesel-powered riff worship of Fu Manchu and the beer-soaked, good-time boogie of Orange Goblin and early Queens of the Stone Age.

Just as Rise Above had codified the doom scene with their *Dark Passages* compilation in 1991, so Roadrunner Records' 1997 *Burn One Up: Music for Stoners* compilation shone a light on bands like the aforementioned, alongside cuts from Queens of the Stone Age, Acrimony, Sleep, Cathedral and the Heads. In reality these bands were often wildly different in their sonic approach. Fu Manchu were 1970s iconography made flesh — a sonic celebration of dune buggies, shwag weed, ornate bongs, wide skateboards, early hardcore, stadium rock and tripping amid the dunes. The Heads offered a scuzzy, Bristol bedsit vibe; Karma to Burn did majestic instrumentals straight out of Sam Peckinpah's nightmares while Queens of the Stone Age, rising from the ashes of Kyuss, went on to become one of the biggest bands of the noughties.

Bands like these shared certain attributes with doom — namely the repetitive riffs, weed obsession, seventies iconography and a predilection for down-tuning — however this was music of the sun, rather than the shadows. If doom had a tendency to dwell in the corners of inner headspace and revel in the doleful atmosphere conjured therein, stoner rock looked towards the open road — the *journey* a constant source of inspiration. Fu Manchu are a case in point. Good-times music, *The Big Lebowski* made sonic flesh. *The* quintessential stoner band, their music has been resolutely unchanging down the years. Like AC/DC or Motörhead, say, they've stuck to an immovable template since the start: vast fuzzy riffs and a lyrical obsession with muscle cars, UFOs and surfing. Singer/guitarist Scott Hill famously listens to nothing but 1980s hardcore and 1970s rock and this myopic vision feeds back into the band. Embodying the lackadaisical Southern Californian vibe, their back catalogue is rock solid but largely interchangeable, and none the worse for that: like AC/DC, they offer a sense of stability in a grim and uncertain world.

Then there's Sleep: among the wider stoner canon, Sleep stand majestically — imperiously — alone. One of the most mystical bands of all time, Sleep are a gloriously eccentric proposition whose hypnotic groove, dubwise bass weight and quasi-religious devotion to the riff, Black Sabbath — and ludicrous, heinous, weed consumption — are the stuff of legend.

Formed in early-nineties San Jose by bassist and vocalist Al Cisneros alongside drummer Chris Hakius and guitarist Matt Pike, they recorded a demo — *Vol 1* (1991) — before recording another album-length tape that they sent to Earache Records. Thrilled by what they heard, Earache signed Sleep on the spot, insisting on releasing the demo tape in its raw, unmastered state. The resulting album — *Sleep's Holy Mountain* (1992) — marked a pivotal milestone in the genesis of stoner rock. To say it was Sabbath influenced would be wild understatement. Sleep revolve around Sabbath at a molecular level: everything from Al Cisneros's nasal vocal to Matt Pike's swampy guitar tone connected back on the ley line to 1970s Birmingham. That *Sleep's Holy Mountain* is, at once, the greatest Sabbath tribute ever recorded while remaining doggedly individual is a testament to Sleep's idiosyncratic synergy: great slabs of bleary-eyed riffing, a hardcore, bluesy, cyclopean hoedown.

Always a band out of time, while the early-nineties grunge explosion raged around them — angsty introspection de rigueur — Sleep retreated to their own world, indulging in sonic myth-making on a grand scale. Just check the lyrics to 'Aquarian'. Rich in hallucinatory derring-do, Cisneros conjured mythic realms, ludicrous in the tradition of proper heavy metal, a Dio-esque lyrical bent heavy on fantasy imagery, marrying scenes of aquatic escape, interstellar travel, gypsies with curses and reptilian aliens to Matt Pike's insistent, ragged riffing. Ending on a Sabbath cover ('Snowblind'), *Sleep's Holy Mountain* even gained accolades from Osbourne himself, who stated that the band were 'as close to Sabbath as anything he'd ever heard.'

Touring support slots for Cathedral and Hawkwind helped cement Sleep's status in underground consciousness before they signed to London Records to record a follow-up in 1995. Holed up in the studio with pillowcases full of weed and banks of vintage valve amps, they proceeded on a path of bloody-minded eccentricity. The resulting album — *Dopesmoker* — comprised a single fifty-five-minute song based around a single circling riff that unfolds, breaks down and builds, time and again. It's an exercise in relentlessness, executed with a precision that belies the billowing clouds of weed smoke that wreathed every last note of its production.

Lyrically, Al Cisneros went all out, creating a fantastical fable following the tribulations and fate of the Weedians — a nomadic desert tribe — who form a caravan and travel with 'herb bails' through the 'riff-filled land' to, eventually, deliver their combustible wares to a temple of robed priests. Operating on a glacial timeframe, *Dopesmoker* was a different beast to Sleep's debut. This was *far* beyond Sabbath; far beyond anyone, in fact. On *Dopesmoker* Sleep succeeded in creating a new devotional music, a praise-filled quasi-religious heviosity whose closest spiritual precedent was arguably not doom metal, but roots reggae. Indeed, the biblical signifiers were writ large all over *Dopesmoker* ('Nazareth!'; 'Creedsman'; 'Holy Prophecy' et cetera), weed venerated as the ultimate sacrament. *Dopesmoker* exists very much in its own headspace. It's a work of such imagination, such pretension, such *ambition* — and such deep commercial folly — that it exerts its own strange gravitational pull. As opening couplets go, 'drop out of life with bong in hand, follow the smoke to the riff-filled land' is unique in its directness: *Dopesmoke*r is Zen-like in its knowledge and acceptance of itself. It's completely *of* itself from the outset, an exercise in primal repetition, every chord left hanging, the drone charging the whole record with desert heat.

It's musical and conceptual merits didn't stop it being greeted with horrified incomprehension when the master tapes — as urban myth has it, placed inside a vast skull bong — were delivered to London Records, however. Here was a single song nearly an hour long, with no discernible hook, concerned with a mythical tribe of weed-worshipping mystics. The band had (literally) burnt an inordinate amount of money on weed, guitars, amps and studio time, having been working on the song for four solid years. Around $75,000 alone went on vintage amps — Sleep were tube amp aficionados — customised guitars and a plethora of obscure pedals. London Records, unable to fathom how they were to market the record, told the band that they couldn't release the album as it was and drafted in producer David Sardy to remix it and shorten the final song. Sleep were not pleased, telling the label that the record must be released as it stood, or not at all.

Dopesmoker thus lay unreleased for four years, during which time the band split up, Matt Pike forming High on Fire — one of the most demented and maximal rock 'n' roll bands in the world, a Motörhead-charged, diesel breathed dragon of a band — while Al Cisneros and drummer Chris Haikus reconvened on the superlative Om and continued the mystic, quasi-religious vibe of Sleep, albeit on a far rootsier tip, experimenting with acoustic instrumentation, raga-esque improvisational structures and mystic Buddhist and Christian imagery.

A version of *Dopesmoker* eventually surfaced in 1999 (as *Jerusalem*, on Rise Above) and the mystic atmosphere that surrounded Sleep's bizarre opus grew by word of mouth throughout the noughties. It was released in various iterations by various labels: a bootleg version; a version on Tee Pee Records — now titled *Dopesmoker* — in 2003, before, finally, the definitive band-approved version (boasting a huge, crunchy mix-down from Brad Boatright) on Southern Lord in 2012. Sleep reformed in 2009 for a pair of triumphant shows at ATP festival and have toured sporadically ever since before surprise-releasing a new album — *The Sciences* — in 2018. Starting with a two-minute peal of feedback before the unmistakable bubbling of a ritual bong hit signals the start and the crushing riff of 'Marajanaut's Theme' strikes up like a galactic colossus stamping through dimensions. Thematically, all the hallmarks are present and correct — Black Sabbath worship, weed mythology, cosmic journeying. It's every bit as eccentric as *Dopesmoker*, Cisneros recounting the tale of a lonely drifting spaceman, traversing the universe through the 'hashteroid fields' before receiving the 'riff beacon signal' and making his way towards 'Planet Iommia'. For Sleep, Sabbath remain more — far more — than mere influence. They are venerated as deities: godlike subjects of worship. Iommi is, of course, the high priest, but Geezer Butler is also praised in his namesake song 'Giza Butler' which recounts the tale of a homeless hippy living underneath an underpass, spiritual epiphany reached via the application of heinous bong hits, the underpass framed as some gilded palace — it's some *biblical* shit ('Helms the shopping cart chariot across the access roads, cart moored to tree . . . proceeds the Creek Hippy'), devotional music of the cosmos, smoker's hymnal that, while rooted in Sabbathian doom, always illuminates the very human need for cranial transcendence.

Come My Fanatics

Electric Wizard are a different proposition altogether. A hypnotic, misanthropic, acid-smothered trip into the furthest reaches of primal heviosity, they offer a vision of doom harsher, punkier and rawer than anything else out there. Inspired by Black Sabbath, Venom, Celtic Frost, Slayer, first-wave doom, the Stooges, early Alice Cooper and (equally importantly) a cornucopia of VHS horror, exploitation movies, 1970s Euro-porn, pulp sleaze, H.P. Lovecraft and Robert E. Howard, they've long mined the darker edges of the counterculture, creating a pulpy world all their own. More than any other band in the doom spectrum, Electric Wizard are inseparable from their cultural aesthetic: a dark slipstream of cinema, drugs and literature informs everything they do. Formed in Wimborne, Dorset in 1993 by singer guitarist Jus Oborn alongside bassist Tim Bagshaw and drummer Mark Greening, Electric Wizard were also a product of the bucolic, rebel spirit of the wyrd West Country.

Oborn had initially put together a roughshod death metal band — Lord of Putrefaction — that ran from 1989 until 1991 before taking a doomier direction and changing the name to Thy Grief Eternal, the band that preceded the formation of Electric Wizard. For Oborn, the underground tape-trading scene offered early inspiration.

'The death metal scene started to fragment, which was how I got into tape trading,' he tells me. 'It was a worldwide network, teenagers trading music with each other . . . you'd advertise in *Metal Forces* or other fanzines — you'd have a rare demo tape and there were certain hotbeds — everybody would want to trade with somebody in Tampa or Brazil, for instance (*laughs*). You'd send a ninety-minute cassette and somebody would send you a ninety-minute cassette back. Eternal were out and out doom, primarily influenced by Trouble, Saint Vitus, Witchfinder General, Pentagram — those were the five main bands. When death metal fragmented, people were searching for something that was raw again; doom hadn't become commercialised.'

Electric Wizard's eponymous debut LP was released in 1995. Combining the Neanderthal grunt of Sabbath with a penchant for drawn-out, swirling psych riffery, it was a decent listen although there was nothing to suggest that there was anything particularly special going on. Second album *Come My Fanatics . . .* (1996) was another story. One of — perhaps *the* — rawest take on wanton, bleak, nightmarish psychedelia ever put to tape, *Come My Fanatics . . .* was a record for the true heads. It was loud, obnoxious, sonically *blackened.* Far beyond (over)driven, Oborn's guitar sounds like a bass while Tim Bagshaw's bass sounds like a misfiring snow plough. The whole thing is subsumed by the drone. Undulating waves of distortion cover the mix, swamping Mark Greening's loose, chaotic, free jazz-esque drums, Oborn's crackly vocal like a wet blanket. *Fanatics* was doom debased, the filth factor amped to eternity. A (very) loose concept album, it foresaw — amid the rictus grin of Tony Blair and Britpop gaklands — a planet gasping for breath, a populace fucked beyond hope and looking for escape.

Using a welter of trash movie samples, primitive Hawkwind-style electronics and cheap pedals run through echo units for added layers of skrog, it sounded like the tapes had lain undiscovered in a dusty attic for years before being scraped off and baked. *Come My Fanatics . . .* was also — crucially — infused with the rural vibe that Electric Wizard have long made their own. As they've always said, they don't just make doom, they make *Dorset doom.* And Dorset — far beyond the tourist ideal — is always there, somehow: the churning mud; rusting farm equipment; botched Satanic rituals in tumble-down barns; the shitty weed; the home-made bongs; the psychedelically strong scrumpy; the small-town madness — it's all there, all along the downs.

'Wimborne is a small town, a lot of unemployment — which led to people doing a lot of drugs — it had a big drugs scene,' explains Oborn. 'That's how I got into anything music-related (*laughs*). It is a weird town: there's a lot of history there, the minster and tunnels and weird temples, the Badbury Rings. And you mix that with bored people taking drugs. I got chased by a load of farm hands into a yard with the geese once, when I was a kid. Off on an adventure on the edge of town, getting a bit rural — you'd meet some *fucking* weird people out there. Kids with guns. Actual fucking shotguns (*laughs*) . . . So with *Come My Fanatics . . .* I wanted it to sound like our lives. The drug influence and the Wimborne influence started to come into what we were doing. I wanted to give it a rawer sound, to sound like we came from Dorset, not trying to copy people we admired any more.

'We had influences like Hawkwind,' he continues. 'On "Phase Inducer" we borrowed a Korg and Tim was messing about with delay pedals and stuff like that, just fucking around with weird sounds and primitive loops and a crappy old delay. And the atmosphere in the town; there were a lot of people into techno and people into noisier music like Throbbing Gristle — and they were playing us this stuff and it was all feeding into it. We were thinking "where can we take this without just being a clone of Black Sabbath?" Loop and Spacemen 3 were a big influence, too. We'd do acid and listen to bands like that — so they were in there too, Loop especially.'

Doom is a space where the meditative properties of the drone are deliberately inverted. Electric Wizard emphasise wilful befuddlement. They embody the idea — as Spacemen 3 so memorably put it, of 'taking drugs to make music to take drugs to' and revelling in the bleaker edges of psychedelia; the black freighter of the mind. Turn on, tune in, drop out? Electric Wizard exhort you to turn off your mind altogether.

Ensconced in a self-contained vestibule of crackling Pentagram LPs, heinously strong weed, bad acid (Oborn maintains that he can't actually remember recording the album) and stacks of obscure Jess Franco videos, *Come My Fanatics . . .* was escape music; at their core, Electric Wizard are escapists. The idea of literal and metaphorical ascent from the physical comes up time and again, both in their music and in conversation with Oborn. *Come My Fanatics . . .* riffs both on the idea of a planet fucked beyond repair, and possible methods — occult ritual, drugs, astral projection — of escape. It's a kind of turbo-charged Hawkwind vibe, reimagined in a parallel negative space. Beginning with 'Return Trip' — a statement of sheer nihilistic intent recounting some poor soul's hateful last minutes on Earth ('I hope this fuckin world fuckin burns away . . . and I'd kill you all if I had my way') which carries the heaviest, sludgiest guitar tone ever put to tape, a *ludicrously* muddy thing of cosmic wonder — it ends on the apocalyptic trio of 'Phase Inducer', 'Son of Nothing' and 'Solarian 13'.

'Son of Nothing' is, lyrically, straight out of the Michael Moorcock school of apocalyptic lyricism, recounting a 'dying sun' that 'fades in our sky'; a scrambled goodbye, before racing to construct the 'pods' that will carry the few remaining survivors to the stars (Oborn even gets a Sabbath reference in, bemoaning the 'war pigs left behind'). Like Hawkwind, Electric Wizard marvel at the unimaginable scale of the universe — adrift on the infinite plain — humanity's cosmically insignificant place amid the churning infinity. The song ends with the haunting closing quote from *Beneath the Planet of the Apes* 'In one of the countless billions of galaxies in the universe, lies a medium-sized star, and one of its satellites, a green and insignificant planet, is now dead.' Escape took a practical form, too. They've made no bones about their prodigious weed consumption down the years: again, it comes back to transcendence — smoke and riff forming a psychic barrier, a muffled diving-bell retreat from the daily grind.

'When we were growing up was pre-skunk, a lot of soap bar hash — nasty stuff,' explains Oborn. 'You'd get the occasional bit of weed — there'd be some connections in Sherborne. Actually, one of the first hydroponic systems started up in Wimborne, a guy I knew — but that was mid-late nineties. There was a lot of acid and speed involved, it was cheaper and a bit more reliable. Speed was good for jamming, we'd do two-hour jams speeding. I can't underestimate the importance of drugs to Electric Wizard. Some people might be embarrassed, but it was always part of it — we always wanted to create that trance feeling, getting away from things. It could go back to deeper stuff about trying to erase the modern world, but it was also about getting in that state which is what we were trying to do. And we were pissed off that people were into techno and shit and we thought, "Why doesn't heavy metal have this vibe anymore," everyone is getting a bit poncy (*laughs*). Fuck that! Bring back the whole twenty-four-hour, full-on acid thing, get it to that level again.'

If *Come My Fanatics . . .* saw Electric Wizard exploring cosmic apocalypse, *Dopethrone* (2000) went further into the escape from modernity that Oborn mentions; and into their personal mythos. Setting the vibe from the cover art up (Satan pulling a bong, amid a backdrop of crumbling black towers) *Dopethrone* is a dense, macabre fantasia that draws on all the classic Wizardian themes — nihilism, despair, drugs, occult ritual, pulp lore — but amplifies the atmosphere, wrapping the monolithic riffs in layers of static, fuzz, wah-wah, distortion and movie samples. It's like peeling layers of an onion: everything swaddled in a miasma of audio fog. Widely considered Electric Wizard's magnum opus, *Dopethrone* opens with a snippet of recorded speech from a TV evangelist talking about the dangers of 'satanic' heavy metal in the 1980s, while the title was a thinly veiled pop at stoner titans Sleep. It's a thrillingly debased listen, veering from sloppy, anvil-heavy blues-inflected gear ('Funeralopolis') to venomous, blackened rock 'n' roll ('Barbarian').

'It was really fun to make,' explains Oborn. 'With *Dopethrone* we dropped acid, locked ourselves in the vault and tried to record the heaviest album we could. We wanted something that was like a proper nightmare and we felt like we achieved it.'

Dopethrone also saw the pulp literary references brought to the fore. Oborn is a fan of early twentieth-century American supernaturalist H.P. Lovecraft and pulp master Robert E. Howard, writer of the Conan novels — and the spectre of both haunts the album in the form of 'Weird Tales', an epic in three parts that pays tribute to the notorious 1920s pulp magazine of the same name to which both writers contributed. The lyric alluded to Lovecraft's Cthulu mythos, a fictive universe inhabited by terrible creatures ('the old ones'), ancient alien entities who dwell deep under the sea awaiting the reanimation of the grotesque Cthulhu, their vast, tentacled, octopus-like leader. Lovecraft's fiction is haunted by the spectre of cosmic fatalism: the idea that human beings can never possibly fathom the mysteries of the universe and that the universe, in turn, remains indifferent to humanity. To Lovecraft, human beings had as little chance of understanding the inner mechanisations of hyperspace as an ant does planet Earth. It's a viewpoint that chimes perfectly with the lumbering, misanthropic gait of Electric Wizard: the world cast as a pitiless void, life a cosmic accident.

Indeed, it's all but impossible to separate Electric Wizard from the mélange of cultural references that surrounds them — they're as much living countercultural wormhole as band. The thanks lists on the back of their records offer an oblique insight into their world; you get figures like *Salem's Lot* actor Reggie Nalder; notorious trash mag editor 'Mad' Myron Fass (publisher of 1970s exploitation titles like *Occult Sex*, *Brute* and *Outlaw Biker Gangs*); *Straw Dogs* star Susan George; Serge Gainsbourg; the Baader-Meinhof gang; marijuana (every Wizard album includes a personal dedication); Spanish gonzo master Jess Franco, American trash pioneer Andy Milligan as well as a plethora of individual movies, often rendered in block capitals; it's a world to sink into, should you choose, and the band has been a gateway for many into cinema and books that may otherwise have lain undiscovered.

'It was always about more than just the music,' says Oborn. 'In the nineties it was pre-internet, really. We like leaving little clues, little nuggets for people to discover — pre-internet, you didn't have the same access to things. You could isolate yourself in a very specific world quite easily and you wouldn't have to have any outside influence at all. We try and leave clues for people so they can create a little world too.'

Many Electric Wizard songs allude directly to specific movies. 'Venus in Furs' (from 2010's *Black Masses*) was a paean to the Jess Franco movie, and finds Oborn riffing on that classic doom trope — 'the evil woman' — in all her leather-clad glory; 'Living Dead of the Manchester Morgue' was based on the bleak, rain-soaked 1974 zombie movie of the same name; 'Dunwich' (from 2007's *Witchcult Today*) takes lyrical inspiration from *The Dunwich Horror*, the darkly psychedelic 1970 update of the classic Lovecraftian tale of ritual and summoning. They also introduced their own recurring character — Drugula — who appears in two songs (2007's 'Satanic Rites of Drugula' and 2010's

'Crypt of Drugula'), the count transposed to 1970s LA, where he feasts on blood laced with cocaine and Quaaludes, thus sparking an insatiable thirst for both blood *and* drugs.

But while Electric Wizard aren't afraid of entering the realm of the ludicrous from time to time, their devotion to hypnotic density has grown exponentially since the early noughties. After *Dopethrone*, the original line-up recorded one last album together — the criminally underrated, churning dirge of *Let Us Prey* — before guitarist Liz Buckingham joined on *We Live*. While both *Come My Fanatics . . .* and *Dopethrone* were filth-encrusted, later-period Wizard has leaned less heavily on abrasion and more on an extended, mesmeric aesthetic. *Let Us Prey*, *We Live* (2004), *Witchcult Today* (2007) and *Black Masses* (2010) were all typified by circling riffs, (very) lengthy songs and mantra-like vocals. Recording the latter two records at Hackney's storied palace of analogue fuzz — Toerag Studios — with White Stripes engineer Liam Watson, they captured a sound straight out of the early 1970s. *Black Masses*, in particular, was sub-basement lo-fi — the drums are barely audible — and was recorded on a four-track. When I spoke to Oborn in an earlier interview about the record, he bemoaned the 'pornographic' sonic quality of modern metal whereby you can 'hear every little detail, every little click, totally clean and polished. We wanted something that sounded musty, like you've found it buried in an attic.'

More recently, Electric Wizard have expanded their sound with by turns the bleakest, and most direct, material of their career. *Time to Die* (2014) was sheer suicidal despair, a clarion call to the black dog. Born out of a period of extreme turmoil (the band were going through serious legal strife with their former label, Rise Above, at time of recording) *Time to Die* is a suffocating listen, infused not so much with eldritch atmosphere or B-movie sleaze but sheer, unrelenting *hatred*. In that respect it stands alone in their catalogue. You have to be in a particular frame of mind to get through it; it carries a vibe of such unrelenting negativity that it feels palpably tainted, as if spending too much time with it may be a bad idea. Speaking to Oborn today, he talks about it along occult lines.

'It was a very bleak album — *very* bleak,' he explains. 'By the time we recorded it there was a lot going on in the background — lawyers and shit, and also with the studio, things not working out there. It was meant to be a horrible album but then it kind of fed off itself. We conceived it in an occult way where it would feed off itself, and we'd make things go wrong and make it even more fucked up — because it was starting to become *really* fucked up. Like some kind of vortex. Make the album sink further and further as *we* sank further and further (*laughs*). And I got obsessed with that until I thought I was losing the plot. But that was actually quite exciting! Like, "Yes! This album is going to be even more fucked up!" It's amplified on that level — changing studios and feeding off negativity . . . how much can you put into a record?'

2016's *Wizard Bloody Wizard* was — by Wizard terms — disconcertingly upbeat. Conceived to be what Oborn describes as a sonic 'palate cleanser' for the band after the tumbling abyss of their previous album, it brought Oborn and Buckingham's love of early 1970s Detroit rock to the fore. The MC5, the Stooges, (early) Alice Cooper and the Amboy Dukes are all firmly in the album's DNA, with Oborn's vocals right up in the mix for the first time, and a (slightly) cleaner production job. Indeed, Electric Wizard go beyond the confines of doom. At this stage, they're an institution. Oborn has often spoken of the band personifying an idea — a world — that goes beyond the individual members. They've proved wildly influential and, in a genre as self-referential and myopic as doom, it's perhaps inevitable that they've spawned an army of copyists; soulless doom-by-numbers that adopts the seventies signifiers but misses the venom, black soul and sheer *alchemy* that make Electric Wizard so special. For make no mistake, at their best Electric Wizard offer powerful liberatory magic that blunts the edges of these hideous times of greasy endgame capitalism. The irony of any band taking such idiosyncratic alchemy and attempting a weak reproduction isn't lost on Oborn. Like the blues or roots reggae, doom metal demands authenticity of intent; more than that, it demands grizzled life experience — it doesn't work when played by people who look like they've had an early night followed by dippy egg and soldiers for breakfast.

'Nobody strives for originality any more! It's like they strive for some kind of "market standard",' explains Oborn, '"this is what thrash sounds like; this is what doom sounds like". They collect all the elements, tick the boxes and if you tick enough boxes your band will be successful and you'll get some monetisation on YouTube or whatever. We strove to be original. We didn't want to steal somebody else's image, we'd consider that to be pathetic. We'd steal their riffs or their music, but never their image (*laughs*).'

That Electric Wizard have the White Panthers' mission statement on the landing page of their website — as pertinent an expression of rock 'n' roll nihilism as ever there was — makes perfect sense. This isn't music to piss about with:

We demand total freedom for everybody! And we will not be stopped until we get it. We are bad. There's only two kinds of people on the planet: those who make up the problem and those who make up the solution. WE ARE THE SOLUTION. We have no problems. Everything is free for everybody. Money sucks. Leaders suck. School sucks . . . We don't want it! Our program of rock and roll, dope and fucking in the streets is a program of total freedom for everyone. We are totally committed to carrying out our program. We breathe revolution. We are LSD driven total maniacs of the universe. We will do anything we can to drive people crazy out of their heads and into their bodies.

Lysol

Many bands engaged in serious Sabbath worship carry a misanthropic world view, or are wrapped up in eternal melancholy. There are notable exceptions, however. The Melvins have long combined the Neolithic under-swing of Sabbath with hardcore influences courtesy of Black Flag and Flipper, presenting an absurdist panorama of grotesque, Lynchian Americana shimmering with bizarre imagery.

Inhabiting a surreal suburban vista as viewed through hazy bong water, at their best — as on *Bullhead* (1991) or *Lysol* (1992) — they're weighty to the point of absurdity. These are records that exert physical presence, a palpable gravitational pull. Caught in the maelstrom of hype surrounding Seattle in the early 1990s, they were frequently named — due to their association with Nirvana and huge influence on most bands in the scene — as the 'sludge metal forefathers' or 'godfathers of grunge'. (Melvins drummer Dale Crover had played for Nirvana on *Bleach* [1989] while singer Buzz Osborne was instrumental in the genesis of that band, having introduced Kurt Cobain to Dave Grohl and Krist Novoselic.) But though fond of low tempos and oppressively heavy vibes, they can't be pinned down to the 'sludge' tag that has tended to follow them. Their discography is a labyrinthine sprawl encompassing avant-garde experiments, frenetic punkier fare, electronic noise, stadium rock covers (they're Kiss and Judas Priest obsessives) and countless solo projects and left-field collaborations. In the intimidating Fall-esque density of their back catalogue — not to mention their legendarily fearsome tour schedule — the Melvins also epitomise a blue-collar American work ethic that would floor bands half their age. They put out an album every year — sometimes more — and tour *relentlessly*; the Melvins are, therefore, the lifers' lifers, grizzled veterans out in the trenches of stale beer, tour vans, the drone of ringing feedback, the road eternal.

Formed in 1983 by guitarist and vocalist Buzz Osborne alongside bassist Matt Lukin and drummer Mike Dillard, they quickly gained a reputation for playing slower, lower and sludgier than almost any band on the scene. Dillard quit in 1985 and was replaced by Dale Crover who — along with Osborne — has formed the nucleus of the band ever since, alongside a rotating cast of bassists. Like many others involved in metal's slipstream — Eyehategod, Earth, Sunn O))) — the second side of Black Flag's seminal *My War* (1984), explored in the previous chapter, was a pivotal early inspiration.

'We were *totally* into *My War* side 2,' explains Crover, 'also Black Sabbath and Flipper and Wipers. We were also really into Hellhammer — who were super slow and dirgy — and Venom. Hellhammer and Venom were, like, the heavy metal bands that were accepted in the punk community (*laughs*).'

Propelled by monotonous riffs and an elephantine groove, the Melvins' debut — *Gluey Porch Treatments* (1987) — was a lumbering beast that hit the sweet spot between the time-stretched sonic tar of Flipper and the swaggering absurdity of stadium rock dynamics filtered through a bottle of codeine cough syrup. Hugely influential, both on Seattle's nascent grunge scene and the genesis of what would later be termed sludge metal, *Gluey Porch Treatments* was a two-finger salute to those who would pigeonhole them. Following a disastrous US tour in 1986 that saw them playing to often violent crowds of skinheads and disparaging hardcore kids who weren't used to the monolithic welter, the Melvins were running on empty. The notoriously po-faced West Coast punk scene bible *Maximumrocknroll* loathed them. Seattle was a different story, however — and far more accepting of what the band were doing, as Crover remembers.

'In Seattle, things were ahead of the time compared to the rest of the country,' he tells me. 'Melvins were accepted. When I joined, the band was already established and there were some hardcore bands playing super fast, but the majority had gotten over that and were moving on to other things. The bands on SST, for example, were really popular, and they were all different. The Meat Puppets and Hüsker Dü? They didn't sound like Black Flag. All those bands were completely different, and that was what the scene was like in Seattle. There we could play slow, crazy shit and people loved it. But once we got outside of Seattle on a tour, the rest of the country was *way* behind and it was more "We're not having any of your long-haired bullshit! Get your hippie shit out of here!" (*laughs*) It took a couple of years before people caught up. All of a sudden people were interested in what was going on in the Seattle area.'

Second album *Ozma* (1989) amped the dronal underbelly, hinging on nightmarishly rendered slow-motion riffs and a lyrical third eye tuned to the vagaries of American suburbia. Like all the best Melvins records, it's psyche-delic in cleaving viscosity. *Bullhead* (1991) went further into doomy, downer vibes, finding the Melvins in unabashed metal mode. Opener 'Boris' — the song to which Japanese sludge overlords Boris owe their name — is eight minutes of unrelenting hypnosis, a sinister ode to the mesmeric powers of Buzz Osborne's cat that succinctly captures feline malevolence ('Boris *knows*') while 'Ligature' lumbers forwards with all the grace of a punch-drunk farmer on the ropes at an illegal barn fight.

The Melvins toured relentlessly as the Seattle scene was blowing up. Surrounded by bands like Nirvana, Mudhoney, Tad and Soundgarden — all of whom were inspired by, and often vocal, in their appreciation of the Melvins — the city came under intense media glare as grunge gained traction. Soon, major labels were clamouring to sign any band associated with the city. Soundgarden had the classic rock dynamic, albeit tempered by an off-kilter, raga-inflected hypnotic grandeur; Nirvana were raw, bloody emotion; Pearl Jam ploughed an earnest furrow while outliers like Mudhoney and Tad were a rawer proposition. The Melvins were weirder and weightier than any of them. Their music may have been anxiety making, but it never wallowed in self-pity, their swung grooves at once dead-weight heavy and strangely life affirming. In Dale Crover they had a drummer of brute power — he hits seriously hard — and dizzying creativity, a Miles Davis obsessive who carries the groove with an uncanny command of space and silence, constantly turning rhythmic ortho-doxies on their head — it's often as much about what he *doesn't* play.

Lysol (1992) was an exercise in reduction, boiling the bones of their structure down to a rich, bovine essence. A near-biblical text among drone metallers like Earth and Sunn O))) — both of whom *obsessed* over the record — *Lysol* remains a separate entity in the wider Melvins catalogue. Nothing else that they've recorded matches its ritualistic power or meditative magnetism. Epic ten-minute opener 'Hung Bunny' unfolds at a glacial pace, Osborne's guitar assuming physical form in its glutinous viscosity, each droning chord hanging in the air like a mushroom cloud, by turns devastating and strangely graceful, while Crover's crashing drums breach the hot static air like a wrathful thunderclap every minute or so. As vocal drones and feedback join the mix, the sense of ritual intensity increases; waves of sound building and fading and building before the moment of epiphany arrives at around eight minutes, Crover's drums taking on a tribal power, like the soundtrack to some ancient ritual where you're served your very soul on a plate. The entire genesis of drone metal is right there, in those first eight minutes — there isn't a solitary chance that either Sunn O))) or Earth would have gone on to make the music they made without *Lysol*: it's a year-zero moment. Crover traces the record's dronal genesis back to similarly elemental sounds — Velvets, Stooges and Buddhist chant.

'We were *really* into the Stooges. "We Will Fall" in particular, which comes from the Velvet Underground influence, John Cale had a lot to do with that. And we were into the Velvets too. But another thing a lot of people don't know, was that we were really into the Gyoto Monks, Tibetan chant. That first song on *Lysol* with the chanting? That was the height of when we were into Tibetan music. It felt like all the songs that we did before — all of the slow stuff, at least — was leading up to *Lysol*. It was like the pinnacle. It came together quickly, we did it in one take. We knew that if we fucked it up we weren't gonna go back and do it again — it was too long (*laughs*). There's a structure to it, but the structure is more a feeling of when things are supposed to happen. I remember thinking: "I really like this a lot, this is a really cool thing but *everybody* is going to hate this thing." Nobody was more surprised than us that anybody gave a shit. I would never have guessed that it would have been a record that people would hold in high regard: never in a million years did I think that would happen (*laughs*).'

Caught up in the feeding frenzy that followed grunge — when equally left-field bands like Tad, Jesus Lizard, Helmet and Butthole Surfers landed major deals — the Melvins soon followed suit. Signing with Atlantic Records in 1993, they released *Houdini* in the same year. Ostensibly 'executive produced' by Kurt Cobain (he was, in fact, strung out on heroin at the time and not present for most of the sessions) the album didn't exactly tone down the Melvins' immutable combination of Dadaist absurdity and cleaving heviosity. Crover insists Atlantic were under no illusions about what they were signing, however, committing to offer the band full artistic freedom.

'We went into a meeting with Atlantic Records and played them *Lysol* in full and said: "Look, this is what we're putting out next. Are you *sure* you still want to sign us?" (*laughs*) They weren't thinking "This can really sell!" The reason we signed with Atlantic was because we went in there and the vice president said "Look, you guys are already an established band, you're low budget, you make it work, your music is uncompromising but you've somehow influenced all these bands. We want you guys to sign with us because if you do it will also make us look good and we'll be able to sign other bands (*laughs*). So, do whatever the fuck you want, you'll always have a home here and it'll be great." We had a great relationship. In fact, I don't know *any* other band who has signed to a major label on those pretences. It was realistic all the way down the line. It was a weird time . . . we were friends with Cobain, that helped too.

They knew that we had something. We know our music is uncompromising and totally weird and not likely to sell millions of records. Bands like Nirvana and Soundgarden took what we were doing and put it in a more commercial format with more basic song structures. We understand! There is no confusion here of us having not sold millions of records and not understanding why (*laughs*). We know why! We know *exactly* why. But somehow we've managed to take this thing of making ferocious music and being able to survive. We own houses and raise families — wow!'

The Melvins released two more records with Atlantic — *Stoner Witch* (1994) and *Stag* (1996), signed to experimental noise mainstays Amphetamine Reptile for an album of chaotic electronic noise — *Prick* (1994) — and then to Mike Patton's Ipecac Records for a welter of noisy avant-garde-leaning material including the notorious Throbbing Gristle-esque squalling electronic noisefest *The Colossus of Destiny* (2001). Their influence has been immeasurable. It's unthinkable that Nirvana would have recorded the sludgy *Bleach* without the influence of *Gluey Porch Treatment*s (check 'Floyd the Barber', say — *pure* Melvins): the immutable heaviness, the rain-flecked gallows humour, the tar-thick grooves — it's all there. The Melvins inspired Seattle to down tune and embrace ludicrously thick fuzz tone: the drone was in grunge from the start, and it came from the Melvins, by way of Flipper and Black Flag.

For a certain section of the metal underground, it was *Lysol* that remained the most enduring influence, however: a sacrosanct text to build on.

Special Low-Frequency Version

Earth represent a pleasingly symmetrical convergence of strands covered in the *Monolithic Undertow* sonic universe. They took their name from Black Sabbath (Earth being Sabbath's original moniker) while bandleader Dylan Carlson also took a keen interest in minimalism, wondering what would happen if he 'took a Slayer-style riff and played it at half speed . . . for twenty minutes?'[8] As mission statements go, it's a compelling one, and his initial explorations were startling. Earth condensed the weight of metal — the distortion, the crunch, the aggression — but stretched it like so much black tar; time melting like a Dalí clock.

A magisterial wall of sound — as opulent as it was foreboding — 1993's *Earth 2: Special Low-Frequency Version* was the culmination of two years' refinement of process. Labelled 'ambient metal' at the time by Carlson, the record comprised seventy-five minutes of stratified guitar drones with minimal rhythmic adornment. It changed metal for ever — slower and more minimal than *Lysol*, even. Much was achieved via painstaking studio overdubs — a welter of obscure pedals, vintage amplification and expensive cables creating a rich tonal vocabulary that cleaved to the idiosyncrasies of the gear as much as the chords. Though a self-described teenage metalhead into AC/DC and Black Sabbath, Carlson's tastes circumnavigated everything from Terry Riley and La Monte Young to the Velvet Underground and the Melvins. And it was this combination — brash and bombastic rock with subtler, weirder flavours — that fed into Earth.

'My mom turned me on to the Velvet Underground at a very young age,' Carlson explains. 'It was through listening to them that I found out about La Monte Young and Terry Riley. You couldn't get any La Monte Young, so he was more of a conceptual influence, but I'd found some Terry Riley stuff and really liked that. Then the other big thing was King Crimson and from that I found *No Pussyfooting* (1973) by Fripp and Eno, although it was the second one they did — *Evening Star* (1975) — that I was most into, although it seemed to get totally ignored (*laughs*). So it was a combination of things. I've always liked bands who did longer stuff — I'm a Dead head, I love Allman Brothers — but for the drone thing, it was really the Velvet Underground and the exposure to minimalism and Riley and Young and Crimson and Fripp and Eno, which was where that came from.'

Indeed, one can trace a path from Fripp and Eno's *Evening Star* — particularly the half-hour drone piece 'An Index of Metals', Fripp's guitar treated with distortion and echo — to Carlson's debut LP *Earth 2: Special Low-Frequency Version* (1993). One of the lushest and most expansive drone records of the twentieth century, *Earth 2* was a dramatic change in the drone continuum. While doom metal hinged on sustained notes, it seldom focused on naked drones. Carlson changed this. He took the foreboding atmosphere — and volume — of metal and married it to an extreme drone aesthetic: no vocals, no drums, half-hour pieces charged with serious hypnotic portent.

If the Melvins proved too abrasive for mass consumption, even in the context of the major-label feeding frenzy that surrounded early-nineties Seattle, Earth were an even more extreme proposition. Signed to Sub Pop, *Earth 2* was met with some acclaim but plenty of bemusement. At odds with the roughshod thrashings — Tad, Mudhoney, Nirvana et cetera — that most associated with the label, Carlson appeared on the back sleeve wearing a Morbid Angel T-shirt. A small factor, but one that nonetheless helped place the record in the metal sphere, as opposed to the purely avant-garde. It would be many years, however, before his band would be lauded as drone metal pioneers and *Earth 2* taken as a definitive statement. Earth were a band out of time during the early 1990s, Carlson's music a world away from that of his friends and peers such as Kurt Cobain or Mark Lanegan.

'Seattle was so small then,' Carlson recalls. 'And it was funny: there were certain bands put out at the height of the feeding frenzy from the majors and everyone was like, "Oh, they're from Seattle!" and we were all like "No they're not, because we've never seen them." You knew who was from Seattle because you saw people around town or you'd run into them at a party. It was really strange. I was grateful to have the opportunity to make a record, because not everyone gets to. Now everyone has the ability to record on a laptop, it's more accessible — but back then not everyone got to make a record, so I was grateful to be able to do that because of Sub Pop — and we got more notice than we probably would have. But the flip side was that a lot of the people who would have liked it might not have got it *because* it was on Sub Pop and, then, a lot of people who bought it *because* it was on Sub Pop didn't get it (*laughs*). All of a sudden MTV wanted to film one of our shows, so they came down and filmed and interviewed us and they were obviously *completely* confused and not very happy at the situation. They were expecting the next big thing . . . and it really wasn't (*laughs*).'

From the foreboding hum and roar of 'Seven Angels' to the abyssal half-hour 'Teeth of Lions Rules the Divine' and equally majestic 'Like Gold and Faceted', *Earth 2* represented a reimagining of minimalism. If Rhys Chatham and Glenn Branca had infused minimal structures to the adrenal rush of punk, Dylan Carlson was taking the drone to areas deeper and darker: here was the Theatre of Eternal Music recast as a claustrophobic, moody, rain-soaked wall of distortion and dynamic feedback, as slate grey as the Washington State skies. It also carried a strong ritualistic bearing, prefiguring the 'amp worship' of Sunn by some years. Carlson remembers his idiosyncratic performance aesthetic of the early years.

'When I first started I came to Earth with a concept, it was a conceptual band. When we first started, I played sitting down and I was behind the amplifiers, nobody even saw me. And then later I came out but I still sat, probably because of the Fripp thing, but originally I sat behind the amps, so it was the opposite of the ego . . . there was also a technical function in the earlier days and I had feedback, but the early incarnation of Earth I sat down to play: I was not showy in that way.'

Following up with underwhelming *Phase 3: Thrones and Dominions* (1995) — a rawer vibe, shorter songs, made at the height of Carlson's crippling drug addiction, and a record that very nearly didn't get finished at all — Earth's next LP, *Pentastar: In the Style of Demons* (1996) was more considered and dramatic, and featured Carlson's vocals for the first time, although its release signalled a decade-long absence from music as legal hassles and serious drug issues took their toll. Reconvening in 2005 with new drummer Adrienne Davis on the bluesy, understated *Hex; or Printing in the Infernal Method* — a record Carlson has stated was strongly influenced by Cormac McCarthy's hallucinatory, ultra-violent western novel *Blood Meridian* — Earth's second phase has seen Carlson embrace a wider sphere of influence, drawing on country, psychedelia and American primitive more than metal.

Records like *Angels of Darkness, Demons of Light* were underpinned by a cinematic, Morricone-esque grandeur that Carlson has made his own: the metal influence is more restrained, Adrienne Davis's drums a mournful — though devastatingly precise — trudge (playing this slow is, for the drummer *incredibly* difficult: any misstep can derail the carefully layered vibe, and mistakes are far more obvious than at high tempos); it conjures serious imagery — ancient weather-beaten faces, desolate chapels out on the plains, dustbowls, empty mezcal bottles and cheques cashed in shady saloons in the pitiless heat of the day. Carlson connects in spirit to the primitive lineage — John Fahey, Sandy Bull, Robbie Basho — that we explored in earlier chapters sharing their bloody-minded devotion to wringing maximum emotive drama out of austere elements.

Primitive and Deadly (2014) was equally haunted: if *Earth 2* was claustrophobia and humidity this was the sound of blood-red earth, loneliness at the edge of the canyon. Carlson's long-term friend Mark Lanegan lends his sand-blasted larynx to a couple of tracks — the perfect vocal foil to Carlson's patient riffs. Indeed, Carlson's playing is always tempered by restraint. There are no jagged edges; every note is considered. His playing carries a steadying warmth, even when he's working with serious volume — it's a careful alchemical balance. It's easy to discern an otherworldly atmosphere in Carlson's work. Listening late at night, headphones on, volume up, the sepulchral western licks linger and drone in a way that evokes some presence just out of reach.

Indeed, it's something Carlson knows directly. Although reticent to be drawn on the precise details, he experienced unusual visions in London while touring after a bout of serious illness — an experience that led to the creation of his 'Dr Carlson Albion' alias, a vehicle for his love of British folklore and the more esoteric corners of British folk music (Pentangle, Fairport Convention et cetera) rendered with a certain otherworldly aesthetic.

'Musically, I discovered folk through Led Zeppelin — Sandy Denny being on "The Battle of Evermore". My uncle had an album collection that he was getting rid of, but he gave me the first Fairport record, and then Pentangle and stuff like that. I'd always liked that, it had always been a part of my listening, but after I got really ill — just before we did the *Angels* record — I was on a press trip and I had what were, for lack of a better term, some supernatural experiences. At the time I was listening to a lot of folk and thinking about mortality and origins, but it had always been there in the background, too.'

The Dr Carlson Albion material offers an interesting counterpoint with Carlson's work with Earth: connecting back to herbaceous, occult-leaning folk and offering his own spin on older music still. His cover of Elizabethan composer Anthony Holborne's 'The Faerie Round', for example, carries a particularly haunting quality, rounded drones offset by eldritch finger picking. Carlson remains a roots artist at heart. Accordingly, his concept of the drone is not tied to the metal aesthetic he is generally associated with, nor to tropes of volume or the diminishing returns that come from slavishly chasing extremity; rather, he connects the drone back to older sources and universal spiritual significance — something that occasionally rankles with Earth fans who expect him to repeat *Earth 2* ad infinitum.

'I remember when we were touring the *Bees Made Honey in the Lion's Skull* record. There was this drunk Italian guy and he said "Why do you not do the drone music anymore?"' laughs Carlson. 'And it's funny because the way he was talking made it sound like — to him — drone just meant *Earth 2*. Like, really loud and a ton of amps.

'But to me it's a technique; it's an oblique motion, because you have sound moving *against* the static note; and it's infused *everywhere*. It's in the blues, it's in country, it's in rock. Indian music is all about it. And then of course, people like La Monte Young and Terry Riley. I've always viewed it as a technique: it's not like "Oh, I have 10,000 Sunn amps and a rack!" — that isn't what makes it drone. And I guess I've always deeply responded to it. Even when I first started playing guitar I used to lay in bed with the guitar on my chest and play a string and let it go and just absorb the tone. So it's been there right from the start. For whatever reason, I've always gravitated or responded to that static sense of harmony. I view music as one of mankind's original technologies; it allows communication in ways that language can't, it transports us to other realms — especially with the drone. It's trance-inducing, so it's a combination of a really magical form of communication and — for want of a better term — a teleportation to allow us to travel to other realms. Vibration is the ground of being: everything in the universe is vibrating.'

251

Maximum Volume Yields Maximum Results

While Earth were roundly ignored in their original nineties phase some were listening keenly. Formed in homage to Earth (as guitarist Stephen O'Malley explained to me in 2013, in his case 'the Sunn orbits the Earth') — Sunn O))) offer the most viscerally physical expression of the drone imaginable — raw physical sound, chest-plate vibration.

If tropes of ritual, catharsis and physicality are the hallmarks of much of the *Monolithic Undertow* universe, they reach an apex with Sunn O))). Stephen O'Malley and Greg Anderson treat sound as a physical presence — some grunting Norse behemoth hewn from rock, capable of dislodging cranial matter by dint of face-shaking volume. They speak the language of volume, worshipping at the sonic altar. More than any other band, they glean inspiration from the experience of physical transcendence via sound, and have often referenced it in their iconography — one memorable tour T-shirt asked 'Ever Breathe a Frequency?' — while their wildly excessive tech spec sheet, distributed well in advance to venues and promoters — has entered legend.

More manifesto than instruction manual it reads:

MAXIMUM VOLUME YIELDS MAXIMUM RESULTS: Sunn focuses on low and sub bass tones with intention of heavy physical presence within music beyond the typical concert listening experience. The point is the pure physical power of sound toward the audience. An absolute encounter with sonics. We love frequencies such as 80Hz, 110–120Hz, 180–220Hz. We worship resonance and feedback. Frequencies that you can feel vibrating the environment, air and your body. FOH crew working the event must be prepared and comfortable with high volume/low frequency MAXIMISING of the PA.

Some trepidation surrounds the Sunn O))) live experience. Garish stories abound: that the bass will shake bottles from the bar; that vomit will streak the floor; that you'll dislodge essential cerebral fluid or soil yourself as O'Malley and Anderson harness the force of the 'brown note'.

Regardless of the veracity of such incidents, the fact remains — the sub frequencies at a Sunn show do indeed work on a chest-rattling level — what Bristollian dubstep producer Pinch calls 'chest-plate' bass, whereby your ribcage physically rattles and air is pushed out of your lungs: they're a band you *feel* rather than hear. They present the drone as sonic ceremony. Massive walls of amplification afforded sacrosanct reverence, positioned as a monolithic focal point — sonic obelisks — while the smoke, hoods and robes add ritual gravity.

Anderson and O'Malley were both veterans of the Seattle metal underground by the time Sunn O))) formed in 1998. Both had been members of Burning Witch — a low-lit Seattle doom band — and the pair had also played together in the short-lived Thor's Hammer. Sunn O))) formed after the pair were asked to contribute to a Metallica tribute album, covering 'For Whom the Bell Tolls' without drums or vocals at a muddy, sepulchral, completely unrecognisable trudge. Bonding over a deep, alchemical connection to Earth and the Melvins — two records provided the nucleus for the pair's nascent sound.

'Sunn started as a tribute to the *Earth 2* record, in particular, and Melvins' *Lysol*,' said Anderson. 'Steve and I were also really into a lot of sixties and early seventies jazz — Miles Davis and John Coltrane and Eric Dolphy and stuff like that — but as far as the way that the pieces of music were played — long, drawn out, a lot of repetition, the repetition is what we were drawn to. In Seattle in the 1980s, getting into underground music, the Melvins — that's where the Earth sound came from, that's where Dylan got the sound. Melvins were the band who would come out on stage before an extremely fast hardcore or thrash metal band, and they'd come and play a twenty-five-minute drone with Buzz standing his guitar up against the amp, feeding back as the intro to their set just to piss people off! (*laughs*) They were *extremely* heavy: Dale Crover is one of the greatest drummers ever, which added to the thunder and the heaviness . . . so that's where it all came from. We were both into playing very slow and heavy music and Earth and Melvins were as slow and heavy as you could get (*laughs*). We really emulated that as a starting point — we made no bones about it.'

The GrimmRobe Demos (2000) was particularly blatant in exultation of Earth: one track was called 'Defeating: Earth's Gravity' another, simply: 'Dylan Carlson'. Early Sunn O))) was (far) more abrasive than Earth, though. This was sheer maximal sonics. As we've explored, Carlson tended to apply feedback with restraint and — *Earth 2* aside — has long tempered the metal influence with sweeping, hallucinatory Americana. Early Sunn O))) took the immovable bones — *Earth 2* and *Lysol* — threw them in the cauldron and boiled them into a roiling, gluttonous stock, like Sumo wrestlers building a *chankonabe* soup. The result wasn't so much tribute, as Frankenstein's monster:

a lumbering, elemental beast. And this is key — Sunn O))) tap into the drone in a symbiotic way. They may have been worshipping at the altar of Earth and the Melvins but they were also connecting to the immovable truth that sits at the core of the drone: sonic power beyond reason, something that simply *is*.

The first three records — *The GrimmRobe Demos*, *ØØ Void* (2000) and *Flight of the Behemoth* (2002) — are suffused with a viscous, untethered vibe. This is Sunn O))) at their wildest: the sound threatens to break free at any moment, Anderson and O'Malley only *just* holding on to the roar of the drone, like a medieval guard holding the back slobbering hounds. It feels right up close, the breath of the beast on your face, the frequencies — even on a home stereo, even on headphones — enveloping. Sunn represent the symbiosis between electricity, amplification and artist. The Sunn amps (the band are named after the company, even borrowing the idiosyncratic O))) from the logo) are venerated for their inimitable grain, essentially becoming a third member of the band.

'They were originally made in the 1970s,' said Anderson. 'They carry so much power, so much low end. We became obsessed with those amps: you can feel the vibrations, feeling that on the back of your legs is a really powerful experience. It really added to things, especially when you're playing slower, drawn-out music with the long chords and hangs, it added to the feeling of the music becoming this 3D thing. With Sunn, it became a concept of being able to *feel* the sound so in the early days we'd try to hook up as many as possible.'

Early Sunn O))) was united by the visceral thrill of vibration, Anderson and O'Malley standing in a humid LA studio feeling the frequencies push the air around the room. It wasn't enough for the pair though. After *Void*, they were driven to attempt to put forward what they were doing in the live arena — to understand the band, people needed the volume. Early tours were fractious, however. How best to present a band without rhythmic pulse? Without a singer? Without anything that a majority metal audience would even recognise as a 'song'? A difficult early outing with uptempo stoner rockers (and, at the time, fellow Rise Above signings) Orange Goblin heralded a sea change in their thinking.

'People didn't understand what was going on at the time — no vocals, no drums — it didn't make sense (*Anderson laughs*). Orange Goblin are like a party band . . . playing with Sunn on those shows was rough, because by the end of that tour I wasn't even sure if it was something that should be performed live — and definitely not in a pub or in a small venue. It didn't seem conducive or the right environment. I felt myself wondering what it was about in the first place: three guys up there without any drums or vocals, it didn't make sense. I felt self-conscious up there, extracted from concentrating on playing because I was concerned about what the reaction of the audience was — which for me was the opposite of what the band was about in the first place, because what other people thought was never a concern of ours. But when you're stuck playing in front of a bar and you're wearing jeans and T-shirts in front of your amps, and there are a bunch of people holding their ears with faces of disgust? It took me out of the mindset that I need to be in when I'm playing this music.'

Changing things up for the last show at Camden Underworld, Anderson and O'Malley retreated from view, set the amps in front of the stage and performed from behind them. It was a revelation. Freed from audience expectation, they were focused on the naked drone, able to channel the sound in a more powerful way.

'You couldn't see us,' remembers Anderson. 'From that point on we decided that our identities were going to be concealed. It wasn't going to be a normal rock show with jeans and T-shirts and a singer trying to get the crowd excited about what's going on on stage. That's *not* what it's going to be. And that's how it developed into what it's been to this day: the fog and the robes, an anonymity as to who is performing on stage.'

The live rendering is Sunn in the purest form: physical music, air moving through the room, cavities rattling. It's a familiar feeling to anybody who takes an interest in sound system culture: the rattle is what moves the whole thing forward. It's entirely at odds with the tinny treble of most rock shows, having far more in common with some titanic dub system — the warmth of the valve amps, the perfectly tuned sound, the titanic walls of speakers — than anything else. Indeed, the only comparable sonic experience I've had which has approached the power of Sunn O))) in full flight was Iration Steppas vs King Earthquake at a University of Dub dance at Brixton Rec in the early noughties, where the bass was so strong it physically threw the contents of my unrolled spliff across the room like a poltergeist.

Indeed, although Earth and the Melvins paved the way for Sunn O))), neither approach their bass weight: the frequencies Sunn reach are in a different spectrum altogether. It's also a particularly synaesthetic experience, the distortion, saturation and sustain moving in uncanny synchronicity with the opulence of the lights — chilly blues and blood reds — and the constant stream of dry ice, Anderson and O'Malley wreathed in plumes of smoke for the duration. It's a fundamentally theatrical spectacle — a mass — hairs collectively standing up as they move sloth like, arms raised in reverence, hands held aloft in the smoke for twenty seconds before striking the strings. With the hoods and the beards and the exaggeratedly slow, cumbersome movement there is something primitive and bearlike about the pair.

Despite the heft, however, Sunn O))) are not bereft of subtlety. As the noughties moved on, Sunn records displayed progressively wider influences. *White1* (2003) had a notably rootsier feel due to traditional Norwegian folk lyrics sung by ex-Thor's Hammer vocalist Runhild Gammelsaeter while the bucolically evocative collaboration with arch drudion Julian Cope on 'My Wall' — in which he places Anderson and O'Malley at the centre of an ancient sonic mythology and name-checks everywhere from Wansdyke to Silbury Hill in a gloriously, preposterously Copian manner ('Play your gloom axe, Stephen O'Malley sub bass clinging to the side of the valley') — is one of their most magical moments.

Black One (2005) is by some distance the bleakest record in their discography, talking directly to the pair's longstanding love of black metal, with a notable collaboration with Malefic who recorded his inhuman vocals from inside a coffin for extra malevolent atmosphere, while 2009's *Monoliths & Dimensions* displayed next-level subtlety and shade. A sprawling record that talks strongly to the pair's love of outré jazz, it featured a guest spot from veteran trombonist Julian Priester (who had previously played with Duke Ellington and Sun Ra) and laid down the backing to 'Alice' — a tribute to Alice Coltrane that exemplifies the sheer psychic uplift that Sunn O))) are often capable of — a spacious piece inspired by the spiritual light of Coltrane, Priester's trombone beautifully mournful. *Monoliths & Dimensions* was the moment Sunn fully eclipsed the Earth worship and embraced a more expansive palette entirely their own. Strings, vocals, trombones, electronics — all were layered against the drone with devastating effect. 'Aghartha' added a string section to the rumble while the vocals of ex-Mayhem singer Attila Csihar — a cavernously low, sometimes whispered growl — added grim luxuriance. The saturation of the guitars was more subtle throughout: on 'Aghartha' they're right down in the mix, more prominence given to creaking doors, Csihar's whispered vocal, the piano, strings and atmospherics. 'Big Church' was majestically nightmarish, combining a choral arrangement, staccato strings and Gregorian chant-style vocals from Csihar to evoke dank ritual — albeit shot through with a certain camp, *giallo*-esque soundtrack vibe. Indeed, Csihar has become something approaching a third member, collaborating with the pair on further albums and many tours down the years. 'Everything that he brings is in his reaction and interpretation of the music,' explains Anderson. 'That is one of the reasons that we love to play with him — he really gets it and he got it from early on. Stephen and he were pen pals in the nineties. Atilla was always into experimental music and experimenting with music; even the way he used his voice with Mayhem — it had this Gregorian chant aesthetic to it.'

Monoliths & Dimensions helped Sunn O))) transcend the left-field metal underground, as likely to be playing at arts venues like the Barbican or head-lining avant-garde festivals as on doom metal bills. Likewise they collaborated with an increasingly eclectic group of artists. In 2011 industrial mainstay Nurse with Wound produced a subtle and foreboding set of remixes of *Void* entitled *The Iron Soul of Nothing* while in 2014 the pair collaborated with Scott Walker on his *Soused* LP. It was a rich combination, the density of Anderson and O'Malley's drone subtle but strident, tempered in the mix just below Walker's tremulous, dramatic tenor.

'Brando' was particularly bracing, Walker cracking an American bullwhip to keep time, while 'Herod 2014' transposes the horrific Bible story (the King of Judea ordering mass infanticide in Bethlehem in order to kill Jesus) to any number of modern war zones. Walker's voice was an extraordinary instrument: at once nakedly vulnerable and madly defiant. There is a gloriously overblown aspect to his vocals on *Soused* — the stridence of delivery is, in its own way, sheer metal. On 'Bull', for example, he juxtaposes biblical imagery with a childlike chant of 'bump the beaky!', an apocalyptic scene — fire ants, Jesus on the cross, quilt-covered corpses — tied to this nightmarish, repeated exhortation. Walker was a master of portent: his voice quivers and stutters and warbles and tremors in a state of biblical dread and dark prophecy, like some underworld town crier.

Soused is a darkly opulent masterpiece — both dramatic and, at times, gloriously absurd (check Walker's warbled 'hey nonnny nonny!' towards the end of 'Lullaby'). But despite the rich layering and volume it was originally conceived by Walker as an exercise in *reduction* — a reaction to the head-spin-ning complexity of his preceding LP *Bish Bosch* (2012). As he told the writer John Doran in 2014, he wanted to get rid of the 'cast of thousands' and 'reduce everything. Take it down to the basics. And the basic in music is the drone. So I thought, "Well, it's a reductive exercise": and I thought of those guys and the drones . . ."[9]

Though Walker was tapping the primitive potential of the drone, reduc-tion isn't a word most would associate with Sunn live. For some the weight of sound is oppressive, but for many it's a monumentally uplifting experience. Last time I saw them was at the Paradiso in Amsterdam, early 2019 — a beau-tiful theatre, a high-ceilinged converted church. The feeling of encasement in bass was overwhelming, a juddering blanket of weight that was akin to Deep

South humidity: a wet blanket, heavy-limbed vibe, palpably *warm*. Sunn O)))
is meditative in the extreme but involves active submission to the drone. The
churn unfolds at a glacial pace, the dry ice so thick you can't see your own
hands. The subs, meanwhile, reach into the nasal cavities, chest, lungs, ribs,
shake the hair follicles — your eyeballs vibrate in their sockets — it's a sonic
bodily excavation.

Suddenly, you're aware of micro movements within your own body; yes,
the volume is extreme, but it's a pleasurable extreme: Sunn O))) are as defined
by the transcendence of time as depth of volume. Like the Dream House we
discussed earlier, say, time feels distorted, bent out of jig by the sonic colossus
emanating from the vast stacks. It's as intimate and immersive as a big show
gets, more akin to druidic mass than gig. While most rock music is based on
moments of communal tension and release there is no prescribed reaction at
a Sunn show. Looking around the Paradiso I see people with eyes closed in
rapture, some lying on the floor, some pumping fists sloth-like at the front,
some looking, frankly, terrified, others enraptured or nauseous — the full
gamut of emotion is represented. Ultimately Sunn O))) preside — even in
bigger theatres like the Paradiso — over myriad personal rituals as opposed to
a collective experience.

'I really don't feel comfortable with classifying Sunn O))) in a genre,'
says Anderson. 'Over the last ten years, we've moved beyond the genre tags.
Calling it a "metal" band or a "drone" band or even "experimental" — it's
transcended that, to my mind. One of the things that I'm really grateful
for in this group is that it has connected people from *all* walks of life. For
me, something that resonated early on with our music was the freedom that
it had. My entire life, I'd played in bands that have an orthodox structure
where, along with playing guitar in a band, you have these expectations —
recordings, label, gigs, the tradition of rock music, guitar music. With Sunn
O))) we didn't care about any of that: we just wanted to do it in an unortho-
dox way, without *any* restrictions or rules . . . we're coming from a free space.
There is something very primal — the intelligent caveman aspect (*laughs*) —
it's coming from a space that is very raw: we try to respect and honour that.'

Harvestman

'We had a phase when we were quite percussion heavy,' explains Neurosis
guitarist and vocalist Steve Von Till. 'And — at the risk of sounding like some
hippy drum circle bullshit (*laughs*) — we really did try to use tribal percussion

mixed with noise and drone to achieve an altered state of consciousness. It was aggressive and it was violent: but it brought us closer to a clean state where we were removed of all our mental trappings, a breaking through to the other side. We actually titled a song "Cleanse" because it *was* cleansing — to our souls, to our bodies. We felt that we'd been sweated clean every time we did it. That whole *Souls in Zero* era — of endlessly slogging through the drone; of repetitive crushing darkness — allowed us to purge the shit from our souls and bodies, to find something meaningful in a world of otherwise distracting bullshit.'

Neurosis are responsible for some of the most searingly intense music of the past thirty years. Emerging from the nucleus of the Bay Area hardcore scene in the mid 1980s, they originally played metallic hardcore that cleaved to the abrasive sounds of bands like Discharge, Subhumans, Crass, Black Flag, Flipper and Amebix. Mainstays of the San Francisco Gilman street scene (a legendarily hard-line punk venue operated by late *Maximumrocknroll* editor Tim Yohannon) Neurosis tapped into the darker, bleaker, dronier vein of hardcore explored in the previous chapter. Debut LP *Pain of Mind* (1987) typified the vibe, although there was nothing to suggest the searing intensity that was to come. Second album *The Word as Law* (1990) was more complex, hinging on longer songs, experimental structures and a thicker tone, while *Souls at Zero* (1992) was predicated on a darker, more hypnotic vibe. And while some were shocked by the (seeming) abandonment of their hardcore roots, Von Till mentions the psychedelic potential of punk as a driver that had been there right from the start.

'To me, Flipper were a *very* psychedelic band. Maybe there was some-thing in the water in the Bay Area, where even the punk bands ended up having a little more of a psychoactive edge . . . Lemmy-era Hawkwind was very punk rock, too. Hawkwind had two guys who were there specifically to drone on oscillators — how genius is that? And they did that repetitious riff-ing. They were repeating these simple proto-metal, punk-rock style riffs. And I hear the same in Flipper, also in Chrome — which was weird, art-damaged, industrial punk rock from San Francisco — it's in the grit and the grime, I *hear* the drone. These guys were taking these big, heavy tones but they weren't doing rock music, they were doing something else that was more trance-induc-ing and more emotionally connecting.'

Souls at Zero was a dense slab. Predicated on a staunch, tribal vibe — pounding drums, chants, industrial noise — an atmosphere of severe catharsis carries the record. This was the moment Neurosis started to seriously crank the subs, too. A portentous atmosphere reigns — so claustrophobic as to be almost breathable. Likewise, 1996's *Through Silver in Blood* — generally considered the band's pinnacle — was sheer primal sonics that leant heavier on the electronics and samples (Von Till is a massive Throbbing Gristle and Godflesh fan) while retaining the core idea of hypnotic primitivism. Indeed, Swans are the most obvious point of comparison (Neurosis have since worked with ex-Swans vocalist Jarboe on the 2003 *Neurosis and Jarboe* album) with the volume and face-shaking potentiality of sound of foremost importance. Like Sunn O))) and their legendary sound engineer Randall Dunn, say, Von Till is keen to empha-sise the vital role their engineer — Dave Clark — plays in tweaking the system and getting to grips with the room for optimal sonic obliteration:

'The volume up on stage is really significant. We can't feel the subs in the same way, but we can see their impact (*laughs*) — it's like a shockwave. Dave is a sonic wizard. We can see when he is doing the magic; it's like a wave through human flesh. Maybe people feel a comfort in that? Like going back to the womb.'

The visuals are also a key aspect of the Neurosis show. From *Through Silver in Blood* onwards, the band have created what Von Till describes as a 'rapid-fire, droning collage of humanity in all of its spiritual, psychedelic beauty and terror. We would loop beautiful psychedelic imagery that was more evocative of sixties psychedelic-era geometric shapes and spiritual objects with the polar opposites — war footage. It was holding up a mirror, like "Here you go, humans — *this* is you."' Released during the ascendency of nu-metal — Korn, Deftones et al. — *Through Silver in Blood* was at odds with that movement's hip hop-inflected groove and performative adolescent angst. Emotionally, Neurosis were reaching to a zone of sheer mental discombobulation. Summed up by the twelve-minute title track which pounds along on drummer Jason Roeder's tribal floor tom intro (live he's also often joined by Von Till on a second kit) the grind was all their own: an oddly staccato, industrial rhythm, like an assembly line breaking down and starting up again, underpinned by a ceaseless power line hum. If any album foresaw what was soon to become known as 'post-metal' — bands like Isis, Yob, Boris and Wolves in the Throne Room — then it's *Through Silver in Blood*. This was metal as sound sculpture — some audio dreadnought cutting through the brine — but, though immensely powerful, it wasn't defined purely by aggression. Rather, *submission* — the idea of letting the music take you where it will, subconsciously (often an impossibility when playing the speedier or more technical styles of metal) was of equal importance. Talking to Von Till today, the importance of *channelling*, the harnessing of the subconscious mind in the musical process — comes up time and again.

'Embracing the drone was the real link between those two records (*Soul in Zero* and *Through Silver in Blood*): touring and learning the power of repetition, pounding heavy things into the earth over and over and over until we were reaching a cathartic state — an ecstatic state . . . we're talking repetitious heavy riffs that bring on a trance state; it's a full-on out-of-body experience. You're able to leave your body and become the music . . . we're embodying the spirit of the music: that full-on psychedelically, revelatory, outer-body experience through music.'

Von Till's cerebral, psychedelic side has been equally galvanised in his solo Harvestman guise. Exploring his love of Canterbury folk (Pentangle, Fairport Convention et cetera) alongside the occult-inflected pagan industrialism of Coil and Skullflower, and traditional drone sources ranging from Mongolian throat singing to bagpipes and hurdy-gurdy, Harvestman arrives at a bucolic, atmospheric reading of folk that centres the drone at the core as opposed to the periphery of the circle. Over the course of three records, he's frequently married Celtic drones to a dubwise, live desk sensibility that speaks to his love of Adrian Sherwood and the On-U Sound screwed dub approach — playing the desk, manipulating the sound live on playback and arriving at a mysterious place through symbiosis.

Indeed, Harvestman exists in a sonic universe where many of the strands of the music we've discussed thus far converge to an uncanny degree. Speaking to Von Till is an edifying experience: his awe in the face of the drone and immersive sound is infectious — the ley lines he draws make perfect sense.

'I've always had home studio equipment set up in my house and there was a point at which I was tripping out on Irish and British folk music as well as creating textures with distorted guitars that didn't have anything to do with writing heavy riffs,' he says. 'It was more of a broken electronic feel . . . In my tuning I have three open Ds and three open As and so the drone is central to the way I write riffs: the end of these open strings are always droning. So the sonic inspiration for Harvestman — and it happened by accident — is through collecting reels and reels of tape, and creating multiple levels of sound from tapes; taking that dub philosophy whereby it doesn't matter where you track, because when you mix it you can create a new piece of art. These drones are all just colours. It became a sonic repository — combining it all into something where it might only make sense to me, but where all of these things take place in my imagination: my meditations on folk medicines and folklore and stone circles and primitive sites and megalithic sites — they all make sense to me with British folk music and Mongolian throat singers and Skullflower and Hawkwind — it's all game and it's all coming from the same place of resonance and intuition of something primal that exists within everything.'

Chapter 9

INFINITE LOOPS

I'm leaning back in a chair, a bright lamp shining in my face. Brian Eno is standing over me laughing and frantically waving a magazine in an attempt at inducing Brion Gysin-esque light hallucinations. This isn't an anxiety dream. We've been talking about sensory extremes — the Dreammachine specifically — and black patterns start to form behind my eyes, surrounded by little balls of light, as he flaps away. I was expecting a measured Zen master vibe, but Eno is a ball of energy. He's as erudite as you'd imagine, but wears his intellectual heft lightly, laughing often, and frequently springing up for practical demonstrations of specific techniques during our interview. Indeed, when I'm shown into his Notting Hill studio — an airy white space lined with bookshelves, surrounded by his LED light boxes with a small studio annex for his monitors and computer — it isn't some ethereal drone emanating from the speakers but frenetic breakbeats at ear-splitting volume, as he tests out a new Logic plug-in with gleeful enthusiasm. Though best known in the collective subconscious for his subtly enveloping ambient works, was he ever, I wonder, similarly enthused by absolute extremes of volume?

'I went through a period when I was younger of experimenting with extremes quite dedicatedly,' he says. 'I had a little flat in Camberwell with an 18-inch speaker cabinet that was very powerful. It was a prototype — something they never put on the market. And I bolted these speakers on the bottom of my bed with a chipboard base. I was also fascinated by extremes of light, and had these eight-foot fluorescent tubes. I'd play drones through the speakers. It's interesting: traditionally, drones had to be made by the continual input of human energy — circular breathing, somebody actually working. In Indian music somebody would be playing the tanpura, constantly plucking the strings. But that's different in electronic music. You can switch a drone on and it sits there for the next six months if you want it to (*laughs*). And that tells you something about *perception*. If you know that the drone is absolutely constant — which you can do if you're using a sine-wave generator, like La Monte Young at the Dream House, for example — then you know that if you hear changing, it is you that is changing and not *it*. It's a perceptual change that is going on — and that is very interesting.'

In Roxy Music, Eno had introduced synths and 'tape effects' to a rock 'n' roll setting before leaving and making one of the most idiosyncratic records of the (fading) glam years — the swirling, bruising, psych-inflected *Here Come the Warm Jets* (1974). Equal parts experimental and accessible, the album explored a welter of sounds and techniques (the title's 'warm jet' referred to the guitar tone on the title track) veering from slow-burning chug ('Dead Finks Don't Talk') to cacophonous skewed pop (the title track) and jangling grandeur ('Needles in the Camel's Eye') that married the immediacy of rock 'n' roll to the obfuscation and textural grain of more avant-garde stylings. Eno had no formal musical training (he famously described himself as a 'non musician') and *Here Comes the Warm Jets* was personified by a playful, anarchic spirit — a slinky, animalistic quality. Eno credited himself as playing 'snake guitar' on the album, telling Lester Bangs that 'the kind of lines I was playing reminded me of the way a snake moves through the brush. A sort of speedy, forceful, liquid quality.'

Suffering a collapsed lung after release, he entered a period of recovery, resolving to eschew life on the road for the studio. Convalescing in hospital after a car accident, his girlfriend of the time brought him a record of gentle harp pieces. Lying immobile, he listened at a low volume as the barely audible strings melded into the rain outside. It proved revelatory. Here was a music that didn't intrude but, rather, merged to the fabric of life. On recovery, Eno resolved to explore a new music designed to blend with the ambience of day-to-day life. *Another Green World* (1975) — while not an ambient album, per se — nevertheless marked a step in a different direction. Arriving at Island Studios in Notting Hill with nothing prepared, he spent the first few days with producer Rhett Davies in a state of nervous anxiety, getting little done. Turning to his Oblique Strategies cards — a deck of cards Eno had developed alongside artist Peter Schmidt with short precepts ('Listen to the quiet Voice', 'Ask your Body', 'Gardening not Architecture!') aimed at shaking up the creative process and getting artists who may be blocked 'unstuck' — Eno used the cards to get started himself, as well as on guest musicians on the sessions — John Cale, Phil Collins, Paul Rudolph (the Pink Fairies), Percy Jones (Soft Machine) and frequent Eno collaborator Robert Fripp (King Crimson).

The resulting album was personified by a restless quality, taking in muscular, funk-infused groove ('Sky Saw'), full-on pop ('I'll Come Running') and dronal ambience ('The Big Ship'). The tonal shifts throughout the record were dizzying, Eno having little interest in regular structures or traditional rockist tropes. Robert Fripp — one of the most accomplished guitarists in the world — could put his hand to anything and Eno was typically exacting in his instructions. On 'St Elmo's Fire' he'd asked Robert Fripp to play the guitar in imitation of a Wimshurst machine — an electrostatic generator charged by the spinning of two contra-rotating discs. Again, Eno used poetic descriptors on the album credits — 'Choppy Organs', 'Uncertain Piano', 'Spasmodic Percussion', 'desert' guitar.

While some distance from the beatific atmosphere of his pure ambient works, the latter half of *Another Green World* — particularly tracks like 'Becalmed' and 'Zawinul/Lava' — point towards it with reverb-treated piano, seagull samples, synth drones and an atmosphere of melancholy, albeit slightly more strident than what was to come.

Discreet Music (1975) — his key proto-ambient record, released just two months after *Another Green World* — pivoted on fleeting movement, slowly drifting drones, an *instantly* recognisable lilting melody and pads untethered to the grid, melodic lines bobbing against one another like driftwood. Eschewing the linear narrative of classical music and the adrenal rush of pop, the first thirty minutes of *Discreet Music* comprise a single track — an experiment in generative composition made by setting two overlapping tape loops of differing lengths against one another. The dreamlike melody repeats at unexpected junctures but, instead of manipulating a desired emotional response — a journey of peaks, troughs and prescribed reactions — it's just *there*, not filling up too much space, drifting in and out of focus gently.

This was anathema to much of the rock press of the time who could be scathing of electronic music at the best of times, framing it as cheap novelty or, even, morally suspect, as Eno explains: 'Electronic music could be seen as unethical, or even immoral. I was never concerned about that though. I wanted a music that was more like painting, where you didn't *have* to do a performance any longer; you weren't performing if you were *making* music in the studio. I didn't think it was a problem at all . . . the public found it less of a difficulty than the critics. The public listened to things and liked them or didn't, but didn't worry so much about how they were made. When *Discreet Music* came out — which was my first pure electronic piece, no natural instruments — it was either ignored or badly reviewed. I don't think it got a single good review from England. The essence of the reviews was "Isn't this too easy to do?" I remember one review that said "this is a music that lacks rhythm, melody, narrative, personality" and I thought "Oh, great! Those are *exactly* all of the things that I want to leave out."'

Much of the music we've discussed in previous chapters has been enveloping — visceral, physical music. Ambient — a term first used by Eno on *Ambient 1: Music for Airports* (1978) — presents the flip side: a music that can take the back seat by design. As Eno famously stated in the album's liner notes, ambient can 'accommodate many levels of listening without enforcing one in particular; it must be as ignorable as it is interesting'. At first glance, the notion of an ignorable music seems artistically aberrant: alien to the creative urge to be heard. After all, before ambient, 'ignorable' music had deeply negative connotations personified by mass produced 'muzak' — elevator music designed to be as inoffensive as possible that was, nonetheless, fascinating in its maddening inanity.

Music for Airports was built around sustained chords — piano, acoustic guitar, soft vocalisation — a tinkling piano motif from Robert Wyatt repeating at unpredictable junctures, vocalisation sounds and lilting guitar lines. Initially inspired by Eno's irritation at the dismal and stressful soundscape of Cologne airport during a long delay, it was designed not so much to *mask* the background noise of the airport, but, rather, to mollify its abrasive edges and dissipate the stress and tension of the terminal. As on *Discreet Music*, Eno used generative tape loops to facilitate calm through the idea of eternal drift — the loops set off in a cycle that never allows for clear resolution. Instead, they move in dreamlike circles that never quite connect, never allowing the brain to get used to markers of time.

This music is gentle and passive, but it's anything but static: rather it's built around serenity in *movement* — indeed, in relation specifically to the airport environment, it amounts to a sense of grace under pressure, Eno thus reframes the stress and noise and cortisone-raising undercurrent of urgency to the utopian blueprint ideal of wide-open space, gentle purpose, graceful human flow. This, however, gets to the core of what some find difficult — offensive, even — in ambient music. The sense of complacency; the wallpaper aspect; the mollification of the necessary stresses of life into a 'now breathe' cosiness; a designer calm imposed on a world abjectly chaotic and violent and fraught. The feeling that it alleviates the viciousness of consumerism. Indeed, in recent years, ambient has been closely associated with corporate Spotify playlists specifically designed to 'increase productivity' or some such;

a (gentle) capitalist cattle prod. Eno's ambient works are a world apart from that stuff, however. Aside from anything else, the average Spotify 'ambient' playlist is full of garish new age woo-woo. Eno's ambient records may be gentle, but they're also elegant, quietly compelling. Most people into Eno have a particular record they play repeatedly, perhaps for years, a personal talisman that — by dint of repetition — becomes more than the sum of its parts. They're often used as a backdrop for writing or painting or creative activity, rather than corporate work.

Ignorable they may be, but does he, I wonder, consider his ambient works to be fundamentally *useful*?

'My ambient works are *intended* to be functional, they are intended to have a useful place in your life. I wasn't that concerned whether I didn't make people dance or reduce them to tears or the other things that musicians might like to do (*laughs*). I was always very pleased when I heard from writers or designers or illustrators, though — people who sit in a room for a long time doing something. And they'd often say, "The only thing I can listen to is these albums, because they make a good background for working." I always thought *that* was a big success — when somebody found this thing really useful. I didn't care whether they adored it or whether they thought it was the best thing *emotionally,* but physically it was useful to them . . . I remember meeting a woman who said, "Oh, I just had my daughter listening to *Discreet Music*" and since then I've met several people who've used it as birthing music. There was a maternity hospital in East Anglia that was using it as their birthing music, in fact.'

Initially intended as a site-specific installation piece, *Music for Airports* was made by layering up tape loops of different lengths to repeat at odd junctures, phasing in and out of time in unpredictable fashion. It was the first record to be specifically labelled 'ambient' although there has been much debate surrounding the genesis of the genre. Muzak aside, there are various claims to ambient forebears, not least the 'furniture music' pioneered by composer Erik Satie in turn-of-the-century Paris, a form designed to be played by musicians to blend into the background. Likewise, some of the Krautrock records of the early to mid 1970s — not least the less abrasive edges of Ash Ra Tempel, Tangerine Dream and Harmonia — share certain sonic hallmarks. *Cluster and Eno* was released the year before *Music for Airports* and, while more melodically strident than his ambient works, it shares with them a certain wistful, melancholic air, minimal rhythmic adornment and dreamlike sense of space.

Ultimately, Eno ties ambient to the idea of surrender — specifically, the idea that in any given situation there is a spectrum of possibilities available in how we choose to react and that sometimes surrender can be the way to go. He uses the analogy of a car crash to illustrate the point:

'You might be able to take control of it, but if you aren't able to take control of it, what should you do?' he asks. 'Your best option might be to surrender and prepare yourself as best you can to crash. In most situations you're somewhere between the two — partially surrendering and partially taking control. Because we are a technical culture, which means we live amid the instruments that allow us to take control of things, we tend to overlook the surrendering side — another way of saying surrender is what the hippies used to call "going with the flow" — just becoming part of what is happening and not trying to be the driver. A lot of the aspects we find so graceful in ancient cultures are to do with their ability to interweave their own lives with the bigger processes that they were part of: they had to build their life around surrendering.'

The lack of traditional markers of time — verse, chorus, verse, say, or percussive fills or bridges; elements that say 'now *this* is going to happen' — allow us to get lost amid the sound, freed from expectation. This idea is central to Eno's idiosyncratic use of repetition in his ambient works. Often, as on *Discreet Music* and *Music for Airports*, say, he's working with tape loops that repeat at unpredictable junctures, so that you get familiar motifs happening at unpredictable times. More recently, he produced an app — *Reflection* — that allowed the album of the same name to be played in endlessly variable ways, the stems of each piece never repeating in the same way, no matter how many times you play it. The brain doesn't quite have time to adjust to the markers of predictable repetition, resulting in a pleasantly dreamlike state — not soporific, necessarily, but more the feeling of the familiar rendered uncanny, as when you're dreaming and a familiar place is obfuscated: your house has become moorland, say, but you still, somehow, know that it's your house. In any case, even if we listen to a piece of music a thousand times we'll perceive it slightly differently each time, like driving past a familiar view: the human brain doesn't 'do' exact replication.

'I think of surrender as an active verb, not a passive verb,' explains Eno. 'People *love* surrendering. Think of when we practise surrender — sex, drugs, religion, art. In all of those things we are explicitly putting ourselves in a situation where we let go, lose control. In fact, *all* of the metaphors that go with that are to do with being taken out of yourself — "uplifted", "out of my head", "overwhelmed", "transcended" — we fully accept that this is what we do for pleasure yet we exclude it as a technique for the rest of our lives. It's a little holiday. We go and surrender somewhere. What I want to say is: why don't we just weave it into everything else we do as well? Recognise that our repertoire includes all of those things, not just what we do at the control end. Think of surfers who take control of the situation by getting up onto a wave but are then taken by *it*. In sex, it's the same thing — input and then result, something happens (*laughs*).'

Triptych

Eno's definition of ambient as potentially 'ignorable' — a deeply radical proposition — has ensured that many producers who work with similar sonic palettes have often been reticent to identify as such. In some respects, then, Eno is a genre of one — with a discography of idiosyncratic ambient works to immerse in (or, indeed, ignore) for a lifetime. Nonetheless there are many who work the fertile hinterland around minimalism, ambient and pure drone, for whom submission and passivity — allowing simple tones their place — is key. Éliane Radigue, for example — one of the most single-minded and uncompromising electronic musicians of our age — has spent decades patiently coaxing precise tones from modular synthesisers and layering them into intimate, slowly unfurling drone pieces that hum with a beatific, other-worldly atmosphere.

Working in Paris as a sound engineer at Pierre Schaeffer's Studio d'Essai — the birthplace of *musique concrète* — Radigue spent months at the edit, splicing the spools of tape, processing, looping and archiving. Stopping music for a decade while raising her three children, she returned to Paris in 1967, this time working alongside Pierre Henry on his epic *concrète* piece *l'Apocalypse de Jean* (1967). However, *musique concrète* is a very different vibe to Radigue's solo compositions. It was predicated on the use of found sound — sampling the everyday in a reflection of thrusting, cacophonous post-war modernity. Schaeffer and Henry would record engine noise, trains, doors slamming, background conversations, snippets of radio, television broadcasts, political speeches, screams, dogs barking — whatever they could find. Both were scornful of electronically generated sounds: the technological aspect happened after the fact, in the edit. The source material was always gleaned from the everyday.

Radigue was, rather, experimenting with pure electronics. Fascinated by the hypnotic potential of feedback, she'd stay on in the studio after hours, experimenting, coaxing the most beautiful tones — not violent or abrasive or painful; nothing we would usually associate with the term — but, rather, painstakingly working the delicate balance that arose from respecting the 'behaviour of moving very slowly, not going too near or too far to the loudspeaker because that would make it blow up. I loved testing the limits. And believe me, you only had a hairs breadth to work with.'[1]

In 1970, Radigue crossed paths with figures from the New York minimalist axis we explored in earlier chapters — specifically Morton Subotnick and Rhys Chatham — during a residency at the New York University School of the Arts. There, sharing a studio with fellow composer Laurie Spiegel she experienced the full chaotic potential of the Buchla 100 synth, an experience that left her cold, wondering what she could possibly do with such a 'silly machine'. Nonetheless, interested in the potential of synthesis, she explored other machines, eventually settling on the warmth and haze of the ARP 2500 — a great, big, cranky machine. Focussing on a process of subtraction, Radigue rejected hundreds of sounds — anything she deemed the 'big effects' — instead focussing on what she described as a 'tiny field of sound'. It was the place she'd remain for the next three decades, working with overtones and subharmonics and sounds within sounds that personify her subtle drone pieces.

The vast majority of her work from the early seventies onwards has been focused on pure drones — granular textures shorn of any harmonic progression, owing their singular tones to the idiosyncratic choices Radigue made in programming the synth. On an imposing wall of knobs and faders — it weighs around sixty pounds — she generated drones that pulsed and hummed, great swathes of ominous sub-bass, pin-drop crackle tones and shimmering aquiline movements. Her recently unearthed *Feedback Works* (1969–1970) — selected from tapes that had hung on the walls of her flat in Paris for some forty years — emphasise minuscule change and extraordinary subtlety. Originally recorded for the 1970 Osaka Fair, *Feedback Works* was composed using tones from the ARP recorded onto tape, then spliced into loops and, finally, manually manipulated on playback to either slow down or speed up.

A window into the nature of her painstaking process was captured in the short 2009 documentary film *A Portrait of Éliane Radigue* which showed her working the ARP in her small flat, adjusting the faders and poring over beautifully ornate handwritten frequency charts that showed ring and frequency modulators' inputs and outputs while using her stopwatch — dubbed the 'teddy bear' — to mark exact timings on the synth delays. Unlike other minimally minded composers — the Fluxus artists, or John Cage, say — Radigue holds little truck with chance operations. Her modus operandi favours a razor-sharp focus on searching for *precise*, carefully monitored sounds, refining them and using *only* those. While many modular synth operators favour — fetishise, even — the hand of chance, Radigue operates more like a sculptor or surgeon, relentlessly chipping away at the superfluous. Her music is truly minimal, although the genius of Radigue is that, though process driven to a scientific degree, her music is imbued with an extraordinary amount of soul.

'I never make sounds for nothing. I always make them for something . . . I am guided, like an architect who needs a scaffolding and then removes it once it is done . . . I threw out every kind of stereotyped sound, sounds which bored me. I got rid of them all until . . . "Ah! There's an interesting tiny little thing! Let's see what we can do with that."'[2]

Introduced to Buddhist theology in New York in the early 1970s, much of Radigue's key discography connects to her faith. Her three-hour *Adnos Trilogy*, composed between 1974 and 1982, was an extraordinarily delicate take on pure drone that facilitates a contemplative mood, but changes and shifts so subtly that the effect — when you give your full attention — is startlingly dramatic. The addition of an ominous undertone at around eight minutes on the first movement, say, or the way that the most subtle of hisses and static and crackle are added throughout, only for the main drone to drop out entirely, leaving a void of ominous static: it's an sonic universe defined by absence, but also the impossibility of nothing. As we saw earlier, space isn't a vacuum and here — deep in the Radigue sound-world — microscopic changes become emotional events. Inspired by the metaphor of flowing water for sound — the way it changes, teems with life, reflects and refracts on the surface, and works as a carrier — Radigue's drones are, perhaps, the most narcotically affecting (I have to listen early evening; late evening and it's into sheer soporific overdrive, waking up on the sofa in a state of confusion four hours later) in existence.

She is in absolute control of the journey, knows the precise direction of travel, and listening to her *Trilogie de la Mort* in its entirety — each movement lasting one hour — with the lights off and the headphones on, focusing completely, is a *heavy* emotional experience. By tuning into the infinitesimal permutations the mind is quietened but also heightened: unlike La Monte Young's sine-wave drone pieces, this isn't a case of filling in blanks so much as anticipation; Radigue manipulates tone with a razor-sharp focus. Like the Beatles' 'Tomorrow Never Knows' *Trilogie de la Mort* takes the *Tibetan Book of the Dead* as inspiration, the three movements following the cycle of life and death through the six stages of consciousness: *kyena* (birth), *milam* (dream), *samtem* (meditation), *chikai* (death), *chonye* (clear light) and *sippai* (crossing and return). After the death of her son in a car accident in 1991, Radigue finished the second movement, 'Kailasha', which represented a journey though the sacred Mount Kailash before recording the third and final movement — 'Koume' — in 1993. Ultimately, the *Trilogie* is a rumination on the impossibility of spirit death; the idea that physical death is not the end; the existential continuity of the soul.

It speaks to the mystery of creation, the comfort of faith in the face of tragedy and, above all, the transcendence of the physical, the sheer emotional depth that can be wrought from the drone.

'They act as a mental mirror; they reflect the mood you are in at the time. If you are ready to open yourself up to them, to listen truly and devote yourself to listening, they really have a fascinating, magnetic power. I know this to be true, otherwise I would never have done it! It was the two extremes: one to throw it all away, the other to be captivated . . . above all I listened with the greatest respect, trying to understand what they had to say.'[3]

Chill Out

It's no coincidence that ambient was enthusiastically adopted by the rave generation. Raving is, after all, *built* around surrender: to sound, to chemistry, to the experience and both the literal and metaphorical journey. Ecstasy facilitated a break from stiffness — reluctance to open up, talk to strangers, let go on the dance floor, forget the day-to-day. It's unique in its *warmth*. Most other stimulants — cocaine and amphetamine (caffeine, even) — are chilly, brittle and, after the initial rush, personified by a disquieting detachment. They're substances that promote inwardness: they don't move the human spirit closer to anyone else.

Ecstasy, on the other hand, facilitates empathy and a genuine interest in those around us. The chill-out room thus made perfect sense. Given the newness of the experience, the physical exertion of dancing in the heat, the fact that hundreds of people wanted to talk to each other outside of the volume of the main room, it helped facilitate the communal feeling that personified rave's honeymoon period. Dance music is immersive in a way that few other musical experiences match, in terms of visceral intensity. It is also — given the sleep deprivation, physical exertion and drugs — draining. So it was that ambient — and, ergo, the drone — found itself centred in the rave from early days, the chill-out room a space that enabled knackered ravers to curate their own peaks and troughs, alternating the thump of the main room with the fugue-like womb (now, sadly, an increasing rarity) where they could wig out to weirder, dronier sounds and visuals.

In the chill-out room at the Orbit, say — a notoriously hedonistic and sweaty late-nineties techno session just outside Leeds where the main room would be banging by 9 p.m. and you could hear Surgeon, Jeff Mills, Sven Vath and the like — you'd hear records by Brian Eno and Terry Riley next to

Kraftwerk, Basic Channel, the Orb, On-U Sound, roots reggae and hip hop: a total hodgepodge designed to spangle already confused minds to a state of pleasing mollification. Lights and decoration in chill-out rooms tended to be idiosyncratic but of a homely bent: bean bags, projections, cult B-movies (could go either way: *Eraserhead* seemed to be a perversely popular choice), fractal patterns and the ever present fugue of weed and cheap soap-bar hash. It didn't take long for rave and ambient to meet outside the confines of the chill-out room, however. Producers like Autechre, Aphex Twin, KLF and the Black Dog all experimented with ambient to greater or lesser degrees, drawing on the psychedelic afterglow of the rave — and, equally importantly, the stranger corners of the sleep-deprived mind — for inspiration — the after-hours an open-ended territory to explore, the drone of the club still fresh in the ears, the muffled, diving-bell fugue state; the feedback loop of 4/4 kicks reverberating seemingly for ever.

The Orb, formed by Alex Patterson alongside (later) KLF man Jimmy Cauty in 1986 (now comprising Patterson alongside Thomas Fehlmann), combined lush pads, ambient drones, bouncy techno beats and dub-inflected sub-bass to huge popular appeal. Patterson and Cauty had initially run the chill-out room at Paul Oakenfold's Land of Oz club night at Heaven, mixing up Eno with heavy-duty dub and La Monte Young, Steve Reich and Pink Floyd, alongside psychedelic visuals.

As well suited to sunny afternoons as dark basements, the Orb were festival mainstays of the early nineties, marrying their love of Eno, Kraftwerk, acid house and psych rock to beatless passages and spoken-word samples. Because of their festival links, they gained a significant crusty following that tended to follow the Megadog axis — Hawkwind, Spiral Tribe, Levellers, Back to the Planet, Liberator DJ's, Senser, Eat Static, Ozric Tentacles, speed, acid, pills, hallucinatory scrumpy. Indeed, for the befuddled denizens of the ever-growing free party network, the Orb were a functional mainstay of the comedown. They soundtracked the descent back to Earth for hundreds of thousands in smoky living rooms across the land, although they never appreciated the hippy tag (Paterson was, after all, an ex-Killing Joke roadie). Imbued with warmth, the Orb's music hinged on constant movement and a friendly, spacey atmospherics bedded down by a choice of vocal samples that perfectly suited the saucer-eyed, chemical adventurer vibe of the time — most notably singer-songwriter Rickie Lee Jones remembering the sky as a girl on 'Little Fluffy Clouds'. It hasn't all aged well — they'd sometimes veer perilously close to New Age territory with cheesy panpipe samples and the like — but at their best, as on *U.F.Orb* (1992) they were pleasingly sideways. It's easy to forget just how big the Orb were during the early nineties: like Underworld, Leftfield, Orbital and the Prodigy they occupied that strange — and lucrative — 1990s position as one of the few dance acts enjoyed by otherwise uninterested indie fans.

The KLF's *Chill Out* (1990) also traversed ambient house territory, albeit to very different ends. If the Orb took ambient and festivalised it, sound-systemed it, dubbed it, the KLF *woozed* it — imbued it with the wistfulness of rolling FM Americana. Acting as a dreamlike counterpoint to an electronic music culture in terminal acceleration, *Chill Out* presented an imaginary sonic journey — a night drive down the Gulf Coast from Texas to Louisiana ('Six Hours to Louisiana, Black Coffee Going Cold', 'The Lights of Baton Rouge Pass By' et cetera) — that played out in a sample-heavy wave.

Peppered with a rich tapestry of odds and sods Americana, as if you're twisting the dial on a crackling Winnebago radio in the caffeine jitters of a lonely night, they peppered the record with FM radio snippets. So you get twanging steel guitars, bits of Presley ('In the Ghetto'), echoes of Fleetwood Mac ('Albatross'), news bulletins, outdoors field recordings, the overtone drone of Mongolian throat singers. It's sentimental, but taken at the right moment (and on the right drugs) it's a mollifying swaddle that gives the sensation of being lulled gently to a Mandrax-assisted sleep on some mid-1970s chromium tour bus, rolling through the Texan night, the drone of cicadas outside in the humidity of another parking lot lit by a harvest moon, driver buzzing on cheap trucker speed and the bus scented with premium mezcal fumes and cheap Tijuana weed.

Indeed, *Chill Out* — despite being designed for a situation that is (ostensibly) outside the 'rockist' idiom — is an incredibly rock 'n' roll album, dealing as it does with atmosphere and aftermath. The mythical journey imagined on the album acts as a neatly transposed allegory for the illegal rave scene which was — when the record was released in 1990 — so closely aligned with the open road. It feels as if the KLF were attempting to take the glow of the rave convoy — the motorway, the service station, rolling baccy and king-size blues in the glove box; the tight wraps of speed, hard-shoulder breakdowns, flashing police lights, open-air adventure — and imbue it with a sepia-tinted, cinematic grandeur. It should be noted, however, that the only reason people obsess over the MDMA comedown is that, handled correctly, it has the capacity to be an actively *pleasant* experience, the world afforded a rosy-cheeked glow of good cheer. The same simply cannot be said of *any* other stimulant — certainly not the panicky, clammy embarrassment and feeling of grim, close dread that personifies the coke comedown or the grimly psychedelic, biblical exhaustion that accompanies speed. Also, the KLF being the KLF, nothing was to be taken *entirely* at face value. Despite the satisfyingly lush trip, they understood ambient's downside — namely the complacency, the whimsical smugness — implicitly. Everything they did was peppered with Discordian energy. As such, the sleeve notes to *Chill Out* are peppered with earnest piss takes — 'Ambient house makes love to the wind and speaks to the stars!' — while the cover features a field full of sheep — a reference, Drummond said, that alluded to Pink Floyd's *Atom Heart Mother* but was just as likely to be a sardonic nod to the cult-like aspect of 'together-ness' that underpinned rave culture.

Elsewhere, techno producers like Luke Slater and Kirk Degiorgio also experimented with ambient-inflected gear — albeit with a firmer eye on the dance floor. Eschewing the barrelling, bass-driven techno he makes under his own name or his Planetary Assault System guise, Luke Slater's early 1990s 7th Plain project mixed off-kilter, IDM-esque blips and beeps with emotive pads and spacey drones. UK techno mainstay Kirk Degiorgio, meanwhile, was also highly prolific under his As One pseudonym, releasing a number of albums that touched on jazz and ambient house. No one worked the sweet spot where home listening met club tracks better than Warp Records, however. Home of Nightmares on Wax and LFO, the Sheffield-based imprint had spearheaded the cone-shattering sub frequencies of the city's bleep techno scene, but were also staking out more cerebral territory. Their *Artificial Intelligence: Electronic Listening Music* (1992) compilation featured a crop of artists — the Orb, Autechre, the Black Dog and Speedy J — who submitted tracks that weren't necessarily geared to 'chill out' per se, but rather to continue the night at a lower-lit pace.

Andrew Weatherall once said that he was 'more interested in what hap-pened after the club'. So it was for many others. Rather than gearing towards the sentimental or the mollifying, then, the *Artificial Intelligence* compilation kept energy levels relatively high, albeit with a pleasingly warped sonic pallet encompassing everything from acidic electro ('Polygon Window' by the Dice Man aka Aphex Twin) to shuffling, downer-steeped dronal breaks (Autechre, 'The Egg') and lush, trancey vibes (Alex Patterson, 'Loving You Live'). Prefiguring the IDM (intelligent dance music) boom spearheaded by the same label a year or two later, these compilations were the first time the word 'intelligent' had been used in relation to dance music which, it's important to remember, had gone through *years* of tabloid outrage and public ridicule that painted the culture in base and lurid terms. The sleeve mapped out the psychic territory — the futuristic meeting the domestic

— explicitly with a robot splayed out on a chair in a living room listening to Kraftwerk's *Autobahn*, a nod both to that group's pivotal influence on techno culture but also — again — a metaphorical tip of the hat towards rave as journey and living room as final, weary, terminal destination. The inside sleeve featured interview snippets with key Warp artists. Autechre's was particularly telling. Only nineteen or twenty years old at the time, the pair name-check shamanistic electronic outliers like Coil and Tangerine Dream alongside Detroit artists, writing that 'when people run dry copying each other, a deeper, more creative music will emerge where ideas and originality play a major role'.

Artificial Intelligence thus sat between night and the first light of day. This was, to all intents and purposes, *morning* music. Anyone who has done time at the coalface of techno will be familiar with the strangeness that emerges in the a.m., the feeling of a world at obtuse — sometimes sickly — angles, a few points removed from the peculiar chemically enhanced reality you find yourself in (the fact that out there, just feet away from the living room window, people are getting ready to *go Saturday morning shopping*, say — it seems egregious; a world both familiar and bafflingly alien). These tracks are thus imbued with a psychedelic undertow. Sleep deprivation alone is, after all, enough to render the everyday uncanny. The brain begins to 'dream' of its own accord: the conscious and the unconscious colluding in strange new ways. Add to this a cornucopia of chemicals and the psychedelic angle is a given. Warp were articulating a demarcation line between the functional, DJ tool house and techno that fuelled the parties and a more forensic music equally as suited to the headphones as the dance floor, although it was 'intelligent dance music' — named after an online mailing list in the nascent days of the internet; and a deeply contentious term to this day — that eventually stuck, rather than 'electronic listening music'. Regardless of semantics, it was something of a manifesto: if dance music was to be a 24/7 culture, it seemed to say, it couldn't be 24/7 in terminal velocity.

By 1992 the ecstasy honeymoon period was over. It was ingrained in the fabric of weekend life. People knew what it did, what it didn't do, how to handle it. In its own way, then, this music was as functional as the DJ tools that soundtracked the first half of the night. People who were *living* club culture needed a music that facilitated the drift back down to earth and Warp artists implicitly understood the power of the drone to evoke a sense of psychic drift; as specified on the sleeve, here was music for 'long journeys, quiet nights or club drowse dawns.'

Shadowlands

It was the psychic territory of the 'club drowse dawn' — the creative atomisation of sleep deprivation — tracks primed for home listening rather than the clubs — that provided Warp mainstay Aphex Twin (Richard D. James) with creative inspiration for much of his work, *Selected Ambient Works Volume II* in particular.

Inspired by experiments in lucid dreaming, the tracks were written and recorded on waking; an instant evocation of the mental state that led to their creation, and were also informed by James' intense synaesthesia — a condition which causes the brain to assign colours, letters, shapes, smells or physical sensations to sound. James thus presented an idiosyncratic take on ambient, very different in approach to the ethereal backdrop style of Brian Eno. Many of his ambient tracks were beatific but, at the same time, tripped out, disquieting, sometimes overtly menacing — the music of the shadowland.

Discussing his predilection for extremes of sleep deprivation with the writer Simon Reynolds in 1993, James explained that since childhood he'd decided that sleep was simply 'a waste of your life. If you lived to be 100, but you didn't sleep, it would be like living to 200' and went on to explain how he'd recently gone about 'whittling down' his nightly four hours to a meagre two, with predictably hallucinatory results: 'Your mind starts getting scatty like you're senile. You start doing unpredictable things like making tea but pouring it in a cereal bowl.'[4]

As such, a fair chunk of the tracks on *Selected Ambient Works Volume II* were underpinned by mauve atmospherics — the drone of piercing dread — the same mischievous sprite that has imbued much of his music since the start. A bedroom alchemist if ever there was one, Richard D. James grew up in Cornwall way outside the M25 loop that initially harboured UK rave culture. However, his wasn't the tourist version. James was from Redruth which — along with towns like Launceston, Bodmin and Camborne — is an area of serious deprivation and unemployment; a grim corridor that, far enought away from the coast, is bypassed by most tourists, having more in common with the Welsh Valleys or Teesside than the common postcard conception of the county.

Coming to music 'out of boredom' he immersed himself in the wonkier edges of the free party scene that flourished on the beaches, woods and fields and was exposed to a cornucopia of gabber, Chicago acid trax, Detroit techno, Belgian new beat, dark side hardcore and all manner else. This spangled, acid-fried scene inspired James to experiment with whatever equipment he could get his hands on. By the early 1990s he was making music that delighted in both speaking to and smashing genre conventions. He personified a shamanistic isolationist bent: obsessed with the nascent rave culture, chemicals and music technology but far way enough from the epicentre to approach it from oblique angles.

His tracks were often imbued with a childlike sense of wonder — jittery 8-bit melodies that evoked memories of Atari computer games and the like — but also with an (equally childlike) sense of dread. Aphex Twin amplified the grotesque like few others. Techno could be a notoriously po-faced world: indeed, the very idea of *showing* your face was anathema to many who stuck to the cultural blueprint of anonymous 12-inches and zero press shots. As such, James put his face — often disturbingly reddened and distorted, as if looking in the mirror on acid — on *everything* he did, perhaps most notoriously the grotesque 'Come to Daddy' video by Chris Cunningham which saw his face transposed to a group of children marauding their way — *Clockwork Orange*-style — through the Barbican. Over two decades later it's still the imagery most associated with him. Indeed, he once stated that he liked music to sound 'evil and eerie', and *Ambient Works Volume II* plays with the latter vibe to the nth degree. An eerie drone underpins most of the tracks; the drone of electricity — the inescapable hum — was a galvanising factor in the album's creation, as he explained in an interview in 1994: 'Power stations are wicked. If you just stand in the middle of a really massive one, you get a really weird presence . . . you've just got that hum. You just feel the electricity all around you. That's totally dreamlike to me. It's just like a strange dimension.'[5]

This strange dimension — ambient's shadow zone — has long been explored by producers far and wide. Tangerine Dream's *Zeit* (1973), for example, was a brooding hour of droning, black atmospherics playing out over four movements which each lasted a full side of vinyl. Evoking the cavernous vista of hyperspace and, by proxy, humanity's insignificance in the face of immense celestial forces, *Zeit* pivoted on the moody, sepulchral Moog of Popol Vuh's Florian Fricke. An eerie, dilapidated vibe prevails, particularly on the nightmarishly tense 'Nebulous Dawn', where rising pads, trills and a queasy Doppler effect evoke some rusting hulk orbiting a long forgotten moon. *Zeit* presents an oppressive, dystopic vision of space — less gleaming chrome and fastidious co-ordinates, more staring into a void of shabby nothingness, a creeped out, paranoid, *Heart of Darkness* descent into abyssal dread. There is something strangely fecund about *Zeit* — the queasy drone, the undulating throb, evokes thoughts of viral reproduction out in space, patiently awaiting a host.

Throbbing Gristle's *D.o.A: The Third and Final Report of Throbbing Gristle* (1978) channelled a similarly otherworldly vibe; not in the cosmic sense, but rather the feeling of having slipped into a nearby dimension of drabness and decay. Chris Carter — the most technically minded member of TG — was a big Tangerine Dream fan, and there are definite parallels with *Zeit* on tracks like 'I.B.M.' and 'AB/7A': granular textures, pings, echoes and bleeps coagulate into an alien sonic tapestry that — as always with Throbbing Gristle — holds up a chipped mirror to the carnival bizarre of the everyday.

There are echoes of Hawkwind in the swirl of 'Hit by a Rock' and a weird proto-electro bounce to 'Dead on Arrival'. One can never be quite sure of a sound source: field recordings collide with guitars, home-made circuitry rubs up against radio static. 'Valley of the Shadow of Death' is a different kind of ambient, taking the synaesthetic temperature of some stinking late 1970s locker room, disembodied voices talking about someone 'pushed up against the fucking wall' while 'Weeping' sees Genesis P-Orridge recounting a nervous breakdown against a backdrop of plinking guitars and a Cale-esque scraping viola drone. Listening to *D.o.A* puts one into an uncomfortable position, like watching strange domestic vignettes unfold through a diving bell. Throbbing Gristle belong as much to the dream unconscious of late 1970s/early 1980s Britain as that so viscerally tapped by the film-maker Alan Clarke (*Scum, Made in Britain* etc), only while Clarke was reflecting the reality TG were concerned with the upside down; the dreamlands articulated by means of sonic obfuscation and decay.

Musick to Play in the Dark

If Throbbing Gristle were informed by the gnarled, granular horror of the everyday, Coil — formed by ex TG member Peter 'Sleazy' Christopherson alongside vocalist Jhonn Balance in 1982 — presented a more opulent, fantastical vision. Inspired by magick, rapturous states, sleep deprivation, heinous chemical experimentation, the occult, the London gay scene, acid house and esoteric literature and art (1920s Brixton occultist Austin Osman Spare was a particular favourite), Coil made music of the Delphic shadows created, more often than not, in a state of mentally draining ritualistic focus.

Aligned to the same visionary underground that included like-minded spirits Nurse with Wound, Current 93 and Clock DVA, the 'industrial' tag they've sometimes been lumped with doesn't begin to do them justice. Rather, they ploughed a unique furrow that stretched from abrasive, sample-heavy cut-ups (*Scatology*) to mauve, cinematic ambient (*Musick to Play in the Dark*) and pure dronal hypnosis (*Time Machines*). Their music is about beauty and terror and sex — and an opening of hidden channels (their 1995 album *ELpH*, for example, was named after the invisible presence they felt was 'directing' proceedings), arcane lore.

Sleazy had grown up on early electronic music as well as the more experimental end of the rock spectrum — Captain Beefheart, CAN, Amon Düül et cetera — before joining the pre-TG COUM Transmissions art collective in Hull alongside future TG members Cosey Fanni Tutti and Genesis P-Orridge. Bringing his technical chops to Throbbing Gristle, he experimented ceaselessly with primitive sampling technology and tape loops as a means of breaking the frame of rockist convention during the height of punk. Meeting vocalist Jhonn Balance — a massive TG fan who ran an industrial-leaning fanzine — in the early 1980s after the dissolution of Throbbing Gristle, Coil set out their unique stall with a poetic manifesto in 1983 ('Coil is a hidden universal. A code. A key for which the whole does not exist. Is non-existent, in silence and secrecy. A spell. A spiral. A serpents SHt round a female cycle. A whirlwind. A double helix. DNA. Electricity and elementals. Atonal noise, and brutal poetry.')

Many working in the industrial hinterland were either working on a shoestring, limited by a lack of technical know-how or wilfully pushing towards a lo-fi aesthetic. Coil had the ability and vision to sound *immense*, however. They thrived on tension. Sleazy was a video director by day, working with big bands and expensive ad agencies but keeping Coil entirely separate from the corporate universe he inhabited during daylight hours.

Early Coil was laden with ritualistic focus. *How to Destroy Angels* was 'ritual music for the accumulation of male sexual energy' and featured the layered drone of the bull-roarer — an ancient Aboriginal wooden drone instrument. Coil moved in similar London circles to Derek Jarman, Soft Cell, Einstürzende Neubauten (also living in the city at the time), Michael Clark, Nurse with Wound, Current 93 and Leigh Bowery. It was a fertile, free-spirited scene, and records like *Horse Rotorvator* (1986) hinged on a similarly chaotic tapestry of sound: samples were gleaned from anywhere and everywhere, the ancient drone — bagpipes, hurdy-gurdies, organs — colliding with state-of-the-art drum machines and synths.

Too often painted as dark or debased, the reality was more complex. Much of Coil's music was as divinely beautiful as it was foreboding; for every moment of ostensible darkness there was a passage of transcendent uplift lurking round the bend. *Horse Rotorvator* is all pomp and ceremony — subtle, grotesque and stunningly textured. Opening with 'The Anal Staircase' — a paean to sex and death that samples Stravinsky's *The Rites of Spring* and slowly unfurls in a stuttering electronic groove, a line is trod between bright energy — layered synths, razor-tight percussive loops, Balance's powerful baritone — and bleakly opulent romance.

'Slur' rolls along like a drunken seventeenth-century cartman after a day on the scrumpy, Balance singing of the sun sinking down on the 'blood red edge of a blood red town', while 'Ostia' references the murder of radical Italian director Pier Paolo Pasolini in 1975. A gay man working amid the corruption and prejudice and wild excess of the Italian movie business, Pasolini had just finished directing *Salo* — a hyper-violent and lushly baroque adaptation of the Marquis de Sade's *120 Days of Sodom* — before being murdered in sadistic fashion on the beach at Ostia. Some — Balance included — posited a theory that Pasolini's death was something of an 'organised' suicide: an artwork of sorts, designed to be the peak of a career that frequently obsessed over sadism and death. The song was also intended as a tribute to a friend of Balance's who had committed suicide at Dover cliffs. The layering of opulent synth drones — Sleazy had used the Emulator synth to mix synthetic strings with live instrumentation — and the mixture of fantastical myth with personal pain was *completely* Coil: art everything, everything art.

Indeed, despite being cited as a major influence on angsty American industrialists like Nine Inch Nails and Skinny Puppy, only one track on *Horse Rotorvator* — 'Penetralia' — features metallic guitars. Though emotionally heavy, Coil never got into the angst-porn wormhole that so many American industrialists seem to fall down: Coil's music hums with life and glee.

Moving on from the funereal grandeur of *Horse Rotorvator*, Coil's next record — *Love's Secret Domain* (1991) was a kaleidoscopic trawl through the ragged excesses of London clubland. Both Sleazy and Balance were enthusiastic early adopters of acid house. They loved the freedom of the scene and the chemical chaos that went along with it, using its energy to fuel a record that galvanised the unrelentingness of roughshod house and referenced clubland's seamier edges. Techno producer Regis once described Birmingham techno institution House of God to me as being akin to 'a cruel cabaret' and that is *exactly* what Coil express here. They implicitly understood the grotesque, carnival aspect of clubbing — the melty faces, the ugliness, the sweat and stench and need. *Love's Secret Domain* was like acid house directed by Peter Greenaway: a hall of mirrors where elongated shadows appear and gurning, jaundiced ringmasters fling wraps from top hats.

While others were obsessing over the 'togetherness' Coil cast the club as a vestibule of the last days of Rome; poetic Byronic excess. The recording process was as fraught and excessive as the music — frequent collaborator Steven Thrower remembered spending significant amounts of time rolling around on the studio floor in a chemically enhanced state of discombobulation and frustration after multiple attempts at mixing down the tracks. The chemical experience was pivotal to Coil. Though initially enthusiastic about the rave scene, both Sleazy and Balance eventually came to the conclusion that clubland was not necessarily the best setting for MDMA, preferring to have absolute control over an environment, as opposed to basking in sensory overload. *Time Machines* (1998) thus hinged on hypnotically dense, pure drones, each individual drone chosen to align psychically to a specific substance ('tested and retested') which also provided the track titles.

The album pivots around four synth notes processed and compressed and put through the mangler in various ways, so as to best represent the specific properties of the chemicals that inspired their creation. Each drone is tuned to the psychic 'tone' of the chemical. Coil implicitly understood the power of the drone. La Monte Young provided inspiration — specifically his Dream House works — with Balance describing the album's process as 'borrowing slightly from La Monte Young . . . the perpetual drone. The drugs thing is actually a hook we hung it on . . . you'd realise that you'd had some sort of temporal slip . . . We tried lots of drones . . . It's a very rough science if it is a science.'[6]

British Murder Boys

While Coil occasionally flirted with the immediacy of dance music, few in the techno scene approached their oblique sensibility. Techno was generally tied to futurism and immediacy: it simply wasn't the place for the hidden hand, arcane signalling or erotic esotericism.

The mid-nineties Birmingham sound changed all that, however. Taking the functionality of techno, layering it with a bleak dronal undertone and applying a very English DIY sensibility — one that frequently displayed a keenly chiselled sense of the absurd and a willingness to explore the grotesque — the Birmingham sound was centred around the productions of Surgeon and Regis and the ludicrously debauched House of God club night. Informed by elements of post-punk, synth pop and industrial music alongside a vital inspiration from the harder side of Detroit (i.e. Jeff Mills and Robert Hood), the techno coming out of the city in the mid nineties was jarring, hypnotic and relentless: stripped of any fat whatsoever, based around incessant loops and — almost always — underpinned by a dronal element.

Regis (Karl O'Connor) started Downwards Records in 1993. Named after a visit to Coil's studio with producer and ex-Napalm Death drummer Mick Harris (aka Scorn — himself an absolutely key figure in the Birmingham underground) in which Coil singer Jhonn Balance had appeared after a wait of some hours complaining that everything was 'going downwards!' O'Connor was initially inspired by the single-mindedness of indie labels like Mute and Some Bizarre. Although generally associated with Regis's run of austere, barrelling mid to late nineties 12-inches and LPs, Downwards has never been a purist techno label. The very first 7-inch release — an abstract low-bpm growler by Antonym — was a far way off from the belting sound most associate with the label, while in recent years he's put out hardly any techno, instead focusing on everything from DVA Damas's sepulchral Americana to late-period Eyeless in Gaza and William Bennett's Haitian-inspired rhythmic Cut Hands project: for O'Connor, hypnosis is the key.

'Hypnosis is central to everything I was aiming to do,' he tells me. 'I was always on that track. John Cale: when me and Surgeon go to a festival or club or whatever, we'll always ask "How much John Cale is in the room?" (*laughs*) And it's usually only about one per cent. But the drone is central to what I do. The way I try to execute it is by layering it underneath something familiar. So the techno is doing everything that people think that it is supposed to do — some sort of rhythmic structure — but the drone will be *underneath* what is happening: it modulates or it undulates or it does nothing, it just sits there and does what it does by its very presence. And I do that on all my tracks — it's a *presence*, you can feel it. And I love that.'

O'Connor was coming at techno from an outsider position from the start. He had scant equipment in the early days — a single drum machine, one synth, one effects unit — and, though drawn to the immediacy of techno, was unschooled in its conventions. He knew that he wanted to make music free of conventional structure — 'giant slabs of sound', as he once described it — and it was this disavowal of conformity (no intros, no outros, no breakdowns, no remixes) that led to the jarring immediacy of his raw early tracks. Debut LP *Gymnastics* (1994) was as minimal as anything Jeff Mills or Robert Hood were doing but psychically aligned to the weird corners of late 1970s England: lino flooring, empty swimming pools, piss-soaked stairwells, stale fat coagulating in the fryer. You either got it or you didn't. He once told me that playing any track off it in a DJ set would 'fuck up the last three tracks you've played and ruin the next two as well'. Though functional and grindingly repetitious it's impossible to mix any of the tracks from *Gymnastics* smoothly: they're imbued with an unhinged mischief, elbowing their way into a set. Tunes like 'The Black Freighter', 'Careless

Pedestrian' and 'We Said No' entered the techno pantheon with a punkish intent: both Jeff Mills and John Peel were enthusiastic early supporters.

'When I recorded *Gymnastics* I used to run things really hot: I had a really primitive set-up and my amp used to blow. Back in those days nothing was on computer: you used to do things straight to tape. And the mix was what it was. I used to do things in a dub reggae way, hands on the board. It wasn't tracked, it was all live — and if you listen to a lot of that stuff, about one minute before the end the amp would go, so I'm mixing in a precognitive way. Maybe something takes over when I'm not consciously mixing? You can't hear what happens; then you play it back and you don't know what's happening. And there were little mistakes that obviously I left on. Things weren't edited to death in those days.'

Talk to O'Connor about some of the narratives that surround rave culture — particularly the idea that great swathes of the population were fundamentally changed by ecstasy — and you'll get a different perspective to the usual. Into electronic music since the early 1980s, and travelling far and wide to see the likes of Fad Gadget and Einstürzende Neubauten, he maintains a healthy degree of scepticism as to how far house music and ecstasy actually changed the general psyche, more interested in how techno could potentially subvert rockist complacency.

'I'm very snobbish about music,' he tells me. 'I loved what I loved. I didn't used to talk to people who wore trainers (*laughs*) — we'd dress a certain way and communicate through music. I'd look at people in the early acid days and think, "But there's no John Cale in it; you're not into the Stooges! You're dancing to electronic music but a year ago you'd be beating me up for liking Fad Gadget!" And this is the problem I have with dance music: "Oh, it brought people together! It brought football hooligans together!" But, at the end of the day, when they came down on a Monday morning they were still a bunch of scumbags. They didn't live the art all the time. With techno at that point there wasn't really an industry, there weren't any rules. I had nothing invested in the scene or the gathering of people or all that communal nonsense. What I *did* really like was that it broke the DNA of rock 'n' roll completely. It broke it all up — verse, chorus, verse — everything. Even the industrial music, Throbbing Gristle and everyone — it was still four people making it and they still had breaks in between the songs. It was still in the rock format. But techno just stripped *everything* away. And I saw the potential in that. It didn't have any commercial value. It was the first time that anything experimental or avant-garde could be applied in a popular way; you could play it in a club and people who wouldn't be into experimental music could still dance to it.'

This oblique undertow was brought to the fore on the infamous early noughties British Murder Boys project. Formed by Surgeon and Regis just on the cusp of the minimal techno boom in the early noughties — whereby bpms were lowered and labels like Kompact and Perlon were pushing a sleeker, more progressive sound — British Murder Boys were out on a limb (and, in hindsight, *way* ahead of the times) from the outset. Unlike anything else on the techno scene of the time, BMB were theatrical and ritualistic and noisy and absurd. Moving away from the 'faceless' techno clichés, they put on a show. It was all gloriously overblown, flipping the script on techno functionality and mainlining pure drama — pure Tap — onto the dance floor.

Ramping up the industrial influence, tracks like 'Learn Your Lesson' and 'Don't Give Way to Fear' (the deathly clarion call of commanding officers sending battalions of doomed First World War soldiers over the top) hinged on a sense of clammy, rising dread. More rhythmically complex and densely layered than any of the pair's early solo 12-inches, they foresaw the industrial techno boom (much of which was cartoon nosebleed in comparison) that gained popularity ten years down the line. This wasn't an exercise in mindless brutality. BMB implicitly understood the essential yin-yang of dynamic tension and release that made the music of their youth — Fad Gadget, Coil, Whitehouse, Cabaret Voltaire, Throbbing Gristle — so compelling.

'Techno can be a carrier wave for something else,' explains Tony Child (Surgeon). 'The tonal elements and structure that is used to deliver the *rhythmic* carrier wave — that's techno. I've used this style of music for a long time now and I find it an incredibly effective delivery method. You can get five thousand people to dance to a drone if you put drums underneath it (*laughs*) whereas you may only get one hundred people to listen to it without the drums.'

Child's early productions on his Dynamic Tension and Counterbalance imprints matched belting, hypnotic movement with a playful lightness of touch. His classic self-titled EP came out on Downwards in 1994 and Surgeon was brought to underground consciousness due to its success (Jeff Mills including two tracks from the EP — 'Magneze' and 'Atol' on his legendarily intense *Live at the Liquid Rooms* mix a couple of years later). Over myriad releases, Child's music has ranged from purist techno to ambient, field recordings and live analogue improvisations. Recent years have seen him push further into the realms of avant-garde experimentation with 2013's *Breaking the Frame* including a selection of intensely uplifting drone pieces alongside depth-charge techno.

'When I did *Breaking the Frame* I did a lot of research into what I could sum up as abstract devotional music,' he says. 'I was listening to a lot of Alice Coltrane, La Monte Young, Terry Riley, Éliane Radigue, John Coltrane

— and looking into the idea that abstract music was used to express a devotional feel. Alice Coltrane was so powerful; it's amazing how she managed to transmit and convey that love and devotional atmosphere through her music. It's very powerful work.'

The devotional — in the non-denominational sense — has been increasingly central to Child's music in recent years. He's long harnessed a razor-sharp focus in techno, standing calm amid the chaos during his sets as if in the eye of a storm. For the past decade he's also been a keen practitioner of intense ashtanga yoga, while more recently his Transcendence Orchestra project (alongside Dan Bean) has focused on lush meditative drones, their two albums — 2017's *Modern Methods for Ancient Rituals* and 2020's *Feeling the Spirit* — both channelling a sense of palpable well-being via slowly unfurling drones and ambient soundscapes. Live, Child finds the ritual bent of the Transcendence Orchestra — where hoods are donned, incense is lit and lights are lowered to near darkness — an even more intense experience than his techno sets.

'I've thought a lot about the idea of drone and really elongated sustained tones and it relates to the idea of infinity to me. I have vivid early memories . . . When I was around seven years old, I lived in a village just outside of Northampton and when I went to sleep at night I could hear the sound of the M1 and — because it was fairly far away I could only really hear it at night — I'd go to sleep with this drone sound and I remember that having really bizarre psychedelic effects on me, falling asleep in that semi-conscious state. I feel like I was pre-programmed to tune into that. Another early reference for me was Spacemen 3. I was a big early fan of theirs — also Suicide, the repetitive nature of it. I think it seeped into my subconscious as a producer. I'm not a religious person but, to me, the idea of infinity connects to a very abstract idea of god: infinite sound connects to something deep and primal. A really important part of the Transcendence Orchestra is that we become psychically involved in the music: it's very much an altered state of consciousness. That's what we experience while we perform it, and that's what we're trying to elicit in the audience. We are equal participants when we perform it — it's far more powerful than a techno performance, the degree to which I'm psychologically affected by it.'

Zonal

'Jamaican music culture in Birmingham in the 1970s was everywhere,' says Justin Broadrick. 'I lived on the border of neighbourhoods with blues parties going on: you'd hear the most almighty bass in the distance and the smell of sweet dope. I was attracted to both (*laughs*). The weed and those humungous basslines that used to take your guts out. I'd get into these hallucinatory, trance-like states from dub reggae in a tiny room with an uber-sized sound system. It was an otherworldly experience.'

Justin Broadrick has spent his musical life working the sweet spot between the abrasive and the foundational. In Godflesh he married punishing sheets of noise to the bass weight of dub and clanking, hip hop-inflected beats; as Jesu he layers walls of soaring guitars against hypnogogic, melancholy melodies while Techno Animal (alongside the Bug's Kevin Martin) presented a narcotised take on industrialised, droning instrumental hip hop. His beat is a very English urban dread fuelled by what he once described as a 'horror of the everyday', and tied together by monolithic bass weight and crushing heaviness.

Living on a hippy commune on the outskirts of the city between the ages of two and four, then on an east Birmingham estate, Broadrick's childhood was often harrowing. His mother and stepfather were into drugs (his stepfather was a heroin addict) and he was exposed to extreme situations — and music — from an early age. He recalls a particular light in Birmingham outside his flats — 'a sickly yellow light from the street lights and the buzz of the lights' — the claustrophobia of being surrounded by concrete, the need to escape into an interior world.

Music was a sanctuary and Broadrick absorbed a plethora of sounds — dub, early hip hop and industrial, early house, hardcore punk, with TG and Cabaret Voltaire bootlegs from a record stall in the Rag Market providing particular fascination. By 1984 Broadrick — still in his early teens — was making primitive noise with 'shortwave radio static through an echo chamber' as Final, before joining an early iteration of Napalm Death on guitar in 1985 and playing on the first side of the seminal *Scum* (1987). Soon tiring of the creative dead end of untapped aggression and speed, he left Naplam Death and joined — for a short time — the industrial metal band Head of David on drums. His long-standing obsession with electronics and dub were calling ever stronger, however, and Godflesh was the culmination of years of obsessive, wide-ranging, listening.

'I remember hearing the early Human League records and being blown away. And Cabaret Voltaire — early Cabs was *it* for me. After my obsession with Throbbing Gristle I consumed the whole industrial music culture. So I got stuff like *Cabaret Voltaire Live at the Lyceum* and was exposed to drones and drum machines, essentially (*laughs*). And then you had these pseudo dub basslines. Cabaret Voltaire are really unsung — even now, it's like we have all the obsession with Throbbing Gristle but Cabaret Voltaire were ridiculous!

A lot of us old-school people love them — speak to Regis about them! I still listen to them and marvel at how they did it.'

Exposed to acid house though Birmingham's Swordfish Records, Broadrick heard the owner's take on acid house — a cranky, raw 12-inch entitled 'Jesus Loves the Acid' — and immediately tied it back to 'later Throbbing Gristle . . . when you think of a track like "Five Knuckle Shuffle" or "Something Came Over Me" they were proto-techno tracks, essentially.' Swordfish had an in-house label and released the first self-titled *Godflesh* album in 1988. Melding dubwise bass, Broadrick's gruff vocal, drum machine rhythms, drones and repetitive riffs, *Godflesh* was the sound of Birmingham, distilled through the contours of Broadrick's muscle memory — the 'sickly yellow street lights'; the distant hum of blues parties; the shock and awe of Swans and Big Black; the hollow thud of the drum machine; time-stretched samples — it was all twisted up into an audio zone that spoke of *ceaseless* inner pressure. There was a metallic element at play but — more often than not — the guitars were used as either a rhythmic gristliser or dronal texturiser, chugging along relentlessly with zero leads, down-tuned to a subbed-out, gut-rumble sludge. The spaces *between* the beats were of paramount importance and, though aggressive, there was a vulnerability to Broadrick's vocal delivery: his charnel-house bark imbued with a haunting, mournful edge.

Signing to Earache for the seminal *Streetcleaner* (1989) Broadrick found himself in a difficult position. On the one hand, Godflesh were exposed to a (much) bigger audience; on the other they found themselves playing to conservative metal crowds. Earache were the biggest metal indie in the world, and had made a name by introducing the more extreme ends of metal's increasingly fragmented subgenres to a wider audience. As such, Godflesh soon found themselves on tour with bands like Carcass and Morbid Angel, playing to crowds who latched on to the aggressiveness but missed the wider sonic subtlety — the dub, the bass and hip hop. Sonically, Godflesh lived and died by the sub frequencies. Playing on top-heavy rock venue PAs, if the subs were missing half the story was gone. Godflesh were thus often — and erroneously — put into the 'industrial metal' bracket alongside bands like Ministry, Nine Inch Nails and Skinny Puppy. The sound system aspect was completely ignored; the fact that Godflesh was a foundational sound born of the unique sonic symbiosis of Birmingham went flying over people's heads. They got the aggression, but not the vulnerability; the power but not the meditative core. For Broadrick, it remains important to attempt a joining of the dots.

'When I first reformed Godflesh, Regis came to DJ at some of our US gigs. Even in this age of saturation I still want to present audiences with our tastes. Expose people to stuff. I had people coming up to me saying, "That Regis was amazing! What *is* that stuff?!" And how do you explain it to somebody who only listens to micro genres of metal? People say things like, "I only listen to blackened shoegaze made by people in the early noughties." It kills me, it's preposterous! (*laughs*) Back in the day people referred to us as "industrial metal" . . . even now people say things like: "Godflesh made the best industrial metal album of the year!" For fuck's sake! I don't even know what "industrial metal" *is!* I don't listen to that shit. It's horrible.'

Over the decades, Broadrick has remained dedicated to exploring the outer reaches of sonic intensity both within Godflesh and elsewhere. His discography is cavernous. Aside from the projects and pseudonyms we mentioned earlier, he's made drum and bass as Tech Level 2, covered grimy analogue synth workouts as Council Estate Electronics and bleak, skeletal ambient as Pale Sketcher. Most recently, as JK Flesh, he's mastered a narcotised, dubbed-out, dreadnought techno that evokes a feeling of lumbering through stinking, gaseous, canal-side mud. Often working at a crawl-pace shuffle — as low as 80–90 bpm — records like *Rise Above* (2016) were a lesson in claustrophobia and clammy tension while his latest project with Kevin Martin and Moor Mother — Zonal — was equally tumultuous, their *Wrecked* LP (2019) hinging on shattered bass, mighty drones and Moor Mother's apocalyptic vocal.

'People who hear Godflesh and then meet Justin, there's probably a massive disparity,' laughs Kevin Martin. 'What I liked about him was that there was an anti-machismo in him. A lot of people involved in metal are way too macho for my liking — the testosterone levels are too much. But Justin is, like me, *over*sensitive if anything. When we started talking and touring Techno Animal and became good friends I was drawn to the fact that we both had terrible backgrounds. That's why we were drawn to music. Music was our escape mechanism, our coping strategy, our absolute obsession and compulsion. Justin's frustrations with how Godflesh were perceived was partly the reason we started working together. He's like my little brother. We've worked together for so long and had so few cross words. In fact, the only argument we've ever had was when I said I wasn't really feeling a guitar part he was recording. He got a strop on and said, "Look Kev, the difference between me and you is that I like Hawkwind and you don't!" And he was right — I still don't like Hawkwind (*laughs*).'

Like Broadrick, Kevin Martin has an incredibly intense relationship to sound. Early sonic epiphanies were intimately tied to painful family situations. Like Broadrick, he recalls escaping to an interior sonic world, pulling the speakers off the wall onto the floor and lying down with them 'as close as possible to my ears to drown out the sound of my parents fighting. Discharge, Crass — like a jet playing drone — to exclude the fact that my dad was a wife- and child-beating arsehole. That's what I would trace the idea of immersion into sound back to; punk spoke to me. I wasn't too impressed by the world. Punk was a big wall of "fuck you" to the world. A comfort zone of "I can't hear the madness".'

As the Bug, Martin has spent over two decades twisting the outer reaches of UK sound system culture into any number of cone-shattering permutations. Dub, jungle, grime, noise, drones, fierce ragga and industrial textures have all found their way into his productions, always rooted by a wall of bass. Indeed, his sound is often as physical as it's possible to get. His sub frequencies match the smothering bass blanket of Jah Shaka or Sunn O))) in full flight, while his spacious beats hit like a breeze block, although — as we'll see — recent years have seen him experimenting with subtle drone work every bit as emotionally resonant.

A conversation with Martin is intense. He carries the air of a man in a constant state of sonic awe, running through a selection of musical epiphanies with such palpable wonderment that they may as well have happened yester- day. Moving from punk to dub reggae via the jagged contortions of Killing Joke and Adrian Sherwood's On-U Sound Records, he was spellbound by the way that dub reggae provided an 'unstoppable throb, that heartbeat, that bass, that blood-pressure pulsation — it had a relentlessness to it. For me dub was the nature of deconstruction and the elements of chaos . . . with live dubs on a classical mixing desk they'll be muting things on the fly or flying the faders up really quick to get what sounded like random delays or random effects. There was this unpredictability of chaos.'

He found similar excitement elsewhere, describing the first Godflesh album along dub lines while signalling the primal bludgeon of Swans as a particularly formative experience — their infamous mid-1980s ICA shows in particular.

'They didn't have a support act. They just had a stage full of body builders, with no music (*laughs*). And they came out and it was fucking *brutal*. At least half the audience left between the first and second song. On one hand, it was the most hellish experience — but I found it exhilarating. My body and soul had found the sound that I was looking for. I was deaf for a week — I had terrible tinnitus for a week. I remember walking home with a friend and the whole walk was just us doing impersonations of it on the walk home — "bwww clangbww- wyuurrbbuuurrr" — the whole thing had imprinted itself on my body.'

Making industrially inflected, avant-garde noise as GOD, Martin eventually formed Techno Animal with Broadrick, releasing *Ghosts* (1991) then

Re-Entry in 1995. Presenting a lumbering, psychedelic and menacing take on down-tempo beats, Techno Animal fused their love of hip hop, post-punk, (proper) industrial and techno in a limber framework and quickly positioned the pair outside their comfort zone of the regular circuit that both GOD and Godflesh operated in.

Instead of indie venues and festivals, they found themselves playing underground clubs with massive systems to crowds of spangled ravers, on bills with everyone from Atari Teenage Riot to DJ Rush. It was an immensely energising experience, although — as Martin notes — it could be a disorientating experience for the ravers who were 'there to dance while we were there to obliterate.' The experience of recording and touring as Techno Animal was nonetheless formative, particularly for Martin who 'became hooked on studios, became obsessed with the texture and tone of the sound. I fell out of love with bands. There was no way back for me after that.'

This obsession — with the grain of sound and the infinite possibilities afforded by the studio — has been writ large on everything he's put out since. The Bug was initially a project undertaken alongside DJ Vadim, the pair's debut LP — 1997's *Tapping the Conversation* — a sombre, smoky affair, some distance from the ragga-inflected chaos that was still to come while 2003's *Pressure* (released on Aphex Twin's Rephlex Records) saw Martin, now solo, presenting a noisier, more aggressive sound with the ragga influence front and centre, marrying acidic digital chaos to abyssal dub and glitched beats.

The seminal *London Zoo* (2008) was a huge leap forward and something of a line in the sand. A maelstrom connecting the wider continuum of British sound system culture from its West Indian dub roots through grime, dubstep and hallucinatory ragga, there was an untapped energy at play on tracks like 'Skeng' and 'Jah War' but, as ever with Martin, texture was key. Working alongside a plethora of MCs and vocalists — Flowdan, Space Ape, Warrior Queen and Tippa Irie, to name a few — Martin ramped up dancehall tension to breaking point and coated it in swathes of pummelling bass, rattling snares and skewed, queasy synths. In comparison, *Angels and Demons* (2014) was a (marginally) subtler affair that featured — alongside rapid-fire spitting from Flowdan, Miss Red and Warrior Queen — haunting vocals from Liz Harris (aka Grouper) and Inga Copeland. Divided into two halves — 'Angels' and 'Devils' — the first half of the record hinges on waves of static, delicate vocals and pin-drop tension, the latter half on maximal sound pressure.

While the Bug negotiates maximal dancehall pressure, 2019 saw the release of two drone-centred records — *Sirens* (as Kevin Richard Martin) and the fourth King Midas Sound LP *Solitude* — in which Martin navigates loss and trauma. *Sirens* had its genesis in a one-off experimental show based around minimal permutations of rumbling sub-bass and siren and foghorn sounds. However, shortly after performing it Martin suffered the trauma of his newborn son — who'd already had a complex and traumatic birth — having to undergo an extensive (and, thankfully, successful) series of intestinal operations and weeks in an ICU.

'The whole thing changed me,' explains Martin. 'When it came to making an album of *Sirens* I realised that what I'd done in the live context was more of performance piece or installation piece — excessive volume, excessive bass, excessive smoke; when I came to making an album, I wanted to do justice to the whole experience, do justice to my family to make a piece of music that stood as a piece of music. I had to start from scratch and write the album as if I'd make a film score of the whole life experience. Cinematic themes that would repeat over and over with drone as the gelling agent. Tension as the overriding emotion . . . Drones can be therapeutic — like a sound massage — but can also convey paranoia or tension, to a massive degree.'

Track titles — 'There is a Problem', 'The Surgeon', 'Mechanical Chatter in the ICU', 'Loss of Consciousness', 'The Deepest Fear' — allude directly to the unfathomable stress and heartbreak of the situation while the music — low, subtle drones, far-off reverberating pings and bleeps — sonically channel and, ultimately, process the trauma. It's Martin's most personal record and, knowing the story of its genesis, an incredibly difficult listen, shot through with terror, loneliness, sorrow and dread. As King Midas Sound — alongside poet Roger Robinson — he also delivered the emotionally devastating *Solitude* in the same year and both *Sirens* and *Solitude* work in musical (if not thematic) symbiosis.

Pitched as a 'meditation on loss' *Solitude* is an unbearably intimate portrait of relationship breakdown and the void of loneliness, mental disarray, jealousy, bitterness and emptiness left in its wake. Tracing the arc of a relationship before and after the fall, Robinson's spoken-word vocal exhumes a partnership that turns inwards to the point of unhealthy obsession before turning the mirror on the narrator as he describes the weight of his own descent into solitude. The details — vocalised in Robinson's hushed monotone — are rendered in such a way that you feel effectively pinned against the wall, unable to move for fear of giving away your presence. It's so personal as to feel like an exercise in voyeurism, as well as intimacy. Bitter vignettes unfold ('We float through different parts of the house like a chess game') before he descends into darker territory, all rendered with an unflinching, naked honesty poetic in its absolute truth. Martin underpins Robinson's monotone delivery with desolate drones that supplement the feeling of emotional dereliction. It's a beatless album but, in its own way, more sonically devastating than anything he's done as the Bug, even — a ghostly minimalism, the music of an absence so keenly felt as to be all-enveloping.

Ghost System

While Martin's drone evoked the ghost of absence, the haunted corners of (counter) cultural memory have been equally thoroughly excavated by other electronic producers in recent years. Unfurling skeletal frameworks that tread claustrophobic, uncomfortable or melancholic paths, submerged rave memories have held a peculiar fascination in recent years, specifically the narrative of the rave as a black box of engulfing flashbacks, emitting stifled pings in the blunted synapses of the producer's memory; a ley line to halcyon days never forgotten, never to be repeated.

Lee Gamble's *Diversions 1994–1996*, for example, was assembled entirely from his teenage cache of jungle mixtapes, splicing together a hazy selection of samples that speak to mid-nineties Midlands raving. Diva shrieks are elongated into volleying drones and buried underneath layered pads, juddering subs are turned into aquatic atmospherics, the frenetic energy of the rave replaced by a wistful melancholy; tracks originally produced for maximal dance-floor impact lovingly reimagined as a lo-fi time capsule. On *Diversions* Gamble focused largely on the beatless breakdown sections, amplifying the tape hiss as another layer of the sonic onion skin. Tunes like 'Digbeth' and 'M25 Echo' hone in on single sounds — a reverb-laden stab, say — and loop it until it takes on a mantric quality evoking not the adrenal rush of the night, but the tinnitus-muffled drone of the train home — paranoid, sweaty and having to face the square world in all its unblinking, uncomprehending hideousness.

Elsewhere, the hauntological axis — broadly speaking, electronic music that trades on memories of an imagined past — was one of the most interesting developments of the late noughties. A term originally coined by the philosopher Jacques Derrida in the nineties as a means of discussing what he described as 'a dislocation in temporality' — the past returning to the present. Running as an audio counterpoint to the psychogeographical landscape staked out by writers like Iain Sinclair, labels like Mordant Music and Ghost Box imagine a Britain of, by turn, grim, hallucinatory menace and whimsical eeriness, conjuring a land stuck in an eternal feedback loop of sinister iconography dawn from the hinterland of subconscious memory: a fusty cornucopia of public information broadcasts, folk horror, radio static, library records, imagined theme tunes, empty car parks, false memory and folklore. The central idea — a hyperreal dreamscape just out of reach but psychically accessible via carefully curated audio and visual talismans — proved potent, particularly in an England so readily predisposed to obsess over mythical pasts.

Mordant Music was a vital hub for world-building hauntological journeying. Run by producer Baron Mordant (who also made the majority of the tunes put out on the label) and ploughing a Chris Morris-esque furrow of gallows humour and unflinching everyday observation, records like *Dead Air* (2006) imagined a parallel universe of eerie domestic dread: a fusty brown- and orange-wallpapered living room, Ceefax flickering on the telly and an unnatural hue to the sky outside. Enlisting ex-Thames TV continuity announcer Philip Ellesmere to narrate a surreal commentary in chipper, local TV style, *Dead Air* took the idea of a ghost TV station still, somehow, transmitting into the ether and fused quasi-industrial soundscapes, naive melody, test card themes and pealing drones to evoke the veil of everyday reality slowly lifting to reveal a surreal dreamscape slightly skew-whiff. The *Travelogues* series was equally disquieting, taking field recordings — anywhere from a Southend car park to the west London streets around Craven Cottage — and turning the sonic screws with creeped-out flutes, white noise, tape hiss and synth drones, like slowly twisting the dial on a radio tuned to collective subconscious disquiet.

Elsewhere a commission from the BFI — *MisinforMation* — saw Baron Mordant rummaging through hundreds of hours of archival material for an audiovisual remixing of the sinister UK Central Office of Information films of the 1980s. Against a backdrop of barren drones, the films played out in reassembled form — disturbing archival images that those of a certain age have for ever burnt onto the retinas: snot-encrusted glue sniffers staggering around on chilly industrial wasteland, swarms of magpies ravaging a suburban home (a metaphor for burglary), nuclear explosion advice, John Hurt narrating a film called *Monolith* that used an iceberg as a metaphor for the spread of AIDS. *MisinforMation* felt like the last word in domestic anxiety — a cryptic crossword of shuddering symbolism soundtracked by the drone of dread.

Others working the hauntological fields ploughed a more whimsical furrow. Ghost Box Records took the idea of a parallel universe where it's the late 1950s to the late 1970s for ever. Drawing inspiration from old Penguin and Pelican spines, sixties municipal buildings, domestic interiors in vivid hues of orange and brown, library records, forgotten soundtracks, secret numbers stations, dowdy laboratories, cipher code, uncomfortable knitwear, village folklore and hidden ley lines, Ghost Box have released everything from the narcotised late-night chug of Pye Corner Audio to the uncanny whimsy of Belbury Poly and Focus Group, their aesthetic illuminating a Britain that exists not in concrete reality but, rather, in the dream unconscious of those who grew up in the sixties, seventies and eighties, mining the fertile hinterland between whimsy and dread. Musically, we're talking the uncanny valley of electronics, a symbiosis of the BBC Radiophonic Workshop and Brian Eno and the more cerebral moments of Cluster and Tangerine Dream. The BBC Radiophonic Workshop — the layered, alien modular synthesis of Daphne Oram and Delia Derbyshire, in particular — is writ large over most everything Ghost Box have put out. Theirs is world-building par excellence, the beautifully observed covers and titles often imagining novels and TV series and plays, an evocative cultural haunting that encourages imagery to form in the mind of the listener: *The Séance at Hobs Lane*, *The Owl's Map*, *The Belbury Tales*.

Perhaps inevitably when dealing with imagined pasts, the more flagrant excesses of the hauntological oeuvre can tend towards sickly 'jumpers for goalposts' tweeness as personified by the woeful Public Service Broadcasting and their tiresome 'Keep Calm and Pass the Biscuits' shtick, a wearisomely sentimental melancholy — think shipping forecast samples over bland motorik-lite — that evokes John Major's drooling assertion in a 1993 speech that 'Fifty years from now Britain will still be the country of long shadows on county cricket grounds, warm beer, invincible green suburbs, dog lovers and — as George Orwell said — old maids cycling to Holy Communion through the morning mist.'[7] It's notable that the hauntological axis spread predominantly pre-Brexit: would there be as strong an underground appetite for it now, given what has since transpired? Or are the toxic effects of obsessing over an imagined past now all too painfully evident?

Leyland Kirby — a wildly prolific producer who, as the Caretaker, made countless hours of hazy, often sad, hauntological gear sampling crackly recordings of 1920s ballroom tunes in evocation of passing time and dementia — has also spent significant time reconfiguring his own musical epiphanies. His Death of Rave project — released under his V/Vm alias — mines the dreamscape of his formative early rave experiences, a fantasia of swirling hoover pads and the like slowed down beyond all recognition and formed into a dense dronal fog. The track titles may be personally evocative — 'Acid Alan, Haggis and Scott', 'Big Eddie's Van — Bowlers Car Park', 'Monroes Stockport' — and the music wistful, but it comes from a place of disillusion, rather than sentimental warmth. Kirby's drone is cast not as celebration but techno's death knell, a lysergic memorial device leading down a long dark tunnel. As he explained in 2011: 'the idea for *The Death of Rave* was conceived in early 2006 after a visit to the Berghain club in Berlin. At the time Berghain was about to explode on the international club scene as a temple. The feeling was in the air that something special was happening. I went and saw a pale shadow of the past. Grim and boring beats, endlessly pounding to an audience who felt they were part of an experience but who lacked cohesion and energy. For me personally something had died. Be it a spirit, be it an ideal, be it an adventure in sound. Rave and techno felt dead to me.'

Wistful memories underpinned by a darker edge — the passing of time; halcyon days lost; epiphany gone for ever — it can all start to grate. In some respects it's a deeply egocentric view: the 'you should have been here in the sixties' pub bore vibe, made dismal sonic flesh. The fact remains that clubbing will *always* provide epiphany (though, as I write this, Covid-19 has sadly put the scene on indefinite hiatus) but there is no such thing as a golden age. The serotonin-depleted will always whinge that it was better back in the day. It isn't true: the uncomfortable truth is that *you* were better — i.e. less jaded — not *it*. There remains a creeping suspicion that much of the deconstructed club music that proliferated throughout the late noughties represents a mawkish attempt to academicise the visceral; to get under the bonnet but, in the process, rip out the engine. Much of it seems to be made by people who haven't danced for a very long time. In that respect it can be read as sanitised musical exhibition; like when New York City council decided to clean up the subway graffiti only to install a special graffiti train exhibit to pootle round the tunnels.

That isn't to say, as we explored earlier, that the narrative of rave culture as eternally rosy arena of shared togetherness can't be robustly challenged. Of course, for every magical moment of warmth there were always night-marish, grotesque edges that took equal precedence. Everyone who has been involved in the culture — then or now — will most likely have a palpitation-inducing memory bank of paranoia-inducing train journeys, sweat-soaked, teeth-grinding come-downs, self-loathing and panic. Rave temples that have been eulogised long after the fact — places like Bagley's, Stratford Rex and Milton Keynes Sanctuary — could, in reality, be seriously grim: psychotic bouncers, fights in the car park, organised gangs selling shit gear, questionable puffer jackets, pale-faced gurners blinking into the queasy morning light as if wrenched from Dante's third circle. Regardless, though, the *epiphany* — the ritual, the theatre, the glorious absurdity of it all; dancing in the dark; the drone, the bass, the altered states — that's eternal.

'All discos are is humanity tapping into a need that has been around since the chimpanzee ate the mushroom and consciousness developed: it's smoke, coloured lights and music,' explains Andrew Weatherall. 'There were ancient Greek ceremonies that involved a square room, lights and chanting. My last ever psychedelic experience was on top of Silbury Hill so I'm a little bit obsessed. There is a great book called *On Silbury Hill* by Adam Thorpe and he posits the theory that they'd shine torches and create shadows on the side of the hill as part of a ceremony. And when you've taken acid and you think on that — that you're tapping into some 4,000-year-old energy — you do think: "This is probably as far as I can go psychedelically. I shall stop my psychedelic adventuring forthwith." My outlook on these things can be summed up with the Terence McKenna quote: "I'm a rationalist with weird edges."'

It feels both strange and incredibly sad to be writing about Andrew Weatherall in the past tense. He tapped an eternal groove; few connected the dots like him or created pivotal dance-floor memories for so many. As a record collector and DJ he roamed everywhere from bowel-shaking dub reggae through raw acid tracks, techno, rare rockabilly 7-inches, slow motion disco, psychedelia of every vivid hue and all points west aside. His production for Primal Scream's *Screamadelica*, of course (alongside remixes for everyone from My Bloody Valentine to Happy Mondays) ensured his name was known far outside the confines of underground dance culture in the early nineties — but that was only ever part of the story. In the Sabres of Paradise — alongside Gary Burns and Jagz Kooner — he explored hypnotic, dub-infused after-hours beats; Two Lone Swordsmen (with Keith Tenniswood) specialised in sleazy, sound system electro; in the Woodleigh Research Facility he honed in on wistful, hauntological vibes while the Asphodells (alongside Timothy J. Fairplay) fused driving house with a sideways, Krautrock-referencing sensibili-ty. Over three decades of activity, collaboration remained key and he remained a connector — of people, sounds and scenes — to the end.

As a DJ, he was all about hypnotic groove, one of the most patient and hypnotically focused in the game. He'd use every inch of a record, rolling out a track from beginning to end, a master of long, mesmeric, perfectly EQ'd blends. You'd hardly ever hear Weatherall indulge in rapid-fire mixing: his was the pilgrim's path — a slow, sustained chug. Of course, he could — like so many of his peers — have taken the money and pursued the superstar DJ tra-jectory, playing bland tech house in Ibiza. He considered such garish concerns a fool's errand, however. That he choose an idiosyncratic path of backroom pubs, modestly sized clubs, perfectly tuned sound systems and smaller festivals was testament to the fact that he intrinsically knew his calling — a purveyor of gnostic sonics; an enabler of dance-floor transcendence. Indeed, the mystic aspect of dancing — the 'disco' as he invariably had it — was a source of endless inspiration and he remained scornful of those who attempted to fuck with the ritual. As he explained, his idea of a perfect night remained 'DJ'-ing for eight hours so that I can set the control of the night and set the mood. In an underground club where people can take control of the universe and have a transcendent experience? That's the real shit. But people who go and see Tiësto at some massive thing and it's all about Facebooking yourself? That's the disco equivalent of TV evangelism. Touch the screen and I'll send you five dollars. That ain't the real deal, that ain't psychic energy — that's something else. Just as with religion, you can sniff out the bullshit from the real thing.'

For Weatherall, the obsession with acceleration and futurism and originality that so often surrounds electronic music discourse was anathema. He viewed house and techno more like his beloved dub reggae: a form of eternal roots music untethered to the fickle vagaries of fashion: 'Electronic music has history going back to the Italian futurists,' he said, 'and further back, even. You can trace it back far. Of course, it *can* continue to become original. But there is a terrible urge to be original (*laughs*). Originality comes through judicious plagiarism.'

Anybody who has been involved with electronic music in any capacity will have their favoured Weatherall era. I distinctly remember friends in Hull — die-hard techno heads — fretting when he moved away from his banging, utilitarian techno stage — what he famously termed 'panel beaters from Prague' — in the late 1990s, a sound he was drawn to as a functional, anonymous antidote to the showier vibes that were proliferating all around.

'When I was playing harder techno it wasn't really because of the drugs,' he explains, 'it was more that I'd had a look at that whole superstar DJ thing and it was getting a bit cheesy. I'd been a big Factory head — I saw Throbbing Gristle live — I'd very much partied in the death disco, so to speak, pre-acid house. And then it got a bit fluffier again and it was a quite nice release, to be honest. Playing Trax records instead of "Hamburger Lady" (*laughs*). But then it all got a bit vacuous and I wanted to go back to what I really liked, which was the darker stuff. Maybe it coincided with me stopping taking ecstasy — although in a sense that was more of a career decision. I only ever thought I'd be a DJ for a year, and then get another job. It was only when it started to dawn on me that I was completely unqualified to do anything else — after about ten years — that I thought I'd actually better stop taking ecstasy at work (*laughs*).'

He could convey equal levels of intensity whatever the tempo and for many, his Love from Outer Space DJ partnership with Sean Johnston was the pinnacle of his DJ'-ing. A magical symbiosis of low-slung sleaze with a manifesto to 'never knowingly exceed 122 bpm', A Love from Outer Space was framed as an audio counterpoint to a world in ever-increasing acceleration, and could amble everywhere from the weirder corners of progressive house to the seediest Belgian new beat; chest-hugging dub techno to slow motion disco. It became a sanctuary of sorts for grizzled rave veterans and quietly built a die-hard cult following with a vibe quite unlike any other on the scene — focused, meditative, epiphanic.

'Sean and I had been friends for many years,' explained Weatherall. 'He was driving me to gigs and we'd spend the whole time in the car listening to this 104–110 bpm stuff. We thought: "Well, we like it — let's hire a pub." First night we had fifty people, next night seventy-five. Now we're doing festivals, but still the spiritual home is in the pub with three hundred people. Any artistic experience is best experienced in a small room, in my opinion. Obviously that isn't to take anything away from the big gig experience — that's why people go to football, to be part of something much bigger than yourself. But there is also something to be said for being part of something a bit different from everything else; your own private thing. The fewer the people the more gnostic, in some respects. It isn't people whooping and hollering all night. A groove is established: the slower the music, the more space there is, physically — 104 beats per minute is it. And if you listen back to the early house records, they were 110/120 bpm. It's only with the advent of techno, really, and the change in drugs that the tempo kicked off . . . I got asked "How has clubbing changed?" The only thing that changes is the technology, the method of delivery. The basic human need for transcendence through coloured lights and music goes back thousands of years. And whether that's delivered with flaming torches or state-of-the-art lighting equipment it's the same thing — without a doubt.'

Chapter 10

THE CLOSING OF THE CIRCLE

'I remember having this moment . . . I'd stopped playing piano in a serious way and I was still wanting to compose music and figure out how to do that and I was obsessed with Chopin and I was listening, and heard a chord. And I remember wanting the rest to stop so that I could hear that chord, just hear that for a while,' explains Sarah Davachi. 'In classical music you hear notes and they go away but that was the beginning: thinking, "Why isn't there a music where you just listen to something for a while and appreciate it for what it is?"'

Tapping into the cavernous reverberation of sacred spaces, the unpredictable frisson of cranky old synths and the mesmeric potential of the organ, Davachi's haunting productions fuse a baroque atmosphere with eternal ambience. Most of her records tend towards pure drones augmented with acoustic instrumentation — string, organ or flute, edited post-production. Mostly working in the electro-acoustic sphere, Davachi's music is informed by a willingness to interrogate the inner grain of sound, to get right inside a chord and stay put for as long as necessary.

Influenced by baroque music and, later, the minimal compositions of La Monte Young, Davachi had access to an enviable archive of rare, out of circulation synthesisers while working at the National Music Centre in Calgary. In charge of tour groups, during the foreboding Canadian winters she'd often find herself in an empty museum where she'd take advantage of the sonic bounty. Picking a different instrument every week, Davachi would research its idiosyncrasies before getting to know it on a practical level. Synthesisers held a particular fascination. Sitting in the basement in the empty museum one freezing afternoon, she happened upon the Buchla 100 modular system (explored earlier with Morton Subotnick) and set two of the oscillators in tune. They started drifting out of tune of their own accord and the next day — playing an acoustic organ — she noticed the same occurrence. 'These older machines from the 1960s and 1970s — they weren't intended to be unstable,' she explains. 'It was the best equipment that they had — primitive electronic equipment — so the fact that these machines were always drifting in and out of tune was a problem for most players. But just as acoustic organs are not perfect, neither are synthesisers. They are built by a person; they're never going to be precise. The organ is the synthesiser of the classical world, and I found that analogue synthesisers were the same — those little fluctuations make the music more immersive and intimate and different.'

Debut LP *The Untuning of the Sky* (2013) tapped into this unpredictability with rich, slow-burning drones from synths such as the ARP, Buchla and Mellotron intertwined with organ and harmonium; her sonorous drones feel imperious, immovable. While sometimes put in the ambient bracket it doesn't feel appropriate for music of such viscous presence. Indeed, it's not a term she appreciated in relation to her own music: 'I've always felt weird about the word ambient,' she says. 'People assume everybody is happy to be categorised as ambient, but I think when people use the term now they don't fully understand what it's referring to — it's become this blanket term for drone music, but it's never been a word that's sat well with my music. I think minimalist music can be overlooked in that it's very simple music on the surface, but that doesn't mean that the listening experience is simple at all.'

Davachi's music is imbued with a solidity and presence that sits in opposition to the Eno definition of ignorable by design. Even on non synth-based albums like *All My Circles Run*, Davachi's drones are palpably *present*, filling every corner of the room — 'for strings', for example, is intensely maximal, drawing on her usual technique of recording and then layering and manipulating post-production, treating the studio as a separate instrument. Listen to the way the voices on 'Chanter' are layered atop one another in ethereal harmony — it's evocative of choral movement, at once haunting and beautiful. The following year's *Gave in Rest* explored Davachi's love of church acoustics more explicitly, alongside early music influences. Inspired by a period of relentless worldwide touring, where Davachi increasingly found herself seeking refuge in cathedrals, *Gave in Rest* connects early Renaissance music to the minimalist drone continuum. Ultimately, this is what Davachi's music so readily taps: a non-denominational sacred atmosphere whereby the drone is cast as a means of exploring the mystic in the everyday, as she explains: 'I was interested in taking sound and structure from early music — specifically late medieval music, the way that it didn't really move in the same way. When you get to the Renaissance it starts to get a little more active and modulating, but I've always found it interesting that medieval music is so still and stays in the same place. I tried to tap into it a little bit more. I was in a transitionary time; I had this period when I was touring the whole time and had a lot of time off and a lot of space between shows and I'd always visit old churches. Because my life was a bit more chaotic, the sense of quietness and calm that I felt in these large acoustic spaces became more important in slowing things down and getting something that was completely separate from the outside world. That I was trying to imbue on that record.'

'I used to play at medieval banquets at a pub in Bungay,' laughs Laura Cannell. 'I guess the start of the medieval stuff was a school trip to an Elizabethan house. There was a selection of early instruments — recorders and hurdy-gurdies and things like that — and then when I was about eighteen I did the medieval banquets and learnt how to improvise around chords and drones. We covered a set of medieval Italian dances — there was a set of around twelve, the popular ones — that were accompanied by drones and, because there was so little material, you had to find a way to expand and develop the sound.'

Cannell draws on early music, British folklore and the landscape of Suffolk and Norfolk in foreboding, droning, windswept improvisations for violin and recorder — a bleakly majestic sound at serious odds with the high camp, 'chicken in a basket' vibe of medieval banqueting. Over the years, she's explored the resonance of lighthouses, churches and — most recently — the wild reverb of Wapping Hydraulic Power Station. Using an idiosyncratic double recorder technique, she explains that she has long 'tried to get as much sound as I can out of performing solo. The double recorder is actually a really ancient technique where one is used as a chordal instrument. With the violin, the whole piece becomes a slow moving, monolithic thing. The drone is never fixed in one place.'

Though not religious, church acoustics have long provided particular fascination to Cannell. Over the past decade she's spent countless afternoons exploring lonely rural churches with a portable recording device ready to go, setting up, playing and hoping nobody will walk in mid take. 'Originally, it was about having a space that is free,' she laughs. 'I know that sounds incredibly unromantic. They're accessible, there are loads of them and the warden opens them in the morning and closes them at dusk so you can just drop in and out.'

Combining an ancient bearing with an obtuse, modern minimalist sensibility, *Hunter Huntress Hawker* was recorded in the ruins of St Andrew's Church in Covehithe, Suffolk while *The Sky Untuned* (2019) was made at another St Andrew's (in Raveningham, Norfolk). In both cases, the individual reverberations were more important than the spiritual echo, as she explains:

'The space becomes like another player, because it affects the speed, how you listen, how you perform, what you do next; this was also a time when I was exploring the idea of "no mistakes", letting myself be free enough to improvise, and know that you *can't* actually do anything wrong: there are no "wrong notes" or "wrong answers" — you can just play and be, there is no idea of perfection. I was trying to get away from the classical stuff that I had ingrained. Quite a lot of the time in my music and recordings, there will be something that the first time might be a bit out of key or that I didn't have the intention of playing — but then I'll just reiterate and reiterate; it's the baroque idea of rhetoric where I ask a question over and over again but you never get the same response. Or I'm asking the question slightly differently every time. Taking something and changing the inflection, or the accent, means that I can have tiny differences in things that are quite minimalist and if things go in an unexpected direction — which I love — then I can explore the space with that, and lean into it more and sometimes find something interesting . . . every time I'll do it differently, it depends on the space. And there might be a note — like a wolf note — that really comes out and resonates with the space and then I'll build something around that.'

Simultaneous Flight Movement was recorded in one take inside Southwold Lighthouse, the mournful scrape of Cannell's violin evoking local avian life in flight. It was rendered doubly evocative, however, due to the fact that it was recorded on the eve of the Brexit vote, Cannell inwardly ruminating on the sadness of a country drawing in on itself, while looking out of the lighthouse towards the European mainland. Describing the album as being akin to a 'duet with reverb', it's an idea explored equally strongly on *The Earth With Her Crowns* (2020). Recorded in the decommissioned Wapping Hydraulic Power Station, the album sees her violin interacting with the damp air and cavernous walls, creating music that speaks to the recent industrial past without resorting to twee sentimentality. Crucially, this is the sound of *now*, rather than a simulacrum of the past: ancient technique and space reverberating back through time to the present, part of a constantly shifting continuum.

Richard Skelton also hones in on singular aspects of landscape — the ambience of specifics — in his subtle drone work. A wildly prolific producer (some twenty albums and counting) *Lastglacialmaximum* (2020) took the last ice age as a pivot to explore glacial, ominous tones; the *Wolf Notes* series (alongside Autumn Richardson) took the landscape of the Duddon Valley in Cumbria as inspiration; *Border Ballads* was a melancholic evocation of the Scottish borderlands. Skelton tends towards a channelling, rather than a reflection, of the spirit of a place. In interviews he's refuted the idea that his music is a 'vehicle for emotion. Whatever is transmitted "is" and I have no control over it, nor would I want any. I've always viewed music as life affirming, transformative energy.'[1]

The ley line linking place, organic instrumentation and visionary folk music has delivered some of the most magical music of recent years. Artists like Laura Cannell and Richard Skelton all derive inspiration from specific places, the shifting counters and acoustic resonance of landscape and building. Others have attempted to get inside the head of the past in a magical-realist sense, building a world around an imagined vista. Richard Dawson's masterful *Peasant* (2017) is a case in point. Rejecting the term 'folk' in favour of 'ritual community music', the record depicts Dark Ages life in the north-east, Dawson assuming the narrative role of different villagers — 'Soldier', 'Weaver', 'Prostitute' — in gritty vignettes, brutally shorn of mawkish sentiment. The drone here is hinted: subtly distorted chords, chants and atonal fiddle evoking the brutal realities of Dark Ages life with tenderness and black humour.

Likewise Gazelle Twin (Elizabeth Bernholz), whose brilliant *Pastoral* (2018) took the seething malcontent, pettiness, rage, idiocy, bad faith, irrationality and bloody-minded arrogance of Brexit Britain and transposed it to a turbulent maelstrom of splattering beats, distorted vocals, rattling snares, drones, rave sirens and arpeggios while reaching back to the past with heavily treated recorders, harpsichords and organ. It's an album steeped in disgust, mutant paeans of a lost land drowning in the spittle of its own malevolence, flailing around in a tangled-limb folly dance. Track titles — 'Better in My Day', 'Little Lambs', 'Tea Rooms', 'Glory', 'Jerusalem' — allude to glory while the lyrics present vignettes of bitterness that will be Pavlovian in intensity to anybody who has spent any time here over the last decade or so — on 'Better in My Day' she channels the rage at the core of the flag-waving jingoistic *Daily Mail* curtain twitcher ('Just look at these kids / No respect') while 'Little Lambs' explores the art of the queue — that absurd, self-satisfied English comedy of manners that carries an undercurrent of barely repressed rage ('Jump the line! / No, that's just fine! / Charming!'). The cover sees Bernholz crouching amid the bucolic ideal of an English meadow watercolour in her stage attire, a red jester suit — some mischievous sprite come to lead the dance, destroy complacency in the face of encroaching sentimental authoritarianism. Recently working with London 'drone choir' NYX, Bernholz presented a new piece called 'Deep England' which described her move from Brighton to the countryside, meeting head on what she described as the 'danger lurking beyond the quaint'. Indeed, *Pastoral* — while very much of today — reaches back through time with themes that resonate throughout history: it's a raw, punk protest music. 'I was thinking of the Romantic art form of the pastoral especially — the classical symphony, the landscape painting, and how that romanticism still very much continues to inform the contemporary branding of rural life here. I know I wanted this to be my parody on that longstanding mythology.'[2]

Others have recently taken a similarly jaundiced view of little England. Gnod — a collective living and working at the Islington Mill community arts space in Salford — harness the chaos energy of spontaneous collaboration, psychedelic excess, hypnotic noise and electronic experimentation to gloriously dizzying ends. The suitably titled *Just Say No To The Psycho-Right Wing Capitalist Fascist Industrial Death Machine* (2017) was a caustic howl at the rage-inducing, stultifying, slack-jawed idiocy of the Brexit era, drawing on a layered barrage of detuned guitars, feedback, submerged noise and chanted vocals that called to mind the despondent desolation of early Swans, tribal rhythmic drive of Test Dept and hypnotic storm of Hawkwind.

Mirror (2016) — a shot of equally caustic noise rock written and recorded in the wake of the 2015 general election — was driven by disgust at the British political landscape and, equally, the addictive digital shadow that most of us feed compulsively. Elsewhere — in a sprawling discography — Gnod have traded in everything from ambient drone (*The Somnambulist's Tale*) to skewed techno (various 12-inches as Dwellings and Druss) and barrelling psych rock (*Chaudelande*). The drone, improvisation and extended jams are constantly recurring themes, however, and the cavernous *Infinity Machines* (2015) showed Gnod at their most mesmeric: a raw, intensely psychoactive trawl that took in narcotised beats, mournful foghorn-esque sax, guitars that plink rather than rage and all manner of creeped-out echo box effects and vocal samples — a masterful dragnet through Salford's shadowlands.

Indeed, in terms of community vibe, ceaseless experimentation and indefatigable spirit, Gnod are arguably more closely aligned to the sonic freedoms of the Krautrock era than almost any other band, a DIY punk ethos running through everything they do — the essence of which is, as band member (and qualified sound therapist) Alex Macarte described it to the *Quietus*, 'essentially trance music . . . music is a self-healing tool for so many people, even if they're not consciously aware of it — whether it's the metalhead getting all their aggression out by thrashing to blast beats or being really quiet and still within yourself from some gentle, soothing sounds . . . all of it is facilitating transcendence beyond their normal day-to-day state.'[3]

The drone — via its infinite pliability and accessibility — represents the ultimate folk music: a potent audio tool of personal liberation. In 1977 *Sniffin' Glue* verbalised the musical zeitgeist with their infamous 'this is a chord; this is another; now form a band' illustration. The drone requires neither chord nor band. Indeed, the subtitle of this book — *In Search of Sonic Oblivion* — refers not to some destructive audio force but the potent ability of sound — in this case slow-moving sound — to help dissolve the fragile trappings of ego. The drone is a psychedelic talisman; immersion in hypnotic and repetitive sounds allows us to step outside of ourselves, be it chant, a 120-decibel beasting from Sunn O))), standing in front of the system as Jah Shaka drops a fresh dub or going full headphone immersion with Hawkwind. These experiences are akin to an audio portal — a sound Tardis to silence the hum and fizz of the unceasing inner voice.

Crucially, the drone allows you to take *control* of time. Humanity is tethered to the inevitability of time. The awareness of its passing informs almost every decision we will ever make. The certain knowledge of death is the source of a baseline torment that, to some degree, defines what it means to be human. Modern ideals of 'living in the moment' — or the experiential economy — retains such vital currency because it hints at a freedom, albeit fleeting, from fate itself. The drone facilitates a focus on the present by limiting the constant of change. Capitalism demands that you remain tethered with technology and keep stride with the shifting vagaries of the free market. It demands that you keep moving and strive for material gain, fetishises change for change's sake — the Darwinian concept of adaptation as the highest natural state. The language of capitalism decries stagnation as sin. The Protestant work ethic presents work — any work — as an end unto itself. After all, the devil makes work for idle hands.

The drone is fundamentally subversive when taken in relation to capitalist doctrine. It subverts every tenet of music as consumer commodity. You're unlikely to find any commercial radio station playing a full half-hour Sunn O))) piece. Likewise, the very notion of authorship — and therefore ego — is called into serious question. Do you 'write' fifty minutes of feedback? Do you 'own' an A chord that reverberates for a full half-hour?

It's no coincidence that many protagonists in this book eschew the preening dynamic of normative rock 'n' roll stage performance. The stadium rock show is exciting precisely *because* it emphasises a fundamental disconnect between band and audience. It makes you feel smaller — thrillingly so — by dint of bombastic theatrics, the overwhelming scale of the spectacle. The unwritten rule? Never forget you're a spectator. This isn't an 'equal' transaction. Nor should it be. It's bread and circuses — and you aren't the emperor. I'm not claiming that the stadium experience is invalid. A good stadium show — be it Lady Gaga or Iron Maiden — fosters a feeling of togetherness by dint of communal awe and shared wonder presided over by a master. Drone is less transactional. It allows for individual transcendence to the extent that I want to ask the question: do we play the drone or does it play us?

It exists outside of us, an aural expression of a universal hum we can only hope to fleetingly channel.

Notes

Prologue

1 Sword, Harry. 'The Strange World of Surgeon', *Quietus*, 28 February 2017.

2 McLuhan, Marshall. *The Medium is the Massage* (Penguin, 1967), p. 63.

3 NASA, 'Interpreting the "Song" of a Distant Black Hole', https://www.nasa.gov/centers/goddard/universe/black_hole_sound.html, 23 February 2008.

4 Harkins, Sophie. 'The Sound of Black Holes Colliding', *Electronic Beats*, 16 January 2018.

5 Becourt, Julien. 'Éliane Radigue: The Mysterious Power of the Infinitesimal', *Red Bull Music Daily*, 2015.

6 Foucault, Michel. *Discipline and Punish: The Birth of the Prison* (Pantheon Books, New York, 1977), p. 82

7 *Sounds Inside*, Prison Radio Association, 2017.

8 Ibid.

9 Russolo, Luigi. 'The Art of Noises', https://opasquet.fr/dl/history/music/ztt/etc/russolo-artofnoises.txt

10 Marinetti, Filippo. *The Futurist Cookbook* (1930) (Penguin Modern Classics) makes fascinating reading. This was the cuisine of the terminal aesthete. One dish — 'aerofood' — is described as follows: 'The diner is served from the right with a plate containing some black olives, fennel hearts and kumquats. From the left he is served with a rectangle made of sandpaper, silk and velvet. The foods must be carried directly to the mouth with the right hand while the left hand lightly and repeatedly strokes the tactile rectangle. In the meantime, the waiters spray the napes of the diners' necks with a perfume of carnations while from the kitchen comes contemporaneously a violent sound of an aeroplane motor.'

11 Keenan, David. *England's Hidden Reverse: A Secret History of the Esoteric Underground* (Strange Attractor Press, 2016), p. 7.

12 Hensley, Chad. 'The Beauty of Noise: an Interview with Merzbow', esoterra.org http://www.esoterra.org/merzbow.htm

13 Watson, Chris. *Stepping into the Dark* liner notes (Touch Recordings, 1996).

14 Das, Santanu. 'Sensuous Life in the Trenches', British Library, at https://www.bl.uk/world-war-one/articles/sensuous-life-in-the-trenches

15 El Sarraj, Waseem. 'The Sounds in Gaza City', *New Yorker*, 19 November 2012.

16 Stanford Law School Report, 'Living under Drones: Death, Injury, and Trauma to Civilians from US Drone Practices in Pakistan' (2012), p. 80.

17 Ibid

18 See http://thehum.info for the full map.

Chapter 1: Enter the Chamber

1 'The Xaghra Hypogeum', *Malta Independent*, 10 January 2010.

2 Griffiths, William Arthur. 'Malta and its Recently Discovered Prehistoric Temples', *National Geographic*, Vol. XXXVII, No. 5, 1920.

3 During the siege of Malta in the Second World War — when the Luftwaffe blitzed the tiny island for 158 continuous days and nights in the heaviest sustained attack of the entire conflict — the Hypogeum acted as temporary air raid shelter. A number of the chambers were seriously damaged. In the proceeding decades, a heavy footfall of uncontrolled tourism further corroded the soft limestone.

4 Deveraux, Paul. 'A Ceiling Painting in the Hal Saflieni Hypogeum as Acoustically Related Imagery: A Preliminary Note', *Time and Mind: The Journal of Archaeology, Consciousness and Culture*, pp. 225-231.

5 Cox, Trevor. *Sonic Wonderland* (Vintage Books, 2015), pp. 13-26.

6 Interview with G.K. Michalakis, http://analogion.com/site/html/Isokratema.html

7 Fricano, Mike. 'Measuring the sound of angels singing', UCLA newsroom, 14 September 2015, http://newsroom.ucla.edu/stories/measuring-the-sound-of-angels-singing

8 Todd, Bella. 'Tim Hecker: 'I make pagan music that dances on the ashes of a burnt church', *Guardian*, 5 April 2016.

9 Elsewhere — in the Maeshowe Neolithic burial chamber on the Orkney Isles — other interesting acoustic phenomena has been observed. Dr Aaron Watson found both 'standing waves' and infrasound activated at the site. Standing waves are produced when low-and high-intensity sound waves interact, either cancelling each other out or connectively boosting the sound. The effect is disconcerting: volume can oscillate in such a way that appears to have no relationship to the sound source. Infrasonic frequencies are below the human threshold of hearing. However, they have a physical effect. At Maeshowe, a drum was used in acoustic experiments, triggering infrasound. Test subjects in the cairn reported feeling that sounds were

emerging from inside their heads and bodies. Feelings of dizziness, nausea, headaches, moving sensation and elevated pulse rates were also noted. See Watson, Aaron. 'The Sounds of Transformation: Acoustics, Monuments and Ritual in the British Neolithic', in Neil Price (ed.), *The Archaeology of Shamanism* (Routledge, 2001).

10 Clarke, Arthur C. *Mysterious World* (Fontana, 1982), p. 137.

11 'Newgrange Burial Chamber Reveals Haunting Sounds of the Past', *Sunday Times*, Irish edition, 15 July 2001.

12 Dr Derbertolis's research was undertaken as part of the 2014 'Archeoacoustics: Archaeology of Sound' conference.

13 Derbertolis, Coimbra and Eneix. 'Archeoacoustic Analysis of the al Saflieni Hypogeum in Malta', *Journal of Anthropology and Archaeology*, Vol. 3, No. 1, June 2015, p. 59.

14 Cook, Pajot and Leuchter. 'Ancient Architectural Acoustic Resonance Patterns and Regional Brain Activity', *Time and Mind: The Journal of Archaeology, Consciousness and Culture*, Vol. 1, Issue 1, March 2008, p. 104.

15 Watson, Aaron. 'The Sounds of Transformation: Acoustics, Monuments and Ritual in the British Neolithic', in Neil Price (ed.), *The Archaeology of Shamanism* (Routledge, 2001), p. 178-93.

16 Grow, Kory. 'Judas Priest's Subliminal Message Trial: Rob Halford Looks Back', *Rolling Stone*, 24 August 2015.

17 Martino, Ernesto De. *The Land of Remorse: A Study of Southern Italian Tantrism* (Free Association Publishing, 2005), p. 87.

18 Reynolds, Simon. *Energy Flash* (Faber and Faber, 1998), pp. 167.

19 Jones, Hilary. *Doctor, What's the Alternative?* (Hodder & Stoughton, 1999), p. 42.

20 Cox, Trevor. *Sonic Wonderland* (Vintage, 2014). See prologue (pp. 13-26) for Cox's idea of aurally reading your surroundings.

21 Stanislavski, Konstanin. *An Actor Prepares* (Bloomsbury, 2013), p. 63.

22 Williams, David-Lewis. *The Mind of the Cave* (Thames and Hudson, 2002), p. 126.

23 Boorstin, Daniel J. *The Creators: A History of Heroes of the Imagination* (Knopf Doubleday Publishing Group).

24 Brown, Barnaby. *Blast from the Past* documentary, European Music Archaeology Project (2017).

Chapter 2: Chant Ecstatic

1 The Mandukya Upanishad scripture is devoted to Om (represented as 'Aum'). The scripture defines the four primary states of consciousness, each linked to an attendant letter — waking state by 'A'; dream state by 'U'; deep sleep and peaceful

consciousness by 'M' while the fourth state — Turiya, or 'transcendental consciousness' — is represented by the three letters together.

2   Oliveros, Pauline, Satz, Aura and Spiegel, Laurie. *Dial Tone Drone* (Burlington
House, London, exhibited 5 September 2014 to 9 January 2015).

3   UNESCO documentary, *The Mongolian Traditional Art of Khoomei*.

4   Prosik, Daniel. 'Morocco: An American Perspective of Tangier', https://sites.psu.
edu/northafricacomm410/tag/william-s-burroughs/

5   The psychedelic potency of Joujouka music is also underpinned by the millennia-old
kif culture that thrives in the Rif mountains. A mixture of cannabis bud from tough,
spindly sativa plants that are cultivated commercially in the valleys cut with strong wild
tobacco, kif is as indivisible from daily life as sweet mint tea, its preparation a careful
ritual. The thin flowering heads are painstakingly shaken, the seeds removed before
being chopped to fine powder with black tobacco. Kif is seldom smoked in joints (that
is reserved for hash) but, rather, taken in ornate wooden *sebsi* pipes which hold only
a tiny amount. Frequent blasts are taken alongside draughts of incredibly sweet mint
tea (ten sugar lumps per pot) which counteracts any soporific effect. The influence on
Jajouka music shouldn't be underestimated: it underpins what is happening — on every
level — musically. 'They've been smoking their entire adult lives — and smoking whilst
playing music — so the trance aspect is not just music induced, there is a strong drug
aspect that goes along with it,' explains Rynne. 'The two of them are very important in
terms of where the music developed from.'

6   Gysin, Brion. *The Process* (Tusk Ivories, 2005 edition), p. 103.

7   Aside from Gysin and Bowles, he also introduced Frank Rynne to the village,
after Rynne put on the 'Here to Go' exhibition in Dublin in 1992 — a celebration
of the work of Burroughs and Gysin — which featured paintings from Hamri and
performances by the Masters.

8   Bowles, Paul. 'The Rif to Music', *Their Heads are Green* (Abacus, 1963), p. 114.

9   Burroughs, William S., and Gysin, Brion. *The Third Mind* (Viking Press, 1979), p. 10.

10   When living in London in the early seventies Burroughs became angry at rude
service at the Moka espresso bar. He stood outside making field recordings for two
days which he then played back in an attempt to 'place the Moka Bar out of time'.
For a full philosophical explanation of his ideas on tape recorders see his essay:
'Feedback from Watergate to the Garden of Eden', https://archive.groovy.net/dl/
elerev.html

11   Burroughs, William S. *The Revised Boy Scout Manual: An Electronic Revolution*
(Ohio State Press, 2018), pp. 48-9.

12   Savage, Jon. Brion Gysin interview, Paris, 1986, https://www.ubu.com/papers/
gysin_interview_savage.html

Chapter 3: Midnight Raga

1   Gemie, Sharif, and Ireland, Brian. *The Hippie Trail: A History* (Manchester University Press, 2017), p. 16.

2   As we saw in the previous chapter, it's the *constant*: underpinning melody, and connecting musician and listener back to the one. Musically, the drone sits beneath the *raga* — a melodic improvisational framework that translates to 'colouring'. Each raga corresponds to a mood or time: a raga may evoke, for example, 'love', 'midnight' or 'monsoon'. The sitar has twenty-one strings, four of which produce a drone. A simple sitar drone might consist of a single note repeated, while more complex harmonics are made by placing two or more notes in the drone spectrum. The overtone buzz is elevated to the state of *jivari*, which corresponds to 'life'. In Hindustani and Carnatic traditions alike — the former the music of the north, the latter the south — the drone is also frequently played on the tanpura. A member of the lute family, it is around five feet long with four strings. It has a deeper, more rounded tone than the sitar and a long hollow neck ending in a bowl (generally fashioned from a gourd in the north or jackfruit in the south).

3   Simpson, Dave. 'The Byrds: How we made Eight Miles High', *Guardian*, 16 September 2014.

4   The Kinks attempted to emulate the drone of the sitar a year previously on 'See My Friends', Ray Davies's trademark laconic drawl stretched out to a nasal whine alongside a sustain-laden twanging guitar line. However, this was imitation.

5   *The Beatles Anthology* (Apple Corps, 2000), p. 210.

6   I've only experienced it once, after smoking salvia. I was in Hull. It felt like flying through hyperspace. There was an immense sense of motion. I had no conception of myself. No memories. 'Harry Sword' was disintegrated, completely. I remember leaping 'back' through an embroidered sun cushion on my bed, over-whelmed by a sense — implicitly felt, deep in my bones, as real as anything I had up to that point or ever since felt — that reality, in the material sense at least, is a false construct. I found it strangely comforting. Others less so. A friend who had a similar experience — again on salvia — had to be walked up and down Newland Avenue for an hour, tapping railings to 'check everything was still real.'

7   Hollingshead, Michael. *The Man Who Turned on the World* (Blond and Briggs Ltd, 1973), p. 122.

8   Roberts, Andy. *Albion Dreaming: A Popular History of LSD in Britain* (Marshall Cavendish, 2012), p. 100.

9   Leary, Timothy, Metzner, Ralph and Alpert, Richard. *The Psychedelic Experience* (Penguin, 1964), p. 121.

10   George Harrison, quoted in *The Beatles Anthology* (Apple Corps, 2000), p. 177.

11   McNeil, Legs and McCain, Gillian. 'An Oral History of the First Two Times The Beatles Took Acid', *Vice*, 4 December 2016.

12   *The Beatles Anthology* (Apple Corps, 2000), p. 210.

13   Ibid.

14   *The Frost Programme*, 4 October 1967.

15   Pearlman, Sandy. 'Patterns and Sounds: The Use of Raga in Rock', *Crawdaddy*, December 1966.

16   Voger, Mark. *Groovy: When Flower Power Bloomed in Pop Culture* (TwoMorrows, 2017), p. 36.

17   Meshel, Jeff. 'Sandy Bull: Blend', https://www.jmeshel.c om/275-sandy-bull-blend/

18   Janos, Adam. 'G.I.s' Drug Use in Vietnam Soared — With Their Commanders' Help', https://www.history.com/news/drug-use-in-vietnam 29 August 2018.

19   Grow, Cory. 'The Doors Reflect on Early Shows, Jim Morrison's Genius', *Rolling Stone*, December 2016.

20   Check the blistering rebuttal of the movement's restrictive practices, written by an ex-devotee, here: https://harekrishnacultexposed.blogspot.com/

21   'Swami in Hippie Land', *San Francisco Chronicle*. Quote accessed at https://theharekrishnamovement.org/2011/03/13/swami-in-hippyland-chapter-7/

22   See 'The Hare Krishna Thing' Blog Pages for further information: http://harekrishnathing.com

23   Goswami, Mukunda. Interview with George Harrison 1982, https://www.beliefnet.com/faiths/hinduism/2001/12/the-mantra-keeps-me-in-tune-with-reality.aspx

24   Porter, Lewis. *John Coltrane, His Life and Music* (University of Michigan Press, 1999), p. 209.

25   Ibid., p. 211.

26   Williams, Richard. 'Free Rage: Albert Ayler', *Guardian*, 25 September 2004.

27   Porter, Lewis. *John Coltrane, His Life and Music* (University of Michigan Press), p. 203.

28   Khan, Ashley. 'Alice Coltrane: "The Gifts God Gave Him"', *Jazz Times*, June 2001.

29   'I am the sire of the world, and this world's mother and grandsire / I am he who awards to each the fruit of his action / I make all things clean / I am *Om*!'

30   Pharaoh Sanders would explore similar spiritual territory — albeit generally less fiery — on his solo records, particularly on his *Karma* album, which included a chanted mantra on the half-hour 'The Creator Has a Master Plan'.

31   Baham, Nicholas. *The Coltrane Church: Apostles of Sound, Agents of Social Justice* (McFarland & Company 2015), p. 60.

32 Cook, Richard. *Jazz Encyclopaedia* (Pengiun, 2005)

33 Satchidananda, Swami. *The Yoga Sutras*, https://dippingintolight.com/saraswati-satchidananda_scriptures/

34 Coltrane, Alice. *Transcendence* liner notes (Atlantic, 1977).

Chapter 4: The Drone of the Holy Numbers

1 In 2015 he told *Vulture* magazine that 'People have written that I'm the most influential composer in the last 50 years, and I think that's true . . . what's more, when I die, people will say, "He was the most important composer since the beginning of music."'

2 In 1972 by the American writer Tom Johnson in a review of composer Alvin Lucier. Before then 'New York hypnotic school' was sometimes used.

3 Zuckerman, Gabrielle. 'American Mavericks: An Interview with La Monte Young and Marian Zazeela', *American Public Media Radio*, July 2002. Transcript here: http://musicmavericks.publicradio.org/features/interview_young.html

4 Maciunas, George. *Fluxus Manifesto*, 1963, http ://georgemaciunas.com/about/cv/manifesto-i/

5 Cage, John. *Silence: Lectures and Writings* (Wesleyan University Press, 1961), p. 1.

6 Zuckerman, Gabrielle. 'American Mavericks: An Interview with La Monte Young and Marian Zazeela', *American Public Media Radio*, July 2002. Transcript here: http://musicmavericks.publicradio.org/features/interview_young.html

7 Strickland, Edward. *Minimalism: Origins* (University of Indiana Press, 1993), p. 231.

8 Pouncey, Edwin. 'John Cale interview', *Wire*, April 2001.

9 Perreault, John. 'La Monte Young's Tracery: The Voice of the Tortoise', *Village Voice*, 22 February 1968.

10 For further information on Young's ideas on tuning, scales, improvisation etc. check his 2000 essay 'Notes on the Theatre of Eternal Music and The Tortoise, His Dreams and Journeys', https://www.melafoundation.org/theatre.pdf

11 Conrad, Tony. 'LYssophobia: On Four Violins', sleeve notes to *Early Minimalism Volume One* (Table of the Elements, 1997).

12 Ibid.

13 Chaffee, Cathleen (ed.). *Introducing Tony Conrad, A Retrospective* (Albright Knox Art Gallery, Buffalo, New York), p. 111.

14 Yue, Genevieve. 'Interview: Tony Conrad', *Lincoln Center Film Review*, https://www.filmcomment.com/blog/loose-ends-an-interview-with-tony-conrad/

15 Licht, Alan. 'Flaming Creature Reborn: Angus MacLise', *Wire*, December 1999.

16 Fred Frith — avant-garde musician who founded the band Henry Cow.

17 Riley, Terry. Notes on *In C.*

18 Potter, Keith. *Four Musical Minimalists* (Cambridge University Press, 2000), p. 116.

19 JD Twitch. '"A Particular Glow" — On Loving Terry Riley', *Boiler Room*, 3 April 2015, https://boilerroom.tv/a-particular-glow-on-loving-terry-riley/

20 Oliveros, Pauline. 'Deep Listening' issue, soundamerican.org

21 Oliveros, Pauline. *Sonic Meditations* (Smith Publications, 1974), p. 5.

22 Oliveros, Pauline. Red Bull Music Academy lecture, 2016, https://www.redbullmusicacademy.com/lectures/pauline-oliveros-lecture

23 Oliveros, Pauline, Satz, Aura and Spiegel, Laurie. *Dial Tone Drone* (Burlington House, London, exhibited 5 September 2014 to 9 January 2015).

24 Oliveros, Pauline. Sleeve notes to *Deep Listening* — Pauline Oliveros, Stuart Dempster, Panaiotis (New Albion, 1989).

25 Information on Nath is hard to come by. Aside from talking to Terry Riley about his first-hand experiences, I am indebted to Marcus Boon's excellent essay on Pandit Pran Nath found in the *Wire*, September 2001.

Chapter 5: Do the Ostrich

1 Doran, John. 'A Quietus Interview: Lou Reed Metal Machine Music Revisited', *Quietus*, 28 October 2013.

2 Bockris, Victor and Malanga, Gerard. *Uptight — The Velvet Underground Story* (Omnibus, 1983), p. 16.

3 Sword, Harry. 'The New English Library Was the Sleazy King of British Pulp Publishing', *Vice*, 16 December, 2014.

4 Bockris, Victor. *Transformer: The Lou Reed Story* (HarperCollins, 2015), p. 75.

5 Ibid., p. 90.

6 Bockris, Victor and Malanga, Gerard. *Up-tight: The Velvet Underground Story* (Omnibus, 1983), p. 22.

7 Ibid.

8 *Beat* magazine, 28 May 1966.

9 Savage, Jon. *24-Hour Arty People: Andy Warhol's Explosive Collision with the Velvet Underground*, *Guardian*, 18 April 2009.

10 Bockris, Victor and Malanga, Gerard. *Up-Tight: The Velvet Underground Story* (Omnibus, 1983), p. 47.

11 Epstein, Dan. 'Inside White Light/White Heat', *Rolling Stone*, 18 January 2018.

12 Bockris, Victor. *Transformer: The Complete Lou Reed Story* (1994, Harper), p. 156.

13 Dadomo, Giovanni. Nico interview, *Sounds*, 29 April 1978.

14 Doran, John. 'Lou Reed Interview: Metal Machine Music Revisited', 28

October 2013.

Chapter 6: Kommune

1   Pouncey, Edwin. 'Communing with Chaos', *Wire*, February 1996.

2   Stubbs, David. *Krautrock and the Building of a Modern Germany* (Faber & Faber, 2014), p. 287.

3   Ebert, Robert. *Herzog by Ebert* (University of Chicago Press, 2017), p. 36.

4   Sword, Harry. 'Reasons We Should All Love Hawkwind', *Vice*, 1 March 2015.

5   Johnson, J. 'The Truth About Hawkwind', *New Musical Express*, 5 February 1972. Retrieved 23 May 2020, from http://www.rocksbackpages.com/Library/Article/the-truth-about-hawkwind

6   Stevens, Andrew. 'Taking Drugs to Make Music to Take Drugs To', *3:AM Magazine*, 10 October 2002.

7   Carruthers, Will. Edited extract from *Playing the Bass with Three Left Hands* (Faber), *Guardian*, 26 September 2016.

Chapter 7: Reverse Hardcore

1   Quote from *Gimme Danger*, Jim Jarmusch, 2016.

2   Quote from *Gimme Danger*.

3   Ward, Edmund. *The Stooges* album review, *Rolling Stone*, 18 October 1969.

4   Cameron, Keith. 'The Stooges: Return to the Fun House', *Mojo*, April 2007.

5   His own 'Notes for *Guitar Trio*' — given to musicians taking part in performance — make clear the importance of volume: 'Because the overtones generated by the guitar are quite soft, it is for this reason that we play *Guitar Trio* at relatively high volume levels, in order to hear the subtlety and poetry of the soft overtones (i.e. we play this piece LOUD!). You'll want to significantly boost your guitar in the frequency area of 1.2k (mid-range frequency) if you have a bandwidth booster box, or on your amp. Otherwise, set the midrange on your amp to a high setting. Set the treble boost on your amp to "high", if you have one. Those with sensitive ears or tinnitus can use earplugs.'

6   Quote from Lydia Lunch, *Blank City* documentary (Celine Danhir, 2012).

7   Sword, Harry. 'Suicide and Henry Rollins in Conversation', *Quietus*, June 2015.

8   Masters, Mark. 'An Interview with Glenn Branca', *Wire*, May 2018.

9   Sharp, Elliott. 'Glenn Branca 1948 — 2018', *Premier Guitar*, 16 May 2018.

10   Harmonicait. Kim Gordon interview, *Complex*, 22 April 2013.

11   Sullivan, Jim. 'Flipper: The Channel, Boston', *Boston Globe*, 29 April 1983.

12   Rollins, Henry. 'I Am a Stoner at Heart', *LA Weekly*, 9 February 2017.

Chapter 8: Beyond the Electric Caravan

1   Bangs, Lester. Black Sabbath review, *Rolling Stone*, 17 September 1970.

2   Sword, Harry. 'Like the Early Seventies Forever', *Record Collector*, issue 410, January 2013.

3   Marshall, Brandon. Bill Ward interview, *Sonic Excess*, http://www.sonicexcess. com/BILL_WARD_BLACK_SABBATH_interview.html

4   Smith, Mark E. *Renegade: The Lives and Tales of Mark E Smith* (Penguin, 2008).

5   VH1 animated short, *Fingers Bloody Fingers* (2015), https://www.iommi. com/2015/02/vh1-history-of-heavy-metal/

6   The third being the bludgeoning 'Symptom of the Universe' from *Sabotage* (1975).

7   Sword, Harry. 'Like the Early Seventies Forever', *Record Collector*.

8   Bacher, Hanna. 'In Conversation with Dylan Carlson', *Red Bull Music Academy*, Berlin, 2017. https://www.redbullmusicacademy.com/lectures/dylan-carlson-lecture

9   Doran, John. 'Enter the Furnace: Scott Walker Soused: Scott Walker', interview, *Quietus*, 25 March 2019.

Chapter 9: Infinite Loops

1   Éliane Radigue, IMA Portrait documentary, 2012.

2   Ibid.

3   Élaine Radigue, IMA Portrait documentary, (dir. Primosch, Cornelia), 2009.

4   Reynolds, Simon. Aphex Twin interview, *Melody Maker*, 27 November, 1993.

5   Toop, David. 'Lost in Space', Aphex Twin interview, *Face*, March 1994.

6   Keenan, David. Coil interview, *Wire*, July 1998.

7   Major, John. Speech to Conservative Group for Europe, 22 April 1993.

Chapter 10: The Closing of the Circle

1   Burnett, Joseph. 'Nature Eclipses Culture: An Interview with Richard Skelton', *Quietus*, 12 March 2014.

2   Hyde, Daisy. 'A New Dark Age', Gazelle Twin interview, *Wire*, September 2018.

3   Neale, Matthew. *Untangling the Galaxy: AHRKH's Alex Macarte*, interview, *Quietus*, 9 March 2020.

Acknowledgements

My thanks to all the following incredible spirits, alive on the infinite plain…

To Tamara Sword for her encouragement and love — and for always saying a resounding yes to the universe. To my editor Lee Brackstone and agent Natalie Galustian for their unwavering energy and support, and for getting this book right from the start. To David Keenan for his early enthusiasm — and whose words 'trust in madness' resonated with me throughout many late nights writing. To Luke Turner for his encouragement throughout — and for all the early evenings at Mangal 1 and early mornings at Corsica Studios.

Thanks always to Mum, Bill Powell, Dad and Di and Oliver, Irene and Sophie Cotton.

Huge thanks also to Tom Noble, Ellie Freedman, Alex Layt, Lucinda McNeile, Natalie Dawkins, Katie Espiner, Lucie Stericker, Seán Costello, Lauren Barley, John Doran, Karl O'Connor, Tony Child, Jennifer Lucy Allan, Jus Oborn, Zoe Miller, Barnaby Brown, Rupert Till, Laura Cannell, Paul Deveraux, Andrew Weatherall, Justin K. Broadrick, Sarah Davachi, Morton Subotnick, Dylan Carlson, Greg Anderson, Stephen O'Malley, Beck, Henry Rollins, Lee Ranaldo, Frank Rynne, Rhys Chatham, Steve Von Till, Dale Crover, Oliver Ho, Justin Robertson, Lee Dorrian, Brian Eno, The Secret DJ, Hawkwind, Michelle Coltrane, Professor John Cramer, Jean-Hervé Peron, Manuel Göttsching, Katya Stroud, Dr James Giordano, Terry Riley, Kevin Martin, Stephen Mallinder, William Doyle, Toby Cook, Dharambir Singh, Dean Brown, Andrew Paine, Oisin Lunny, John and Riona Horley, Alex Freeman, Pete Boatfield, Chloe Meredith, Ed Robertson, Alex Stark, Johny Davis, Ben Beaumont-Thomas, Walter Roadburn, Becky Laverty, Laura Snoad, Rory Gibb, Sophie Colletta, Lilith Whittles, Dan Papps, Robin Turner, Carl Gosling, Mark Pilkington, Drift Records, Robin Allender, Andy Bell, Spider Stacey, Tim Burrows, the *Quietus*, *Guardian* Music, Record Collector, Strange Attractor Press, Tusk Festival, Roadburn Festival, Corsica Studios, Mangal 1, The Red Bull Cambridge, Wilkins Cider, John Robb, Richard Norris and Rock 'n' Roll book club.

Index

339

Picture Credits

Chapter 1: Hypogeum in Malta © Heritage Image Partnership Ltd
Chapter 2: Master Musicians of Joujouka © Frank Rynne (L-R Rynne, Terry Riley and Ahmed El Attar, Tokyo 2017 © Frank Rynne, all rights reserved)
Chapter 3: Alice Coltrane © Getty Images / Michael Ochs Archives
Chapter 4: La Monte Young © Getty Images / Fred W. McDarrah
Chapter 5: Velvet Underground © Getty Images / Fred W. McDarrah
Chapter 6: Faust © Getty Images / Ebet Roberts
Chapter 7: The Stooges © Getty Images / Michael Ochs Archives
Chapter 8: SUNN O))) LIFE METAL photo by Ronald Dick © 2019 SUNN O)))
Chapter 9: Surgeon © Doris Woo
Chapter 10: Sarah Davachi © Sarah Davachi / Photo still from film by David Reiman (October 2019)